THE DOG BY THE CRADLE, THE SERPENT BENEATH

THE DOG
BY THE CRADLE,
THE SERPENT
BENEATH

SOME PARADOXES OF
HUMAN–ANIMAL RELATIONSHIPS

ERIKA RITTER

KEY PORTER BOOKS

Library and Archives Canada Cataloguing in Publication

Ritter, Erika
    The dog by the cradle, the serpent beneath: some paradoxes of
human-animal relationships / Erika Ritter.

ISBN 978-1-55470-076-9

1. Human-animal relationships. 2. Animal welfare. I. Title.

QL85.R58 2009   304.2'7   C2008-902370-6

The publisher gratefully acknowledges the support of the Canada Council for the Arts and the Ontario Arts Council for its publishing program. We acknowledge the support of the Government of Ontario through the Ontario Media Development Corporation's Ontario Book Initiative.

We acknowledge the financial support of the Government of Canada through the Book Publishing Industry Development Program (BPIDP) for our publishing activities.

Key Porter Books Limited
Six Adelaide Street East, Tenth Floor
Toronto, Ontario
Canada M5C 1H6

www.keyporter.com

Text design: Marijke Friesen
Electronic formatting: Alison Carr

Printed and bound in Canada

09 10 11 12 13 5 4 3 2 1

For the animals—in all of us.

CONTENTS

PROLOGUE

I T'S ONE OF THE OLDEST STORIES in the world. Before leaving the house
with his wife, the master sets his faithful dog to guard their only child,
slumbering in its cradle. Soon after the parents' departure, a servant enters
the child's chamber and makes a horrifying discovery: the dog spattered
with blood, the cradle overturned, and the infant nowhere to be seen.

When the master and mistress return to confront this gruesome evidence, the man immediately slays the treacherous animal. Only then is
the cradle turned upright—to reveal the child, still slumbering peacefully
and entirely unharmed. A moment later, the bloodied, tooth-marked body
of a venomous snake is found in the corner where, after killing it, the dog
had apparently flung it.

That succession of bitter reversals has haunted me for years: the
master's complete trust in his dog so easily broken; the animal's valiant
service so cruelly repaid; the superficial evidence so woefully at odds with
the truth the creature has no voice to tell.

The more I have thought about the story, the more its simple specifics
have come to embody some of the contradictions I see at the heart of
humanity's relationship with all animals. The fact that we claim to love
what we so often end up killing. The guilt that the abuse of their innocence
can inspire in us. The impulse to assuage that guilt by making animals
seem complicit in their use, abuse, and even death. Our need to pamper
and celebrate the chosen few as a means to offset our unease about our
casual dispatch of the many.

What follows is my adult journey into the implications of those and
other paradoxes. One branch of the trail takes me to the heart of the story
of the dog by the cradle, and a real-life cult of blasphemous worship that
arose literally from his corpse. Another track of my journey leads to

9

conversations with animal advocates, philosophers, activists, and academics about their personal methods for dealing with the disparities between the fortunes of humanity and non-humankind. Yet another fork in the road takes me into some of the factual, fictional, and downright mythical ways in which humans seek to resolve the contradictions in the bonds between us and them.

In the end, all roads converge in a misty woodland in the Dombes area of rural France. There, what remains of a seven-hundred-year tradition of clandestine communion with animals beckons me—and you, I hope—to what I have come to think of as the very heart of Ark-ness.

INTRODUCTION

E VIDENCE OF OUR GROWING PREOCCUPATION with animals is all over our media—from comical accounts of stubborn skunks under the porch, to scarifying headlines about avian flu, to reports on pampered pooches at doggy "spaws," to laments for the fate of polar bears on disappearing ice floes. Perhaps, behind both the humour and the near-hysteria, there lurks a rising element of human guilt about our widespread despoilment of the natural world. At the same time, our media may be signaling an increased, if somewhat perplexed, sense of fellow-feeling toward the animals among us.

But rising affinity—if this is what it is—comes at a price. In practical terms, we are spending more money on pets, pet food, supplies, and training now than at any point in history. And the political cost of animal companionship may be even higher.

After all, if they think like us, feel like us, or simply (as nineteenth-century philosopher Jeremy Bentham opined) suffer like us, why shouldn't they enjoy our access to civil and legal rights? Be spared the horrors of scientific experimentation and routine slaughter? Choose where and how they'll live? Even to pose those questions is to open one of many doors marked "Paradox."

On one hand, in a world that is becoming more and more industrialized, we depersonalize animals like never before—in huge factory-farm operations, in medical and commercial laboratories, and through the wide-scale devastation of their habitats. On the other hand, organic food movements, wildlife protection associations, and animal rights activism are also on the rise. As well, more and more of us care about where our food comes from, how the creatures who feed us lived and died, what they ate on their way to market, and in fact whether we should be eating animals or consuming animal products at all.

How can we reconcile the seemingly irreconcilable contradictions in our relationship with animals? How are we to bridge the gulf between our growing sense of alienation from the natural world, and our burgeoning desire for kinship with creatures we see as closer to nature than ourselves? And, most of all, how can we explain that desire for kinship, which runs so inconveniently counter to human self-interest? After all, it's far easier for us to use and abuse animals without a qualm if we don't look them in the eye and see something reproachfully similar to us staring steadily back.

What I am seeking to do in this book is investigate these and other questions, by calling upon the paradoxes innate within the ancient tale of a greyhound named Guinefort. The theme of my investigation—whether we are talking leash laws, four-legged victims in fiction, animal welfare, cognitive research, or ritual sacrifice—is found within the contradictions that story embodies.

My method—especially in interviews with experts and advocates in various areas to do with our moral, emotional, practical, ethical, and spiritual relationships with animals—is one of open inquiry, rather than categorical pronouncement. The scope of my inquiry encompasses everything from human prehistory, to animal adoption, to veganism. And the breadth of my investigation covers children's literature, cattle-branding, bear hunts, warhorses, ape sanctuaries and much more. Yet, while the subject under scrutiny is animals, the main focus of my interest is human beings.

How can we speak of "humane slaughter"? Why do we regard some animal species as so much more than kin but so much less than kind? Who appointed us stewards of the Earth and to whom are we accountable for any dereliction of duty? What impels us to seek assent from animals in the outcomes we force upon them? Where do we draw the line between licencing urban animals and giving them licence to behave according to their natures? And when do the disrespected bodies of non-humans become holy objects of human worship?

Despite increasing social and scientific focus on animal consciousness, legal rights, welfare, and more, we have not, to date, answered any of those contradictory questions. Nor have we allayed the powerful feelings of discord and dissonance they imply. Perhaps these paradoxes can't be resolved, because human beings lack the fundamental willingness to relinquish control over the natural world and break the cycle of exploitation and guilt exemplified by our stewardship.

I hope that's not the case—not only for the sake of humanity but for the non-humans under our aegis. I admire animals; I delight in their occasional foolishness; I am impressed by their peculiar wisdom; I exult in their existence among us, and at the same time fear for their future at our hands. Although the following quest was undertaken for myself and for fellow humans who share my interests, I also sincerely hope I have done something useful, as advocates of direct action on behalf of non-humans like to say, "for the animals."

PART ONE

Killed with Kindness:
Humane Slaughter

M OST OF US EAT MEAT and use other products derived from animals. Yet, increasingly, we keep ourselves separate from the gory details of livestock rearing, transport, slaughter and butchery. More and more, cattle, hog, and poultry farms resemble impersonal factories, both in scale and methods of operation. And farmers, who used to do their own killing, now routinely send their stock away to be slaughtered.

The removal of animal death from our daily lives is a process that has been ongoing from the beginning of our appropriation of animals to our use. In ancient times, hunting rituals served to set apart human predators from their victims and from their own guilt. When livestock agriculture developed, special observances connected to slaughter performed the same purifying function. Nowadays, as we select a pristinely packaged cut of barely identifiable beef or pork (not "cow" or "pig") and drop it into our shopping cart, perhaps we find ourselves sufficiently remote from the animal to keep our guilt in check.

Yet that element of discomfort is still there, in constant conflict with our sense of entitlement. Sport hunters envelop the act of stalking and slaughtering in an almost religious mystique. Urban food writers feel sanctified when they go on organized expeditions and personally take down their own dinner. Even experts who earn their livelihood devising more efficient methods of livestock rearing and killing feel compelled to stress the humane component in their chosen careers. Why?

If slaughtering and eating animals is our right as well as in our nature, why have humans always been so driven to justify, codify, ritualize, and euphemize what we do and have done to animals for millennia? Welcome to the paradox of killing with kindness.

I

I'M A LITTLE LATE ARRIVING for Temple Grandin's Humane Slaughter class. But nobody notices as I thread my way to a vacant seat. All eyes are on Dr. Grandin, who paces back and forth in front of the class, deep into the question of how to properly stun cattle with a captive-bolt pistol. Occasionally, she shakes her head, as if to admonish the unseen image of some sloppy practitioner she's met.

"You've got to get the *brain*," she declares emphatically. "And to do that, you've got to know where the brain *is*." She stabs a lethal forefinger at a picture of a cow's head. "Right here! Not there. *Here*. In a cow. Sheep you shoot in the *top* of the head."

The zest of her presentation verges on the comical. In fact, some in the audience of mainly female students titter. But you can tell they're used to her style, and feel relaxed around the topic at hand. Almost as relaxed as the legions of cows and sheep and pigs who pass willingly through the chutes of the slaughter systems she designs—and up the fateful ramp she's nicknamed the "Stairway to Heaven."

As for Temple herself, "relaxed" isn't quite the word for her constant pacing. But neither does she appear self-conscious at the front of the lecture hall, with her PowerPoints on the overhead—and a meathook dangling nearby for the purpose of more visceral illustration.

Why would she be uncomfortable? She's been delivering versions of this lecture—to students, to stockmen, to welfare groups, to executives of McDonald's and Wendy's, and to members of the media—for twenty years or more. The fact that she's also autistic shouldn't lead me, or anyone, to expect someone more tentative, less confident.

These days, Dr. Grandin is as renowned for her "high-functioning" autism as she is for her high-minded dedication to humane livestock slaughter. "The most famous person on this campus," according to friend and philosophy professor Bernie Rollin—himself no slouch in the animal welfare pantheon, even if he lacks the cachet of a woman who's been on *Larry King Live*, as well as in *The New Yorker* and *Time* magazine.

Temple Grandin writes books on what it's like to think like a cow and how the world appears both to animals and autistic humans. Her writings about her own autism have turned her into a role model for autistic kids and their parents across North America and beyond. As well, she churns out monographs on breeding pigs to withstand the stress of slaughter, papers on the neurological complexities of animal welfare, blueprints of restraints better adapted to kosher and halal killing, and materials for DVDs on the preceding topics and more, which you can buy directly from her website.

And in her spare time...well, there isn't any. When she's not lecturing in the Animal Sciences building here on campus, she's on the road, either visiting slaughter plants to make sure her system of auditing performance is being maintained, or lecturing at autism and Asperger's conferences and livestock symposiums.

In each of her succession of hotel rooms at the end of the day, she snatches moments to return methodically the copious calls to her answering service. And no doubt thinks about being back home in her own Fort Collins, Colorado, apartment, where she can unwind in her self-described "hug machine"—a kind of comforting squeeze chute she designed to deal with her own distinctive tactile requirements.

Is that as lonely a row to hoe as it sounds? More than a decade ago, neurologist Oliver Sacks spent an entire weekend with Temple for the title essay in his book *An Anthropologist on Mars*. In addition to observing her in her hug machine and even trying it out for himself, Sacks took a close look at her uneasy relationship with human emotion.

Back in the late 1960s, he tells us (and Temple's own writings corroborate Sacks's account), she had an opportunity to meet the legendary behaviourist B. F. Skinner. "It was like having an audience with God," is how Temple recalled it to Sacks.

But in person, she was "let down" by Skinner, and his reduction of brain function to "just a matter of conditioned reflexes." Even more disillusioning was how the grand old man of stimulus-response tried to touch her legs. "I was shocked," she remembers. "I was in a conservative dress. I told him: 'You may look at them, but you may not touch them.'"

Sitting in her class in Room 114 at the Animal Sciences Building on the campus of Colorado State University so many years later, it's still easy to see in Temple Grandin vestiges of that young graduate student shocked by Skinner's vulgar overture. What's more difficult to imagine is that young grad student in a dress.

Nowadays, her uniform—and I don't know what else to call an outfit that has been so unvarying over several decades—is a neckerchief, an embroidered cowboy-style shirt, stiff-looking blue jeans covering the legs that once stimulated B. F. Skinner, and black lace-up boots. For today's class, she's chosen a red neckerchief and a shirt bedecked with red roses. At our previous meeting, her neck scarf was blue and the shirt, decorated with a stitched motif of cattle heads, also blue. In photos and videos stretching back years, there are slight variations, but always slight, on this very definite ranchland theme.

She's a tall, solid-hipped woman of sixty, very straight up and down in the body, like a tightly-packed cotton doll. Her short hair is graying somewhat, but still reddish and curly. She wears it shoved behind her ears and smoothed back from her high pale forehead.

Somehow, her face reminds me of Marjorie Main's—especially her mouth, which works vigorously as she talks, like an old mountain woman's. But in the next moment, she stops pacing to comment proudly on the success rate of her audit system at fast-food empires like McDonald's. And a sudden, sly smile transforms Marjorie Main into a mischievous little girl.

Then, just as abruptly, the smile is extinguished and it's back to business: the business of stunning sheep this time, done not with a pistol but with electricity. Back and forth she walks in front of the class, clicking a slide onto the screen of a sheep with "stunner" prongs on either side of its face, like a telemarketer's headset. She drags down the meathook on its pulley to show how an animal, once stunned, can be hooked and lifted effortlessly to the "bleed rail."

"Electric stunning only makes the animal unconscious for twenty-five seconds—like a grand mal seizure—so you have limited time to bleed them before they wake up."

During one of her long-ago conversations with Oliver Sacks, Temple told him she'd once raised genetically "enriched" pigs as part of an experiment. She became "so attached" she couldn't kill them when the time came. However, she did manage to accompany the animals on their last walk, calming them on their way to slaughter. But after their deaths, she recalled, "I wept and wept."

It's hard to put that tearful recounting together with the efficient professional I'm observing in front of her class. Yet, there's a sharp emphasis in the way Temple speaks that hints at another, more emotional self beneath the tough persona.

In Mexico, she tells her students, they stab a knife into the back of the head, which doesn't render the animal insensible, only paraplegic. "Stupid!" she spits out with an anger that could be read as outrage on behalf of livestock, or perhaps disgust at the general incompetence of humans.

"Stupid" is a word she finds cause to use again and again, whether she's deploring practices that produce unnecessary animal suffering, or taking potshots at what she perceives as the misguided convictions of the vegan set—sometimes with a kind of angry, jeering impatience that seems to be about something else. As if "stupid" might be an insult she knew too well as an oddball child, and even now can exorcise only by hurling it back, hard and often.

Some slaughter-plants—the ones without her systems in place—she deems "horrendous." Some are great. "It's like the little girl with the curl," she says. The class nods at what is obviously a familiar reference. It takes me a moment to remember the little girl in the nursery rhyme, with the curl in the middle of her forehead. When she's good, she's very, very good. But when she's bad, she's horrid.

In fact, the little girl with the curl is only one of Temple's standard references. Sometimes, she repeats whole paragraphs word for word. Yet it's never in a rote or mechanical way, but always with the freshness of initial iteration. Like an actor following the Stanislavsky method, she seems able to recapture the emotion reliably again and again, always as if finding it for the very first time.

She links this trait to her high-functioning autism. In our conversation, she told me she hates what she calls "small talk," and gets criticized by friends for always talking about her work. And perhaps for always talking about it in exactly the same way?

She also mentioned being called "the tape recorder" as a teen. And in her books, she critiques her first forays onto the lecture circuit, when she was wedded to notes and repeated herself word for word at every public appearance.

Later, however, she learned to embrace the "tape recorder" epithet as the basis for a successful speaking career. "I have so many stock phrases and sentences I can move around in new combinations," is how she explains her method in her book, *Animals in Translation*.

At other times, she has compared the filing system in her brain to a computer's. Whatever the technical analogy and regardless of repetition, watching her in action in front of a class makes it clear: over the years, the words may stay the same, but humane slaughter is a subject for which her enthusiasm never flags.

It's all in the system, she is continuing to explain to the class as she paces. If you have a curtain to keep them from seeing what's waiting ahead, a leg spreader they can straddle in comfort on their way, the right shape of chute, and a firm but calm means of urging them inside ... you can kill them like clockwork.

Proper maintenance of equipment, adherence to strict standards of how many are allowed to fall down on their way to slaughter, how many "hot shots" with the electric prod you permit, and what percentage of "vocalizing" per hundred animals is deemed acceptable are essential elements of her method of auditing slaughterhouse performance. "But most of all, as I get older," she tells the class, "it seems to me more and more important to have good management—even more than good equipment, more than anything."

If stunning is poorly done, or any other benchmark of the audit is missed along the way, blood-spotting in the meat can occur. This is an outcome to be avoided, although exactly why, she does not elaborate. "Now, in New Zealand they can use electric stunning on cattle, because those cattle aren't grain-fed like here. For some reason, electric stunning works on grass-fed cattle without spotting the meat."

Click! On to a picture of pigs in an elevator awaiting descent into a chamber of carbon dioxide. "Generally, CO_2 works fine for stunning pigs," she assures us. "Death isn't instant, but that's only a problem for pigs with a stress gene. You gotta breed that gene out of pigs, and then they're fine with CO_2."

Click! "How can we know for sure they're dead?" Now it's a photo of a slaughtered cow hanging, head down, tongue lolling out. "Loose and flaccid." Temple puts out her own tongue by way of contrast, and speaks with effort around it. "See? I can't even stick mine out like that. Mine's stiff and curly. So, loose and flaccid is what you're looking for."

Of course, she continues, you want to make really certain the creature's passed beyond all pain, so you also poke its eye. "You can use your finger in a big animal's eyes," she cautions, "But not little animals. You poke those eyes with a pencil."

The students diligently make note of this, and so do I. You never know, it might come in handy. It might turn out be the very piece of information I need to solve an apparent paradox, one which Temple Grandin personifies: How can any of us claim to love what we kill, whether with kindness or a captive-bolt pistol?

———————

IT'S A QUESTION I'VE BEEN asking for a long time. Certainly long before I came to be scribbling notes in my airplane seat, on my way home to Toronto from Room 114 of the Animal Sciences Building on the campus of Colorado State University in Fort Collins. From time to time, I feel I am getting closer and closer to an answer. But even after all these years, I still find myself at least one wise man short of an epiphany.

The nobleman had been a bachelor when he and his greyhound first forged their bond. . . . Every journey, they say, begins with a single step. In my case, it was a single opening sentence in a storybook. Which particular book, I can't remember—nor the title of the story, or whether any author's name was given.

That opening sentence and all the ones that followed it are mere hazy approximations in my adult mind of what I must have read on the page all those years ago. *In time, however, the man took a wife. As more time passed, along came a child—his father's pride and joy. But his loyal dog remained precious to him, too. On a day when business beckoned him and his lady away from home, the lord didn't hesitate to entrust his infant son to the dog's keeping.*

How old am I? Nine, maybe. Ten? Eleven at most.

In my customary reading pose, on the living-room sofa, with the open pages close to my face because my thick glasses, as usual, have been misplaced. In my hands is a big, battle-scarred volume, with the title hand-lettered in white ink on the spine some librarian has carefully re-taped. *The Big Book of Dogs? The Fireside Collection of Dog Stories?* Something like that. Or maybe not. All I'm sure of—looking back on myself at the age of nine or ten or eleven, on the living-room couch with my nose literally in a book—is that I am taking the first step down a trail from which there is no turning back.

The nobleman and his wife were barely a league along the road, when a servant from their castle came galloping up behind them, full of dire news: no sooner had the hound been left alone with the child, than he had attacked him in his cradle!

Immediately the parents turned their horses and hurried back home. There, they came upon a damning scene: the baby's cradle overturned, blood everywhere, and the child nowhere to be seen. Yet more horrible, there was the dog standing beside the fallen cradle, coat spattered with blood, tail a-wag, and not a flicker of remorse in his steady gaze.

This betrayal was too much for the nobleman. Without a moment's delay, he drew his sword, and slew his beloved dog on the spot.

Next to me on the plane, my seatmate stirs. Sorry, ma'am. I must have flinched in some noticeable way. Half a century has come and gone, but the memory of the impact of that story on my nine- or ten- or eleven-year-old self is ... well, never mind. You had to be there—back in my childhood, right inside that story. There, inside those cold castle walls, where a man has just killed the thing he loves. Which more or less explains why I'm *here*, on an Air Canada D-C Whatsis, somewhere roughly over Minnesota. On my way back from Temple Grandin's class on Humane Slaughter, and just beginning to follow the story, to learn how it comes out.

It was only after the greyhound lay dead that someone thought to right the overturned cradle. Beneath it was the child, slumbering peacefully. And beside him, the remains of a serpent, punctured with bloody tooth marks. Too late, the truth of the situation came clear to the nobleman: far from seeking to do his child ill, the dog had in fact saved him from a snake crawling into the cradle.

Or maybe I'm not so much hoping to see how it comes out, as to understand why.

Stories about animals are the oldest kinds of tales, the means by which humanity in its infancy took its first stumbling steps to understand the world. The oldest kind of journey is the quest. And reading signs and markers we encounter along the way is surely the oldest form of detective work. In my case, the journey began in my childhood with that old, old story of a dog and the man who both loved and killed him. The quest, however, is a more recent enterprise. Fortunately, the trail—although long and winding as a trail should be—is well marked, with legible signage. It's only a matter of working out what the markers might mean and what the signs say.

———◆◆◆———

LOOKING OUT FOR ADVERTISED SIGHTS and alleged markers is nothing new for me. You might even call it my life—as opposed to "leit"—motif. I am someone who always feels that if I can just find that oddly-shaped rock, that peculiarly-worded gravestone, that elusive spot of hallowed ground promised in the tourist brochure, I will confirm not only the significance of the specific trip I happen to be on, but also the point of my own existence.

Often—like the meaning of life itself—the locations of those rocks and stones and spots of ground have proven elusive. On a trip to Edinburgh in the early 1970s, I trudged for miles in hopeless quest of the statue of Greyfriars Bobby—perhaps the most famous landmark in the city centre.

Unfortunately, a faulty tourist map had located it in the boonies. That's where my travel companions and I wound up, until some kindly suburbanite put us on the right bus. He promised us that we couldn't miss the statue: just next to Greyfriars church, and directly outside the pub named after the faithful terrier.

The kindly suburbanite was right, of course. Even so, I was surprised to find the memorial exactly as advertised: beside the churchyard where Bobby had stubbornly refused to leave his dead master's grave—and where he is immortalized with a monument far more lavish than his owner's.

How often does that happen, after all—that the site of an animal's burial is denoted with such prominence? When it does happen, something out of the ordinary has apparently occurred; some admission of a long-time oversight, perhaps. Some special intervention plucked an individual animal from the obscurity in which most non-human creatures dwell most of the time, in order to offer something in death not accorded in life.

In Wales there's a monument to an ancient variant on the dog-cradle-snake story. In this case, a wolfhound named Beth Gelert saves the child of his master from a wolf. Gelert winds up the victim of the same kind of misunderstanding as the nameless greyhound, condemned to death by the false evidence of his bloody jaws and an overturned cradle.

In a soppy narrative poem of the late eighteenth century, the Hon. William Robert Spencer identified Gelert's master as a nobleman named Llewellyn (presumed to be Llewellyn ap Gruffyd, the last prince of an independent Wales prior to English conquest). Spencer's treatment of the story is well on the way to melodrama with the obligatory rosy-cheeked cherub of a child, an idealized Gelert ("So true, so brave—a lamb at home, A lion in the chase!"), and Llewellyn as a grieving master desperate to make amends for misjudging his faithful dog. In fact, so guilty is the prince that he constructs "a gallant tomb...With costly sculpture decked" to house the slain body of his canine companion.

In the mid-nineteenth century another British poet, named Richard Hengist Horne, took a crack at the "Beth Gelert" story. In his version, the master (identified merely as a "rural lord") also leaps to the conclusion that the wolfhound killed his child. He not only batters in the dog's brains with his staff, but for good measure "stamped him dead with frantic laugh!"

Not too many lines later, the child is located safe and sound asleep in the heather, near where "a haggard Snowdon wolf, stark dead and glaring, Lay on its back." In this case, the tomb is a chapel the remorseful lord constructs to atone for the wrong done to his dog.

Neither of these modern accounts of Beth Gelert is much better than, well, doggerel. But in the Welsh village of Beddgelert, which prides itself on being named for the slain dog, there has always been a determined effort to believe in the story as authentic medieval history. Especially after the statue of Greyfriars Bobby erected in Edinburgh turned out to be a solid hit with nineteenth-century tourists.

An enterprising hotelier in Beddgelert spearheaded efforts to construct a memorial to the town's canine hero. Not a statue of the dog as such, but an attempt to replicate the stone marker Llewellyn ap Gruffyd had supposedly erected centuries before in memory of Gelert. Sure enough, the tourists come in droves.

It doesn't happen all that often, this kind of public commemoration of the death of a mere animal. When it does happen—as with both Greyfriars Bobby and Beth Gelert—perhaps the impulse speaks more to human needs than to canine deeds. Maybe it says more about our view of death than theirs. Yet, the fact that the impulse exists at all might be, in and of itself, reason enough to seek out an accurate map and follow the signs to the spot.

II

THE ANIMAL SCIENCES BUILDING on the Colorado State University campus in Fort Collins boasts a mural of domesticated animals and their ancient forebears marching across the front. A line of horses at progressive stages in equine evolution runs above a row of various types of pigs. Cows walk in procession with prehistoric bison, over the heads of a string of sheep. On my way to an appointment with Temple Grandin, I stop on the steps to admire this tribute. Later, I learn this frieze is collectively titled "Range to Research." That's a little less fanciful than my initial impression, a little more to the point.

In the photos on her website and on the covers of her books, Dr. Grandin is often presented in some sort of communicative pose with a livestock animal: lolling companionably beside a cow, or with her face nuzzled against the cheek of a horse, in a way that speaks volumes about non-verbal understanding.

Yet it's that very gift of understanding that's enabled her to deal with animals' humane dispatch. When Oliver Sacks first met Temple, he noted her particular affinity with cattle, and her self-declared need to take breaks from the regular task of overseeing their slaughter. At the same time, he observed her lack of emotional response when addressing other highly-charged topics. As is common among autistic people, he concluded, she showed "overwhelming concern in certain areas," but was highly "selective" in her passions and involvements.

To a less trained observer, the contradictions in Temple Grandin are no less stark. Sometimes she is strikingly intense in her convictions and criticisms. At other times, she appears to approach the entire topic of slaughter—even of her beloved cattle—with an air of detachment more suited to an efficient executioner than someone you might pick out as "an animal person."

How I plan to engage that apparent contradiction, I'm not entirely sure. At the very least, meeting her will be an opportunity to confront my own ambivalence about us and animals. A private audience with someone who, in her own specialized realm, is a figure of almost papal authority— as legendary as her one-time "God" B. F. Skinner.

In Temple's case the audience takes place in an inconsequential office in the basement of the building. At first, I think I've misunderstood the receptionist's directions. But there's no mistaking the distinctive voice drifting along the basement corridor to meet me before I reach her open door. There's a peculiar twang to it, somehow simultaneously flat and inflected, especially when she's being emphatic.

"Do you eat meat?" I had asked her in an earlier conversation over the phone.

"I *gotta* eat 'em!" Her voice had snapped back in my ear, rebuking as a rubber band. Now, as I approach her office, I can tell that she's once more on the phone, and no less definite with the person on the other end.

"...And those books better be there for my talk," she's declaring firmly, like any author used to taking care of business for herself. "'Cause people are gonna want me to sign 'em on the spot."

The depth and breadth of her office clutter is a surprise. From phone conversations and reading her work, I knew her to be highly organized. In fact, she has frequently described her mind as a series of "computer file folders" from which information can be readily retrieved.

But here are plastic horse figurines, with their heads protruding through what look like miniature restraining stalls, competing for shelf space with plaques of commendation from cattlemen's associations and medical research companies. An action figure of Albert Einstein (a kind of patron saint of high-functioning autism) stands not far from a Frederick Remington bronze sculpture of a horse and cowboy. As well, there are representations of cows in many sizes and styles, from the realistic plastic type, to fey critters fashioned from fabric, wire, or wood, to a whimsical painting of a calf, the frame still wrapped in its gift bow.

I wouldn't call them "props," precisely. But they don't seem to represent her *real* animal passion: the desire to make the "good death" ever better through continual upgrades in system design, measurable methods, clearly defined goals, practical action, and constant vigilance. That's who she is, I am about to find out, in a conversation that begins the moment I walk in the door and then goes on for the many hours she generously apportions to me from a schedule I know is jam-packed.

Part of her machine-gun delivery of information might be attributable to the fact that she genuinely does not tire of the topic of humane slaughter. Another aspect, perhaps, is the comfort of those touchstone topics she returns to and reiterates. Above all, though, she seems possessed of a fierce certainty that she knows best about what's good for animals— and for interviewers.

"You're from up in Canada," she tells me, "so you want to look into the plants that may be taking the horses we're exporting for slaughter, now that there's that damn bill."

I know what damn bill she's talking about: the American Horse Slaughter Prevention Act, which by this point has made its way through the US House of Representatives, but is still awaiting passage in the Senate. Temple is a vocal critic of the proposed legislation, and more than ready to explain why.

"I've lived in Arizona. I've seen cattle and horses starving on the desert. I know what abattoirs are like down there in Mexico. There's lots worse than humane slaughter. Lots worse than slaughter."

That phrase is a mantra to which Temple constantly returns. Perhaps it's as consoling in its way as the muscular embrace of her hug machine.

"Do you ever think about focusing your attention solely on ways to better their lives, rather than their deaths?" I ask.

She shakes her head. "It's enough to do, teaching and overseeing implementation of my systems, and lecturing. I can't do everything."

But, she adds, she is in favour of some of the direct action that groups like People for the Ethical Treatment of Animals have taken, going under-cover to video substandard slaughterhouse conditions, in order to raise public awareness. (That favourable regard is reciprocated by PETA. In 2004, they gave Dr. Grandin their "Proggy" award in the "visionary" category—to the outrage of organizations that oppose any work on behalf of animals that is predicated on their slaughter and consumption.)

Not that PETA is by any means perfect, in Temple's opinion. Take the comparison they've made of animal slaughter to the Holocaust, for instance. She dismisses this as "stupid."

And on the subject of PETA's recent "Unhappy Meal" campaign against McDonald's—the first giant fast-food empire to sign on to her system of slaughter-plant management—she is downright scathing. "Handing out 'Unhappy Meal' packs, with little bloody knives in them, and little toy farm animals smeared with fake blood? Upsetting kids that way is plain wrong."

It occurs to me, fleetingly, that with a little work on their stress genes, maybe kids wouldn't act so upset when presented with the animal-slaughter aspect of their McDonald's lunches. Aloud, I suggest: "So it would be fair to say you're more concerned about children than animals?"

Her answer is prompt and, of course, emphatic. "I accept that I'm a speciesist. I don't have a problem with killing animals, if it's done right. But we don't kill our own."

She tells me she's been asked what she would have done, had she been called upon, in Nazi Germany, to design better systems for killing human beings. Her response, she says, is that she would have designed systems to self-destruct in some way, but undetectably—in order to allow her to continue creating faulty systems that would spare many lives.

She is, of course, speaking hypothetically. Yet, there is a flicker of impudence, the sly, secret smile of the little learning-disabled girl with the curl, who grew up to outwit them all.

I, meanwhile, am still pondering her assertion that "We don't kill our own." I wonder if feeling or not feeling that distinction between species is what demarcates the biggest distinction between *people*. But it doesn't seem like the right question for Temple. Instead, I ask: "Are you someone who believes there's a growing sense in our society that animals have consciousness, much like us?"

She agrees with that to some extent, especially when people are made forcibly aware of the "reality" of animal life and death. But, she says, she doesn't like to see the issue polarized by the "radicalism of left and right." Things have to happen to people personally, she tells me, before they make a real impression. Such as with an oil executive she met, who became motivated to complain about environmental degradation when his favourite hunting spot was ruined by oil rigs.

"That's how I changed the minds of those McDonald's executives, pre-1999." (She frequently dates events from that watershed year when her audit system was made mandatory practice for suppliers of meat to McDonald's.) "Although, there was this executive one time, who shall remain nameless—" That's another of her favourite bywords, whenever she cites veterinary schools with bad policies, animal activists with bad politics, and others whose motives or behaviour she questions—"Let's just say he represented a national chain of casual-dining restaurants you'd know right off if I told you.

"There was this one time he flew with me to look at a chicken supplier's plant, and on the way there, he was very chatty." However, on the way back, after seeing the "deplorable" state of the plant, the executive didn't talk to her at all. "He just buried himself under his headphones and pretended to be the pilot."

"What do you mean?" I ask.

"You know, like the pilot on an airline, talking to the passengers about the flight conditions and calling out the names of what you're flying over. This man just couldn't deal with what he'd seen."

For all her forthrightness in expressing her views, for all her tireless availability to the theory and practice of humane slaughter, for all her impatient dismissals of the many instances she encounters of human stupidity, Temple is surprisingly sensitive about anything she perceives as an attack on her position. Not only does she eagerly answer the challenge, she is ready to arm herself for fresh assaults.

"A certain well-known vegan who shall remain nameless," for instance, has lately drawn her into an email correspondence about the environmental threats posed by the livestock industry. But after Temple took the trouble to write him back, pointing out that raising crops requires animal fertilizer, "he had no answer for that!" She reiterates triumphantly: "No answer!"

Yet, on some level, she also seems disappointed that the vegan has un-accountably dropped the electronic ball without lobbing it back, by opting to meet her irrefutable logic with mere silence. Possibly, at this moment the nameless vegan's concerns exemplify the sort of fuzzy abstraction she has deplored all her life. What she does approve of unequivocally are the priorities of the common man: the kind of person who has no time either for abstract principles, or what she refers to as "hot-button issues," because he's too busy struggling to meet his basic needs.

To enforce that point, Temple invokes both Maslow's Hierarchy of Needs—with food and shelter at the wide base of a pyramid, and philosophical issues at the narrowest point—and her own comfortable familiarity with "the Wal-Mart crowd" whose commonsensical views mirror her own. That identification may be what's behind the oddly down-home twang (she was born in Boston and raised mainly in the East), the no-nonsense blue jeans, the tell-it-like-it is tone.

Essentially, the kinds of people Temple likes and approves of are people who come face to face with the consequences of animal slaughter.

"Back in the late seventies," she says, "when I was first working out a better system, there were these 4-H kids who personally walked their cattle up the Stairway to Heaven." She's referring to calves raised by hand, treated like pets. Yet, she suggests, these kids were comforted by walking those last steps with their animals. And later, made proud by seeing how insulin could be extracted for medical use from the cattle carcasses.

From range to research. It's hard for me to know what to say about the unarguable courage of those kids, leading their own animals to slaughter. Could I, or any other self-described animal lover I know, do that? Not likely. Nor even undertake the basis task of all 4-H club members—and, for that matter, any small-scale livestock producer anywhere in the world—to raise a creature from infancy and come to know it as an individual, all the time aware of the intended outcome of its life.

During the day I spent with Temple, she shared a number of anecdotes—about the oil executive, about the misguided vegans, and about slaughter-plant operators, good and bad. But it's the one about the 4-H kids and their calves that comes back again and again into my mind. That was the tale that rose above its purpose as an illustrative parable, to attain the stature of an archetypal story about us and animals; that is to say, a real story about love and death.

———◦•◦◦•◦———

"ANIMALS ARE GOOD TO THINK," declared anthropologist Claude Levi-Strauss. Animals are good to tell, he might also have said. And for some, good to hunt. However, Man the Hunter need not be a carnivore in order to want to search out the story that is Animal. Sometimes all that's required is the persistence of a certified bibliophile and the soul of an amateur sleuth.

Originally, whatever truth there was about anything came wrapped in a story. Stories of how the world came to be, for instance—whether as an idea in the mind of a lonely Creator, or carried on the back of a giant turtle. Then, there is the story of how humans as a species came to be in charge of all the other creatures. Many elements of that story often end unhappily for the animal, with the noble steed collapsing at the finish line, the stag at bay brought down by the huntsman—or the luckless greyhound who kills the snake and is in turn killed by the master who once loved him.

The earliest English-language version of that story I can find is "The Dog and the Adder." It's a poem in rhyming couplets by an anonymous bard, probably of the late Middle Ages. Master and dog are as nameless as the poet. "A rich man of great might" owns a "greyhound that was good and snel" that he loves "so well." He and his wife have a year-old child whom the father also dotes on. There are also some nurses who attend the child less diligently than the dog does. One day, when the good greyhound is on watch and the human help has slipped out to watch a joust, an adder slips in and slithers toward the child. The serpent is fought to the death by the dog, tipping over the child's cradle in the process.

When the nurses return to their duties, there is no sign of the child. They find only the greyhound, lying stretched out in the hall, winded and bleeding. To cover up their own negligence, they rush to their mistress with the mistaken intelligence that the child has been "eaten flesh and blood" by the dog.

Not surprisingly, the parents hotfoot it to the scene of the crime. When the guileless greyhound spies his beloved master, he jumps up and puts his paws on the man's chest—as if to reassure him that his wounds from the skirmish are minor. But in a panic of misunderstanding, the poet tells us, the master "drew his sword anon" and stabbed the dog to the bone.

Of course, once the cradle is righted, the knight realizes that he's slain the dog that killed the snake that menaced the child. Grief-stricken, he staggers out to a fishpond. Into which, the poet tells us, "for dole of his hound, He leapt in, and sank to the ground."

Since the dog's master chooses to drown himself, he foregoes the opportunity to construct a monument or a chapel to express his remorse. Unlike the wolfhound Beth Gelert, the anonymous greyhound of "The Dog and the Adder" has no traditional burial place, no memorial of any kind (ancient or contemporary) to house his earthly remains.

However, like the wolf-versus-wolfhound variation offered in "Beth

Gelert," the tale of greyhound and adder probably originates with a two-thousand-year-old Persian collection of stories similar in set-up to *The Thousand and One Nights*, comprising a series of yarns told to beguile a tyrannical king. In the centuries since, all kinds of other versions have been spun off, involving mutable animal adversaries and the occasional recasting of the canine hero as, in India, a mongoose. There is even, in one variant from Greek lore, a noble *serpent* that slithers in to save the child.

The fact that this basic dog-snake-cradle storyline crops up in so many cultures over several millennia, in numerous languages and several distinct parts of the world, might indicate there never was a real-life basis for the tale. On the other hand, the persistence of the legend could suggest the very opposite: that in the course of human-animal affairs, this kind of tragic misunderstanding happens all the time.

Most of the time, when it does happen, the animal is the one who pays the price. Leaving the humans behind to tell the tale, mourn the dead and—in rare instances—erect a lasting memorial.

———·•·———

MAYBE MORE THAN ANYTHING, the story of Animal is about our childhood—both as individuals and as a species. The bonds children naturally make with animals stem from an instinctive recognition of animals as equivalent species—in the true sense of equal value.

In children's own stories, animal characters are seldom presented as inferiors, but as equally potent personalities with interior lives easily as important as those of humans. Literature written *for* children evokes that same sensibility. As well, within many of us so-called "grownups," some sense of that lost animal-human relationship continues to lurk deep in our bones—perhaps deeper than our individual recollections of childhood, and as deep as the memory of our earliest ancestry.

Marjorie Kinnan Rawlings' Pulitzer Prize-winning novel *The Yearling* (adapted as a film with a fair amount of fidelity) is a story primarily about childhood. A boy named Jody Baxter steps out from the backwoods of Florida to forge a tender bond with a newborn fawn. But there is something profoundly ageless in the encounter and its aftermath.

The fawn comes into the Baxter family's dirt-poor life at a crucial moment. Out hunting for food with his son, Jody's father, Ezra (called "Penny") Baxter is bitten by a poisonous snake. Penny shoots a doe in order to use her warm liver as a poultice to draw out the venom. Jody glimpses her orphaned fawn, and later he begs his father to let him go back to the woods to find it and bring it home to raise. He argues it's the least he and his father can do, since the doe's death has saved Penny's life.

The father agrees with Jody's sense of justice, and overrules his wife's objections to having a wild creature in the house. As an infant, Flag the fawn makes a wonderful pet. But as he matures into a yearling, he becomes less biddable and more destructive, particularly of the family's crops.

Eventually, Jody attempts to drive Flag off the Baxter place, and back into the woods. But it's a life the yearling is no longer fit for. In the end, he has to be eliminated. Which is how Jody winds up squinting down the barrel of a rifle, forced to draw a bead on the bright eye of his best friend, and squeeze the trigger.

Afterward, Jody flings down the rifle, and flees both the act he's committed and the family for whom he carried it out. Rawlings' account of Jody's solitary, delirious journey through swamp and scrub after he's killed the fawn is as stirring as anything that's ever been written about loss:

> He found himself listening for something. It was the sound of the yearling for which he listened, running around the house or stirring on his moss pallet in the corner of the bedroom. He would never hear him again. He wondered if his mother had thrown dirt over Flag's carcass, or if the buzzards had cleaned it. Flag—He did not believe he would ever love anything, man or woman or his own child, as he had loved the yearling. He would be lonely all his life. But a man took it for his share and went on.
>
> In the beginning of his sleep, he cried out "Flag!"
>
> It was not his own voice that called. It was a boy's voice. Somewhere beyond the sink-hole, past the magnolia, under the live oaks, a boy and yearling ran side by side, and were gone forever.

As a child, I read *The Yearling* repeatedly. No matter how often I approached the ending, those final words invariably made me cry. It was not only the bleakness of the boy's emptiness that struck me then—and still does. More than anything, the real source of sorrow was that heavy implication of loneliness as a man's "share": a commodity necessarily purchased by obliterating the boy within.

With her presentation of boy matriculating to manhood through killing a beloved animal, Rawlings may have tapped into something particularly American. A slightly later classic of hardscrabble rural adolescence—*Old Yeller* by Fred Gipson—strikes some similar chords. Like *The Yearling*, Gipson's novel was turned into a successful film. In fact, *Old Yeller* ranks as one of Walt Disney's most palpable hit movies of the 1950s.

As with Flag the fawn, Yeller, a dingy blond cur, steps into the picture at the perfect moment. Jim Coates, the father of a family in rural Texas, is away on a cattle drive. His struggling wife, Katie, and her two sons can certainly use some help around their small acreage. And with no visible means of support of his own, the stray yellow dog who happens along can clearly use an opportunity to be helpful.

In the "no- 'count, egg-suckin'" tradition of American dog lore, Yeller is at first roundly rejected by Travis, the elder son in charge. The dog's initial bid to gain acceptance is saving the younger brother, Arliss, from a mother bear. Later, more conclusively, Yeller comes to Travis's aid, by fighting off an angry wild pig that has attacked the boy. After earning his stripes—literally—in the form of slashing wounds from the boar's tusks, Yeller is allowed to take his place on the family hearth, and in Travis's heart.

Unfortunately, it's a similarly heroic act that later proves both the dog's and the boy's undoing. When a lone "loafer" wolf menaces the family, Yeller fights it to the death. But such an unprovoked assault by a wolf can only mean that it's rabid.

In the film version of *Old Yeller*, Travis persuades his mother to wait and see whether the dog will actually get sick. He confines Yeller in a corn crib and checks daily for signs of the disease. Inevitably, the day comes when Travis peers into the pen to be met by the sight of a snarling, slavering beast only barely recognizable as his dog.

Katie offers to spare Travis the terrible task of shooting Yeller. But Travis takes the gun and tells her: "He's my dog. I'll do it." Which he does, "just like a man," as his father commends him upon his return.

Jim Coates has come back from the cattle drive with a horse for Travis. The idea is to move on, literally as well as figuratively, from the death of the dog. As well, a shy neighbour girl, Elizabeth Searcy, tries to contribute a puppy from a litter sired by Old Yeller.

But Travis doesn't want or expect another dog like Yeller. He leaves his little brother Arliss to romp with the pup. Like Jody Baxter before him, Travis Coates has taken his place in the adult world through the necessary sacrifice of his boyhood companion. As his father assures him, no man could have done any better.

In both *Old Yeller* and *The Yearling*, the boy is the one required to do the killing. Jim Coates is away from his family when the rabid wolf strikes. In *The Yearling*, Penny is injured and unable to get out of bed at the point when it becomes necessary to shoot the destructive deer. When Jody's mother botches the job, the son has no choice but to finish off the wounded Flag.

In both tales, the son is forced to be the executioner of the animal he loves. But, in so doing, he winds up securing the approval of his father through this all-important act of slaughter. At the end of *The Yearling*, as well as *Old Yeller*, the father is back in his rightful place at the head of the household, with a manly son at his side.

As well, in these two novels (and the films made from them) female characters exist, for the most part, to abet their boys on the road to manhood. In the film *Old Yeller*, Travis's mother Katie is the one who points out to him it "was not so lucky for Old Yeller" that he came into contact with a diseased wolf. Katie is the one who produces the rifle to dispatch the dog, prompting Travis to take it and do what he must do.

In *The Yearling*, it's also the mother who brings out the gun, when it's clear there is no choice but to get rid of Flag once and for all. But she aims badly, and it's only the sight of the poor animal floundering on the ground that compels Jody to take up the rifle and put an end to his pet's suffering.

In the film *Old Yeller*, Elizabeth Searcy brings Travis the new puppy that Yeller allegedly sired, out of her own spaniel Miss Priss. Regardless of whether a dog like Yeller can be replaced, young females like Elizabeth—and Miss Priss—have a regenerative part to play, by offering proof to grieving young men like Travis that life will go on.

In the equally revered American classic *Charlotte's Web*, author E. B. White allows his title character to provide the same reassurance. Charlotte the spider has saved the life of a young pig named Wilbur by weaving eye-catching messages about him into her web. However, a spider's lifespan is a short one; it's Charlotte who turns out to be the character doomed to die within the pages of the book.

But before she goes, Charlotte has time to weave one final master-piece, what she calls her "magnum opus": a sac full of her own eggs slated to hatch in the coming spring. Wilbur, who loves Charlotte, is devastated at the prospect of losing her. And he's adamant in his refusal to be consoled by the promise of her future offspring.

But Charlotte knows better. In the superb curtain speech he crafts for her, White makes clear that it's from the very inevitability of rebirth that comfort comes. More importantly, the death of the old is a prerequisite for that business of renewal that is the major point of existence.

"These autumn days will shorten and grow cold," Charlotte tells Wilbur in a failing voice.

> The leaves will shake loose from the trees and fall. Winter will pass. The song sparrow will return and sing, the frogs will waken, the warm wind will blow again. All these sights and sounds and smells will be yours to enjoy, Wilbur—this lovely world, these precious days . . .

White and Charlotte are right, of course. When spring hatches out, so do Charlotte's eggs, and the tiny spiderlings who salute an astonished Wilbur prove to be as wise, as whimsical, and as verbally nimble as their departed mother. The queen may be dead, but long live each new gener-ation of arachnid anointed. Or, as the cornball lyrics on the *Old Yeller* soundtrack have it during the closing credits: "Young Yeller's like his pappy; he's frisky and he's happy. And that's how a good dog should be."

In *Charlotte's Web*, E. B. White presents a clear distinction between the roles of human males and females with respect to animals. When we first meet eight-year-old Fern Arable, she is already in the act of intervening to save Wilbur's life. Her father, farmer John Arable, intends to dispatch a runty piglet with an axe. Like *The Yearling*'s Jody, Fern entreats her father to play fair with a little animal, who, as she points out, "couldn't help being born small, could it?"

Fern's ten-year-old brother Avery is introduced to us only a few pages later as "...heavily armed—an air rifle in one hand, a wooden dagger in the other." Avery's first reaction to the runt piglet is to deride him as "a miserable thing," with the unspoken suggestion that being born small means he's unfit to live.

Whether E. B. White intended it or not, these quite gender-specific responses to the pig have their origins deep in human consciousness. In *The Singular Beast*, anthropologist Claudine Fabre-Vassas tells us that in the Middle Ages in many parts of Europe, little girls were the family members charged with raising the pigs.

Boys, on the other hand, were encouraged to form a rowdier and often bloodier relationship with swine, especially in everything associated with their demise. From imitating the animals' cries of panic while being slaughtered, to bleeding themselves in obscure rites based on the ritual bleeding of the dead pig, it was the male offspring in the family who groomed themselves for future adult roles as Lord High Executioner. Just as their sisters, coddling and cosseting the little piglets, were readying themselves both for motherhood and the women's traditional task of tenderly coaxing the last drops of blood from the hanging pig carcass, to make sausage for the family feast.

In places as "modern" as twenty-first-century urban North America and Europe, direct personal contact with animal slaughter is the exception for most of us, rather than the rule. The meat we eat usually comes from the store, pre-killed and swathed in cellophane. When animals that we know and love have to die, it's generally the vet who dispatches them, not us. Even so, somewhere deep in our background, that age-old gender divide between destroyer and preserver occasionally lurks.

As a child, one of my most enduring desires was to have my own horse. However, until the real thing came along, I was prepared to make do with invented alternatives. Even at the age of eleven—embarrassingly old, according to my thirteen-year-old brother, for that sort of thing—I rode to and from school every day on an imaginary horse named Hightail.

The route of my twice-daily canter frequently took me past my brother, standing on the corner kibitzing with his friends. As Hightail and I thundered past, I would observe him, red-faced and mute with humiliation, while his friends derided him for having a crazy sister.

His pleas to my mother availed nothing. My mother always came down foursquare on the side of Creativity and Imagination. So eventually, my brother took matters into his own unlawful hands.

One evening, he accosted me in the family garage, where I stabled Hightail, just as I was currying the horse to put him away for the night. "Where is he?" my brother demanded. "Where's the horse?"

Scenting no particular danger, I pinpointed the place where he stood. From behind his back, my brother produced an ancient BB gun, and shot poor Hightail—who fell down as dead as any flesh-and-blood stallion would.

It was fantasy's darkest but most impressive hour.

Satisfied, my brother took his gun and went his way. However, the next day, as he and his friends clustered in their favourite spot on the corner not far from our school, he was horrified to glimpse me riding by as usual.

"I shot your horse!" he later raged at me out in the garage where I was busy, as always, grooming my steed. "I shot him dead!"

"You shot Hightail," I told him calmly. "This is Black Magic, Hightail's son."

III

EVEN IN CHILDREN'S CLASSIC BOOKS and movies like *The Yearling* and *Old Yeller* and *Charlotte's Web*, some animal deaths are more meaningful than others. After all, Jody Baxter and his father are out hunting the day their lives are forever altered by their encounter with the fawn they've made orphan. Similarly, in both the novel and film versions of Fred Gipson's *Old Yeller*, the Coates family routinely depends on what they kill—both livestock and wild game—in order to survive.

As well, in *Charlotte's Web* the Arable family's farm is rife with animals slated for the fate that Charlotte helps Wilbur the pig to avoid. To the cows, sheep—and no doubt especially to Wilbur's mother and siblings—the rules of birth, growth, slaughter, and consumption apply.

Or so we assume. Young Fern Arable, as far as we learn, has never previously felt motivated to intercede for any animal's life. Neither did Charlotte the spider act to save any other creature, before Wilbur came along.

And if Avery Arable's wooden dagger and air rifle are any indication, the boy in the family is already in training for his adult role as hunter and butcher. In none of these books or the films made from them does anyone ever suggest that the death of an animal you *don't* love might come at some emotional cost.

Meanwhile, in the real world, the love of actively taking animal life has enthusiastic proponents. Back in 2006, not long after the anniversary of his first five years in office, US President George W. Bush gave an interview to the German weekly *Bild am Sonntag*. He was asked to name both the worst and best moments of his presidency.

Not surprisingly, as his worst moment, Bush chose the morning of September 11, 2001, when he learned that hijacked planes had crashed into the World Trade Center in New York and Washington's Pentagon building. And his best moment?

"I would say the best moment of all," the president replied, "was when I caught a seven-and-a-half pound perch in my lake."

Some people might be taken aback by the revelation that catching a fish in his own carefully stocked lake would rate as a peak moment for anyone, particularly a world leader. But in other dedicated anglers—as well as with hunters—I would imagine the president's small piece of self-congratulation about the big one that didn't get away struck a chord of fellow feeling, regardless of party affiliation or point of view on 9/11.

For a period of time in the 1990s, I lived in the heavily populated countryside north of New York City, where the fall deer hunt was—and no doubt still is—an annual rite. Around mid-November, "Welcome Hunters" signs would go up in Day-Glo lettering outside roadside eateries and inns along the local highways. "Guns and Ammo," advertised outside stores year-round, featured even more prominently during deer season. And with inevitable concurrence, the "sanctity of hunting" rhetoric would heat up to the boiling point in the local papers.

Letters to the editor attested to the power of hunting as a way to bring together today's fractured families. Cracker-barrel columnists and backwoods philosophers poured on the purple prose, as they extolled the merits of shooting deer as a means of getting closer to God, or saving the local retail and service economy—or both.

Oh sure, the destruction wrought by the abundant deer population also rated a few column inches. "Giant vermin" and "oversized rabbits" were the epithets most commonly hurled at these devourers of hedges and decapitators of corn-tops. "Responsible stewardship" was the most frequently cited rationale for heading out on a frosty fall morning with guns and ammo.

But the way it looked from my front window and along the road, some folks just like to hunt. Weekend warriors in sedans with New Jersey plates, already lubricated against the chill of November in the Taconic Hills, would arrive loaded—in both senses of the word—for deer, ready to fire at anything that looked biggish or brownish, be it barn or Buick or billy goat, and intently hoping something besides themselves might get bagged.

Surprisingly, there were seldom any young sons in evidence, getting their first lesson in manly outdoorsmanship from Dad. Few proud sportswomen either, drawing a bead with the quiet competence of Annie Oakley. Just packs of cost accountants and car dealership owners and middle managers at large utilities in orange hats and camouflage fatigues, waving chummily from their cars as they drove by with a bloodied doe slung over the hood—or retreating, surprised and indignant, when confronted by a homeowner pointing out a "No Trespassing" sign.

Yet, even in a place like that—where prey animals were in over-supply

and gullibly approachable—it was "Love of the Chase" that was most frequently invoked to justify what passed for sport. That, according to
American anthropologist Matt Cartmill, is not much a surprise.

In *A View to a Death in the Morning: Hunting and Nature Through History*,
Cartmill writes about what he calls the "murderous amorousness" of hunting: a sort of reverence for killing that implies an affection for the victim
which is, in fact, false and even contemptuous.

Cartmill also views hunting as a symbolic attack on women, almost an
acceptable form of rape. Another social observer of the American scene,
Brian Luke, agrees that there is veiled sexuality in the hunting of animals.

However, Luke adds, the "sportsman's code" of killing quickly and
taking only as much game as needed at least involves some recognition of
the value of individual animals and an obligation to minimize their suffering. Canadian philosopher Angus Taylor remarks on this code as something of a "paradox." In his opinion, those goals could best be realized by
not hunting at all.

Of course, when questions of love and death arise, women also want
to weigh in. As far back as the seventeenth century, Margaret Cavendish,
the Duchess of Newcastle, turned her feminist gaze on hot pursuit of the
humble rabbit. She laments in her poem "The Hunting of the Hare":

As if that God made Creatures for Mans meat,
To give them Life and Sense, for Man to eat:
Or else for Sport, or Recreations sake,
Destroy those Lifes that God saw good to make.

Poet Andrew Marvell, almost an exact contemporary of Cavendish,
put himself into the psyche of a similarly animal-friendly woman. In "The
Nymph Complaining for the Death of Her Fawn" Marvell's nymph declares:

The wanton troopers riding by
Have shot my fawn and it will die.
Ungentle men! They cannot thrive to kill thee.
Thou ne'er didst, alive,

Them any harm; also nor could
Thy death yet do them any good.

Later in the poem we learn that the maiden's faithless lover Silvio has
left her in the lurch. In fact, it was Silvio who gave her the fawn. Clearly,
the death of the animal suggests more to her than the loss of a pet she has
taken charge of mostly as a token of her departed sweetheart's love.

Still, she makes clear that she has never blamed the little creature for
her circumstances. "O, I cannot be Unkind t' a beast that loveth me," she
declares—in an obvious jab both at Silvio and at those "wanton" male
strangers who shot her pet.

Generally, the love of killing is something we associate less with
women than with men. The media frenzy surrounding the hunting
prowess of 2008 vice-presidential candidate Sarah Palin only underscored
how unusual it is to see photos of a woman proudly holding up the
antlered head of a caribou she has personally shot, or hear the ability to
"field-dress a moose" included in her list of qualifications.

But even if women are found more rarely than men in the forefront
of the hunting party, that doesn't mean they've had no other role to play
in the capture of prey. Young maidens in particular have a long, if not
exactly honourable, history of showing apparent willingness to serve as
bait for the animals men seek to kill.

The Unicorn by Lise Gotfredsen is a wonderfully complex study of that
mythic one-horned animal. Along the way, much attention gets paid to
the virginal human being as the love interest who entices him to her lap,
for easy capture and subsequent death.

As early as 200 CE, says Gotfredsen, the anonymous bestiaries written in Greek and collectively called The Physiologus depict a virgin first calming a unicorn, then getting it to suckle, before holding it in place for the
hunter. (Physiologically, it's hard to feature how a virgin would have breast
milk to offer to a unicorn or any other being. It makes me wonder if Mary,
the virginal mother of Christ—to whom the unicorn myth later became
linked—prefigures that image of a lactating maiden?)

By the Middle Ages, according to Lisa Gotfredsen, the animal's horn symbolized penetration. The idea of the virgin holding the unicorn in her lap was now established as something clearly sexual, almost romantic. But it was a romantic relationship that led to the animal's death, with the virgin as accomplice, witting if not necessarily willing.

More recently, both in life and art, big-game aficionado Ernest Hemingway included gun-toting women on hunting trips. As well, in the film version of Isak Dinesen's *Out of Africa*, one of the most romantic scenes features a pith-helmeted Karen Blixen and her lover Denis Finch-Hatton surprising and shooting a pair of lions—and then becoming erotically charged by this high-risk experience.

Around that same time, in the early twentieth century, Delia Akeley, first wife of naturalist Carl Akeley, accompanied him on elephant-hunting expeditions. She also took part, seemingly gleefully, in the kill. In a photograph of Delia, a servant holds an arch of severed tusks over her head, as she is "anointed" with pulp from the tusk of the first elephant she shot.

By contrast, in his writings, Delia Akeley's husband Carl revealed ambivalence about killing animals. He described "feeling like a murderer" as he looked down on a silverback gorilla he'd felled. In an account of another expedition, he expressed relief that it was a cameras-only shooting party, from which the gorillas headed off "none the worse for having met with white men that morning."

In fact, Akeley's attitude to exotic animals comprised a complicated mixture of love and bloodlust. He first made his name in taxidermy circles in the 1880s, when he undertook the stuffing and preservation of Jumbo, P. T. Barnum's world-famous, oversized African bull elephant.

Jumbo had met his end a few days before in a collision with a train in St. Thomas, Ontario. By the time Akeley could get himself from New York to the site, Jumbo's enormous corpse was in a fairly unsavoury state. Six butchers had to be called in to help with the rapidly rotting carcass. But eventually, Akeley remodelled the remains into a form that ensured Jumbo could continue to make money for Barnum, even after death.

Akeley went on to a career in hunting, shooting and then stuffing dead exotic animals, mostly for dioramas he created in the American Museum of Natural History in New York City. This livelihood engendered in him a lifelong conflict.

On the one hand, there was Akeley's Great White Hunter persona, which manifested itself in his friendship with and admiration for his frequent hunting companion Theodore Roosevelt. Even by the rough and ready standards of those rapacious days, Roosevelt was a man outstanding in his zest for bloodsport. Yet, Carl Akeley's writings reflect another self, with genuine reverence and even empathy for the animals he hunted, killed, and later mounted in authentic-looking jungle sets.

Ambivalent aspects of the relationship to both animal love and animal death also show up in Ernest Hemingway's work and life. Hemingway was only two years old when Rough Rider Theodore Roosevelt ascended to the US presidency. But in some ways, he was as much a product of those times as Roosevelt and his good friend Carl Akeley.

Certainly, elements of Hemingway's work seem to exemplify that prevailing cultural pressure to become a "man among men," by taking up arms against a sea of troubles—be they in the form of the German Kaiser, the fascists of Spain, or an enraged elephant—and by opposing, end them. Along with, perhaps, some of your deeply internalized doubts about your own rough-and-readiness.

In all aspects of human life, the need to inure oneself to the pain of death can sometimes have a corrosive effect on the ability to open up oneself to love. And in the long history of humans' involvement with animals, learning how to kill kindness in *oneself* as a means of killing the love we feel for them has often been the only means to manage our emotions surrounding their slaughter.

At the extreme end of the spectrum, people who actually go out of their way to hate, abuse, or even kill animals may be reacting to their own darkest terrors. In *The Dreaded Comparison: Human and Animal Slavery*, Marjorie Spiegel analyzes the basis of violence toward "the oppressed" (whether animal or human). Denial of irrational aspects of our own selves, such as fear of animals, or even "an unnatural fear of nature itself," can lead to projecting those fears onto others, Spiegel writes. "Through violent actions towards the symbol, the oppressors unconsciously try to destroy those qualities in themselves which they find so threatening and wish to deny."

However, in his study of Hemingway, American critic Cary Wolfe points to a softer side that comes out in *The Garden of Eden*, a novel unfinished at the time of Hemingway's suicide. While still a boy, the protagonist, whose name is David, witnesses the killing of a bull elephant by his over-bearing father and his black African guide. For David, one of the most terrible aspects is that he was the one who innocently alerted his father and the guide to the elephant's presence. Even as an adult, David still can't rid himself of the recollection of the eye of that elephant fixing him with a look of reproach, just before the huge animal collapses into a wrinkled, inert pile—an image which might come readily to the aging, impotent Hemingway, shortly before he pulled the trigger on himself.

Cary Wolfe is struck by both the compassion and the ambivalence about animal death that Hemingway displays. His character David's tor-tured response to the death of an elephant is a far cry from the ballsier perspective of some of Hemingway's earlier protagonists—as well as Papa's own more typical point of view.

For instance, in *Death in the Afternoon*, a reverential treatise on bull-fighting, the author makes much of the almost sacred aspects of the show-down between bull and matador. However, the disemboweling and deaths of horses in the bullring is apparently another matter. "[I]n the tragedy of the bullfight," Hemingway writes dismissively, "the horse is the comic character."

There is no doubt that tough-minded inculcation has always been required to form boys into future men of action. Particularly in the boy-hood era of men like Hemingway—as well as Roosevelt and Carl Akeley, only slightly earlier—hair-raising books of hunting lore had a role to play in that inculcation.

One day while stalking the stacks of the University of Toronto's Gerstein Library, I happened upon a book I'm sure Teddy R. himself would have regarded as a real rip-snorter. It was a morocco-bound volume titled *Curious And Instructive Stories About Wild Animals and Birds*, published in Edinburgh in 1897.

Curious in itself is the fact that the name of the author appears nowhere. However, the charge slip the librarian handed me when I checked the book out gave the name of the author as William White Cooper. He seems to have been an employee or director at the Zoological

Gardens in London in the mid-1800s, although the animals stories he collected for the reader's delectation range from trapping tales of the Canadian North, to the antics of exotic animal mascots at Oxford, to ravening wolves on the Russian steppes.

"Ripping yarns" would be the category into which most of these stories fall, and it's easy to imagine a young English boarding schoolboy, electrified right up until lights out by tales of predatory eagles and man-eating tigers. While the author takes pains to deplore pastimes like bear-baiting as "unsportsmanlike," he seems to find nothing amiss in snaring, stabbing, and whacking innumerable animals in all kinds of ways.

However, in the copy of the book that came into my temporary possession, there is one element that strikes me as almost poignantly askew. A printed bookplate pasted on the fly-leaf informs us the book was won by one David Walker, a pupil of the John Neilson Institution, from the Session 1899–1900. And it was a "Prize Given by John Polson Esq. . . . of Castle Levan, For Learning the Names, English and Botanical, of All Our Common Trees and Shrubs."

Good God. Picture a youthful, tree-hugging David Walker, arboreal enthusiast and gentle connoisseur of botanical Latin, leaving the podium after shaking John Polson Esq's hand—with a book that regards stories of stalking, shooting, and skinning our four-footed and feathered friends as "curious and instructive."

We're a long way from the John Neilson Institution of Paisley, Scotland, circa 1900. But it's curious to wonder whatever became of David Walker. And surely it would be instructive to find out exactly how it was his copy of *Curious and Instructive Stories About Wild Animals and Birds* found its final resting place in the Gerstein Library in Toronto, Canada.

OF COURSE, THE ROLE OF BLOODLUST in shaping men's relationships with animals goes much farther back in time than written lore of any kind. In his interesting but downright peculiar book, *Hunters, Herders and Hamburgers*, Richard Bulliet, a professor of History at Columbia University in New York, does not gently invite us to journey back with him to prehistory.

He grabs the reader by the throat in his first paragraph.

Back in the good old days of "pre-domesticity," Bulliet declares, seeing animals copulate, as well as capitulate to bloody slaughter, was an essential element of human life. Even in the succeeding era of "domesticity" (i.e., from the dawn of agriculture to the rise of the industrial age) every farm boy had a hunting knife or, later, a rifle—plus a calf or sheep of his own to initiate him into the mysterious ways of love.

Sadly, in our "post-domestic" times, Bulliet laments, kids are forced to slake their bloodlust with slasher films, and make do with simulated on-screen sex, or clumsy experiments with human peers—the latter usually at a far later date than those earlier adolescent encounters with available animals down on the farm.

Leaving aside consideration of barnyard bestiality (something I find surprisingly easy to do) it's interesting to look at Bulliet's lament for the passing of the age of direct, everyday contact with animal death in countervail to the "murderous amorousness" Matt Cartmill writes about. Hunting, according to Bulliet's way of thinking, is a far more respectful—even loving—relationship with animals than what's arisen since, first with domestication, and more recently with the successor to the family homestead, the factory farm.

American ecological philosopher Paul Shepard would agree. In *The Others: How Animals Made Us Human*, Shepard argues that it's the disrespect and dishonouring of meat animals inherent in agriculture that forces us to stamp out our own feelings for them in order to kill them—or to conceal what we're about by hiding the abattoirs and even the animals themselves in enormous faceless facilities.

Like Bulliet, Hemingway, and other writers whom I've encountered, Shepard posits a "holiness" possible in "killing them," or in "celebrating them by wearing their skins." He also criticizes what Richard Bulliet has more recently dubbed "the post-domestic" society in which we live. As well, Shepard piles on the animal rights crowd, who, he claims "do not recognize the flesh of animals as a food sanctity or perceive animals as a means of speculative thought, referential analogy or immanent divination."

Respect for the animals we kill, holiness in their death, subsequent celebration of their now-inert hides and body parts. . . . For most of us in modern society, that interface of love, slaughter, and posthumous reverence in our dealings with animals would be tricky enough to finesse. But for those who deal directly and daily with animal life and death by working in humane societies and shelters, finding such feelings of posthumous sanctity or celebration require even more rigorous mental gymnastics.

For one thing, the fact that shelter-workers come to their careers mostly through love of animals frequently puts them in a conflict about animal death that American sociologists Arnold Arluke and Clifford R. Sanders have termed a "paradox" in and of itself. In *Regarding Animals*, Arluke and Sanders looked at a shelter whose "open intake" policy of accepting all animals, whether adoptable or not, made euthanasia of some inmates an inevitable part of the job. There, experienced staff members tried to help newcomers resolve this paradox. "You will want to care for the animals, but you will have to kill some of them," senior staff would explain, and then add, soothingly, "It seems so bad, but we'll make it good in your head."

Making it good in new staffers' heads was not a process of stamping out any emotional attachment to the animals. It was a procedure of teaching workers to see the inmates as "virtual pets"—something between living creatures and inanimate objects.

Another technique involved characterizing the animals as a population of refugees, and seeing them as en route either to homes—or to Heaven. In the institution's record books, initials placed beside the names of departed animals denoted each one's particular fate: "PWP" stood for "Placed With People"; "PWG" meant "Placed With God."

Sometimes, Arluke and Sanders found, workers in open-intake facilities designate particular animals as "mascots." Mascots are never killed, and are allowed to run free on the premises. Therefore, workers can risk getting close to them and treating them as real pets—rather than as remote, caged objects whose uncertain fate makes attachment too emotionally dangerous to contemplate.

In cases where animals cannot be adopted out, staff devise rituals to ease the emotional toll on those workers who must euthanize them. In advance of the necessary execution date, the cat or dog is given special treats and extra time for petting and consolation by staff members who don't have to do the actual killing.

That enables those workers to participate in the mourning process, and share the emotional burden of the person actually designated to euthanize the animal. The workers also reassure each other that the case of the pet in question was "hopeless." In this way, their status as caring and "authentic" shelter workers remains uncompromised by their inability to save every animal under their care.

However, in other cases, the euthanasia of a particular animal may generate an unusual amount of distress and disagreement among staff. In such circumstances, Arluke and Sanders note, ordinary rituals of consolation don't suffice. Shelter personnel become markedly resistant to the idea of further killings, and start to petition more vigorously for the sparing of other animals whose "hopelessness" is now suddenly in question.

AS E. B. WHITE'S WONDERFULLY STRAIGHTFORWARD essay "Death of a Pig" discloses, the author occasionally raised pigs for slaughter. But in his children's classic *Charlotte's Web*, the point of view of the farmer is seldom defended—and even occasionally condemned. Nowhere more so than when White has Wilbur learn from a tactless old ewe about a "regular conspiracy around here to kill you at Christmastime."

"Wilbur burst into tears. 'I don't *want* to die,' he moaned. 'I want to stay alive, right here in my comfortable manure pile with all my friends.'"

When Charlotte the spider gets wind of this plan, she decries it as "the dirtiest trick I ever heard of. What people don't think of!"

Of course, as Wilbur has already learned, Charlotte herself lives by killing and eating flies. But it's the duplicity of human beings that seems to outrage her, and galvanizes her resolve to save her little friend from the axe. Perhaps it was his urge to examine that duplicity in himself that prompted sometime hog farmer E. B. White to inform his character Wilbur about man's plan for pig.

These days, livestock animals are most commonly killed in abattoirs—

usually by people who don't even know them, much less harbour any emotional attachment. However, according to anthrozoologist James Serpell, throughout the long history of our interaction with livestock, farmers and even slaughterhouse proprietors have been required to adopt tactics to enable them to kill animals without guilt—or at least as little guilt as possible. That is as true in modern meat plants as it was on the old-fashioned farm.

Most time-honoured among methods of reducing guilt, says Serpell in *In the Company of Animals*, is "distancing." That may be in the form of the old stockman's maxim "Don't ever name 'em," or through concealment of the site of slaughter, or even shifting the blame for the necessity of the cycle of animal life and death to God or some other external agency. By whatever means it's achieved, detachment from one's own emotion or the opprobrium of others is a vital requirement of the killing enterprise.

For those uneasy with the concept of animal death by any means, it's hard to find a comfortable level of involvement. Would you rather a) shoot a deer with a bow and arrow or gun? b) personally escort the calf you raised in a 4-H club up the Stairway to Heaven? c) select a lobster from a restaurant tank and leave someone else to boil it to death? d) settle down to a bucket of fast-food fried chicken, willfully unaware of the short, stunted life and uncaring, assembly-line death of the young animal whose body parts coated in batter are yours to enjoy? Or e) none of the above?

Of course, if you answered "none of the above," you're going to have a harder time than anyone else comprehending those who speak of loving animals *and* killing them, in the same sentence. Yet even a cheerfully unreconstructed carnivore might well find it difficult to understand how the man or woman who sends a captive bolt into the brain of the cow in the abattoir, or who trains retriever dogs to fetch dead birds without damaging them, or who raises the sheep he or she personally serves up to the family as rack of lamb could identify him or herself as an "animal lover."

However unfathomable to some, those claims are made by others. And even if we are not, ourselves, that sort of animal lover, each of us knows someone who is.

IV

ON THE WALLS OF THE MEXICAN RESTAURANT Temple Grandin has chosen for lunch are murals of what look like Aztec priests or chieftains, bending over ornately arrayed maidens supine on a mountain peak. "Human sacrifice," says Temple succinctly, leaving me to wonder if *this* is what she had in mind when she claimed there's lots worse than humane slaughter.

"The beef and shrimp fajitas are really good," she tells me. "That's what I'm having, only without the tortilla 'cause I'm wheat intolerant. Autistic people need animal protein." (I hear an echo of her sharp, snappy response to me over the phone: "I *gotta* eat 'em!")

"In fact," she continues, "Everybody does. Vegans are Vitamin B-12 deficient, did you know that? They gotta take supplements 'cause there's no natural source of B-12 but meat. Of course, even those chimpanzees the vegans like to talk about as 'vegetarian'—they eat meat! Nobody wanted to believe that, until Jane Goodall said so."

"If you didn't need animal protein for your own particular dietary requirements," I ask, "would you still be a carnivore?"

"Yes, I would be," she replies without hesitation. And then adds, "Anyhow, I went through all that vegan stuff in the early seventies. No meat, no milk, no eggs. It doesn't *work.*"

By this time, I am accustomed to her vehemence. What startles me is this brief glimpse of another Temple, in another day—possibly around the same time that she was deciding which conservative dress to wear for her audience at Harvard with B. F. Skinner.

"But all those vegans," I begin, "Don't they—"

"It doesn't work. For anybody."

Case closed. Veil drawn. Is she disappointed by where she's ended up on the spectrum, even though she considers her reasons for meat consumption easily defended and has made her life's work easing animals as gently as possible down the road to dusty death?

Of herself, Temple Grandin has written: "I don't have an unconscious." In *Animals in Translation*, she goes on to explain that thinking in pictures, not words, makes it impossible for her to repress ideas and images the way non-autistic people can. "That's why I can't watch any violent movie with rape or torture scenes," she writes. "The pictures stay in my conscious mind."

By that logic, it can't be that she has repressed the memory of whatever impulses led her, so long ago, to abjure meat-eating. No more than she has successfully submerged those images of horses starving in the desert or cattle being paralyzed, rather than anaesthetized, by the pointed knife blades of Mexican slaughterhouse workers.

Now, on the other side of the restaurant table, it appears to me that she has gone somewhere into her conscious mind impossible to follow or fathom. "Anyway," she observes after a moment of silent contemplation, "a pet dog who's confined to a crate twenty-three hours a day in someone's apartment is worse off than a cow raised for beef and humanely slaughtered. Besides, we're talking about animals who would not exist if not for us."

That's a rationale I've encountered before, and it always puzzles me. Is she suggesting that life is a gift we've given livestock which remains ours to rescind at will?

To help me through my confusion, she directs me to *The Omnivore's Dilemma* by Michael Pollan—in particular the section on the ethics of eating meat. Pollan pretty much gets it right, she says.

The next day, I go to a bookstore in a Fort Collins mall, purchase a copy of Pollan's book, settle myself in the in-store café with a big cappuccino and flip immediately to the chapter entitled "The Ethics of Eating Animals." In it is an account of the author's conversation with Temple, which reassures him about the effectiveness of her methods of ensuring most animals are slaughtered with a minimum of panic and pain. Yet he is troubled too, because of those allowable exceptions to the rules of measurable audit that end up dying a more traumatic death.

What Pollan concludes for himself is that eating meat is ethical if he can see how it was raised as well as how the animal was slaughtered. Even though the vast industrial complex in which most livestock are raised and slaughtered in America, he says, could not withstand such scrutiny of its operations.

In general, he decides the lives of well cared-for domesticates are such an improvement on the short, nasty, and brutish deaths many animals suffer in nature, that we do them a favour by putting them under our stewardship. And do them no harm by humanely relieving them of their lives at the end of the day.

Besides, he observes, some species, like chickens, have no real role in the world *unless* we eat them. "The surest way to achieve the extinction of the species would be to grant chickens a right to life."

From Michael Pollan, that line of reasoning makes no more sense to me than when it comes from Temple. Still, I appreciate the depth of his concerns. And also appreciate Temple for recommending an author who's referred to some aspects of her work as "troubling."

When I pull out my wallet to pay for our lunch, I observe to Temple—by way of injecting something light-hearted into a mainly heavy day—that I'm lucky to have cash. I explain how I'd arrived the day before, at the Denver airport Budget Rent-A-Car, only to discover that I'd left home without my VISA card and hardly any US cash. Fortunately, I was able to persuade the Budget folks to let me use their phone to reach the VISA emergency line, and VISA orchestrated delivery of cash for me to a Western Union. Temple, the savvy traveler and frequent flyer, is not impressed. "Why'd you have to ask Budget to let you use their phone?" she immediately wants to know. "What was wrong with your cellphone?"

"I don't have one," I confess meekly. "I must be the last person on the planet over the age of six who doesn't."

"You must be," she agrees. *And I'm supposed to be the one with cognitive issues?* is her unspoken subtext. "So how come you didn't just use another credit card to rent the car?"

"I only have VISA." I explain more meekly still. "Up until yesterday, it was all I ever needed."

As I grow meeker, she grows sterner in her assessment. "When I'm on the road, I always make sure my cellphone's charged, and I got an extra credit card, plus cash on hand, just in case."

Her evident pride in her organizational ability is understandable. It's like the way she's described her mind, sorting information into various file folders, and what she's had to overcome, in order to attain such a level of internal control.

Clearly I have failed her measurable audit of my practices, as surely as if I'd used the electric prod one too many times per hundred head, or allowed too high a percentage to slip and fall en route to the Stairway to Heaven. However, despite my deficiencies, Temple is kind. After lunch, she drives me back to my hotel. As she lets me off at the curb, she looks me in the eye—something she has already told me people with autism aren't always eager to do—and says, "I'm about practical solutions."

For a moment, I don't know what she means. Then, I perceive the intent behind the words: when it comes time to write up our conversation, I should put her on record as one dedicated to kinder alternatives to pain and fear for livestock animals slated to die, as livestock animals inevitably are.

Whatever else she says or does or advises or engineers is only a further way of declaring what she is about: practical solutions, rather than abstract concepts or feel-good philosophies or hot-button issues. If I get nothing else right about her, she wants to make sure I am correct about that.

I nod and smile and thank her for her generosity with her time. And I tell her I understand. Because in my own groping way, I believe I do.

FOR HUMAN BEINGS WHO FEEL COMPELLED to kill animals—even, in some cases, animals they profess to love—there is justification to be found in nature. "Nature red in tooth and claw" connotes the realm of kill-or-be-killed. It's a realm where, as we like to say, "the law of the jungle" holds sway. By which we mean no rule of law at all, just the unvarnished exigencies of prey and predator, weak versus strong, fit against fitter.

"Like a wild animal," is something else we say, to characterize a vicious murderer or a particularly brutal assailant. That very term "brutal" links acts of wanton savagery to the animal world. Since that's the way non-humans deal with each other, is the implication, why shouldn't we deal with them just as remorselessly?

That must have been the impulse uppermost in the mind of the master, after he and his lady came home to find the cradle overturned, the child nowhere to be seen, and the trusted family dog with bloody jaws. What further proof did he require of a savage beast lurking beneath the hide of a creature he'd taken for his friend?

Small wonder then that the man instinctively seized his sword and stabbed without mercy at such a merciless brute. In that moment of rage, he was no more complex in his response than a murderous dog: obedient only to the law of strong versus weak, predator against prey. But the greyhound had not harmed the child; in fact, the dog had saved him from a deadly serpent. Red in tooth and claw, as you might say, with the reflexive fury of the family protector—or just the particular savagery snakes seem to provoke in canines.

Does it matter whether the greyhound killed for love of his master's child? Perhaps we can settle on a motive less lofty, more in keeping with the justice of the jungle: kill-or-be-killed. We're talking about a dog, after all. The thrill of the hunt, the love of the chase is a longing far older than the devotion he feels for his master. Even on a day like today, with the lord and his lady unaccountably away from home, and the child left under his watchful eye. Dozing, head down on his paws, long lanky limbs stretched out fore and aft. Yet only seeming to sleep. That's the trick of a sentry attentive to his post. One ear is cocked for trouble, one eye always ready to see—

See what? Head up with a jerk. Or, has he heard it first—that shifting, slithering sound? A snake, a large one, sliding out from between those chinks in the stone, boldly on its way to investigate the cradle. And the child.

The dog feels the short hair rising on his neck, a sensation that serves to drive his anger. This, of course, is what he has waited for. The thrill of the hunt, the love of the chase. Although it's not love he feels toward the snake he means to kill; it's red-hot rage. And in the heat of a moment like this, any love he has ever felt for the child in its cradle, or the absent master, is neither here nor there.

Instantly, the greyhound leaps for the snake. But in leaping, knocks over the cradle. For a moment, he freezes, terrified he's done something terribly wrong. But as the snake hisses and starts to slither beneath the overturned cradle, the dog comes to life again and quickly pounces.

Crack! His jaws close tight on the snake. He feels the crunch of the spine as it snaps. Then he shakes and shakes and shakes it, until the sickly-smelling blood of the snake is spattered everywhere. At last, he flings the snake's body as far from himself as he can.

Now, from beyond the chamber, he hears the footsteps of someone approaching. Instantly, the dog recollects himself *as* a dog: no longer the savage beast, but guardian of the hearth, beloved servant of his master once more. He draws himself up tall, and looks eagerly toward the door. In a moment, just one more moment, someone will arrive. Someone who will notice the upended cradle, and turn it upright, to disclose the master's child, sleeping safe and sound—as well as the serpent lying motionless in a far corner, silent as a secret.

PART TWO

My Keeper's Brother:
More than Kin, Less than Kind

T HE EXPRESSION "DAMNED IF YOU DO and damned if you don't" might have been invented for the animals most like humans. On the one hand (and in the case of primates, we really *are* talking about hands) the striking resemblance between humans and apes argues movingly for their consideration as our kin.

On the other hand, those genetic and psychic similarities between us and them have often operated to their detriment. We have turned them into subhuman experimental objects, pioneering astronauts, and human surrogates whenever we require someone like us—but not *too* like us—to precede us down the mineshaft, into the nose cone, or up onto the gurney for injection with a deadly virus.

Chimpanzees, gorillas, and monkeys are not the only non-humans who both benefit from and suffer for their similarity to us. Dogs appeal to us with their eloquent eyes, eager personalities, and apparent desire to participate in our lives. Yet, because of their nearer kinship to wolves, they also inspire our deepest mistrust.

Perhaps in no other area does the damned-if-you're-similar-damned-if-you're-different paradox operate so tellingly as in advocacy for abused animals. The need for sympathetic "poster animals" to head fundraising campaigns or spearhead pet-adoption drives is a fact of life for animal welfare organizations and sanctuaries. At the same time, advocates for abused donkeys, homeless dogs, and "retired" research apes worry about further exploiting the already-exploited by selling them on their humanoid qualities.

How like us is close enough, but not too close for comfort? How unlike us can animals remain without incurring our suspicion and hostility? Those questions are at the heart of the paradoxical relationship of kin and unkind.

I

ABOVE THE ENTRANCE TO THE COMPOUND at Fauna Farm that houses "retired" research chimpanzees stands a narrow metal cage, looking something like a phone booth with bars. The cage is empty. But it serves as a potent reminder of these animals' past, and perhaps also as a wordless summary of humanity's entire relationship with our nearest kin.

"This is the kind of cage these chimps would live in, sometimes for years and years on end," explains Gloria Grow, co-founder and administrator of the Fauna Farm and Foundation. "We got it from the same facility as some of the chimps. I had it mounted right here to make a point even before you go in. Sure, they're still in prison here. But it's a better prison."

The Fauna Farm is a big, beautiful spread outside the village of Carignan, Quebec. "Once the chimps are gone, I want to turn the farm into an arboretum open to the public," Gloria tells me. She gestures to a large, handsome farmhouse as we whirr past in a golf cart. "That's where we live"— as if the home she shares with her veterinarian husband Richard is simply another of the numerous landmarks on this guided tour. In a way it is.

At the moment, I'm seated on a bench outside the chimps' compound with my notebook, grateful for a brief interlude to jot down some of what I've seen so far from the golf cart. Gloria has left me here while she goes inside to lure some of the chimps to the outdoor enclosure, where there are climbing frames and ropes and trees. It's a warm September day, but breezy. On windy days, she explains almost apologetically, the chimps prefer to hang around inside in their cages, to watch their lunch being prepared in the open kitchen. Still, she's hoping she can move the act outdoors with the enticement of a bunch of bananas.

The farmhouse, the land, and the office buildings have all been deeded to the Fauna Foundation. Gloria and Richard live here as tenants. Although the gardens and the proposed arboretum will eventually be made public, none of the chimps or other rescue animals are for gawking at.

The one hundred-acre farm with assorted horses, cattle, pigs, chicken, ducks, geese, dogs, and, cats—as well as the enclosures that house the various monkeys, a lone baboon, and more than a dozen retired chimps—is available only for pre-arranged viewing. That select audience includes folk like me, as well as media people, money people, and anyone else Gloria and her Foundation family genuinely think can help keep Fauna afloat, until such time as it's given over to tour groups to wander along the paths among the flora.

From my bench, I have a good view of the walkway to a not-currently-accessible island, where a couple of groundskeepers are at work. Presumably, they are trying to deal with the landscaping problems that have kept the island from being the haven Gloria originally envisioned for her collection of battle-fatigued chimps.

I do, however, recall the island from a scene shot at Fauna for a PBS documentary I'd seen about chimp sanctuaries. Tom, one of the oldest chimps, was filmed there, when he first set foot on its open expanse. It was an affecting moment: Tom's sad eyes blinking in the sun, his splayed toes planted in living foliage, possibly for the first time in his long life. When he eventually climbed a tree and surveyed the world below, his sagging lower lip and furrowed face made him seem like some thoughtful tribal elder, pondering the prospect of living out his last days in solitary unconfinement.

Still, for Gloria the plan is not to perpetuate the arrival of new Toms at Fauna. "My goal is to end all this," she stresses. "To see the last chimp leave. But until then ..." She shrugs.

Until then, the shrug implies, there will be more chimps, turned "dirty" from too much experimentation, to be bought or begged from research companies. There will be other unwanted primate specimens offered to Fauna by zoos and university labs. There will be fresh financial benefactors to be wooed, media requests to be sifted through, and the same key points to be made to visitors, as often as required.

All because chimpanzees, among the many species of rescue animals at Fauna, speak to Gloria Grow in some particularly urgent way. What way that is, she has already promised me, I will see when I meet them.

"There's something about them. I can't even describe it. I mean, it's not as if I would say they're my favourite animals in the world. Over there—" From the golf cart she directs my gaze to a distant fenced pen enclosing what in the sun look like a couple of large shiny stones. "Pigs. They're my favourites."

"I like pigs myself," I concur. Much better than primates, truth be told, though I don't want to admit as much to Gloria.

"Wait'll you meet my guys . . ." She turns from the broad green fields toward the primate enclosures. "They're . . . Well, you'll see. They're chimpanzee *people*. There's really no other way I can put it."

It's fun whizzing around the farm, past horses flicking their tails in the pasture, kittens tumbling together in the sun, and sheep and cows grazing in the fields—not to speak of those pigs. All creatures great, small, and indisputably animal.

Now, waiting by the outdoor enclosure to meet chimpanzee people face to face, I know I should feel more anticipation than I do. But apes and monkeys. . . . Well, the resemblance feels, paradoxically enough, like a barrier to wholehearted engagement.

I begin to recollect, somewhat too vividly, one day when I went as a small child to the Moose Jaw Zoo. It was an awful facility in those days— even *for* those days. Stark, cramped cages with bare concrete floors meagerly strewn with straw, like a bad comb-over, and the stench of urine. Then, of course, there were the animals either following you with dispirited eyes, pacing with an air of private urgency, or else apathetically gazing at nothing because there was nothing to gaze at.

As I dawdled behind my parents and brother, I became attracted by a cage full of monkeys. I went close to the bars to have a better look. A monkey looked back at me. He had a hard, evaluative expression, like a tough kid. Suddenly, he startled me by swinging over to stick his hand through the bars, palm up.

I was fascinated by that palm. It was small and crisscrossed with lines, like an old fortune teller's hand somehow shrunken to baby size. I stared down at it, and then up at the animal it belonged to. He stared down at his empty palm too, then back at me, expectantly.

I extended my own hand, to show him it was equally empty. Instantly, his hand darted out to seize my forefinger. His grip was leathery, tight and determined. I stood there terrified, not making a sound.

There was nobody else around the cage. Now that he had me in his grasp, the monkey's expression seemed fierce. His round, blinking eyes searched my face with a kind of impatience. *Well? What are you going to do about this?* By which I understood he meant all of this: the bars, the bare concrete, the awful smell.

It's not my fault, I tried to tell him. It's not my fault you live in a stinky, barren-looking monkey house with nothing to do all day long but terrify little girls for your amusement.

The bars were too close together for me to pull him out of there, and way too close together for him to pull me in. So please, I wanted to say, can't you just let me go?

It was what I wanted to say, but somehow couldn't. If the monkey had been a mean old crone, or a big bullying kid, or even an angry dog, I probably would have pulled the time-honoured little-girl stunt of wailing and begging for mercy.

Yet, whatever there was between me and that monkey seemed of a different, wordless order. He and I were foreigners to each other, not so stupid we couldn't recognize each other as fellow beings. Still, we were not smart enough to overcome our lack of a common language.

Suddenly, it was at this moment—with that dry little fist closed around my finger—that I remembered a book my brother and I had recently enjoyed: *Caps For Sale*. In the story, a peddler carried the caps he sold in a stack on his head. One day, they were stolen by a pack of monkeys who refused to return them. It was only when the man threw his own hat on the ground in frustration that the monkeys responded in kind, and he got all his caps back. "Monkey see, monkey do," was the moral of that story.

I shook my forefinger—the one not in the monkey's grip—in a violent, scolding gesture. The monkey took sharp note, hesitated for a moment, and then relinquished my finger to shake his back at me.

It was almost as if he knew it was a mistake. As I turned to run away, he gave me a look of bitter disappointment. *Just my luck*, that look seemed to say. *Just my luck to run into another kid who's read that goddamn book.*

"HI..."

It's Gloria, back with a banana in each hand like a six-shooter. "No luck luring anybody outside. The wind, like I said. Plus, it's pretty close to lunchtime. Come on in."

As we enter the building, there is the aroma of onions frying in butter, mixed with a strong, indeterminate animal smell. Along the wall in the hallway leading to the kitchen is a succession of paintings, sketches, and photographs of the various residents—most still current, a few sadly not.

One photo in particular catches my eye, as it apparently does everyone's. "That's Billy Jo." Gloria smiles. "They're all special, but Billy was... well, that photo doesn't even do him justice. Such presence. So handsome. You probably remember him, from the show on PBS."

Billy Jo has since died. I nod in respectful acknowledgement of one of the late and great. In fact, the gallery of chimp faces is somewhat like those signed celebrity photos show-business-oriented restaurants display. Some of the faces—like Billy's—are winsome, compelling in their gaze. Some are challenging; others are unremarkable and mild. Just regular schleppers, special only because they ended up in a place where they get to have their likenesses mounted—as well as onions fried in butter for their lunch.

Nevertheless, as Gloria has said, this is a prison—although it's a nicer sort of jail, where nobody straps them down to inject them, or draw their blood, or wrap them in restraints. Here, they are free to turn their backs on us, or head to the outdoor enclosure without asking permission. The cages, though spacious, are in a multi-storied range and closely barred, except for a small opening in the door that allows the occupants to extend their hands to us, and permits Gloria to reach in to give them a handclasp in return, or a banana, or both.

Most of the dozen or so animals feel inclined to make their way over to the bars to check me out. Some linger, but not because I'm an object of any great fascination. For most, overseeing the preparation of their food is the real draw. Like inmates in any sort of institution, they have learned to build their day around mealtimes.

In many ways, this feels more like a seniors' home than a prison. The occupants, with their long, creased faces, are overtly curious. But in the challenging manner of old folks long past the niceties, they stare directly as if to say: *Well? What's so interesting about you?*

Regis, one of the most persistently forward of the group, hunkers close to the bars, all the better to spit periodically—with no apparent hostility but with great accuracy—at me and Gloria. His saliva is sugary from the fruit drinks, Gloria says. Whenever she fails to wipe it from her cheeks, it forms a glossy sheen.

She jokes that she's thought about turning Regis's spit into a cosmetic product. She improvises a breathless endorsement: "What gives my face such lustre? Why, it's Regis Spit, available exclusively at Fauna."

At the long stainless steel table not far from a stovetop range where the onions are caramelizing, Janet, a volunteer, is struggling to peel leaves from a large raw cabbage. The leaves split in her hands, and she throws them down, frustrated. "Do you happen know how to make cabbage rolls?" she asks me.

As a matter of fact, that was one dish from my German grandmother's otherwise complicated repertoire I was able to master. Parboil the cabbage, I tell her, before trying to peel it.

"Ah!" Happily, she plops the cabbages into a pot of water on the stove.

I wonder if the cabbage rolls will be for the chimps, but am afraid the question might sound stupid, whatever the answer. (Later in the afternoon, Janet showed me the finished result: a plateful of perfectly formed cabbage rolls, with rice and tomato and onions all furled up inside. She was taking the leftovers home to her kids; the rest had indeed been eaten by the chimps. Would my German grandmother have been pleased or insulted?)

Gloria introduces another woman named Kim, a staffer. When I ask Janet if she too will eventually graduate to paid status, she laughs. "Oh no. Gloria's too smart for that."

Kim and Gloria join in the laughter, but I sense Gloria is in a delicate spot. She needs to maintain good relations with all the staff—paid and otherwise—yet also needs to put the chimpanzees *uber alles*. Which means keeping everyone gung ho to do their bidding, often with no greater recompense than a chimp's enthusiastic response to the smell of something new in the kitchen.

Gloria has already told me about her difference in operating philosophy with one former staffer. The disagreement culminated in his departure from Fauna, insisting that Gloria was "spoiling" the chimps.

"But why should we deny them anything?" Gloria demanded of me, as if carrying on the argument with the departed employee. "To build their character? We *owe* them for those awful lives they led. I regard them as heroes!"

For her heroes and heroines, stainless steel trolleys of snacks are in easy reach outside the cages. To make it even easier, Gloria places oranges, juice containers, and fistfuls of cellophane-wrapped suckers into any and all of the open, black, wrinkled palms extending from the small aperture in the bars.

She cannot do enough, cannot begin to make up for their past sufferings or their present tedium. The best she can offer is continual distraction from the fact—as she's expressed it to me outside—that "they've come here to die."

The chimps readily accept the food and cartons of juice, or help themselves from the trolleys *ad libitum*. Sometimes, however, they throw their juice boxes—empty or full—or petulantly toss oranges and bananas from on high.

It could, of course, be worse, Gloria remarks. Some sanctuaries have plastic curtains hung in front of the bars to catch the feces the animals fling. When a male chimp pees on us from above, Gloria excuses him. "He's diabetic," she says, as she moves to mop the urine toward a drain. The diabetes, presumably, is a legacy of his life in research. As for the peeing, it's much like Regis's spitting—not to be taken personally.

An engaged group of chimps continue to cluster by the bars, looking steadily at us, neither hostile nor overtly friendly, merely meeting our gazes. As Gloria rubs her thumb on a forehead here, strokes a leathery, long-fingered hand there, definite personalities begin to emerge.

Among the more sociable is Pepper, a thirty-seven-year-old with remarkably neat little ears, but a look of dejection in her eyes. Sue Ellen is tiny, snub-faced and elfin. Binky is a young ruffian, big on threatening poses and sudden, looming appearances over our heads.

At one point, Gloria reaches into her pocket, produces a tube of lipstick, takes off the top, and applies colour to Pepper. Pepper purses her lips—then snatches the lipstick and begins to rub it on her mouth herself. After a brief effort to take it back, Gloria shrugs. "Oh well. It's a better shade on you anyway."

The exchange has the feeling of a familiar schtick. Chimps like Pepper who play-act with cosmetics, or with handbags and parasols, may have been sold into research from a circus background. "It's the young ones you see riding unicycles, or wearing propeller beanies in TV commercials," Gloria explains. "The adults are ... well, like this." *This* describes unexpectedly large, heavy-set animals who look to me more like gorillas than body doubles from *Bedtime for Bonzo*. Their earlier histories—as infants stolen from their mothers in Sierra Leone, or as hammy circus stars, or as long-suffering lab inmates—are nowhere in evidence in their stolid faces.

How these chimps might feel about the contrast between then and now is even more of a mystery. Despite all that animal science has learned about the evolution of their species and the working of their bodies and even the structures of their brains, humans understand little about what they think of their current lives, and what they might remember.

After Gloria made her decision—"on my fortieth birthday"—to take chimps on board at Fauna, she set out to learn everything she could to prepare for what lay ahead. Part of that preparation took place in the state of Washington, at the Chimpanzee and Human Communications Institute run by famed primate expert Roger Fouts and his wife Deborah. The institute was the final home of Washoe, the first of the American Sign Language-trained chimps.

"I learned a lot there," Gloria remembers. "We got to spend time with the chimps, even Washoe. But one thing that bothered me at Roger's place: those ASL-trained chimps were constantly signing for things like an apple or a cookie—but they hardly ever got them. What kind of reinforcement is that? Like, give them the apple already!"

The standard comparison of chimpanzees to five-year-old humans, she believes, is wrong. She experiences these animals as adults—much deeper, much more introspective than any human kindergarten class. Unfortunately, the only environment which could truly test their intelligence, their wisdom, their ingenuity, and their resourcefulness is the wild. And that's an environment most of them have either never known, or were taken from too young to recall.

No wonder Roger Fouts, the folks at Stanford University who work with the gorilla Koko, and all the other advocates of communication between humans and primates, are so unceasing in their efforts to get these animals to "talk." How else are we ever going to find out what stories they have to tell us? If, in fact, they can remember any stories at all.

Gloria and I leave the chimps to their lunch and head out to find our own. With the animals' eyes following our departure from behind the bars, the freedom simply to leave at will and go where we wish suddenly feels like a pleasure too embarrassingly guilty to share.

————◆◆◆————

THE LEVEL, UNBLINKING GAZE of an animal can be unnerving. Something in the eyes suggests an expectation of understanding. Yet, it's an expectation we can't always fulfill.

What was it like, I wonder, for the person—most likely a servant—who opened the door to the baby's chamber, and was met by the face of the dog? That long, narrow greyhound's face, with its steady, searching, untroubled eyes.

Perhaps the servant has been drawn by sounds of a scuffle, perhaps not. Maybe all she intended was a quick, routine check on the chamber where the master's baby supposedly slumbers under the watchful eye of the master's dog.

Either way, as the door swings open, she is met by the greyhound standing right there, staring, as if expecting her. Then, quite suddenly, she is jolted by the sight of bloodstains around the dog's panting tongue and along his muzzle. From there, the servant's eyes dart to fresh splotches of red on the stone floor. With rising panic, she scans the entire room. Blankets, torn pillows all in a welter. More blood. And the child nowhere to be seen!

She might be hardly aware that she's started screaming. The dog, no doubt, is startled by this. Yet, so far as he knows, he's done nothing wrong. In a moment or two, the woman will surely understand that—once she's righted the cradle and come upon the body of the snake.

Or maybe that kind of thinking is too complex, too human. Perhaps in the mind of a dog, all that might form would be a simple desire to calm down the woman, by wagging his tail.

The truth is, I have no idea—nobody does—how much an animal understands of human behaviour, or how earnestly he might or might not wish he could make himself understood. Even in his last moments, once his master has been summoned and the dog has been stabbed to death for reasons he can't comprehend, who can say whether an animal would have any inkling what death is about?

Yet, there is something in that simple scene—in those last few anguished seconds of interaction between misunderstood dog and misguided man— that speaks loudly and insistently. So much so, that people have been telling the story in its various versions for almost two thousand years.

WHAT WE CAN'T KNOW ABOUT ANIMALS and the way they think, we try to supply. The British poet William Cowper made several earnest efforts to get inside the mind of his spaniel, Beau. In "Beau and the Bird," Cowper despairs of a dog "well-fed and at his ease" who would be heartless enough to kill a fledgling bird, against his master's express orders.

Then, in an attempt to be fair on behalf of his dog, the poet penned a response titled "Beau's Reply." There the spoiled spaniel declares in his own defence: "'Twas nature, sir, whose strong behest Impelled me to the deed." Cowper strives to understand a dog's motives better than Beau will ever comprehend his master's consternation over a mere bird.

However, as a human being, Cowper can't just leave it there. In the poem, Beau goes on to point out that even a dog is capable of making moral distinctions, and reminds his master of a previous occasion, when Cowper's pet linnet escaped its cage and lay exhausted on the floor. Then, the spaniel, "knowing him to be a sacred thing, Not destined for my tooth," had merely licked the bird's feathers.

Cowper deserves credit for setting aside his own human perspective and making a sincere effort to see things the way Beau would. Still, there's something ironic about the enterprise.

After all, Beau was only an over-indulged house pet who attacked birds purely for diversion. Yet, his master conferred a kind of glory upon him by making him the title character of several poems.

Meanwhile, there is that nameless greyhound of the ancient story who undoubtedly saved the life of a child by his assault on the snake. Unlike Beau, he has only posterity to speak up on his behalf—and not a word to say for himself.

NOT LONG AFTER MY VISIT TO FAUNA, a small but prominently-placed item appeared on the front page of my morning newspaper. Washoe, described as "a female chimpanzee believed to be the first non-human to acquire human language," had died of "natural causes" in Ellensburg, Washington.

Washoe was born in Africa, captured in infancy and brought to America, at exactly what age, nobody could be sure. Her language acquisition—however impressive—was insufficient to quiz her about such details. Therefore, her exact age at time of death could only be estimated as around forty-two years old.

The president of Central Washington University in Ellensburg issued a statement assuring the world that "the entire CWU community and the Ellensburg community are feeling the loss of our friend, Washoe, one of our daughters." Presumably, the other chimps at the Chimpanzee and Human Communications Institute on the Ellensburg campus also felt the loss. Not only was Washoe the senior female in the group, she was the one who taught several of the other chimps the American Sign Language she herself had learned over a period of forty years.

For her first three years in the United States, Washoe was trained by Drs. Allen and Beatrix Gardner, who named her for Washoe County in Nevada, where they lived. In 1980, the chimp was transferred to Washington State to become the founding matriarch of the Chimpanzee and Human Communications Institute headed by Roger and Deborah Fouts.

Washoe was as well-known outside the research community as she was within it. Her name was synonymous with the concept of animal-human communication, and her ASL vocabulary of 250 or more words made her an international celebrity.

In the world of primate-human communication, only Koko, the Stanford University lowland gorilla, has rivaled Washoe's eloquence with American Sign Language. It was Koko who famously expressed in signs her grief at the death of one of her pet kittens. Washoe, meanwhile, gained her greatest acclaim for her alleged ability to recombine existing signs for nouns and adjectives into original phrases to describe novel objects and situations presented to her.

However, the famous chimpanzee also had her doubters and detractors. Harvard cognitive scientist Steven Pinker, for example, frequently expressed doubt that Washoe could actually use language in any meaningful way. He wondered if she was merely "aping the hand gestures taught to her by humans."

Implicit in Pinker's question is whether the ability to pick up hand signals, or to work with spelling blocks, computer keyboards, or other human communicative devices genuinely offers proof that animals can acquire our language. After all, in the wild there has never been evidence, within any group of apes, of language development employing any of the means humans have devised with captive animals.

Coincidentally, about a month before Washoe's death, another animal pioneer in interspecies communication passed away unexpectedly. That was Alex, an African grey parrot trained and studied for almost thirty years by Dr. Irene Pepperberg of Brandeis University and Harvard.

Washoe had been in the public consciousness longer than Alex. Even so, the reaction both in the press and on blog sites to the parrot's passing seemed more emotional.

That may be because Alex squawked his communications in words rather than signing them. It may also have had something to do with the fact that a bird is much more accessible than a chimp to most people's minds, because it is a pet. Or, perhaps Alex's special cachet derived from his close personal association with Irene Pepperberg, his lifelong companion as well as the researcher who made him a household name.

Certainly, anybody who has ever raised any kind of caged bird—be it a parakeet or a canary or an African Grey, like Alex—can probably identify with Irene Pepperberg. As a child, she had trained her own budgies to speak. Then, in the 1970s with a PhD in theoretical chemistry under her belt, this young and independent-minded woman decided to branch out into animal communication. She went to a New York pet shop and purchased Alex for six hundred dollars. The rest, as they say, is history.

Eventually, Alex became renowned for his ability to put together words—in his case, vocally—in original ways, to express fresh meanings about the sounds and colours and shapes he'd been taught to identify and use. By the end of his life, Alex knew about fifty words for objects—far fewer than Washoe could sign.

However, like the chimp, Alex came up with new terms of his own. Those that Pepperberg and her assistants could recognize as words were reinforced with rewards. Those combinations of sounds that were not meaningful in English—such as "cheenut"—were discouraged through a lack of reinforcement.

Even within the cautious scientific community, Alex's efforts earned some commendation forever denied to Washoe. After the parrot's death, Yale linguist Stephen Anderson remarked that there was "apparent evidence that Alex did actually regard at least some of his words as made up of individual recombinable pieces, though it's hard to say without more evidence. This is something that seems well beyond any ape-language experiments, or anything we see in nature."

Or, maybe it was just that there was something more endearing about Alex himself, with his perky parrot manner and his croaky little voice. The last words he was reported to have uttered were to Pepperberg the night before he died: "So long, be good. I love you. See you tomorrow."

Washoe could sign "I love you." She embraced those she cared for, just like a human being. Nevertheless, it may be she lacked the animal magnetism of bright-eyed little Alex. Perhaps Washoe was *too* human somehow—in all the wrong ways.

After reading Washoe's obituary, I got out my notebook to look back over the notes I'd made on my day at Fauna. I had no difficulty recollecting the chimpanzees' eloquent but inscrutable eyes. And their long, black fingers with those beautifully sculpted nails reaching out to stroke Gloria's hand, or to take a treat from her with a quiet air of entitlement.

Prisoners, senior citizens, battered survivors of a stress-filled, joyless "career" in medical science . . . it doesn't much matter which anthropomorphism comes to mind. The fact is, I could best describe those animals to myself at the time—and can best describe them now—in terms of my own species.

Part of that, of course, is explained by their humanoid appearance—or, as chimps might express it, how very much humans look like them. Especially when we're dressed alike, in sweaters and sneakers and bonnets and beanies and OshKosh coveralls. The effect is some sort of visual joke—usually at the animal's expense—like those paintings of dogs dressed up to play poker in waistcoats and watch-fobs, with pipe stems clenched in their teeth and monocles screwed in their eye sockets.

But surely there is something more urgent going on between their species and ours than that, just as with that rather terrifying little monkey I'd met as a small child, at the zoo. He'd acted as if he had a right to reach out to me—as if he'd felt entitled to point out that his incarceration in such a barren, bleak, odious place was entirely inappropriate.

It may be in their very wordlessness that animals have the most to say to us, in that level gaze that expects understanding and commendation. Or in that skeptical glare through the bars that seems to demand: *Why is it I'm in here and you're out there?*

II

GAZING AT THE GALLERY OF CHIMPANZEE FACES on the wall at Fauna, Gloria Grow lamented the deaths of three of her chimps over the previous eighteen months.

"Were they elderly?" I asked.

No. All three died "before their time."

"Oh," I nodded, aware that all had spent most of their lives as research animals, "HIV-AIDS?"

"No," said Gloria. "They were HIV-free. That's the irony. Even if they're deliberately infected, chimps throw it off. They have to keep being re-infected."

I looked up from my notebook in surprise.

"You heard me. They really aren't good models for HIV-AIDS. What they die of is just the accumulation of too many chemicals, over too long. They're no longer clean, or 'naïve,' as the term is. That's the reason they're allowed to wind up in places like this. They're no good to the industry any more."

Back home in Toronto a few weeks later, I'm at dinner with friends. When I'm asked about my trip to Fauna, I hear myself waxing indignant about the chimps' ability to "throw off" HIV. "To me, that just underscores the sad futility of so-called 'research.'"

"Not at all," replies one of my friends. Briskly, she goes on to tell me what she's read about the point of re-infecting chimps with the disease again and again: "To help us learn the secret of their recovery, so we can apply it to humans."

Oh great, I think, struggling not be one of "those" people who rage on and on about animals. *So that's how it is for non-humans: Damned if you're like us, and damned if you aren't.*

Hey, that might work as a snappy slogan for some of those laboratory supply company catalogues, to extol the merits of animal models able to serve humanity equally well, whether or not they were resistant or susceptible to whatever a researcher might want to throw at them. Like the ad for a restrainer Peter Singer describes in *Animal Liberation*, designed to hold a lab rabbit in place while caustic liquid is squirted in its eye. "The only thing that wriggles is the nose!" the ad copy declares jauntily.

Damned if you're like us and damned if you aren't. Even those who seek to act for animals—the advocates of animal rights—can get caught up in conflicting views about what is called animal "modeling" in areas of research intended to help humans.

Singer, for instance, has long criticized the use of animals to test drugs or products to which they react differently than we do. His favourite citation is the drug Thalidomide, developed in the 1960s through testing on primates to quell symptoms of nausea in pregnant women. Nothing in the animal experiments offered evidence of the horrific human birth defects that were to result once the drug had gone to market.

In response, the research community points to hundreds of pharmaceuticals—as well as consumer products—that have been verified as safe for humans by using guinea pigs and other laboratory animals. More recently, science has developed new methods to utilize animals not as models but as hosts for human diseases. Human micro-organisms, tumours, even entire human appendages such as ears, are now grown on the bodies of mice and other small mammals. As well, so-called "purpose-bred" rodents come genetically pre-programmed for human forms of cancer and other diseases.

That said, researchers are not immune to all contradictions. Let's say you're a research scientist who insists that animals don't experience pain, confinement, fear, hunger, or boredom the way we do. What's your answer when an animal advocate points out that, if such differences exist, they invalidate the experiments you've been doing on animals to develop drugs to treat pain, confinement, fear, hunger, or boredom in humans?

For many of us, the larger question is: How much do we want other animals to be like us? And if so, how do we determine which ones? And how should we treat them?

Most humans, I think, do want to feel a kinship with animals. "Higher" animals, anyway. Almost automatically, to say "higher" means to us "smarter," and "smarter," in turn, signifies "most like us." Those most like us, we assume, think like us, feel like us, and are therefore entitled to lives that resemble our own idea of the good life.

But if that's true, what are intelligent animals like pigs doing in sow stalls and CO_2 chambers and on restaurant menus? Apparently, more or less the same thing as our closest rivals in intellect, the great apes, are doing in research cages and sensory-deprivation tanks and circus rings. Far from buying them our endless esteem, the indisputable intelligence of primates—that is to say, the similarity between their intellectual powers and ours—has often proven to be an even greater liability than the high percentage of genetic material their various species share with us.

For animal rights philosophers like Peter Singer, the higher a non-human's cognitive skills (i.e. the more their intelligence reminds us of our own) the more it merits human consideration. The Great Ape Project, of which Singer is one of the founders, dedicates itself to procuring rights for primates on just that basis.

However, The Great Ape Project's aspirations notwithstanding, being brainy so far has not actually gotten apes anywhere—except in Great Britain, New Zealand, and some parts of Europe, where they are exempt from experiments that are still routine in North America and elsewhere. (In June of 2008, a committee of Spain's parliament went so far as to recommend that apes not only be exempt from experimentation but also be released from service in circuses and on TV commercials.)

Evaluating the worth of animals on the basis of their intelligence is a double-edged sword. On the one hand, we feel a natural sympathy for intellects that seem to resemble our own. On the other hand, evidence of that similarity comes with ethical consequences we seem unprepared to deal with.

Not long ago the PBS series *Nova* offered a surprising look at the problem-solving abilities of the cuttlefish, a close relative of the more familiar cephalopod, the octopus. The *Nova* program highlighted the enormous brain-to-body ratio these eerie-looking underwater beings boast, and what that kind of cognitive power looks like in action. For instance, when encountering unexpected obstacles, cuttlefish quickly learn to alter their behaviour, in order to navigate around them with remarkable speed.

Talk about your inconvenient truth. If this is what is actually going on inside the ugly, hydroencephalitic heads of squids and octopuses and cuttlefish, how do we justify flinging their live bodies on the ice at hockey games? Or leaving them to die on the dock, or cutting off their tentacles to fry in olive oil?

The fact is, we don't justify it. We simply go on and do it, even as we tune into TV programs premised on new discoveries about the prodigious intellects of cephalopods and numerous other unlikely species. Paradoxically, it appears that human beings like to affirm the intellectual powers of animals, even those creatures we slice, dice, use, abuse, zap, and wrap.

For some of us, the consequences of the knowledge of intellectual kinship with animals can be uncomfortable. After an hour of exposure to the cognitive abilities of cuttlefish, I caught myself wishing I could go back to those innocent days when I believed—and hoped—these creatures were barely sentient. If an animal's intelligence can't save it from the worst our species can and will do, wouldn't I be better off not knowing about the complexity of its inner life?

Nevertheless, there is an ever-widening world of ethologists, biologists, and psychologists out there, bringing fresh news about the surprising consciousness of ever more species to our TV screens and the science pages of our daily papers. Some of these researchers are mainly concerned with the knock-on benefits to humans of this new knowledge about other animals. However, there are also animal scientists intent on exploring animal consciousness for its own sake, as well as advocating for species on the basis of their intelligence.

Ethologist Donald Griffin, who died in 2003, became increasingly controversial over his long lifetime for his developing opposition to what he called the "cold, clammy influence" of behaviourists and other empirical thinkers. He decried the insistence of these scientists on "describing a behavior solely in terms of stimuli response and adaptive advantage."

In *Animal Minds: Beyond Cognition to Consciousness*, Griffin promotes a much richer view of animals' ability to meet new situations with original responses. He claims that herons, for instance, will begin to use bait like twigs or crumbs to attract small fish, after observing humans employ that trick.

Griffin also condemns assessments made of animal intelligence by our criteria rather than theirs. Chimps and birds can be taught to perceive numbers, at least to the extent of learning correct responses to numerical questions. However, since numeric literacy isn't of much use to them in the wild, why would we regard this skill as proof of cognitive potential? Nor does Griffin think it makes much sense to measure an ape's intelligence by testing its ability to recognize its own image in a mirror—an object in short supply in its natural habitat.

As well, in *Animal Minds* Griffin points to what he perceives as a de-emphasis on evolutionary similarities in the development of human and animal consciousness. This trend, he feels, may be due at least in part "to an unrecognized reaction against the deflation of human vanity by the Darwinian revolution."

Griffin continues:

> The acceptance of biological evolution and the genetic relation-ship of our species to others was a shattering blow to the human ego from which we may not have fully recovered. It is not easy to give up a deep-seated faith that our kind is completely different in kind from all other living organisms.

One of those other living organisms is the chimpanzee, who parted evolutionary company with us a mere six million years ago. That's a drop in the phylo-genetic bucket, compared to the 280 million years that have passed since our last common link with, for instance, the snake.

Chimps and bonobos are genetically closer to us even than to other apes. And we're closer to chimpanzees than the gray wolf is to the domes-tic dog, or a donkey is to a saddle-horse. However, it's only recently that human beings have begun to consider how much our own early develop-ment as a species may have had in common with theirs.

"We used to think that culture and, above anything else, technology was the exclusive domain of humans, but that's not the case," explained University of Calgary researcher Dr. Julio Mercader, in the *Proceedings of the National Academy of Sciences* early in 2007. Based on the discovery of rocks used to crack nuts in the rainforest of the Ivory Coast, Dr. Mercader and his colleagues deduced that even before humans came to that area more than four thousand years ago, chimps were not only using these rocks as tools, they also passed this knowledge down. Two hundred generations later, modern chimps continue to wield rocks in the same way for the same purpose.

Jane Goodall has been telling the scientific community and the wider world all this and more about wild chimpanzees since she first began to observe them in the 1960s at Gombe National park in Northern Tanzania. Goodall saw them breaking off twigs and modifying them in order to fish in anthills and nests of termites. Chimps also fashioned sticks into spears to hunt bush babies and smaller primates—and even other chimpanzees.

But what perhaps even Jane Goodall can't explain is the conflict humans feel in accepting the cognitive abilities of what Gloria Grow has dubbed "chimpanzee people." That delight for some humans in the recognition of patterns of reasoning, methods of problem-solving, and even styles of personal presentation that remind us of ourselves is, for others, offset by what Donald Griffin referred to as "the shattering blow" to the human ego of questioning our own uniqueness.

At the Babraham Institute in Cambridge, England, Professor Keith Kendrick has spent more than twenty years studying the ability of sheep to distinguish photos of their own family members from those of other sheep. Not only do research subjects appear able to remember up to fifty faces of their fellow sheep, they recognize ten or more snapshots of different human beings they've met.

Why does Professor Kendrick spend his time flashing photos of faces at his woolly-haired subjects? Some of his interest, he said in an interview, centres on what sheep can teach us about our own brains. But he also expressed the hope that new insights about the cognitive abilities of sheep might help to ensure their humane treatment.

LIKE KEITH KENDRICK, Donald Broom is based at Cambridge University. In 1986, Dr. Broom became the first professor of animal welfare at any academic institution, in the Veterinary College at the Madingley facility, a few miles from the centre of town. Nowadays, he also consults on behalf of various committees and bodies of the European Union connected to the welfare concerns of livestock animals.

When Dr. Broom arrives to collect me at Reception at the Vet College building, I think how much he looks like someone Central Casting would come up with to play a distinguished professor in a film. He is tall, tweedy, attractive—and gravely English. Like one of those lanky British actors from the forties or fifties, whose names you can't quite remember, who always looked good with a pipe.

But Professor Broom isn't merely of interest to me because he's perfect for the part. I've come to the Cambridge Veterinary College to talk to him about a phenomenon in cows he has termed "the Eureka moment."

In 2004, Broom and fellow researcher Kristin Hagen set up a series of experiments involving a group of Holstein-Friesian heifers. They devised a chute and a panel with a button that cattle could press to open a gate offering access to food. Half of the group of heifers did actually activate the gate by pressing the button; the control group got the food reward on a random basis, independent of whether they pushed the button.

With heart monitors and visual observation of the behaviour of each of the heifers in the two groups, Broom and Hagen measured their responses to success or failure in opening the gate. Cattle who controlled events perceived the connection between pushing the panel and opening the gate. Their increased heart rates and high kicks of excitement connoted pleasure at the connection. Not only the pleasure of the food reward itself, but also that "Eureka!" thrill of being in charge. Meanwhile, the control group—powerless to influence events—registered pleasure only in getting the food.

Even expressed in the dry, calibrated language of a research paper, there was something touching about the happy heifers' increased heart rates and their high-kicking frolics, as they figuratively exclaimed "Eureka!" at their discovery and reveled in their accomplishment.

"But what would be the practical application?" I ask Don Broom, after he meets me at Reception.

On a crisp, sunny February morning, he is leading me, at a fairly breakneck pace, across the bright green sward of grass that stretches from the main Vet College building to the one-storey brick structure that houses his office. In fact, I am panting a little, as I try to keep up with his long-legged, purposeful lope.

He pauses, mid-lope. "It's not a question of application," he says. "It's simply that if cows can demonstrate this ability, then we are less likely to treat them badly."

"Do you mean, the more we see that they're like us, the more sympathetic we'll be to them?"

"They don't have to be the same," he replies. "It's not a question of them being exactly like us, but only more like us than we thought."

For Broom, the implications of this qualified similarity are reflected in his view of his personal obligations to animals. For instance, he advocates high standards in livestock handling, but eats meat.

In his own research, he says, he will do "non-invasive" procedures, like drawing blood, but he won't "cut out bits of brains." However—now sitting behind his desk in his office, he makes this point very precisely—he will make use of research obtained by others through invasive procedures.

"I guess that's kind of an ethical question," I suggest. "The same question in its way as the morality of making beneficial use of medical research done by the Nazis?"

"Quite," he says, and nods. Obviously, he has already formed a position on this issue and is comfortable with it.

Overall, he is cordial but far from effusive and volunteers little insight about how his own emotional relationships with animals developed over time. As a university undergraduate doing animal research, he tells me, he had already drawn his personal line as to what he "would and would not do to them."

Now that he's a higher-up himself, he speaks of "being useful by educating people in animal welfare." It was a career decision that arose out of his first exposure to intensive farming—"a real shock." Out the window went his plans to pursue behavioural research for its own theoretical sake. Instead, his concern turned to finding ways to apply research to solving animal welfare problems—by, for instance, quantifying the joy of Holstein-Friesian heifers in having a small measure of control over their own feeding schedule.

I open my mouth, and start to ask if—

"Shall we go for coffee?" he pre-empts me. It's not a question. Dr. Broom is already on his feet, jingling the change in his pocket.

On our way to the cafeteria, he stops to poke his head into a larger office, and generally addresses the occupants: "We're going for coffee. Anybody want to come?" Obviously, these folks have been pre-selected to want to come—either to help me out with the interview, or to help him out of it.

At the counter, I offer to treat him.

"Oh, that's all right," he says. "I can get my own. Or ..." He pauses to look at me more closely, as if assessing what my outward behaviour might indicate about my inward inclinations. "I get the feeling you *want* to buy my coffee. Is that right?"

"It would be my pleasure," I tell him. For a moment, I'm tempted to kick up my heels, heifer-fashion, and cry "Eureka!" just to confirm it.

At the table, Broom introduces me to two of his graduate students—one from Japan and the other from Brazil—as well as a visiting veterinarian, also Brazilian. All have come to Cambridge to study various aspects of animal welfare, and all profess themselves dissatisfied with the level of concern about these issues in their home countries.

Sachie, the Japanese student, is eloquent about the state of shelters back home. In Japan, she says, dogs and cats are still euthanized with CO_2— usually after only seven days. Hilena, who is studying cognitive abilities in pigs, is disgusted by their treatment in Brazil, as compared to the UK.

"How do you account for your own responses?" I ask them. "You're both products of those cultures, yet you feel a level of concern, clearly, that most people don't."

Both women merely shake their heads and shrug.

"The average person avoids knowing about it," Don Broom observes— meaning, the conditions in which many animals live and die. He goes on to describe a recent RSPCA campaign in Britain to make the public aware of a condition called "hock burn" in chickens sold in supermarkets.

Hock burn is a painful condition live chickens develop on their legs and breasts from being forced to nestle in their own alkaline waste. Posthumous evidence of hock burn on butchered chicken parts denotes substandard welfare practices, he explains. Welfare advocates encourage consumers to learn how to detect the condition on pieces of chicken and complain about it to store managers.

That kind of consumer education and consequent pressure Donald Broom believes in absolutely. He credits the public for many of the concessions UK supermarkets, abattoirs, and individual farmers have made to welfare reforms. As well, he points with pride to the RSPCA's entire line of Freedom Foods, encompassing not only chickens, but a variety of meat, milk, and eggs guaranteed to be humanely produced.

In fact, his own research on hock burn was funded by the RSPCA, with whom he is clearly on the same page, in terms of improving conditions for the animals we use. (However, questioning the basis for that use is no part of the Freedom Foods initiative. That's a sore point for the very vocal animal-liberation constituency in Britain, I later learn. Activists regard the notion of an animal protection society abetting consumption of meat and milk products as anathema.)

When he is not teaching classes, conducting research and writing up papers, Donald Broom is globe-trotting—so far, he says proudly, to thirty-eight countries. Next week, he's off to China.

He professes himself pleased with the high standards he's helped set for the European Union, and notes the EU now requires vets in training to take a course in animal welfare. Since the beginning of the nineties, he adds, there have been no veal pens in the UK.

"It's not like that in Brazil," Hilena observes sadly.

In the part of rural Ontario I know best, small white wooden crates, no bigger than doghouses, sprout like mushrooms beside the cow barns. Tethered inside each one is a tiny black-and-white Holstein calf, separated from its mother and subsisting on milk formula to keep its meat tender.

"It's not like that where I live, either," I tell her.

Soon, Broom says, there will be no more battery cages for chickens in the UK. It's not that Britons and Europeans are better people. It's simply that they've been made to be more informed consumers.

Even in Taiwan, he adds, exporters are learning that if you want to sell to a large British supermarket chain like Tesco, you have to meet EU standards. (Some months after this conversation, voters in California approved Proposition 2, requiring factory farms in that state to provide pens and crates large enough for animals to stand up in, turn around and extend their limbs. This ballot measure, the first of its kind in North America, goes into effect in January 2015.)

Before we part, Dr. Broom shakes my hand formally. Equally formal, I ask him to send me some of his most recent papers. He promises me they will be waiting for me on my computer by the time I'm back in London. And indeed they are.

In one of those papers, he has written that "improved efficiency in plant and animal agriculture, resulting from genetic selection & other scientific developments, was in my view one of the two most important successes in the twentieth century, the other being improved communication amongst people."

In another, he underscores the importance of offsetting that drive for increased efficiency with a long, well-considered look at specific cases. "Animal welfare refers to a characteristic of the individual animal rather than something given to the animal by man. The welfare of an individual may well improve as a result of something given to it but the thing given is not itself welfare."

His reference to "the thing given" hints at impatience with the lofty way humans set themselves up as the unimpeachable arbiters of all things animal. In contrast, "improved efficiency" and "genetic selection and other scientific developments" ring out like proclamations of the wonders of technological progress.

Donald Broom, I conclude as I shut down my laptop, is as complicated as his own definition of animal welfare. On the one hand, there is that personal "shock" he spoke about, on his first exposure to intensive farming. On the other hand, there is his very evident faith in rules and standards, and the power of knowledge to inform public consciousness.

Altogether, he exhibits a kind of mixture of orderliness and idiosyncrasy that strikes me as unequivocally British: unmeasurable, indefinable, but as undeniably manifest as any "Eureka!" moment.

III

"THE PATTERN OF BLOOD VESSELS at the back of the animal's eye is called the retinal vascular pattern (RVP). This pattern is more unique than a human fingerprint, is present from birth until hours after death and does not change over the life of the animal."

A promotional brochure from Optibrand Secure Source Verification Solutions is tucked into the small spiral notebook I take with me to Colorado State University's agricultural research farm, a few miles outside Fort Collins. On an otherwise blank page of the same notebook, I make a ballpoint-pen sketch of a young white-faced heifer, waiting for her retinal scan.

In my sketch, her neck and body are held fast in a hydraulic squeeze chute, a huge iron maiden of a contraption from Moly Manufacturing, suggested by some hasty lines of ink. I print the word "Silencer" on the machine in my drawing.

"Silencer" is what's written on the machine itself. Kevin, an employee of Optibrand, which developed the biometric identification I am about to observe in action, assures me that the name refers to the quiet operation of moving parts—not to any lethal "silencing" of the animal under restraint. From the padded edges of the clamshell door closed against the heifer's neck to the plasticized bolts, the Silencer is designed to minimize noise and consequent animal panic.

I remember reading Temple Grandin's description of building a squeeze chute for herself, back in her high school days. Over the years, she's re-christened it her "hug machine" and modified the design a few times to make herself increasingly comfortable in its mechanical embrace. She's also applied the same principles to designing better restraints for cattle and other livestock.

For all I know, this Silencer is modeled on one of Temple's concepts. Certainly this young heifer seems calm in its iron grip. There was no bawling as she was hustled into the machine. No panicked reaction when Kevin pulled the lever that closed the clamshell door around her and tightened the Silencer against her sides. Only her eye—shortly to be scanned with a lighted wand—betrays her uneasiness.

"A knowing eye," I scrawl in ballpoint, beside my rough sketch of her snubby profile, her tiny buds of horns nestled among the curls on top of her head, and her large, pale-lashed eye. One thing this little dogie doesn't know is that she has less reason to be apprehensive than most.

In the United States and Canada, ranches number in many thousands, and cows are reckoned at more than a hundred million. Traditionally, identification has been a rough-and-ready business of either hot-iron branding or freeze-branding with dry ice. Both methods, traditional to the cowboy way of life, are painful and traumatic to the animal.

Even more important to North American ranchers are ongoing worries about what BSE—"mad cow disease"—has done to their business. The idea of creating a permanent, incontestable record of an animal's identity and medical history from birth to death—and even beyond—holds potentially enormous appeal.

Enter Optibrand Secure Source Verifications Solutions, a privately owned company in Fort Collins, Colorado, which offers retinal vascular scans—along with GPS and other state-of-the-art technologies—to identify, trace, and manage data on cattle. The company was founded in 1998 by three professors variously involved in animal health and welfare at Colorado State University, with the expressed desire to provide "secure, biometric and humane" alternatives to traditional branding and record-keeping.

From the point of view of philosophy professor Bernard Rollin, one of Optibrand's three founding CSU faculty members, it's the "humane" aspect that remains front and centre. This is why he invited me out to the Agricultural Research, Development and Education Center (ARDEC for short), located on a large piece of farmland about eight miles northeast of the CSU campus in Fort Collins, to observe this technology in action.

Like Don Broom at Cambridge's Veterinary College in England, Bernie Rollin believes in promoting humane treatment of animals by highlighting the ways in which they are similar to us. Otherwise, the two men are as unlike as chalk and cheese.

My first indication of Bernie's take-no-prisoners personality came in a phone conversation with him from Toronto, back when I was firming up plans to go to Fort Collins and see the retinal-scanning process in action. Weather permitting, Bernie told me, he'd take me out to "the farm" on his Harley. "Unless, of course, you've got a problem with that."

His voice had the heavy-duty rasp of a Brooklyner born and bred. My problem was picturing a guy who sounded like that on a college campus in northern Colorado—as well as picturing myself on the bitch-seat of a Harley-Davidson.

"This will be the first in a long series of disappointments," I told him. "I am not exactly a huge fan of motorcycles."

His Harley, I knew from earlier phone conversations, is an important prop. Whenever he drives up to meetings of cattlemen complete in leather motorcycle jacket, he immediately establishes himself as a straight-talking tough guy. As opposed to some wispy West Coast animal-rights type, wearing cruelty-free plastic footwear and an expression of earnest inter-species advocacy.

There was a perceptible pause on the other end of the line. "No problem," Bernie said at last. "We'll take my car. Unless you got a position on Cadillacs?"

"I DRIVE IT BECAUSE IT'S A GOOD CAR," Bernie says of the Cadillac, which is, like him, upholstered in leather. It's a sunny day, though cool enough to keep the windows mostly up. What with all that enclosed sunshine beating on Bernie's black jacket and the car's high-gloss interior, it smells like a tannery in here. "I also drive it to piss off the bedroom Bolsheviks of my acquaintance, with a gas-guzzler symbol of American imperialism."

Bernie, in person, is much shorter than he sounds on the phone. The heavily developed upper body of a weightlifter (which he is) is attached to the lower limbs of a much smaller man.

He is, nonetheless, a larger-than-life presence, with a black bushy beard like the Captain in the "Katzenjammer Kids" and a quality of amiable belligerence that to me is quintessentially New York. "Bedroom Bolsheviks" come up frequently in his conversation, as do "gun-control" and "feminists." He's against them all. Bernie enjoys appearing outrageous, a contrarian, an anomaly.

His aggressiveness is part of his role as a conciliator, bringing the animal welfare world together with cattlemen, for example, by embodying within himself both the animal softie and the practical hard-head. The anti-gun control stuff, the disparaging comments about feminists seem like shibboleths to get him past the front gates and admitted into the corral with the cowboys.

At the same time it's important to him that I understand how much he cares. When I called him earlier on his cellphone from my hotel to confirm our appointment, he sounded brusque, preoccupied. I'd caught him "in the middle of an experiment."

"So, what was the experiment you were in the middle of?" I ask him now, on our way out to the university research farm in the Cadillac.

He sighs. Unlike Temple Grandin, he declares himself uncomfortable with carbon dioxide suffocation as a means of stunning or killing, and is looking for a more humane way to put down lab animals at the end of experiments. His own nightmarish recollections of childhood asthma prompt a too-ready identification. "It's the panic. Of not being able to catch your breath. In my opinion, the worst thing in the world."

He says his preferred alternative to CO_2 originated in a recollection of those old test-pilot movies, where oxygen deprivation causes the aviator simply to black out. Basically, says Bernie, it's a case of simulating that deprivation in a rat, for example, in hopes of a quicker, less traumatic demise.

"And how did it go yesterday?" I ask.

"Good." He sighs again. "I don't like seeing animals die in any way," he adds. "Believe me, I don't. But this is definitely preferable."

His goal of diminishing—if not extinguishing—suffering extends to his work with ranchers and regulators. "Cattlemen are often in denial of animal pain," he explains. "However, if they think you know your shit, they can be made to agree with the idea that some procedures are inhumane. So can government officials."

By way of illustration, he tells me that the free flow of cattle north from the Mexican border after implementation of the North American Free Trade Agreement made the US Department of Agriculture uneasy, because of concerns about brucellosis, TB, and other diseases associated with cows from Mexico. Therefore, the Department of Ag proposed that Mexican cattle should be branded on the face with an "M" to make them stand out clearly and immediately from American herds.

"Have you ever seen a cow with a brand right on its face? PETA filmed a cow with its cheek smoking from the hot iron and its eye boiled out. Awful."

Like Temple Grandin, Bernie clearly has had both good and bad days with People for the Ethical Treatment of Animals. On this occasion, he and PETA were on the same page in urging the Department of Agriculture to reverse the face-branding policy.

"Optibrand," it occurs to me, is a very Bernie kind of name for the non-invasive branding technology we're going to see. It radiates the aggressive optimism that characterizes his philosophy about the direction in which animal welfare is headed.

"Do you feel there's been progress in the past few decades?" I ask him as he steers the Cadillac through the gates at ARDEC.

"Yes," he replies without hesitation. "People used to have no knowledge of what a 'factory farm' was. Now they do. Oregon has acted to abolish sow stalls. It's not so much that I'm a cock-eyed optimist. But at least what I call the 'searchlight of stupidity' is now shining on animals as well."

IT'S NOT A SEARCHLIGHT EXACTLY, but it's shining out of the end of the scanning wand in my hand and deep into the open eye of the little white-faced heifer. The light shines through the pupil and beyond, illuminating the tree-branch pattern of vessels on the back of the retina. Each pattern is unique, even in cloned cattle, as well as in each of the eyes of individual animals.

A snapshot is taken and the image freezes on the monitor of the small computer. All kinds of auxiliary data can be punched in, including ear-tag number if any, global positioning at the time the photo was taken, vaccination records, and much more. It's a foolproof registry of identity, unique and immutable.

As I try to position the wand the way the ARDEC and Optibrand technicians are telling me to, I wonder whether this beam of light is uncomfortable for the heifer, along with the squeeze-chute. A far cry, obviously, from a hot brand on the face or flank, or even an identifying tag drilled through her ear.

But even by this method there's still no denying that this little dogie and all the others are being identified and sorted for our benefit, not theirs. The information that I'm gathering at this very minute about her health records and provenance would lead to the efficient sale of her body parts after death—were this not merely a hands-on demo with a real-live model and the patient assistance of this group of men. "Real cattle guys from real cattle backgrounds," is how Bernie has described them in advance.

Huge cattle guys, too. Kevin, from Optibrand, and Casey, who heads the beef research area at ARDEC, are big and (you should excuse the expression) beefy linebacker types. They tower over Bernie and me and even over Alan, also from Optibrand. But there is a mildness in these two big men that is miles from what I think of wranglers.

"We like to coax 'em in quietly," Casey tells me as three little heifers come clattering from the barn and are urged inside the chute to wait their turn in the Silencer for scanning, "with a minimum of cowboy."

And there's a quality of understated admiration in Casey and Kevin when they talk about cattle. "You can't help but like cows," Kevin observes. "They're damn nice animals mostly."

For all their enthusiastic regard for cows, Casey and Kevin appear more doubtful than Bernie about how quickly this technology might supplant the tradition of hot-iron or freeze-branding. For one thing, they say, the cost-effectiveness has to be demonstrated. Securing each animal in the squeeze chute in order to conduct an optical scan and then entering the data adds up to a lengthier process than the seconds required to throw down a calf and apply a hot brand. There is also the fact that some cattlemen are just plain technophobic—while others are phobic of government.

Bernie agrees wholeheartedly. "Black helicopters," he says. "Conspiracy theories, government surveillance, invasion by some new world order...." Plus, says Kevin, retinal vascular imagery lacks the "romance" of old-fashioned branding-iron symbols, each design connoting a particular cattle ranch. He may believe in this system, but he won't deny the fact that some cowboys want to tell their own cows at a glance, just like in the old days.

Besides, even those who acknowledge the painfulness of burn-branding insist cows get over it quickly. According to Kevin, that's an article of faith among ranchers who still perform castration on male calves and dehorning without anaesthetic. Although, Casey adds, some are beginning to move away from castration with a knife. Tying off the calf's scrotum with rubber bands is considered more humane. Eventually the budding testicles wither and drop right off...

Progress? You bet. Still, at the very thought, these big, beefy cattlemen shift uncomfortably and look a little sick. I recall something else Bernie told me on the way here in the car. How he'd once asked a cattleman whether he believed castration caused the animal any pain. "How'd you feel," the rancher answered, "if I got out my Buck knife and did it to you? Damn right you'd feel pain."

"See, they all know it," Bernie concluded to me. "But they don't all admit it like that."

I watch Casey push the hydraulic levers that release the heifer from the Silencer. As the clamshell doors open, she lurches like something sprung from a trap, and leaps kicking and bucking down onto the ground. Perhaps not in "Eureka" recognition of being in control, but with the relief of one moment's absolute freedom.

"WHAT ABOUT THAT DECEREBRATED BEEF IDEA?"

Bernie and I were on the way back to town in the Cadillac. The notion of breeding beef cattle with only the most rudimentary brain function—impervious to pain, boredom, and confinement—is something I'd read about in one of Bernie's books.

Decerebration would be a novel way around the ethical agonies of raising animals for meat, leather, and other useful products. I pictured them being harvested like so many hide-covered melons on a vine.

"That's not going to happen," he said. "Creating meat protein in a lab is now a much likelier alternative."

I thought about what Casey and Kevin had said, about cowboy attachment to the romance of tradition. "Can you envision cattle ranchers wanting to raise meat blobs in a lab, though?"

No, Bernie could not. However, there will always be a gourmet beef market, he assured me. People with big bucks willing to pay for the real ranch-raised thing.

"But it's kind of moot." He gestured out the window of the Cadillac, at the brownish expanses, dotted more and more with houses and strip malls the closer we came to Fort Collins. "Back in the nineties, they moved ARDEC from the campus in town, all the way out here. Pretty soon, they'll have to move it even farther out.

"The countryside's all disappearing. And the ranchers who are hanging on only average about thirty-five thousand bucks a year. There's a huge spread over that way a few miles that got bought not long ago by Ralph Lauren. So why not sell out to some rich guy looking for his private fantasy camp?"

I thought back to the small heifer lunging like a dolphin the instant the hydraulic restraints were released. How would she feel about a future either on the vine, or off the menu completely? Of course, as Temple Grandin observes, that heifer wouldn't exist in the first place without the meat industry as currently configured. So, no matter how you looked at it, the heifer with the knowing eye was not in a good position to choose.

"HOW WOULD YOU LIKE TO BE TREATED, if you were a milk cow?" I once had the opportunity to inquire of Dr. Ian Duncan, Chair of Animal Welfare at the University of Guelph. It seemed like a natural question for a man who's devoted his career to "asking" chickens about their choices in food and living conditions, and proving to dairy farmers that docking the tail of a milk cow in order to keep it out of the faces of farmhands actually impedes milking and milk production. (Dairy animals become frustrated when afflicted with flies they can't brush away.)

Duncan responded by detailing what sort of mat he'd like to stand on, what temperature he'd like his barn to be kept at, and other stipulations to do with comfort and a sense of well-being. Of course, his answers were based on his research with animals, not on his own preferences, if any, in such matters. But the impulse to do the research in the first place appeared to originate with a genuine sympathy for the cow's point of view, as well as a clinical interest in improved production.

Like Bernard Rollin, Temple Grandin, and Donald Broom, Ian Duncan is out to improve the system, not to alter it fundamentally. Given that cattle are going to get rounded up, branded, milked, and very likely eaten, the essential question is: How can their time on this earth and their means of dispatch be rendered as pleasant as possible?

This line of inquiry hardly bespeaks pure altruism. Very often, what is good for the cow—a tail left uncropped for switching flies, a comfortable stall—will also result in benefits for the farmer.

Even within the animal world, behaviour among members of a species that we might describe as respectful or moral or altruistic or even empathetic is not necessarily virtue that seeks no other reward. Just like us, animals are in it for themselves. Sometimes, however, what is good for the individual benefits the group.

That's certainly what primatologist Frans de Waal believes about moral and empathetic behaviour he detects in chimpanzees and other apes. He cites examples ranging from mutual grooming to assisting young or frail members of the community, to female chimps removing stones from the fists of angry males in order to disarm them.

De Waal insists such behaviours provide building blocks for the more complicated empathetic interactions of human societies. In these animal societies, he says, actions undertaken solely for the good of the group are precursors to a morality that also encompasses our person-to-person relationships.

Ethologist Mark Bekoff, of the University of Colorado at Boulder, has focused on a number of species, including wolves and rats. Both, he believes, are capable of playing fairly, cooperating socially, and even cutting each other some slack, through acts of altruism.

Dogs and wolves follow the rules of play and very seldom betray each other by, for instance, offering the exposed neck in a gesture of submission, only to launch a surprise attack. It's not so much because of some innate sense of personal honour, in Bekoff's view, as knowledge that violation of the code will bring justified reprisals. Meanwhile, sharing food or exhibiting other such virtuous behaviour produces benefits.

"A wolf who is generous can expect generosity in return." At the same time, he observes, the pack as a whole benefits from socially adjusted members who play fairly, cooperate on the hunt, and look out for each other.

Rats in laboratory experiments will purposely refrain from pushing a lever that drops a pellet of food, if they see that doing so will cause an electric shock to another rat. Tender-hearted it may sound, but such an action, Bekoff believes, also has the benefit of buying cooperation from the other—in case the electrodes and food levers are re-allocated between the two rats.

At the University of Bern in Switzerland, researchers have come to similar conclusions. Once more, rats are pressing levers, but this time to provide food to each other, not themselves. Even with no immediate personal benefit, a rat will push the lever for another rat who has done the same for her or him.

"Generalized reciprocity" is what this behaviour has been dubbed. The lead author of the Swiss study cautions against making assumptions about humans from this cooperative behaviour in rats. However, a paper based on the study does cite research showing that people who have been helped in some way are more likely to help others immediately afterwards.

Whether human or otherwise, shouldn't we all treat other beings as we'd like to be treated? Even if animals aren't rational or intelligent or capable of what we call language, Bernard Rollin writes in *Animal Rights and Human Morality*, those are not reasons to disqualify them from moral consideration. Morality is not assessed on intellectual worthiness, and trumps all other criteria.

In the end, Jeremy Bentham's criterion for compassion—"Can they suffer?"—may be the only means to determine how any creature of any species ought to be treated. Even in the Rome of Caesar and Pompey—famous for bloodthirsty spectacles of gladiatorial combat between humans and every kind of animal—there was, according to historian Pliny the Elder, one remarkable example of moral outrage on behalf of suffering animals.

In 55 BC in the Circus Maximus, Pliny tells us, Pompey set out to delight the crowd by arranging to pit twenty elephants against a group of Gaetulians armed with javelins. After several of their number had been stabbed to death and maimed by the men and their weapons, the remaining elephants attempted to break out of the enclosure in a panic.

But there was no way out, and once the animals had, in the words of Pliny, "lost all hope of escaping, they implored the compassion of the multitude by attitudes which surpass all description, and with a kind of lamentation bewailed their unhappy fate."

So moved were the spectators that, ignoring the fact that Pompey had organized this spectacle of slaughter for their delectation, they "rose up in tears and showered curses on Pompeius."

Whether the anger of the crowd saved the elephants, Pliny doesn't go on to report. Nor is it apparent that this one brief, singular outburst of compassion had any future effect on the frequency and brutality of the exhibitions of combat and slaughter that continued at the Circus under subsequent Roman emperors.

But if Pliny's second-hand account is accurate, for one moment in time, some sort of empathetic barrier between humans and animals in Rome was breached, so that elephants and Romans experienced something that briefly resembled fellow feeling.

BACK ON CAMPUS, I'm meeting with Bernie Rollin in his office. Actually, his wife and fellow academic, Linda Rollin, has volunteered her office; his own is too much of a mess to meet in, Bernie explains. He proffers his opinion that animals actually experience pain more intensely than humans. The reason? "They don't understand it."

Bernie's colleague, Temple Grandin, has told me she believes the experience of fear—for animals as well as autistic humans like her—is actually more traumatic than pain. That and the terrors of CO_2 are not the only points on which the two academics disagree. Temple is dead-set against the anti-horse-slaughter bill on its way to the US Senate. Bernie, on the other hand, finds "some merit" in legislation that prohibits killing unwanted horses for their meat.

I can't tell if he is motivated by his sentimentality as a man who keeps horses himself. Neither can I can get a fix on his attitudes toward animal slaughter in general. On the subject of whether he eats meat, Bernie offers none of Grandin's justification for being a carnivore. All he will say is that when negotiating with cattlemen, "you have to be able to eat with them."

Back in the sixties, Bernie was living way uptown in New York City while doing graduate work at Columbia University. He had to sweat out the summer working at a parking lot on a very tough corner in Harlem. His boss counseled him to carry a tire iron with him at all times—which Bernie concealed in gift wrap but kept at the ready. Bernie's well-to-do roommates laughed at his "little tough guy" demeanour. "'You have the mentality of a Wyoming rancher,'" Bernie tells me they told him.

"And you know something?" he continues. "They were right. So I started sending out my resumé to philosophy departments all over the West. Linda and I moved here in 1969, and bought ourselves a spread out of town. If I didn't exactly end up as a Wyoming rancher, I came pretty close."

"But you don't think exactly like a rancher. Where did your concern for animals come from?"

"Where else?" he replies, as if it's self-evident. "From the movies."

As a young boy in the late 1940s, Bernie was told his father had died. Later, he learned the man had simply left. In any case, Bernie says, at that point "my life was devoid of male role models—except for the movies. You remember the movie heroes of those days?"

Into my mind pops John Wayne, roughshod but fair. Along with Gary Cooper, aloof, yet straight-shooting. And John Garfield, struggling for decency against the odds. "I certainly do."

"Well, that's where my ethics came from. And this need to be protective."

"But why of animals, in particular?"

The response is prompt and practiced, but no less sincere for that. "As Cesar Chavez said: 'Nobody's more fucked over than animals.' And you know something else? Animals don't return evil for good nearly as reliably as we do."

What he perceives as helpless—a cow with a smoking "M" on its face, or a sow forced to lie supine for weeks on end in a sow-stall, or a laboratory rat scrambling in panic to escape suffocation in a chamber filled with carbon dioxide—he cannot help connecting to himself: a little boy in Brooklyn waking in the night with no dad and bad asthma attacks.

For Bernard E. Rollin the philosopher, the urge to avenge helplessness manifests itself in his pleasure in skewering the attitudes of behaviourists who dismiss any notion of animal consciousness. In particular, he sets his lance at the contradictions implicit in their view that experimental subjects do not cry out in pain, but merely "vocalize" in response to negative stimuli.

Rollin's paraphrase of the behaviourist position purposely invokes the absurdity of *Alice in Wonderland*: "We can't make moral judgments about what we do to animals, because such judgments must ultimately hinge on some imputation of consciousness, which behaviourists declare to be illegitimate."

Meanwhile, Bernie Rollin, the tough guy from Colorado by way of Brooklyn, might put it differently: "That's just bullshit."

Those forerunners of modern behaviourism, like seventeenth-century French philosopher René Descartes, disposed of the notion of animal consciousness by relegating all non-humans—including his wife's dog, whose paws he is alleged to have nailed to a board—to the category of machine. In Descartes' view, animals were incapable of feeling pain. What more soft-hearted souls like his wife might interpret as a cry of distress, he regarded as a kind of automated vocal eruption, comparable to the regulated chiming of a gong in a clock.

Whatever collateral pleasure Descartes and his associates got from torturing animals and reportedly laughing at their torment (pain they allegedly didn't credit), their real mission was to resolve a theological dilemma of the day: how to reconcile belief in a just God with the suffering of innocent creatures who would not even get to experience an afterlife where suffering might be redeemed.

Something had to go, and in Descartes' canon, that something was animal suffering. One of his immediate successors, Nicholas Malebranche, contributed a further argument. Since God is just and omnipotent, said Malebranche, it follows that animals could not possibly suffer—the evidence of our senses notwithstanding.

It's a logic as tortured as the creatures these men systematically abused. Yet, it represents a way of thinking humanity has not entirely outgrown. We can't afford to outgrow it—not when faced with circumstances that require us to regard and employ animals as objects with usable parts.

The pet dogs of philosophers' spouses may nowadays enjoy a more widespread assumption that they have feelings, but other non-humans remain in the category of gongs and clocks. However, there have always been times when the struggle to be "scientifically objective" about research animals is a convoluted—even painful—one for the researcher.

Years before the publication of *On the Origin of Species* in 1859, Charles Darwin was already well-known as a naturalist and a formidable man of science, thanks to the work on natural selection and species variation inspired by his round-the-world odyssey aboard *The Beagle*. In Patagonia, gauchos showed him how to rope rheas with bolos. In the Galapagos, he killed and collected so many birds and other animals that the specimens had to be sent back to Britain on other vessels. In South Africa and elsewhere, his investigative efforts with many species he encountered seemed to be first to kill the creature, then to cook it and attempt to eat it.

Devoted in boyhood to "shooting and dogs," and in adulthood to studying animals post-mortem, Darwin was very much a man of his time—albeit among its most brilliant. And yet, when it came to some of the uglier practicalities of investigative work, he occasionally revealed a surprising delicacy of feeling.

In an 1856 letter addressed to a poultry expert named William Tegetmeier, Darwin requests an Angora rabbit for purposes of research. He takes pains to instruct Tegetmeier:

Could you get the Porter to stick her, for I do not want her alive, and she would get knocked about and half starved in our cross country Roads.

I find that it ruins the skull to kill a rabbit in the ordinary way by a blow, & I shd think it would be difficult to break the neck below the atlas—I really do not wish or expect you to do so disagreeable a task as to stick the poor beast, but I daresay the same Porter whom you employ to carry her...would do it.

If anyone ever perfectly embodied contradictory attitudes about us and animals, surely it was Charles Darwin. His affection for all sorts of creatures was well-known. He spoke of "degree, not kind" as the nature of the differences between us and them. He declared man's "arrogance" as the only stumbling block in our recognition that we are more closely akin to the animals than to (in his view) a nonexistent deity.

Late in his career, in a hopeful outburst, he wrote:

If we choose to let conjecture run wild, then animals, our fellow brethren in pain, disease, suffering, and famine—our slaves in the most laborious work, our companions in our amusements—they may partake of our origin in one common ancestor—we may all be melted together.

Yet, back in 1856, when he required a rabbit for experimentation, Darwin had no hesitation about writing Tegetmeier to send him one. And while he clearly scrupled about subjecting the animal to the hardships of travel to his door, he found a ready solution to her suffering by proposing that she be killed beforehand.

However, the best method of dispatch was not something he expected Tegetmeier, presumably a fellow gentleman, to inflict on the "poor beast." A mere deliveryman, Darwin assumes, would not be fazed by "so disagreeable a task."

By 1856, Darwin was already an associate of the Royal Society for the Prevention of Cruelty to Animals—the RSPCA. Twenty years later, he allowed himself to become involved in drafting anti-cruelty legislation to protect animals used in experimental and medical procedures. However, when the anti-vivisection movement sought signatures to strengthen the provisions of that legislation, Darwin could never bring himself to append his own, for fear his experimental work would be too restricted by an outright ban on vivisection.

For people whose life's work is with animals, the kind of conflict between personal affinity and businesslike detachment Darwin experienced often proves similarly problematic. In *Regarding Animals*, sociologists Arnold Arluke and Clifford R. Sanders present a portrait of two very different workplace cultures exemplified by two neighbouring primate research laboratories in the American Midwest.

At the facility Arluke and Sanders designate as the "Ivy" Lab, a kind of cowboy culture holds sway. Workers take a utilitarian, often hostile view of the animals. They control them mostly through fear or—when the situation seems to warrant it—a whack with a shovel.

Meanwhile, over at what the authors dub the "Urban" Primate Lab, the workforce predominantly comprises individuals who characterize themselves as "animal people." The primates in their care undergo the same kind of experimental procedures as the animals at Ivy. Nonetheless, the Urban workers foster personal relationships with their charges, give them names, coddle the animals' offspring in what's termed the "nursery," and generally treat them as they would pets, or even people.

On one level, the Urban workers appear to have found a way to make their jobs bearable. On another level, they reveal how much harder it is to do this work, when you care so much. To Arluke and Sanders, some confide that it feels like "racism on our part" to keep these amazingly human creatures in cages.

Meanwhile, over at Ivy, the cowboys show absolutely no tendency to confuse these creatures with lovable people, or even pets. Instead, they define their time among these animals as "working with retarded children that have homicidal tendencies."

Nor do Ivy workers trouble to try making the inmates happy because, as the workers say, they're in cages anyway. And like guards in a human penitentiary, these workers have learned the benefits of emotional distance and personal detachment.

At Urban, on the other hand, the staff describe the chance to work with primates as their main motivation for being there. Among those engaged in research as well as animal care, some admit they wish no experiments were conducted on the primates. In order to assuage that conflict, they socialize with the animals as much as they can, spend off-hours with them, and derive their sense of status not from how efficiently they wrangle their charges, but from how warmly the animals respond to them.

The emotional price for what Arluke and Sanders call "dissolving the boundaries" between the Urban workers and the animals they care for is high. But is it higher or lower than what it costs the staff at the Ivy lab to keep the barriers intact and their sensibilities numb?

On the one hand, it may feel better to look an animal in the eye than to beat him on the head with a shovel. On the other hand, leading him by the hand into the experimental lab might well engender a kind of pain akin to hitting yourself with a shovel, again and again.

IV

FOR OUR LUNCH, GLORIA GROW HAS CHOSEN a rural restaurant overlooking the Chambly Basin and the low mountains behind it. Because this is Quebec, the menu is mind-bogglingly various. After some shared self-recrimination over helpless allegiance to fish, eggs, and dairy, Gloria and I each order the smoked trout salad with goat cheese, I in my restaurant French, and Gloria—though a lifelong resident of the south shore of Montreal—in English. I wonder whether it's a case of not speaking French or simply choosing not to.

I do know from what Gloria has told me that she has endured a certain amount of flak from some locals about the chimps. Especially at first. Her neighbours in Carignan heard in advance about the HIV-positive status of some of the animals. They also worried aloud about the possibly of escapes from Fauna.

"Early on," Gloria recalls wryly, "they had 'chimp drills' at the local school. I'm not kidding." The concept invites some amusing images of preparedness: children practising duck-and-cover or rehearsing lockdown, in case of chimpanzee attack. But perhaps at the time, not as amusing as all that.

After the intense level of noisy activity at the chimps' quarters, there is a welcome sense of lull in this fairly unpopulated restaurant. It was hours ago that Gloria drove from the south shore to pick me up in Montreal, brought me out to Fauna, and began showing me around the enormous grounds.

I'm exhausted, but if Gloria feels the same way, she doesn't show it. She's a handsome blonde woman with a summer tan, in a t-shirt and pants that show off her toned arms and attractive figure. She's animated in her presentation and a storyteller with a natural narrative style.

Gradually, she begins to talk about some of the toll this work takes. She has, she says, from time to time needed motivational tapes, self-help, therapy, and the assistance of her family and friends to get her through periods of real despair. Her husband, Richard, I know, is at this very moment in his veterinary clinic not far down the road from Fauna, and he is prominently featured on the Fauna Foundation website. But she doesn't talk much about him, and I don't ask.

Gloria's brother-in-law handles the website, as well as PR. Her sisters and mother, who live nearby, are also involved. But mostly, Fauna seems to be about Gloria. Not only is she an appealing spokeswoman for her cause, she's someone with a good backstory to tell.

A onetime dog groomer, she first met Richard Allan, D.V.M., when she came to his clinic looking to rent space for a grooming operation. They became a couple and bought a farm with no plan beyond stocking it with animals. Little did they suspect, way back when, that opening up their acres to an emotionally unhinged Montreal *calèche* horse was opening themselves up to a seemingly endless stream of other animals in need of sanctuary—from other unwanted horses to shelter dogs, donkeys, sheep, pigs, beagles from research labs, and on and on.

The decision to add retired research chimps to the list of residents also added to the list of would-be donors of surplus animals. Nowadays,

Gloria says, she is petitioned almost daily by zoos and universities eager to pass on monkeys and other primates no longer useful for research and likely be euthanized.

One of those she did take in was Little Man, a capuchin monkey. When she introduced us, Little Man observed me from a lofty perch. Then wrinkled up his face, to expose a set of wicked lower incisors he clearly felt were among his best features. He came closer, stood up to face me and began to masturbate happily.

"That's a compliment," Gloria told me.

"Aw," I said, "I bet he does that to all the girls."

"No, honestly." Gloria was laughing. "He doesn't. I think he likes you."

Uh oh. Remembering that childhood encounter with the monkey at the Moose Jaw Zoo, I gratefully let Gloria lead me away, to an enclosure housing Theo, Fauna's only baboon.

With his long muzzle, deep furry chest, and roundly muscled hindquarters, Theo bore a striking resemblance to a big, clipped poodle. His loose four-legged gait as he prowled was also somewhat canine. But his detachment was purely that of a wild thing, and the expression in his small eyes ineffably sad.

Theo had been caught wild in Kenya and brought to the United States for research, Gloria told me. At her coaxing, he came over to the bars, looked at her face, then gravely turned his muscular bum to her. She obligingly scratched his haunches with her finger, and Theo sighed—mollified, if not actually content.

Later in the day, Gloria told me, we would have found him staring out at the cornfields beyond his enclosure. Every day as the sun went down, he gave voice to a long, sad lament.

"Jane Goodall is on my board," Gloria went on. "One day when she was visiting, I told her about Theo's little ritual, and I asked her what she thought it meant. She said: 'He's calling for his troupe.'"

There was, however, no troupe in the offing for Theo. Repatriation to Africa was out of the question for a male in his prime. Other males wouldn't let him live to join a colony. Equally, he'd fight to the death any other male brought here to Fauna, and bringing a female baboon here was no answer either. The last thing she wanted, Gloria said wearily, was to develop a colony of captive baboons.

Now, over lunch, there is an intimation of that same weariness as she talks about what she terms "compassion fatigue." She worries, she says only half-joking, about winding up a cat lady. "You see them all the time. Those well-meaning women—and they always *are* women—running cat shelters, wearing stretched-out sweaters, letting themselves go, because they're too busy trying to get homes for this endless supply of stray cats.

"When they're talking to you, you know they're not really listening. They're only waiting for a place in the conversation where they can try to press 'just one more' on you, or your friends. They're wonderful women; don't get me wrong. But I can't let myself go that way."

With her careful attention to her appearance, Gloria doesn't look in any imminent danger of going "that way." Still, I understand what she means. ("Addicted to rescue" is the term another animal advocate will use in a future conversation with me.)

"There's also an image you have to maintain, isn't there?" I suggest to Gloria. "An investment in looking good, being positive, not presenting the situation for animals as hopeless?" It must be such a fine line, I suggest. Between using media for publicity and letting yourself or the animals get used by it, between personalizing the creatures for the public and turning them into shills for their own worthy cause. What the sociologist Arnold Arluke terms "a beautiful case."

"A beautiful case?" It's not a term Gloria has run into before.

I explain that it's what PR people at animal shelters told Arluke they call a particular dog or cat they choose to feature in a fundraising event or adoption campaign: an animal whose story is touching, but not too grue-some, a pet who's just the right kind of cute, whose plight will touch hearts and open wallets.

Gloria nods, and tells me about the experience of having a film crew come to Fauna, to shoot the documentary I had seen on PBS. "I had to agree to some things I thought were frankly hokey, beneath the chimps," she recalls.

One scene the filmmaker insisted on featured Billy Jo eating an ice

cream cone. Gloria says it struck her as all wrong. It wasn't that Billy
didn't like to eat ice cream, she explains, or didn't look endearing as he
did it. It was this need for the ice-cream shot, to help punctuate the happy
ending.

"I wound up deciding, 'Okay, I'll do it. I'll do it for the chimps.' I even
said to Billy: 'If walking off into the sunset eating ice cream will put Fauna
on the map ...'" But her sigh indicates it was a tough call she still second-
guesses.

As we drive back along the road running through the farm, I glance at
the cows and horses and sheep and pigs, dotted among the various pastures
and fields on a bright, windy September afternoon. Like the chimps, they
are in sanctuary, a form of friendly captivity, far from whatever hardships
they faced in their earlier lives. Like the chimps, they are kept in enclosures
because there's no other way to keep them.

But unlike the chimps, they are domesticates, long bred to stand out
in a pasture, doing not too much of anything, day in and day out. And unlike
the chimps, most of them have long since lost the will to roam hundreds
of kilometres in the wild, searching out their own food, settling their own
disputes, making their own plans.

"GOODNIGHT, PEPPER. Bye, Regis. Be good now, Binky, you hear me?"

It's Friday afternoon, and Janet the volunteer and Kim the staffer have
left for the day. Over the weekend, the chimps will be fed, played with,
and invited out into their outdoor enclosure.

Still, Gloria hovers, reluctant to check that cupboards are locked, make
sure food is put away in the kitchen, and switch off the lights. It's as if she
can't quite bear to turn her back and close the door behind her, without
offering something more. Whatever might be in her power to offer, in
compensation for what she cannot.

It's not nearly twilight. Still, I find myself listening for Theo the
baboon. Along with the chimps, he's enough like me that I can imagine
how profound his dislocation must feel. Yet, he's also sufficiently *not* like
me that I am anxious to be on my way. With any luck at all, I think, Gloria

and I will pass through the gates and head out onto the road back to town long before he sets up his sad, bootless twilight cry.

PRIMATOLOGIST FRANS DE WAAL cautions against either glorifying or vilifying any species out of hand. But he also warns against what he calls "anthro-denial"—a kind of *a priori* rejection of qualities our species might share with one another, leading to "willful blindness to the human-like characteristics of animals, or the animal-like characteristics of ourselves."

When it comes to our attitudes toward primates in particular, human beings are inclined to lurch between extremes of familiarity and contempt. On the one hand, there's King Kong, the quasi-tragic Beast yearning slavishly after Beauty. On the other hand...well, there's also King Kong— the slavering, licentious monster, literally licking his lips as he ogles the helpless form of a human woman through the window, then reaching out his unclean paw to claim her.

According to ethologist Paul Shepard, humans' notable unease with apes stems from the fact that "the Western mind distrusts appearances and change in nature, all signs of overlapping and confused identity, such as man and ape. The uncanny similarity of higher primates to ourselves triggers cognitive dissonance, and challenges the moral, God-ordained discreteness of his order. Our culture denies the value of paradox and censures anomaly as evil. The ape imitates man just as man confuses himself with God."

Yet, the dissimilarity between us and non-primate species hardly recommends them to us, either. As Arnold Arluke observes: "The less an animal is regarded as 'like us,' the more we will tolerate, ignore or even condone its mistreatment."

At the same time, in human beings there appears to be some persistent need to seize upon certain species and briefly elevate them to almost saintly ranks—then just as quickly, drop them back down to earth with a splat. Over the past few decades we've gone through various species, from dolphins, to elephants, to Galapagos tortoises and—most recently—

bonobos, always looking for that one elusive creature who will, for all time, represent us satisfactorily to ourselves.

This tendency is as prevalent in art as in life. In 1980, renowned British critic John Berger wrote an essay called "Why Look At Animals?" accusing us of having "co-opted" animals as the anthropomorphic heroes of books and cartoons. Thereby, Berger contends, we have deprived them of their central role as animals. The animals in Beatrix Potter's books, for instance, he decries as "human puppets," embodying "the pettiness of current social practices" in human society which are thereby "universalized by being projected on the animal kingdom."

Yet, whether in books like *The Tale of Peter Rabbit* and *Charlotte's Web*, or some nature documentary on TV, many of us find it impossible not to anthropomorphize animals, regardless of how we choose to depict them. The very fact that our kind has always interpreted their kind through stories necessitates presenting them as characters, with impulses and emotions in some way like our own.

"If a lion could talk," the philosopher Ludwig Wittgenstein famously warned, "no one would understand him." Even so, the temptation to put words in the lion's mouth is impossible to overcome. And the more representative of the best or the worst in us is the animal in question, the stronger the impulse to cast it as a central figure in the stories we tell about ourselves.

Naturally, any animal that appears to embody both the best and the worst of humanity makes for particularly interesting human drama. The ape is certainly one candidate for that role, but perhaps too genetically close to us for comfort. The dog may better fit the bill. His kind has always been kin to ours in an emotional sense. But genetically—while close—he is at a more companionable remove than apes.

"On the one hand," Paul Shepard has observed, "the dog is 'man's best friend'.... On the other hand the dog is the alien monster and hypocrite, fallen and hateful, the most corrupt of animals."

The fact that the dog has this double aspect makes it easy to place him at the centre of our storytelling involving animals. If not always as the hero, he can function as an antihero, or—at worst—as the schlemiel. Meanwhile, in the role of ultimate villain, another animal altogether is required. A creature in whom there is nothing for us to identify—except those qualities within ourselves we most crave to trample underfoot.

Enter the serpent.

Apart from herpetologists and other reptile enthusiasts, hardly anybody has a good word to say about snakes. Yes, there have been cultures that have worshipped snakes, or at least not held in them in absolute disrepute. As well, the healing art of Asclepius, the ancient Greek physician-cum-deity (in that depiction, maybe not so different from the way surgeons and other medical specialists see themselves to this day) was symbolized by a snake wrapped around a rod. However, in mythology, from whatever time or place in human history and prehistory, serpents are most frequently cast as the villains of the piece.

Each strand of monstrous Medusa's hair was one of his kind. In the Book of Genesis, the serpent is front and centre, the architect of mankind's Fall. When Cleopatra reached out for help in dispatching herself, an asp was there, ready and willing to be clasped. The snake is in the grass whenever treachery is afoot; his tooth is nearly as sharp as the ingratitude of a thankless child; it's his oil that greases the moustache of the mountebank and lubricates the wheels of the corrupt corporate machine.

The herpeton's lack of legs, absence of eyelids, dry glossy scales that appear slimy even though they aren't...something creepy lurks at the core, a quality of ultimate otherness that makes it possible, even in the competitive annals of animal abuse, for humans to outdo themselves in cruelty when it comes to snakes. The most harmless species among them routinely are shot, crushed, pulverized, pierced, and nailed to boards in order to be flayed alive.

Snakes are phallic, yet not sexual in a way that smacks of joy. The smile on the face of the serpent in the Garden of Eden is ingratiating rather than erotic; the shiver he inspires is a tremor of loathing, rather than the *frisson* of desire.

It's not only human beings who appear to harbour a deep-down, visceral loathing of serpent-kind. In the most essential version of the story of the greyhound and the snake and the baby in its cradle, the serpent is understood to be a primal enemy of the dog.

So subversive is the snake that it manages, even in death, to conceal its role in the attack on the baby. By the time the body of the serpent is discovered in a corner, the evidence comes far too late to vindicate the dog, or to save the master from leaping to the wrong conclusion. In death, the snake gets the last—and the only—laugh.

As for the dog, his silence in death is no different from his muteness in life. He remains inscrutable, unknowable; yet in his heart, he is man's best friend. Or else—if the preliminary evidence is to be believed—an alien monster and hypocrite, fallen and hateful, the most corrupt of animals.

———◦•◦———

WHAT IF IT WERE I, instead of the servant, coming to that closed door? First hesitating, then opening it, to be met by those eyes, that gaze—steady, searching, wordless, silent. And inscrutable.

Eh, boy? Good boy! What's up, fellah?

Oh, nothing much.

Along with the impenetrable gaze there is the ready smile. Lips drawn back, tongue protruding, teeth that gleam and jaws that always seem to grin. Just like the servant, I see blood on the lips and on that lolling tongue and those smiling crocodile jaws. Come on, now. Is it just that you're pleased with yourself for making the kill? Or proud of something even more profound?

You're putting words in my mouth.

Of course I am, I tell the dog. I'm a human being. It's what I do.

Why? This is my story.

But it's my story too. Any moment now, as soon as that servant comes and opens this door for real.

How do you know that?

Because it's my story too, I told you. We're in this together.

———◦•◦———

PART THREE

Guilt-edged Security:
Self-serving Stewards

THERE IS NO PRACTICAL REASON for human beings to be overly concerned about our use of other animals, or to feel pangs of conscience
for their abuse. We, after all, are the pre-eminent ones—with self-declared
"dominion" over all and self-appointed "stewardship" of everything that
walks, crawls, flies, slithers, or swims. No judge, jury, or court of public
opinion is likely to find for them at our expense.

But despite animals' lack of clout, some humans worry about appearing fair. Numerous animal species kill others for their food, just like us.
Nonetheless, it is our own predation that strikes many of us as unfair
somehow, irrespective of whether we choose, as individuals, to give it up.

Why is it that the suffering of one, small, vulnerable animal can sometimes outweigh the devastation of an entire theatre of war? Yet at other
times, we manage to count the massacre of thousands of creatures as
nothing, so long as their death suits our own purposes.

As awareness grows globally of impending crises in fuel and food,
practical debates about land used for grazing and feed crops begin to
mingle more and more with moral arguments against rearing livestock for
slaughter. Nowadays, you will as likely hear a vegan preach environmental
sustainability as animal rights.

Indeed, for all of us—vegan, vegetarian, and omnivore alike—there is
increasing discomfort with the idea that human survival is postulated on
the death of other species and ultimately the planet that sustains us all.
No wonder that in our inability to resolve this profound paradox, we feel

both responsible and inadequate—like stewards struggling with an impossible assignment.

I

OF ALL ANIMALS, there is something about birds that speaks particularly to a quality of innocent joy. No other creature sounds as straightforwardly happy as the warbler pouring out his heart from a tree branch or telephone wire. Not even angels in the morning air could rival the unspoiled purity of a dove, or the clear, liquid song of a skylark on high. Which may be why the image of a canary in a coal mine serves as the ultimate symbol of blameless nature befouled by cruel commerce.

The expression is no mere figure of speech. From the early twentieth century until the mid-1980s—when they were replaced by more "economical" electronic detectors—caged canaries were actually carried down into coalmines in Britain, North America, and elsewhere as early-warning detectors for methane gas and other odourless toxins.

Because of the sensitivity of their systems, canaries were favoured over other small animals, such as mice. In the presence of even a small amount of gas, these delicate birds reacted quickly. First, they would sway on their perches. Then, they would fall down dead.

In a well-known eighteenth-century painting by Wright of Derby, titled "An Experiment on a Bird in the Air Pump," an angelic-looking bird is enclosed in a glass chamber. The painter depicts a scientist about to siphon all the air from the chamber, to demonstrate how the bird will die as a result.

Several of the onlookers—the men in particular—appear as avidly caught up in the spirit of scientific inquiry as the administrator of the experiment. However, one young woman covers her face with her hand, as if sympathetic to the bird's plight. And the small girl beside her—possibly her daughter—is also openly distressed at the fate of the helpless creature.

In real life, experimenters of the day like Robert Hooke and Robert Boyle suffocated all kinds of animals in the name of science, including mice, rabbits, and even dogs. Yet Wright of Derby chose a bird as the centre-piece for his picture. And not a sparrow or swift or other ordinary British species, but a pure and exotic white dove—the very epitome of innocence.

In our time—even discounting canaries in coalmines or doves dying in air-pump experiments—birds continue to play a frontline role as early-warning devices. Between the 1960s, when American ecologist Rachel Carson wrote her groundbreaking book, *Silent Spring*, and the recent publication of Canadian biologist Bridget Stutchbury's *Silence of the Song-birds*, our cause for alarm has become ever more urgent.

Loss of habitat to human development, pesticides, and other forms of poisoning; disruption of migratory patterns caused by lighted buildings; electrocution on power poles; death through collisions with automobiles and airplanes; predation by feral cats that number in their millions . . . these are only some of the obstacles facing birds all over the world. More than a thousand of the planet's almost ten thousand bird species are threatened with extinction—thirty-five additional species added between 2006 and 2007 alone. Worldwide, the species most at risk are albatrosses, cranes, and parrots. Meanwhile, just in North America, 50 percent of the twenty most common birds—including evening grosbeaks, meadowlarks, and bo-real chickadees—have disappeared in the past four decades.

In a State of the World's Birds report released in the fall of 2008, the rate of species extinction is described as "exceptionally high"—about one thousand to ten thousand times what would occur if man were absent from the landscape. Even if we are to blame, most of us—like coalminers with their caged canaries, like those avid experimenters with their air pumps—do understand that what happens first to birds happens soon after to us.

As we begin to sense more and more how inextricably our own future is intertwined with theirs, we will find ourselves looking and listening more and more intently for those flashes of colour and snatches of bird-song we have already begun to see and hear less and less. Whether we have left our common concern too late already is another question. If we have, the silence, when it falls, will be deafening. Innocent and guilty alike, we'll experience the impact together.

WHEN I'D PICTURED IN ADVANCE the Avian Science and Conservation Centre at the Macdonald campus of McGill University, out in the Montreal suburb of Ste Anne de Bellevue, I had envisioned an enormous arboreal expanse, dotted with feeding stations and lookout towers, and thick with species swooping to and fro. Instead, now that I'm here on a brilliantly sunny morning, I am walking across a parking lot with Professor David Bird from his academic office to a windowless hangar-style structure nearby. Dr. Bird unlocks the door and ushers me from blinding sunshine into a dark, stuffy interior. Only after he turns on the lights do I discern a row of individual locked stalls fronted with wire mesh.

In one enclosure, a group of loggerhead shrikes perch in severed tree branches that have been set up for them. Some of the twigs are hung with the strangest of fruit: dead, bloody, white mice, impaled on thorns.

All I know about shrikes comes from a recollection of the sadistic newspaper editor Shrike in *Miss Lonelyhearts* by Nathanael West. But these representatives of the species seem to belie that association with merciless cruelty. The caged shrikes are disarmingly cute, like songbirds, and attractively grey and white with rakish black masks "They're very pretty!" I exclaim in surprise.

David is pleased. "Yeah, I think so too." Shrikes, he assures me, are no more vicious than any other animal that kills and eats its prey. It's just that these birds have to compensate for the fact that their claws can't grasp and hold their kill the way raptors do. "It's because they impale them on twigs or thorns that they've got this bad rep."

"Is that why they're endangered—because people hate them?"

He shrugs. "Habitat loss. Toxic chemicals. We're looking at several possibilities to account for the steep decline. That's why they're in here."

"I see." And I do, but it seems sad that they have to be locked away like this, so deeply indoors, in enclosed spaces no larger than some of the floor-to-ceiling birdcages in which people keep pet parrots or conyers. "Did they kill these mice?"

No, he tells me, the mice were delivered dead, and then hung on the thorns for the shrikes to peck at. The image of Dr. Bird and his researchers tacking up limp bodies of mice like stockings on Christmas Eve is peculiarly arresting, even more startling than the image of a loggerhead shrike out in the wild, sticking a small animal corpse on a sharp bramble for easier dismemberment.

We leave the shrikes to their mice and head to another building. Inside, there is an overripe smell, like a school cafeteria where chicken sandwiches have been left out too long. Bird leads me into a room full of wheeling kestrels, and I immediately locate the source of the odour: a long line of dead day-old baby chickens laid out for consumption, smorgasbord style.

People, David tells me, tend not to give raptors credit for much individuality. But once you've observed them for a while, you come to appreciate the different approaches kestrels take to eating raw chicken. Some like to start with the feet, while others nip off the head. In the same way folks at Thanksgiving choose which part of the turkey they prefer.

Dr. Bird—whose surname bespeaks his general area of interest—is particularly passionate about raptors. His website features a photo of him locking eyes with a falcon perched on his glove. And disregarding any betrayal of political incorrectness, he confesses that he is an enthusiastic advocate of legalized hunting with falcons and hawks.

Even in a small, closed room of captive kestrels swooping down on demonstrably dead baby chicks, he seems to me to derive pleasure from any proximity to birds of prey. This despite the fact that, in this case, they're dipping and diving in a caged space, more captive than if hooded and tethered to a glove, utterly shut off from the sky and denied the wild.

The kestrels bred here at the Avian Centre have never known any life but captivity. The purpose of their existence is to receive measured doses of fenthion, a pesticide used on "nuisance birds" such as starling and sparrows, so that wildlife biologists can determine whether or not fenthion is also fatal to the raptors who prey on those birds.

"How do you feel about that?" I ask Dr. Bird.

Personally, he says, he finds it difficult to administer toxic chemicals to species he admires. Even so, there is information to be gained that is of benefit to their own species, as well as ours. That's not always the case for animals involved in experiments.

In his entire approach to research, Bird strives to be relentlessly unsentimental. Earlier, he'd commented on a regrettable increase among students in wildlife biology who "think with their hearts, rather than their heads."

"But has thinking with our heads always provided good solutions for animals?" I asked, and recalled to him policies from government ministries that had been received by environmental groups as ill-designed. "Like the idea that 'culling' is an automatic answer to excessive populations of animals. What about pulling back on human incursion into their realm?"

David dismissed that as being "emotional."

"Haven't you ever been emotional about any of the birds you've worked with?" I wanted to know.

In response, he took from a shelf a polished claw hanging on a fine chain. The talon, he said, had belonged to Frieda, a hawk on whom he'd done research. Frieda was thirty-seven years old when he decided she should be euthanized because she was old and ill. He'd kept the talon as a memento of a bird he wasn't embarrassed to admit he'd loved.

I didn't know quite what to say. I tried and failed to imagine the finger of a revered human being hanging on a chain, or the paw of a departed pet dog.

David escorts me out of the kestrel pen and back to the parking lot where I've left my rental car. A kind of unease lingers between us. He starts off for his own vehicle, then stops, turns, comes back, and gestures to me to roll down my window.

When I do, he explains that he wanted to tell me about an outstanding presentation he heard at a recent conference. An Australian researcher, he said, had used African music to back up his demonstration. "Terrific music. It really inspired me. Just to say," he adds, with the smile of someone who might be kidding and also might not be, "I'm not utterly insensitive. Not all bad."

I recall Temple Grandin's parting words to me: *I'm about practical solutions.* I didn't doubt her for a moment. Nor do I doubt David Bird. Still, back on the highway, under a bright, open September sky, I instinctively press down hard on the gas and let the car fly lickety-split. Farther and farther from those enclosed cages of birds, doing hard time for crimes they didn't commit.

IN HIS NOVEL *BABI YAR*, Russian writer Anatoly Kuznetsov narrates the horrors of life in Ukraine under Nazi occupation through the eyes of a young protagonist. Among the routine torments and daily terrors of such an existence, the life and death of one deformed kitten should, technically, count as nothing. Yet, both for Kuznetsov and his small hero, the act of putting this newborn animal out of its misery takes on overwhelming significance.

The boy sets out to dispatch the kitten—"a moist, warm blob of life, utterly devoid of sense and insignificant as a worm"—with a brick. But the kitten somehow withstands the assault, and continues to cry piteously. "With shaking hands," the author writes, "I picked up the brick again and proceeded to crush the little ball of living matter until the very entrails came out, and at last it was silent, and I scraped up the remains of the kitten with a shovel and took them off to the rubbish heap, and as I did it my head swam and I felt sick."

In the midst of life that is itself walking death, the extinction of this kitten, seemingly cursed from conception by its deformity, is by no means more horrible than the rest of the horrors on show. But it's entirely effective as a small, complete representation of the will of even the weakest to live, despite the worst existence has to offer.

From the beginning of human habitation on Earth, the saddest casualties of wars between armies have always been the most innocent. Not the least among these are the countless animals caught up in the cataclysmic tide of our *casus belli*. And, among the ranks of those incidental innocents, perhaps the most obvious are horses.

Vedic texts from as early as the second millennium BCE contain references to horses as embodiments of conquest. In one recorded ritual, a king would set free a horse for a year and order his men to follow it. All the land covered during that year by the free-ranging horse became the king's property. After proclaiming title to it, the monarch would order that the horse be killed ceremonially. Whereupon, it seems, his queen would get under bedcovers with the corpse of the horse, and simulate intercourse with it—presumably to cement the deal.

For some later conquerors, simply possessing horses when their opponents did not provided an enormous tactical advantage. The prehistoric horse died out in North America about eleven thousand years ago. When the Spanish invaded this continent in the early sixteenth century, they re-introduced its modern counterpart to the New World—for their own exclusive use as a weapon of war.

For years, the Spanish managed to keep their mounts out of the hands of Native Americans, thereby keeping the natives under control. But in 1680, during the Pueblo Revolt in the Spanish province of New Mexico, a number of horses got loose and thundered away. Some were never recaptured. But others became available for riding by any Indian quick enough to catch them.

The capture of these animals altered the lives of their new captors, and also influenced their character. According to ecologist Paul Shepard, after they acquired horses Plains Indians became more warlike and less brotherly, even within their own communities.

Like early Europeans, North American Indians identified horses with their riders, and sometimes inflicted the same fate on them. The Blackfoot Indians decorated the horse of a fallen warrior with paint and ribbons— then killed and interred it with the dead hero. The Nez Perce, meanwhile, skinned and stuffed horses to use as grave monuments for the tombs of their most honoured braves.

Right into the twentieth century, horses went into war with humans, and suffered alongside the men who rode them into battle or hitched them to cannons and ambulances. These animals have always had even less option about being on the field of battle than their riders and handlers, and far fewer inducements to fight. Perhaps it's that quality of innocent involvement that makes the horse a particularly poignant emblem of man's inhumanity to man as well as beast.

In the film version of Ian McEwan's novel *Atonement*, there is a long, sweeping sequence of British and French soldiers awaiting evacuation from Dunkirk. Briefly, the camera pans a line of horses. They are being systematically shot, perhaps because there is nothing for them to eat on the apocalyptic-looking beach. Or perhaps because, when the boats finally arrive, there will be no hope of transporting them back to Britain.

In the camera's wild panorama of human horror—wounded, dirty, drunken, and demented soldiers, destroyed buildings, the remnants of a seaside amusement park still crazily in operation, a group of men singing a hymn in the fragments of a bandshell—those horses stand out as objects of pathos, as each quietly waits its turn to die. The animals' apparent unwittingness as they await their fate sums up the true brutality of war more affectingly than any other elements of this scene of widespread carnage.

Even more powerful in this regard is a stage production called *War Horse*, which premiered at London's National Theatre early in 2008. The story itself, based on a novel by popular British children's writer Michael Morpurgo, is fairly routine. Joey, a horse much beloved of his young master, is conscripted into the First World War and taken from the pastoral calm of Devonshire to the inferno of battle in France.

It's not the plot line but the theatrical depictions of Joey and his fellow warhorses that raise this tale to an epic level of innocence trampled by the hubris of human beings. The horses are represented through life-sized skeletal structures, each with articulated joints, tails, heads, even ears, all operated by puppeteers, visible both inside the horse bodies and outside, manipulating the head and limbs.

Despite the obvious non-naturalism of this presentation, Joey and the other horses are enormously personable and entirely sympathetic. So much so that no live horse would be half as effective—neither as quintessentially equine, nor as transcendently human—as these beautifully suggested creatures. Gradually, as the increasingly unhappy situation of man and beast deteriorates to the level of the truly hellish, the horses' wooden frames degenerate into broken, shredded representations of the war-torn world at large.

Even beyond the battlefield, horses are affecting as innocent accomplices to human misadventure and involuntary actors in the dramas we create. Nowhere is this better illustrated than in the classic 1939 Hollywood film *Gone with the Wind*.

We see Bonnie Blue, the small, spoiled daughter of Rhett Butler and Scarlett O'Hara, on her pony, being urged by her father to take some low jumps. But even these modest hurdles, her mother objects from the sidelines, are too ambitious for a little girl. While her parents argue about the degree of risk involved, Bonnie impulsively goads her mount toward a fence. As the pony breaks into a gallop, the child loses her seat. One of her boots gets caught in the stirrup, and before the eyes of her horrified parents, Bonnie is dragged to her death.

The aftermath of the accident is not shown on screen. However, the events are narrated so affectingly by Hattie McDaniel, as the family's old mammy, that the effect is—oddly—even more powerful.

Tearfully, Mammy recounts to a friend of Scarlett and Rhett's how the couple quarreled over who was to blame for Bonnie's mishap. Captain Butler, says Mammy, seemed to lose his mind. He had grieved his daughter more bitterly than any man, "white or colored," ever took on over the death of a child.

Finally, Mammy tells us, Butler got his gun, went out to the stable and "he shot that poor pony." The words are succinct, but the picture they paint is vivid: a weeping father, deranged by grief, bursting through the stable door; the pony in his stall, turning his head toward the sound of striding boots, utterly unsuspecting of what is to come, unaware of the devastation he's brought down on an entire family and himself.

It's that complete vulnerability to outcomes they can't comprehend that makes animals such powerful surrogates of our own sense of helplessness. Even with our superior understanding of events, we, like them, can be victims of sudden, cataclysmic, totally devastating change. One moment all seems well, and then in the next split-second.... We shake our heads over the stories we read about people who had homes, right up until the moment they didn't, or identities that disappeared in an instant, or a way of life that suddenly ceased to be.

It's not the events themselves that so unsettle us. It's the terrible capriciousness that we all shudder at, that awful ability of destiny to turn on a dime.

For an animal, it's not that utter upheaval necessarily feels the same as it would to a human. Yet, when it happens, the totality of loss, the entire alteration in existence must hit them with an impact easily akin to the force with which calamity hits us. And when we factor in a non-human's lack of comprehension and the total terror that would accompany such complete disruption, it is almost unbearably painful to imagine what overturned existence must feel like to an animal unlucky enough to be adrift in our world.

In her 1995 novel *Behind the Scenes at the Museum*, British writer Kate Atkinson recreates the First World War training and service of messenger dogs. Many of the animals supplied to Britain's Messenger Dog Service came from dogs' homes across Britain—"overflowing with unwanted dogs," as Atkinson explains, because of rationing. Others were pets of patriotic families who donated them with little comprehension of what was in store.

Atkinson presents an appraisal of the lives of these animals through the eyes of a sympathetic character working as a dog trainer for the Messenger Dog Service.

Jack wondered what those families would have thought if they could have seen the way the dogs were selected for training. He'd found it hard enough himself to stomach. The dogs were only fed once a day—they could all see the food being laid down for them but just before they were set free from their kennels, the handlers had to throw grenades into a pit nearby. Of course, the grenades made a terrifying racket and at first not a single dog would venture out for the food. By the third or fourth day, the dogs were starving and the bold ones, the ones that would eventually go to the Front, sneaked out along their own version of No Man's Land to the dishes and wolfed the food down as quickly as possible before dashing back to the shelter of their kennels.

The bold dogs were soon salivating at the sound of the first grenades, and straining to get off their leashes, torpedoes be damned. However, there were other dogs, Atkinson tells us, who did not adapt so readily to the fog of war.

> Jack had sleepless nights thinking about some of those dogs—one little dog haunted him still, a gentle spaniel the colour of chestnuts called Jenny, petrified out of her wits by the grenades and eventually shot behind the parade ground. Even now, back at the Front, Jack could see the little dog's big, soft eyes turned to him in disbelief at what was happening to her.

"Disbelief" perfectly captures what a dog like Jenny might feel in the circumstance. Neither comprehension, nor understanding, nor even fear at what fresh horror waits to confront her; simply disbelief that the world she thought she knew is now so utterly absent, so entirely lost.

II

IN CAMBRIDGE, ENGLAND, the past seems barely out of sight. Punts for rent bob on the River Cam, willows drape themselves into the water, and reflections of the flat fronts of old houses shimmer like memories of a bygone era. At Evensong in Kings College Chapel, five hundred years of stone, candle wax, and incense blend with the youthful voices of the ancient choir.

At Clare College, founded in the fourteenth century by Elizabeth de Clare, I am lucky enough to be lunching at the High Table with Nicola Clayton, a professor of comparative psychology. True to its name, the High Table is elevated, with professors and guests like me ranged along it, overlooking a refectory hall of student tables spread out below. Amidst a dozen other conversations buzzing around us, Professor Clayton is deep in discussion with me about what memory might mean to birds. The fact that we are picking over various delectable desserts provides her with ready, impromptu illustrations for her brisk disquisition on how the structure of the bird brain differs from a human's layered cerebral cortex.

"Think of two pieces of cake," she says by way of comparison, "made of the same ingredients. But one is a six-layer cake, while the other is mixed up like a fruit cake, with bits of material spread throughout the batter. The fruit cake's the bird brain, as compared to ours." But despite those differences, she adds, in both cases how "mind" links to "brain" is the question. "There's neurology, and then there's imagination.

"Do you remember Robert Burns' field mouse? 'The present only touches thee,' said the poet. But what if Burns was wrong? You see—" she fixes me with her large blue-grey eyes—"there are implications if, like us, animals have the ability to imagine the future."

In an article I'd read, the writer described Nicola Clayton as birdlike herself. Now that I've met her, I concur. She is small, slender, energetic, and mercurial. But it's a description that also fits her as the avid dancer she is.

I know about the dancing from photos she's emailed me of herself and her salsa group. The emails were signed "Nicky" and that fact, together with the salsa photos, have prepared me for someone not the sort of person you'd typically think of as a Cambridge professor. Nicky Clayton has long blonde hair, a brilliant smile, and a stunning figure displayed to advantage by a long-sleeved leotard, wraparound skirt, footless tights and spike heel pumps—"There are four more pairs of shoes in my car," she says.

Despite the heels, on our way here to Clare College from her office she set a brisk pace over Cambridge's cobbled streets. I trotted alongside, doing my best to chat with her on the run, like a character on *The West Wing*.

Briefly, one of her high heels got caught in a grate and stopped her short. But throwing a shoe didn't appear to distress her one bit, or cause her to question the footwear she'd chosen for such challenging terrain. Quite matter-of-factly, she wrenched the heel loose from the grating and put the shoe back on, continuing to talk all the while.

It's not that she acts at all unconscious of the contrast between her vivacious exterior and the gravity of her purpose as a prominent research scientist. If anything, it seems important to her to present herself as someone of varied interests and accomplishments—be it sashaying with the girls or plumbing the capacity for memory in corvids, a category of birds that includes jays, crows, ravens, and jackdaws. It's the whole person on offer here, both Dr. Clayton and Nicky, as free with her anecdotes about her parents' love of ballroom dancing as she is with her descriptions of how birds' brains are structured.

I wonder if her interest in dance somehow relates to her research on birds.

"Yes," she replies instantly. "Both involve memory."

Clearly, she's had this question before. But the answer, clinical and flat, doesn't illuminate the passion she brings to both pursuits. Nor is it obvious how someone as emotive and expressive as Nicky could muster the cool detachment required of Dr. Clayton.

She "loves" her birds, she is quick to tell me. Long before she developed an interest in them as objects of research, she raised cockatiels as pets. Now—like her Cambridge colleague, Donald Broom, and Temple Grandin at Colorado State—she has many research and travel commitments that take her away from home and leave no time to allot to pets. For Clayton, daily visits to her corvids at the aviary outside Cambridge seem as instrumental in filling that gap as in fuelling her research.

I ask her about the trickiness of experimenting on species she professes to love. It's true, she tells me. She far prefers to study their thought processes by setting them enjoyable tasks to perform and problems to solve, rather than by dissecting their brains once they're dead.

"Still," she adds, "I would more readily condone the sacrifice of an animal for research and the knowledge that might follow from it, than its sacrifice as food."

She has already told me that she's been a vegetarian since age eleven. Yet she does not connect this childhood choice to her adult preference for a non-invasive style of research. Nor does her vegetarianism appear to have arisen from her general affection for animals. As anecdotal as she is and eager to share her enthusiasms, she does not strike me as nearly so interested in tracing her own behaviours as she is in observing birds and drawing conclusions about what they know and when they know it.

In her office—in a building in central Cambridge grimly designated

"Experimental Psychology"—Clayton shows me a clip on her computer screen from a no-longer current TV program called *Britain's Cleverest Animal*. The premise, she explains, was to show videos of various animal species, wild and domestic, engaged in activities that appeared surprisingly intelligent, and invite viewers to vote for the cleverest.

The winning clip is of some rooks Nicky first observed at a rest stop on the M4 motorway. These birds had taught themselves to retrieve food from deep in a large waste barrel by pulling up the plastic liner bag with their beaks, an inch or so at a time, until the scraps on the bottom of the bag were within reach.

As we watched the rooks going through their painstaking procedure, Nicky exclaimed over their ingenuity with unbridled delight. She'd seen this clip—and the rooks at their antics, live and in person—dozens and dozens of times. Yet her enjoyment, as well as her pride, seemed entirely fresh.

What is it, I wanted to know, that's behind that enjoyment—not just for her, the avid research scientist, but for an entire TV audience glued to clever pet tricks?

"Of course, they can't seem like tricks," she replied. "When I was a child, there was a circus performer named 'Priscilla the Pig' we all loved, who did clever stunts. But you could tell Priscilla was trained. Nowadays, what we want to see are real-live instances of spontaneous behaviour in animals. We want to see them taking in new information and adapting their behaviour to it."

Nicky's, effusiveness adds an element of the personal to her zeal for scientific inquiry. When she points out the cleverness of rooks solving problems of food retrieval from big, deep bins, or takes me to watch her Eurasian jays hiding toys from each other, she is almost parental in the pride with which she regards these feats.

Like any proud parent, she is quick to defend her own. Neuroscientist Endel Tulving, emeritus professor at the University of Toronto, shares research interests with Dr. Clayton in the area of birds and memory. Tulving, however, believes that animals lack sufficient self-awareness to be able to recall personal memories the way humans can. It's impossible, he says, to remember yourself doing something in the past if you have no present awareness that you even exist.

Not surprisingly, Nicky Clayton disagrees with that assessment. For more than a decade, she's been testing corvids (the brainiest of birds, in her opinion) to determine whether they do possess what Dr. Tulving has dubbed "episodic memory." That is, the ability to recall details of personal experience from recollection of oneself in a particular context. In the case of Western scrub jays, she contends their remarkable ability to relocate food they have previously cached comes from remembering not just the location, but the experience of having hidden food there.

In one experiment designed to prove that contention, she moved scrub jays from a room stocked with food supplies to another where the cupboard was bare, and then back again. The experiment was set up that way to determine if the birds would take provisions from the stocked room and cache them in advance in the empty room, in anticipation of the next day's programmed deprivation. According to her findings, they did.

On our car ride from Cambridge to the aviary, I ask her if she worries about the stressfulness both of the experiments and of lifelong captivity on birds she professes to love.

About the experiments, her conscience is clear. "They enjoy learning. It's a game to them—the compensation for their regulated lives in captivity."

To her, the proof is a test that offers birds three choices of environment: One is a room with obviously accessible food; the second room has food that requires some rudimentary searching to find. "And the third room has food they can only get to by solving puzzle boxes—'Sudoku for birds,' I call it. And do you know what? They clearly prefer the rooms where there is a challenge over the room just with available food."

"What about in the wild, though," I ask, "where gathering food is so labour-intensive, and there's no time to get bored. Would those birds prefer a challenge, too?"

"Well, look at those rooks on the M4, choosing to go through rubbish bins and learning to lift up the edges of the liner bags—even when there is more readily accessible food about. Don't you think that's enjoyable for them?"

Nicola Clayton is concerned about the humane treatment of animals in research, and, like her Cambridge colleague Donald Broom, sees research itself as a way of promoting that kind of treatment. But just as Broom speaks of "our obligations to them, rather than their rights," so is Clayton concerned more with the responsibility of creating a rich environment for her birds, than with questioning the justice of raising species from various parts of the world in captivity.

However, she also advocates "respecting each other's beliefs" on matters pertaining to animal rights. It's a brief statement, more politic than illuminating. The Cambridge area—with both university labs and commercial product-testing facilities like Huntingdon Life Sciences—has long been a hotbed for animal rights actions and protest. Anyone engaged in captive animal research of any kind is likely to have a stock response to questions about how those research subjects live and die—even a vegetarian engaged in cognitive research that's non-invasive, like Dr. Clayton.

When I ask her about respecting the beliefs of activists, she replies that her main worry is about having her birds set loose in a misguided act of liberation. Some, like the scrub jays, are not native to and would die in an outdoor climate as chilly and damp as Britain's. Nor would any of her species, hand-raised from eggs, have much of a chance out on their own.

Even at the thought, her tone becomes cold and her manner briefly withdrawn. Presumably, as a scientist she feels annoyed at the idea of anyone meddling with her research. But in her reaction, there is also the anxiety of someone who cares personally for these creatures, worries about their welfare, and can't wait to get out to the aviary at Madingley to tell them so.

In anticipation, she presses her foot on the accelerator of the Audi TT she calls Timothy and takes the road at an even faster clip. She's had to learn the way by rote, she tells me, as a result of being "spatially challenged."

This is a woman after my own heart, given that I used to get lost on my way home from high school. Perhaps another clue to her fascination with the cognitive power of birds—including their spatial memory—lies in her own self-confessed deficiency in that department.

At the Madingley aviary, I follow Nicky across mossy grass made green by a premature February spring to a big wire-fenced area, open to today's crisp sunshine. Basking in the brightness are Eurasian jays, with tawny bodies and bright blue wings almost iridescent in the sun. One, called Quito (all the jays are named for cities, for some reason), caches marbles in the netting of the aviary, making a great display of trying to make sure none of the other birds can see him.

Again with that hint of a doting parent, Clayton points out how assiduously Quito hides the marbles from view. Corvids display the same avidity in caching food, she tells me, and take endless pains not to be observed by other birds when they do so. In fact, in captive situations, they will even "pay" for the privilege of privacy from prying eyes, by learning to push a button to activate a screen that will conceal them from others as they cache their goods.

Nicky's brought some cherries to feed the jays. In preparation to enter the area, she and I both have to put on blue paper booties over our shoes and she also dons a lab coat before entering the birds' actual enclosure. "Regulations," she explains, and I sense they're not entirely to her liking. Still, in the years since she was wooed back to Britain from California, Cambridge has been good to her, building this first-rate facility to her specifications. Therefore, in the matter of abiding by regulations, she is prepared to be good to Cambridge.

Inside the offices adjoining the aviary, several research students are interacting with the birds, albeit less directly than Nicky with her bag of cherries. One young woman shows me film she's taken of a rook repeatedly rewarded with food each time he pushes aside a bolt in order to open a box. There is another rook observing this sequence. This bird, the researcher explains, will not have to go through the same trial-and-error process to learn to open the box, after seeing how it's done.

In a separate office, another young woman is watching a closed-circuit camera trained on birds in the adjacent aviary. The birds are supposed to pull a string and get a mealworm as a reward. However, she reports to Dr. Clayton with some puzzlement, some have shown an atypical unwillingness to "work" today, even after nine or more hours with nothing to do and nothing to eat.

Nicky expresses disappointment at the lack of interest they are showing in her, too. She's warned me there are some days when they are less interactive than others. Still, it's clear she had hoped they'd offer evidence even an outsider could appreciate of the singularity of their memories and minds. Perhaps she'd have liked them to exhibit the pleasure she believes they derive from the work they do, as well as from their rapport with her.

About her own pleasure in this enterprise, she is entirely unequivocal. As we wing along the road from Madingley back to Cambridge, with scant time for me to make the London train, she declares: "I regard it as a privilege, not a right, to work with these birds."

It's another utterance with a quality of formality, as if prepared for publication. As with other academic researchers I've interviewed, Nicola Clayton feels the need to make clear what she is about. I can't tell if she is continuing to rankle at any suggestion of criticism about the birds' captive lives, or merely underscoring awareness of her own good fortune.

Not long after I returned to Canada, I had an email from her, alerting me to a new *National Geographic* article on animal minds. Even without her saying so, I knew that she was likely to be quoted in it.

Sure enough, there she was, with a good comment about how cognitive scientists sometimes "move the goalposts" regarding the intellectual achievements of animals. For instance, her comment continued, it seems whenever an animal demonstrates ability in something like "episodic memory," some scientists will immediately change the definition in a way that excludes what the animal has done.

I like the vigorous way Dr. Clayton championed the achievements of her beloved birds to *National Geographic*. I can easily imagine how she sounded—her voice tinged by the slightly adenoidal North Country accent of her childhood—as she complained about those goalposts being moved. Just as I can still distinctly hear her, over our lunch at the Clare College High Table, chiding Robbie Burns for his failure to see what a field mouse might see, in looking ahead.

AS TO WHETHER A FIELD MOUSE or a bird or any other animal might be able to look behind the way I can ... Nicky Clayton's definite views on the existence of episodic memory in corvids are not the only opinions out there. So far, scrub jays remain unable to convince their toughest critics that their minds are actually able to revisit specific moments in time, so as to place themselves in situations from the past and recollect what they did and how they did it, in order to find food they've hidden or to make plans to cache it for future use.

At Fauna, Theo the baboon calls out across the cornfields at dusk. According to Jane Goodall, he is longing for the troupe he left behind in Kenya. But perhaps not even someone as sympathetic as Goodall can guess whether Theo actually imagines himself separated by distance from a specific colony of baboons. Let alone what conception, if any, he might have of the time elapsed since he saw them last.

When novelist Kate Atkinson paints an expression of disbelief on the face of a pet spaniel thrown into wartime service, she seemingly supposes a dog can measure the contrast between present and past. But what is it really like for an animal to "miss" something or someone? How empathetic should humans be to evidence animals appear to give of mourning the past, deploring the present, or fearing the future? What does the concept of time mean to animals—the difference between then and now, between what's past and what's yet to come?

If you've ever undertaken to imagine existence as an animal might, you've already asked yourself those questions a hundred different ways from Sunday. (Or whatever distinction it is that animals make between days of the week.)

More than a decade ago, I began devoting considerable time (whatever "time" is) to the development of a dog character for a novel I planned to write. But it was not simply a matter of looking at Murphy the dog from a distance and describing what I saw. I needed Murphy to look back at me, from the inside out.

More importantly, he had to describe what he saw from his perspective. In the narrative tradition of Black Beauty and Beautiful Joe, I wanted to give Murphy a chance to tell his side of the story in his own words. Precisely how he would do that in a book—whether with a piece of chalk in his paw and a wooden slate, or at his laptop, or with the help of a tape recorder—I did not attempt to specify. Like authors Anna Sewell and Marshall Saunders before me, I had too many other considerations on my plate to start worrying about details of mere logistics.

Frankly, if I wasn't going to worry about how Murphy might write, I wasn't prepared to worry, either, about whether he could read. After all, I reasoned, a house pet in the modern world has other means of acquiring information. Listening to what human beings say to each other is one way. And then, of course, there's television. Good old television, the greatest democratizing influence on education since the invention of the printing press. If my own dog at the time was riveted to everything on the screen from the O.J. Simpson trial to ads for fabric-softening squares, why wouldn't Murphy be?

Envisioning what the world looks like through a dog's myopic eyes was also, for me, a lead-pipe cinch. I am so short-sighted, I once introduced myself to a golf bag. It was when I tried to imagine what the world might *smell* like to Murphy that I ran smack into a brick wall—an odourless brick wall, at that.

Dogs, I knew, possess a sense of smell at least a thousand times as good as ours—maybe even ten thousand times better. So, what must it be like, to work your nose along the grass in a city park and pick up a hundred different smells—not only of what is there, but also what no longer is? For instance, the squirrel that ran by an hour ago, but has since been hit by a truck. . . . Surely its scent would remain alive there in the grass for a long time, wouldn't it—at least to a dog?

And mightn't it be an odour which would only gradually fade away, long after the squirrel that had engendered it not only lay dead, but had been scooped up by the Sanitation Department and deposited into a litter barrel clear across the park from where its olfactory memory remained traced in outline in the grass—at least to a dog?

To a dog like Murphy, it seemed to me, the effect of that prodigious sense of smell would be entirely to reconfigure the nature of Then and Now. It would be to take the human perception of time, and compress it all into a great big mass. A realm in which odours would live on and on as Now, in a way that the sounds of a bygone squirrel, or the sight of it, or its taste and the feel of its fur don't actually linger on in the present, for any species, except in memory.

If all verb tenses are indeed compressed into the present by a dog's sense of smell, it might explain why canines seem so particularly attuned to their origins: howling at the same moon their ancestors did; turning around and around before lying down on the linoleum, as they formerly broke down twigs and grasses to make their beds in the wild; rolling, nauseatingly, in garbage or worse, to cover their own scent and thus confound enemies—enemies that your average pet Pomeranian hasn't faced directly for fifteen thousand years. (Unless, of course, you count the vacuum cleaner, which your average pet Pomeranian probably would.)

But if time's passing means nothing to an animal, how is it that—even without a watch—every dog or cat or cormorant or cow you and I have ever met seems to know exactly when it's time to eat, or fly south, or expect the farmer in the barn with a milking stool? Yet on the other hand, every dog seems overcome with fresh pleasure each time his master comes home, as if repetition had no place in his calculus. Or else as if repetition itself meant the constant, joyful re-running of an experience that is brand new each time it happens.

"Zen masters of the universe," is how West Coast dog trainer Dale Stavroff characterizes dogs. "A dog lives in the moment; he brings all of himself to that moment. Whereas we look at the past, take into account the historical perspective, and divide ourselves in our responses to the moment."

Perhaps that divided response accounts for the peculiar comfort we depend on from animals—especially dogs, with their fresh responses to routine occurrences. In his novel *The Unbearable Lightness of Being*, Milan Kundera beautifully summarizes the effect of the perspective of the dog Karenin on his human companions:

Karenin surrounded Tereza and Tomas with a life based on repetition, and he expected the same from them. Human time does not turn in a circle; it runs ahead in a straight line. That is why man cannot be happy: happiness is the longing for repetition.

Meanwhile for Karenin, Kundera seems to suggest, every day is a new day. Yet the happiness that attends it is in the recognition that he's met it before and will again and again and again. "You can never step in the same river twice," observed the ancient Greek philosopher Heraclitus. "But if you do," the philosopher's dog might have added, "you should at least always act surprised."

III

⋯⋯⟡⋯⋯

IN THE DIOCESE OF LYONS, wrote thirteenth-century French cleric Stephen of Bourbon, *near the enclosed nuns' village called Neuville, on the estate of the Lord of Villars, was a castle, the lord of which and his wife had a baby boy. One day, when the lord and lady had gone out of the house, and the nurse had done likewise, leaving the baby alone in the cradle, a huge serpent entered the house and approached the baby's cradle.*

Yes, I recognize this story, all right. I know where this story is going.

Seeing this, the greyhound, which had remained behind, chased the serpent and, attacking it beneath the cradle, upset the cradle and bit the serpent all over, which defended itself, biting the dog equally severely. Finally, the dog killed it and threw it well away from the cradle.

It's the same tale somewhat vaguely remembered from something I read in some book as a child. Except, this version of that old familiar story is set in a specific place. The master is a particular person, with a definite title. The baby is a boy and seemingly the only child and heir. He's been left alone under the protection of the family dog, a greyhound.

The cradle, the floor, the dog's mouth and head were all drenched in the serpent's blood. Although badly hurt by the serpent, the dog remained on guard beside the cradle. When the nurse came back and saw all this she thought that the dog had devoured the child, and let out a scream of misery. Hearing it the child's mother also ran up, looked, thought the same thing and screamed too. Likewise the knight, when he arrived, thought the same thing and drew his sword and killed the dog.

Then, when they went closer to the baby they found it safe and sound, sleeping peacefully. Casting around for some explanation, they discovered the serpent, torn to pieces by the dog's bites, and now dead.

So concisely and precisely told by Stephen—or Étienne—of Bourbon. There's no emotional colouring, and no point of view but that of the dispassionate narrator: a thirteenth-century French Dominican priest, reporting with all the cool clarity of a journalist at the scene.

Realizing then the true facts of the matter, and deeply regretting to have unjustly killed so useful a dog, they threw it into a well in front of the manor door, threw a great pile of stones on top of it, and planted trees beside it, in memory of the event. Now, by divine will, the manor was destroyed and the estate, reduced to a desert, was abandoned by its inhabitants.

Having sought out the source of this story down so many elusive byways, I can't yet quite grasp that this is a genuine account by someone who, if not himself an eyewitness, was at least close enough to events to tell us who, where, why, and how. It's true, the basic set-up—the bare bones of the dog-cradle-baby-snake story—is far older than the thirteenth century, and far more ubiquitous than such specific details as Stephen's would suggest. But the fact that the priest's story has so many similarities to the broad-based myth doesn't invalidate the possibility that these particular events really did occur in a certain part of France at such-and-such a time in the past.

As in several other medieval versions of the story, the master's reaction to the truth is regret and remorse. Yet, he builds no monument to the dead dog, as in the legend of Llewellyn ap Gruffyd and his wolfhound Gelert. According to Stephen, this dog's body is merely bundled down a well.

Why? Because, says the priest, the master had "unjustly killed so useful a dog."

"Useful," rather than "beloved." Killed "unjustly." Does that carry the suggestion that a crime has been committed? You might think so, judging by how the master throws the carcass into a dried-up well, piles stones on top, and for good measure plants some trees beside it "in memory of the event." However, none of those measures seemed to save the lord and his lady—or their child—from disaster.

"By divine will," Stephen says, their home and entire estate were destroyed, reduced to a "desert"—that is, an uninhabited, uncultivated tract of land and forest. But why would the Divine, or any lesser entity, feel moved to retaliate for the unjust but certainly not premeditated killing of a "useful" dog?

It was French anthropologist Jean-Claude Schmitt who brought Stephen of Bourbon's long-forgotten account of these events to modern scholars' attention in the late 1970s. According to Schmitt, there would be every reason, even for a nobleman, to soft-pedal the news that he'd wrongly slain an innocent greyhound.

It's not that the laws of those days and in that place—no more than here and now—judged it a crime for a man to kill his own dog. But in the European Middle Ages, custom and superstition imposed harsh rules. Though some sources disagree, Schmitt, along with numerous other modern scholars, believes that only the highborn of the Middle Ages were allowed to own large hunting dogs. Greyhounds were particularly prized. (The lower orders, meanwhile, made do with curs of all work. And those dogs could not exceed a certain height. To prove they were within accepted dimensions, canines had to pass through a "dog ring"—somewhat like the metal frames in modern airports that determine whether luggage is small enough to be carried on board.)

With the right to ownership of dogs like greyhounds came certain responsibilities. For a noble in medieval Europe, killing such a dog, except with good reason, was to invite negative consequences—anything from seven years' bad luck to a subsequent misfortune befalling someone in the house.

In the bloody aftermath of the slaying of his greyhound—and now aware of the injustice of the act—who can blame the Lord of Villars for swiftly moving into damage control? Down the well with the evidence, pile on some stones for good measure, and, quick, plant a few trees to obscure the scene. Even if rumours of the dog's death start to get around, at least greenery planted "in memory of the event" might help mitigate the consequences.

Yet God, it seemed, was not fooled by the coverup. The manor and surrounding lands were destroyed; the land was reclaimed by the forest. As for the lord, the lady, the child and even the servants ... all quite suddenly disappeared. From a real locality, in an actual diocese, at a definite point in time.

Stephen of Bourbon wrote his account of these events, in Latin, some time before his death around about the year 1260, as one of a series of "Exempla" or instructive tales. The text went missing, and was rediscovered in the late nineteenth century.

When the document came to the attention of anthropologist Schmitt in the 1970s, he was struck by the way the story "places the emphasis on remembering the victim, not on the murderer's repentance and on the transcendent intervention of 'divine will,' rather than on the knight's initiative."

Because the greyhound, Schmitt continues, was uniquely valued in a culture that generally disparaged dogs, the knight has in effect slain the animal that embodied a system of values to which he himself subscribed. In other words—or so Schmitt seems to suggest—the man has not only destroyed the dog, he's destroyed himself.

Damned, deprived of house and home through his own actions, expelled from their farmland by the forces of nature, the man had no choice but to take his wife and child to seek their fortune elsewhere. What became of the Lord of Villars and his family is entirely unknown.

What became of the dog who was killed for killing a snake is yet another story. As well as a journey—first for Stephen of Bourbon in the thirteenth century, then for Jean-Claude Schmitt, more than three decades ago, and now, for anyone who cares to follow the trail Schmitt blazed.

It's a journey I long to undertake myself—in time and also in space, back to the diocese of Lyon. Somewhere in those woods not far from villages with names like Neuville and Villars, I would like to rediscover what happened next, way back when, after a certain lord and lady were banished from their own private Eden, thanks to a serpent lurking where they least suspected.

OVER FAJITAS AT THE INCA RESTAURANT in Fort Collins, Colorado, Temple Grandin offered me her thoughts about humanity's age-old relationship to animals. "You know that part in the Bible that deals with 'dominion' over the animals? Well, I have been told by Hebrew scholars that 'stewardship' is the more exact translation. We have stewardship over the animals. We can't just leave them to fend for themselves."

In my own view, whether you translate it "dominion" or "stewardship," the word on this subject isn't necessarily God's. More likely, you're quibbling over terminology that reflects the sincere attempt of mere mortals of those days to construct a Creator who would conveniently declare in print His plan to hand over the keys to the animal kingdom directly to us.

Nowadays, that small ripple of controversy over what God meant when he gave man "dominion" (or was it "stewardship"?) over the animals is nothing compared to the veritable tsunami of debate on what happened after man lost God's trust. How can we truly interpret the meaning of man's fall from grace and subsequent expulsion from the garden to "earn his bread by the sweat of his brow"?

Opinions have always abounded—and continue to abound—about the literal events behind that figurative bite of the fruit that grew on the Tree of Knowledge. Animal ethicist James Serpell suggests that Adam's actual fall was from hunter-gatherer into agricultural subsistence. This vast change, says Serpell, would have occurred in the Paleolithic period, when the retreating glaciers wreaked ecological devastation. It was the subsequent decline in game that forced man into farming.

Serpell maintains that the agricultural lifestyle was vastly inferior from a health point of view, citing studies of the sturdy bones and teeth of Ice Age hunters compared to those of later Egyptians who farmed. Historian Richard Bulliet concurs that the hunter was better off than the farmer. However, in his view, the biggest loss in the shift to agriculture was the opportunity to satisfy bloodlust, through the rituals that attended the hunting and killing of wild animals.

Other historians and ecologists attribute the prehistoric decline in game more to over-hunting than to climate change. Once mastodons and other Ice Age quarry were hunted to the brink of extinction, man would have no choice but to turn to tillage—i.e., "the sweat of his brow"—as a means of survival. The metaphor of man's expulsion from a lush "garden" translates as the disappearance of an unlimited wilderness abounding in unlimited quarry.

As for the animals, there are as many theories about what the Fall of man meant to them as there are authors to advance them. In *Adam's Task: Calling Animals by Name*, American animal expert and poet Vicki Hearne offers her own view of the harmony between humans and animals in Eden. "Before the Fall, all animals were domestic," she writes. It was only after man sinned that other creatures stopped coming when he called. Suddenly, "wildness was possible."

However, Hearne continues, there were some animals who "agreed to go along with humanity anyway," after the expulsion from Paradise—animals who, in effect, gave us a second chance to assert our benign dominion and mend our ways. Only through training, which she believes all animals crave, can we humans "cleanse our authority."

But if "the Fall" does indeed refer to human awareness of our responsibility regarding animals, when did that awareness begin? At what point in evolutionary development did we begin to query our moral relationship to the animals we hunted, sacrificed, enslaved, and befriended? What was it about the nature of those relationships that might have prompted man to question his absolute authority and even begin to criticize his treatment of creatures possessed of some innocence lost to human beings?

"Man is the only animal that blushes," observed Mark Twain. Then added slyly: "Or needs to."

If we're blushing, maybe that's the heaviest yoke of all: to be cursed with scruples utterly unknown by those non-humans who get to predate, mate, and even defecate without a moment's embarrassment.

Environmental activist Paul Watson seldom hesitates to offer his critique of his fellow man, on issues ranging from nuclear testing to the wholesale slaughter of marine mammals. Among the many targets of his angry opprobrium is what our dependency on agriculture has done to us and the animals. A 2007 *The New Yorker* profile piece on Watson contains this quote:

Cain was a farmer, and farmers began to kill off hunter-gatherers. Our ancestors fed from the table of life; in other words, they fed themselves from nature, but we alienated ourselves from nature by depending upon agriculture, which is what I consider to be the forbidden fruit.

However, Abel was as much an agrarian as the brother who slew him—except that Abel was a sheep farmer, rather than a tiller of the soil like Cain. Hunting and gathering were already all over. What's significant in the story is that Abel's offering of the first of his flock was deemed more pleasing to the Almighty than Cain's basket of vegetables.

Cain's consequent banishment to the land East of Eden may not only have been prompted by his primal act of murder, but may also tell us something important about the preferences of those who penned the first chapters of the Old Testament: as well as being firmly in favour of "dominion over animals," they were clearly on the side of the carnivores.

There is, of course, a whole raft of other interpretations of that first recorded murder, including the animal-friendly perspective. In killing his brother, some vegetarians contend, Cain may actually have been trying to strike a blow against the newfangled vogue in meat-eating.

In fact, it is only the Book of Isaiah that condemns animal sacrifice and speaks of "the wolf lying down with the lamb," or the lion eating straw like an ox, instead of the flesh of other creatures. Otherwise, from Old to New Testaments, carnivorousness is the order of business.

Yet, as far back as the first century of what we now call the Common Era (formerly "Anno Domini") the Greek historian Plutarch—a vegetarian—assumed that the carnivorous lifestyle was something humanity had fallen to, from the original heights of a superior vegetarian lifestyle. "And truly," he wrote,

as for those people who first ventured upon eating of flesh, it is very probable that the whole reason of their so doing was scarcity and want of other food; for it is not likely that their living together in lawless and extravagant lusts, or their growing wanton and capricious through the excessive variety of provisions then among them, brought them to such unsociable pleasures as these, against Nature.

Modern animal rights philosopher Tom Regan has suggested that Adam and Eve before the Fall are depicted in Genesis as vegetarian. The "meat" God is credited with providing for them, says Regan, could be easily translated as the meat of nuts and other plant matter.

Peter Singer, also an animal ethicist, points out that it is only after eating of the forbidden fruit and becoming self-consciously aware of their nakedness that Adam and Eve clothe themselves in animal skins. From there, he adds, it's an easy step to Abel's sacrifice of his first-born lamb, and the birth of a tradition steeped in blood.

Among British Romantics of the nineteenth century, like Mary Wollstonecraft, her daughter Mary, and son-in-law Percy Shelley, there was a firm belief that it was the beginning of meat-eating that marked the Fall of mankind, a lapse recorded not only in the Bible but in Greek mythology. Mary Shelley in particular interpreted the Greek myth of Prometheus stealing fire as "a story of the inception of meat-eating"—presumably because fire was required to render raw flesh both edible and palatable.

In Shelley's first novel, *Frankenstein*, the doctor who challenges God by creating life in his lab is clearly intended to embody hubris on a Promethean scale. The subtitle is, in fact, *The Modern Prometheus*. The overreaching Dr. Frankenstein is a meat-eater, who deliberately separates himself from the world of animals. Meanwhile, Shelley makes Frankenstein's misunderstood Creature a vegetarian, who instinctively identifies with non-human species.

What the author implies is that animal consumption is impossible without that mental divide. Yet, even in societies where meat is routinely eaten, association with the animal is not out of the question. That's especially true when there is direct, ongoing contact between consumer and consumed.

In some parts of agrarian Germany, anthropologist Claudine Fabre-Vassas tells us, the cycle of winter slaughter used to begin with a boy delegated to "question the pig." First he would knock on the door of its sty, then rouse it to respond to queries about possible marriages and other likely events in the village.

Why a pig on the eve of slaughter might wish to make predictions about a future about to go on without it is not explained. Nor is it clear why the boy of the family—in training to butcher the pig himself one day—would be chosen to parlay with it.

What we do learn is that the animal was never fed the night before it was killed. In a peculiar gesture of solidarity, the boy would fast that night, too. Just as all the other boys of the village would be fasting. The next day—St Thomas's Day—after each family's pig was put to the blade and as its carcass was bled, each boy would bleed himself.

A world away, a similar identification exists among the Tukanoan tribe of Colombia. The Tukanoans refer both to their own ancestors, as well as a neighbouring tribe called the Arawakans, as "tapirs." The tapir is a sort of wild pig, but the association to this animal is not intended as an insult. Tapirs are hunted and eaten by numerous South American indigenous peoples, yet the Tukanoans regard them as "souls."

Psychologist Brian Sutton-Smith believes the tribe regards the death of tapirs as a counterbalance to the loss of human souls, particularly those who die in infancy. The hunt, writes Sutton-Smith serves an "ecological stock-taking and a balancing of books," as much as an expedition for meat.

Trying—and often failing—to balance the books seems to be almost universal in humanity's long history of dealing with our unequal relationships with other animals. Whatever the culture, however we struggle, we can't seem to put the toothpaste back into the tube, or spool back the tape to that last moment of innocence in prerecorded time: just before Eve let that snake talk her into taking one small bite. That one small bite for woman would rapidly escalate into a giant, neverending chomp of guilty awareness for man- and womankind.

Was it a bite of an apple or the haunch of some sentient cohabitant of Eden? That is only the first of many hotly disputed chapters in the neverending story about animals and us.

THE FIRST EVER NEW YORK Capital Region Vegetarian Expo is a large, milling, friendly kind of place with no end of exhibitors' tables. Men, women, and teens of both sexes sport t-shirts with various slogans and smile as they press brochures, flyers, newsletters, and handouts of sundry sorts to each and every passerby. There is a roped-off dining area with steam trays of numerous vegan delicacies, as well as urns of weak fair-trade coffee, assorted herbal teas, and crates of various juices on ice.

In a fenced area carpeted with straw, a Shetland pony and a donkey-pony cross munch carrots and other treats to draw attention to an abused-animal sanctuary. There is a booth promoting The League of Women Voters; another offers samples of sesame noodles mixed with broccoli. A team of environmentally-friendly architects kibitz with the woman peddling essential oils.

In other words, there is anything and everything one could conceivably associate with kindness to our planet and everybody on it, as well as a few enterprises whose relationship to that concept seems tangential at best. Many, no doubt, are congratulating themselves that no animal was harmed, no child was exploited, and no non-renewable resources were willfully squandered in the creation of this event.

At the Farm Sanctuary booth, I stop to speak with Harold Brown. Harold is a former dairy farmer who had his "epiphany," as he terms it, with a steer shortly after his heart attack at age eighteen. At first, it was the need to eat healthy for his heart's sake that prompted him to go vegan. Then, the changes in his constitution began to work on his psyche as well.

"I was no longer eating fear," is how he describes his suddenly meat-free lifestyle. "So gradually my cellular structure became more receptive to concern for animals." According to Harold, a lot of "unlearning" is required for someone like him, "raised in agriculture."

Animal agriculture as something to recover from is also a motif for Lee Hall, the lawyer and activist I have come to meet at this Vegetarian Expo. No meat, no dairy, no fowl, no eggs. . . . And for her, a vegan diet is just the basic minimum.

As well, I've learned from her polemical book *Capers in the Churchyard*, Hall is an "abolitionist." That means no livestock, no fences, no pets, no zoos, no human interference whatsoever in animals' lives. But that more radical part of her philosophy, I suspect, will not be the centrepiece of the talk she has come here to give.

I meet Lee at the table set up by Friends of Animals, a Connecticut-based abolitionist organization for which she acts as legal counsel and online contributor.

From the photo on her book jacket, I instantly recognize her pointed, elfin face. However, I am not prepared for how tiny and almost waif-like she is in person.

Oddly, she reminds me of Bob Dylan back in his Greenwich Village days—even more strikingly than Cate Blanchett does in the Dylan biopic *I'm Not Here*. Lee wears baggy cargo pants and a sports jacket. Around her neck is a long trailing scarf, and on her head a ball cap with "Save an Animal, Eat a Vegetable" embroidered on it. Misreading it initially as "Eat a Vegetarian," I wonder fleetingly if it's an attempt on somebody's part to make abstention from meat seem sexier.

The heavy black eyeliner etching her eyes is, I am sure, cruelty-free kohl. But, like her whimsical scarf, it's unexpected on someone who writes the no-nonsense prose I've read in her book and online articles. Lee may be here in Saratoga Springs to propound some hard truths about how we treat animals, yet she's not above enjoying a little "show" with her "business."

She greets me with an extra voucher for what she promises is "excellent vegan food" for sale. She is assuming—and rightly—that a fellow free-lancer will appreciate a freebie on the road. On our way to the buffet table, she offers words of rah-rah commendation to one of the volunteers, aware they'll mean something coming from one of the "stars" of this event.

Over lunch, she is all business, brisk, preoccupied with her presentation several hours from now. Only when I ask her about her cats does she soften up and focus on the present moment.

Opposed as she is to pet ownership, she is as personally attached to her seven rescue cats as any animal lover I've ever met. Still, she says, she's genuinely conflicted by the way domestication has distorted the original relationships we have with felines. "I am a primate. They're predators." In a pristine world, she suggests, she'd be running from them, not opening cans while they weave around her ankles.

Clearly, she's proud of having rescued these animals from the mean streets of her Philadelphia neighbourhood. At the same time, she laments the necessary concessions she has to make in order to keep them in her apartment, such as being forced to support agribusiness by feeding them meat. And she's "taking up more space" than she feels entitled to, because accommodating so many cats has required her to move into a larger apartment.

There is a Calvinistic discipline in her abhorrence of excess that is both admirable and daunting. How many acts of self-denial must she perform every day, in order to stay square with her conscience?

Free-range chickens and eggs are a delusion, she tells me. In fact, they require more acreage to produce and thus diminish habitat for the rest of us. Many vegetarians live in a world of compromise, not only by trying to find acceptability in free-range eggs and dairy, but by, for example, endorsing top-end organic mega-chains like Whole Foods, which she feels has muscled in "with their goat cheese" on small, independent operations.

When I suggest some fair-trade chocolate at a nearby vendor's table for dessert, she approaches it circumspectly. "It's not enough that it says 'fair trade,'" she cautions me. "There's a certain stamp you have to look for."

For someone inconsistently well-intentioned like me, Lee's quality of constant vigilance is almost exhausting. She expresses doubt about the value of having the Shetland pony and the donkey on display, and worries about the "addiction" to sanctuaries and rescue work among some of the well-intended. For all of that, Hall describes herself as an optimist, who genuinely believes in real change.

"But aren't the addicted also optimists?" I ask her. "You know, making things better one donkey or chimp at a time?"

No, she says. All most of them do is encourage the status quo.

I think back on Gloria Grow at Fauna. Gloria was warm and crinkly-eyed when she smiled about her chimps, although candid about "caring fatigue" and genuinely conflicted about promoting the cause with poster-animals. An optimist? An addict to rescue? A slave to the status quo? Or none of the above?

Lee, meanwhile, is becoming increasingly anxious about her presentation. She needs a watch to keep strict track of her speaking time, but no one seems to have one. I offer her mine, and she straps it on, gratefully. (For my own part, I'm grateful that the strap is made of plastic, not leather.)

Her speech is booked in a wide, inhospitable room with a sound system occasionally overpowered by PA announcements from the exhibitors' area outside. Her audience is a straggling group, mostly newcomers to vegetarianism, I sense, with the dazed air of folks who've already been attentive to a long roster of previous speakers.

If Lee Hall is discouraged by these performance conditions, she gives no indication. Like any experienced orator, she's laced her stump speech with local references—in this case, to the way Saratoga promotes itself as a "family" community with its bio-research companies, horse racing, and polo. Hardly a dedicated abolitionist's notion of family values, her ironic tone suggests, but does not overstate.

Her basic message is likewise tailored to an entry-level crowd: Non-humans should not have to rely on the "goodwill" of our species, a variable commodity at best. It is our own former status as prey, she says, that makes us think it's acceptable for us now to prey on other animals.

It's a reasoned argument, but a bit clinical, with little of the personal warmth she revealed when talking to me about her cats. If I were to chastise her for that, however, I'm sure she'd disagree. To her, personalizing animals is automatically "exploitative"—a way of demeaning them by turning their likenesses into fundraising gimmicks and using their physical selves (like that Shetland pony and the pony-donkey-cross) merely as means to draw a crowd.

Instead, Hall has chosen to devote most of her allotted hour to the practical consequences rather than to the emotional aspects of human dominion, offering a crash-course on the big global picture. Food shortages, energy demands, and increased meat consumption in huge markets like India and China threaten a planet on which both cropland and forests are routinely sacrificed to cattle grazing.

Only vegan organic farming, she says, can save the world by turning this situation around. I can readily imagine what Temple Grandin, proponent of the importance of animal manure for plant cultivation, would say about this line of argument. Still, this is clearly Lee Hall's version of "practical solutions"—a strategy of setting the question of rights aside in order to argue the sustainability case.

Barely has she uttered her last scripted word than one of the organizers has moved in to thank her and pronounce her presentation over. Lee is distressed; she had hoped for questions, she protests, had allotted time— she gestures with the wrist that wears my watch—for audience input.

But the organizer is firm about bringing in this last session of the day under the wire. When I come up to congratulate Lee, she is still arguing with him, oblivious to the fact that the auditorium has emptied. Without even looking at me, she unstraps my watch, holds it out to me, and heads out to the lobby to sign copies of her book.

However, by the time she returns from the signing, her mood has improved markedly. In fact, she is elated by a convert she's made. "The woman told me 'I came here today as a vegetarian, but I'm leaving here a vegan!'" she exults. "Now *that* makes the entire trip worthwhile!"

In her mind, she has already moved on, is already buckling herself into her car to drive the five hours back to Philadelphia—"for my cats." She knows, of course, that the tires on the car she'll drive off in contain animal products. She is all too aware that the gas she's consumed to get here— and will consume over the long miles back—profits a vast international industrial-agricultural network of interests that exploit animals, human beings, and the environment alike. More than anybody I've ever met, Lee Hall will be conscious, following the network of highways home, that they have been paved over the corpses of countless creatures, plants, and people, and are composed in part of their flesh and bones.

For the vast majority of people—including many of those who came to hear her today—that kind of awareness doesn't come under the heading of inconvenient truth, but is simply an uncomfortable consideration best ignored. Nothing she has yet written or said has so far succeeded in penetrating the mainstream or making obvious inroads into the status quo.

And yet... there was that one person who came forward to say she'd arrived at the event a vegetarian but, thanks to Lee, was leaving it a vegan. Worth the trip, from Lee's point of view? Of course it is. It has to be. She is, as she says, an optimist.

WHEN THE GREEK HISTORIAN PLUTARCH was asked why his earlier countryman Pythagoras had abstained from eating meat, he answered:

> I for my part do much wonder in what humour, with what soul or reason, the first man with his mouth touched slaughter, and reached to his lips the flesh of a dead animal, and having set before people courses of ghastly corpses and ghosts, could give those parts the names of meat and victuals, that but a little before lowed, cried moved and saw... You ought rather, in my opinion, to have inquired who first began this practice, than who of late times left it off.

More than 1,900 years after Plutarch offered that response, we still don't know. However, it doesn't stop us from asking some of the same questions. How and when did human beings first start eating meat? For how many millennia did they snack on carrion left by animal predators before they began to devise methods of hunting for themselves?

Why do our teeth, our jaws, and even our fingernails seem so ill-suited to the tearing and chewing of animal flesh? When did we begin to cook it? And what has prompted us, as Plutarch noted, to name the body parts we eat so as to differentiate them from the living creatures who were their source?

In the view of contemporary archaeologists like Steven Mithen, our earliest ancestor, *australopithecus*, was entirely vegetarian. While we don't know a lot about the day-to-day life of this hominid who existed between 4.2 and one million years ago, it's likely australopithecines were mainly prey for better-adapted predators, like leopards and other large mammals. And, judging from the fossil evidence provided by a 1929 discovery known as the Taung child, eagles also carried off their share of australopithecine young.

If australopithecines hunted at all, it was, according to Mithen, "no more than chimpanzees today." With "massive jaws and chewing muscles fixed onto a crest of bone," australopithecines were well-adapted to vegetarian cuisine; berries, tubers, and seeds were likely among their principal foodstuffs. Also, like chimpanzees, they may have inserted twigs into the nests of insects to extract some high-quality protein.

The moment or era of human transition from a primarily vegetable diet, to scavenging dead carcasses left by more skillful predators, to bringing down fresh meat on the hoof remains obscure. Either our brain enlarged in such a way as to require more protein, or a change in diet to animal protein led to subsequent enlargement of our brain. What's incontestable is that, with a new and bigger brain, we not only came up with better tools for killing, we also learned to cook the meat we are still physiologically unsuited to eat raw.

Yet, how we came to eat meat is not the only pertinent question. What matters more—to carnivores, omnivores, vegetarians, and vegans alike—is how it is, despite our species' long history of either eschewing or chewing animal meat, the issue continues to be argued to the present day, with ambivalence, unease, and uncertainty, as well as anger. Free lunch there may actually be. But guilt-free lunch is another matter.

Back in the eighties, I remember walking past an old Volkswagen beetle parked on the street. On its rear bumper were two stickers. "I ♥ My Collie," read one. "Meat is Murder" the other proclaimed. As a passerby, I could only wonder what the owner of that car fed his or her Collie.

An eighteenth-century engraving of British antiquarian Joseph Ritson shows him at work on a manuscript in his kitchen where a cow munches contentedly on lettuce. Meanwhile, behind Ritson's head, a chained cat strives for a rat, just out of reach.

Ritson was famous for his eccentricities, which included the utter abhorrence of meat. Man, he believed, was driven to corrupt practices—including horse racing, cock-fighting, and other hot-blooded cruelties—by his addiction to "animal food." Judging from the restraint imposed on the cat in the portrait, Ritson seemed equally reluctant to allow his pets to indulge their basest nature.

To many contemporary vegetarian pet owners—even those who restrict themselves to an entirely vegan diet—it probably seems wrong to tamper with a dog or cat's true nature by denying it food appropriate to a carnivore. However, to journalist Michael Pollan, allowing our pets to eat meat we deny ourselves is a position rich in contradiction. "This," he says, "is one of the oldest ironies of animal rights: It asks us to acknowledge all we share with animals and then to act toward them in a most unanimalistic way." In other words, if they're permitted to act like carnivores, why aren't we?

No doubt, treating pet animals themselves in an "unanimalistic" way— by denying meat to those that would consume it in the wild—would strike someone like Pollan as yet more ironic. Even so, there is a small but growing group of vegetarians and vegans who feed their carnivorous pets broccoli instead of beef bones, kohlrabi instead of Kibbles 'n Bits.

Perhaps inherent in all forms of abstinence from meat—whether we impose it on our pets or upon ourselves—is a primal fear of being eaten ourselves. In her perspicacious first novel, *The Edible Woman*, Margaret Atwood takes her protagonist beyond meat products all the way to identification with carrots figuratively screaming when pulled from the ground. But what triggers the character's initial aversion is meat, and its association to her own sense of being carved up and "consumed" by men—and her society in general.

That not-entirely-bygone society of the fifties, sixties, and seventies routinely belittled women with labels like "chick"—or worse—"cow" and "pig." In magazines like *Playboy*, female bodies were segmented into delectable parts, like a butcher's chart pinpointing brisket and loin and rump and flank. (As recently as 1993, a chicken restaurant in Fort Worth, Texas, derided the then-new First Lady by advertising "Hillary's dinner," with "two big thighs, two small breasts and a left wing.")

But I also remember, way back then, how there could be something oddly affectionate in human regard of animal bodies destined to be dinner. In my own childhood, the purchase and preparation of the Christmas turkey felt like a ritual of love, almost like welcoming a new pet into the family.

That bald, bare-assed, raw, headless fowl—with its purplish-pink tinge and almost indecently plump thighs—seemed to lie back, supine, a willing participant in its own stuffing, seasoning, basting, roasting, and browning. The "chookey," my mother invariably nicknamed it, and invited us children to smack the goose-fleshed turkey on its plump thighs, help pry apart those coyly crossed legs, and ram breadcrumbs, onion, apple, and sage into that hollow cavity.

My father would look in on the ritual from time to time, and invariably recall how, in his boyhood, an entire dead pig was brought into the house at Eastertime. Before his mother and father began to carve the corpse, he said, he and his brothers would straddle it and ride it, cowboy-style, right there on the kitchen floor. Nowadays, as I read in books like *The Singular Beast* about the rites attendant upon pig slaughter in the Middle Ages, I wonder if my childhood recollections of my father's even more distant remembrances of his youth aren't linked—like sausages—to some enormous collective memory of Boy and Pig?

Of course, everything is different now. In *Animal Liberation*, first published in 1975, Peter Singer took the twinned concepts of animal consciousness and human conscience to a whole new level of public debate. In the same decade, women's liberation became popularized by hot-eyed— and hot—young feminists like Gloria Steinem and Germaine Greer. For "chicks" of all species, the future had never looked more roseate.

Cut to the early years of the twenty-first century. In Chicago, the city council has passed a law to ban the sale of *foie gras* on the grounds of animal cruelty. Walt Freese, the nominatively determined CEO of Ben & Jerry's Ice Cream, announces that no eggs used in ice-cream production at the company will originate with battery-caged hens. British university studies find that "Children with a higher intelligence quotient at age ten are more likely to become vegetarians later in life."

Around the same time, Canterbury University in New Zealand declares that more and more vegans feel "squeamish" about sexual intimacy with meat-eaters. And, concurrently, that same Hillary Clinton—small breasts and chubby thighs concealed to best advantage by a seemingly endless supply of signature pantsuits—becomes a serious threat to matriculate from former First Lady to President. A brand-new world order, right?

Well, not quite. Chicago mayor Richard M. Daly refers to the *foie gras* ban as "the silliest law the City Council ever passed." The Ben & Jerry's CEO fails to explain exactly how he will insure the "humane treatment" of every cow milked and every laying hen.

Meanwhile, philosopher and animal welfare advocate Bernie Rollin tells me that 95 percent of Americans are still eating meat. Canadian harp seals continue to be bludgeoned annually in numbers that must stagger Peter Singer, one of those who cheered the "disappearance" of the Canadian seal hunt more than three decades ago. And as for the triumphal march of chick-free feminism . . . ask the men at a 2008 Hillary Clinton rally who jeered at her, "Iron my shirts!"

"We have," says Peter Singer, "a strong interest in convincing ourselves that our concern for other animals does not necessarily require us to stop eating them." While *The Vegetarian Times* may not share that interest, the publication has acknowledged how impossible it still is to avoid animal products in consumer items from videotape to car tires, from emery boards to antifreeze.

How deep are the roots of dominion over animals in human culture? As feminist and vegetarian Carol J. Adams has observed, the Dead Sea Scrolls themselves were written on parchment.

"WELL, IT ALL TAKES TIME." Keith Mann bites into his vegan burger, as he considers the world beyond the window of the Red Veg restaurant in London's Soho district. "After all, we've been on this planet no time at all."

For someone who has spent more than a decade of his little more than forty years in jail, he sounds remarkably philosophical on the subject of waiting. Much like Lee Hall on the other side of the pond, Keith seems prepared to take the long view of veganism's eventual triumph. Certainly, he is sunny and cheerful—far more so than you'd expect a convicted animal rights activist to be.

Keith Mann has done his prison time and is, in fact, a high-profile celebrity in the animal-activism realm, with speaking engagements and a book to promote. Even so, when I initially got in touch with him by email, he was reluctant to divulge precisely where he lives. Instead, he suggested we meet near the Tottenham Court Road tube station.

If that seemed a bit unspecific to me, he had every confidence. "Don't worry, you'll spot me. I'll be the one with the black jacket and the big smile."

Right, I think, as I stand near the corner of Tottenham Court Road and New Oxford Street, on a blustery but warm winter day. Like nobody else in this teeming throng of thousands is going to fit *that* description.

Lurking outside the Dominion Theatre, with "We Will Rock You" on the marquee, I glance up at the big gold statue of Freddie Mercury—guitar in one hand, the other fist raised in victory. I envy both Freddie and Keith their optimism, and wish I could share it.

However, when he appears, I do recognize him right off: the black jacket and the big smile, exactly as advertised. As he walks toward me, it's hard to put this youthful figure together with the man described breathlessly on various websites as "the top of the Animal Liberation Front pyramid." In fact, he more closely resembles the "cheeky Mancunian lad" extolled in the cover blurb on his self-published book.

Instinctively, I find myself reaching out to give him a hug—surprising myself more than him. It must be that smile, I tell myself. Certainly, it can't be the jacket, one of those nylon parkas ubiquitous in Britain, with matted furry plush around the hood.

"Now, that's not real fur, is it?" I ask as we head along New Oxford Street in quest of a café.

Although I'm kidding, his response is serious. "No shops in Britain sell fur or fur-trimmed coats, except Harrods. In fact, the fur industry here is sometimes desperate enough to pass off real fur as fake. Can you believe it?"

Not really. To any Canadian who cares about such things, this realm of bans on fur, veal pens, and cosmetics-testing on animals appears utopian compared to current practices at home. How close to Utopia the United

Kingdom might look to a homegrown activist like Mann is exactly what I'm hoping to find out.

It's public pressure, he tells me, once we've settled into our plastic chairs at the Red Veg in Soho. That's what has produced results in Britain. "No more fur farms, no dolphins as marine-park performers . . ." As he ticks off achievements on his fingers, I think that his faith in the power of pubic opinion makes him not much different from Donald Broom or Temple Grandin—if only in this respect.

In other respects, Keith Mann is much more a there's-some-good-news-and-there's-some-bad-news sort of person than Dr. Broom, with his pride in the high welfare standards set by the European Union, or Dr. Grandin, with her faith in her system of measurable audits in the slaughterhouse. On the one hand, says Keith, the ban on product testing using animals is still merely "voluntary" in the UK. On the other hand—he gestures toward a large supermarket across the street—the huge Tesco chain now offers its own line of household and cosmetics products not tested on animals, thanks to pressure from the animal rights movement.

I try to imagine a Canadian retail conglomerate like Loblaws or Sobey's or Shoppers Drug Mart with its own cruelty-free product lines at affordable prices. Even at the upmarket health- and eco-friendly stores I patronize in my Toronto neighbourhood, the staff is not always sure that the shampoos, skin cream, and detergents I pay through the nose for are not just non-toxic and free of preservatives, but were not tested on animals.

"Boy, the level of awareness here," I tell Keith with the brash assurance of a recent arrival, "is light-years beyond North America. Even those Freedom Foods sponsored by the RSPCA—"

"—are rubbish," he interrupts. "The RSPCA has the Queen as its patron. A woman who hunts, shoots, wears furs. . . . And the RSPCA is full of people just like her. I'm not interested in welfare, larger cages."

For a moment, I can hear Lee Hall, contemptuous of Whole Foods "moving in their goat cheese." And before me I suddenly see the man who broke into research labs, sabotaged fox hunts, set vehicles alight, "re-homed" stolen animals, and participated in many other "actions" described in his self-published book, as well as other activities "to help desperate animals to which I can't confess...because I'd be arrested and sent to prison."

But then the angry impatience passes from his face and the sunny, attractive Mancunian lad is back, still boyish at forty-something and looking like any other habitué of a café with a name like Red Veg and a Soviet-style star as part of its logo. Mann himself wears a five-point star necklace.

It's a "vegan symbol," he says, although he admits he's uncertain of the connection. His t-shirt declares him "VEGAN" much more unequivocally, in lime-green caps. There are tattoos all up and down both bare arms, but there's nothing thuggish or homemade about the elaborate scrollwork. I can't imagine, somehow, that he had them done in prison. But it feels rude to ask point-blank. Instead, I inquire how he managed in prison to promote a vegan menu for inmates, as he claims in his book.

"It wasn't necessarily for the animals they went vegan." With a laugh, he harks back to one tough customer who'd killed four people in a robbery. "He just came to realize that in prison the meat is mostly scruff off the slaughterhouse floor."

Worse than scruff. Mann goes on to tell me that it was during the years of BSE (bovine spongiform encephalopathy) concerns in Britain that beef became *particularly* available in prisons. That also served to turn some of the inmates into non-carnivores. "Basically, they came to see you're better off on a diet of veg and knots."

It takes me a moment to realize the word in his Lancashire accent is "nuts," and that snarls of string played no part in his jailhouse menu. Still, it's hard for me to picture some hardened con in a Canadian prison setting up a clamour for veg and nuts.

Nor more easily can I picture this mostly amiable and gentle-looking man as a convict any place. When I ask him what was the worst aspect of incarceration, he says it was missing his dogs.

Unlike Lee Hall, he seems untroubled by the ethicality of pet-keeping. "What do your dogs eat?" I ask.

Vegan food, he replies promptly. "You can get it quite easily here," he adds, as if the only possible impediment might be unavailability.

Nowadays, he says, the dogs live with his former girlfriend. "We broke up because she let out her cats and they killed birds—birds I'd built houses for and all."

Luckily, these days it suits Keith to be free of pet-care concerns. A lot of his time is spent traveling in Europe and as far as South Africa to promote his book, *From Dusk 'til Dawn*, which he wrote over fifteen years, many of them spent in various prisons. He regards it as no small achievement. During some of his transfers from one facility to another, the exhaustive notes he'd accumulated were confiscated or lost. Still, he managed to create a history of animal rights action in Britain, spanning decades and boasting photos, footnotes, and a thorough index. "An invaluable service," is how Keith Mann's colleague in direct action, Ronnie Lee, described the book to me.

As well, at six hundred pages, *From Dusk 'til Dawn* is as thick as a brick, even in paperback. In addition to using his book as a resource, I tell Keith I've found it helpful in as a substitute for the free weights I wasn't able to bring with me to Britain.

"Twenty minutes hefting a copy of Thomas Pynchon in one hand and your book in the other, and I figure my biceps and triceps are getting the same workout as at home."

He laughs, genuinely pleased. "That'd make a great advert for the book, wouldn't it?"

Promotion of the book—through his website, through the small bookshops with a taste for the radical to which he hand-delivers copies, and through his appearances on the animal rights circuit—is a continual preoccupation. No longer on the front lines of illegal activism, Keith seems content with his new life. For the most part, he serves the movement by touring with his book or speaking at events related to the cause of animal liberation. What worries him is preaching only to the committed and resting on the past accomplishments of direct action in furthering animal rights.

After all, it's not as if he feels the battles are anywhere near won. Botox testing, for instance, rankles him. Though much of the use of this chemical is cosmetic, he complains, safety tests of the product on animals are still permitted, because Botox's status as a pharmaceutical exempts it from cruelty-free stipulations.

Pharmaceutical testing, of course, is the tough one—virtually all over the world. "In the case of laboratory testing on animals," American journalist Michael Pollan has written, "all but the most radical animal people are willing to balance the human benefit against the cost to the animals."

The cover photo on *From Dusk 'til Dawn* depicts a shivering baby monkey called Britches, mutilated for the sake of medical research and rescued from the University of California in Riverside. But Keith Mann likely knows all the animal empathy in the world won't take many people that extra mile into absolute condemnation of medical research involving animals.

After all, refusing to eat meat, opting out of milk and eggs, emptying the closet of leather and fur coats, and tossing out products tested for toxicity on the open eyes of animals ... all of those things are within the realm of what most people would call personal choice. But how many among us would look a friend with cancer in the eye and tell him or her: "I don't think you should avail yourself of therapies developed on animals"? And if personally threatened by a serious illness for which drugs safeguarded by animal testing were regarded as the best available treatment, how many of us would say to our prescribing physician: "Sorry, I am committed to a cruelty-free lifestyle, even if it kills me"?

Among members of the loosely affiliated groups and individuals who make up the Animal Liberation Front, there is flat condemnation of animal-testing. Yet, even the ALF's co-founder, Ronnie Lee maintains, "It isn't the fault of a person who makes use of drugs or therapies that those things may have been tested on animals.... A person who does so does not need to approve of such tests in order to justify their actions. Many of the roads in this country were created by the Romans using slave labour. Does that mean I should not drive my car along one of those roads unless I approve of slavery? Of course not."

Like Ronnie, and numerous other activists, Keith Mann rejects the necessity for animal experiments in the first place, as well as the scientific reliability of most animal testing, with respect to its applicability to humans. He also believes that human consumption of animal products is responsible for "degenerative illnesses" that in turn motivate scientists to "torture other animals in a desperate search for miracle cures!"

However, Mann is convinced that most people can be persuaded to choose alternatives better for animals when such alternatives are made available. Perhaps it's that basic faith that has left him upbeat, despite the substantial chunks of time he's done in prison and the scenes of animal suffering he writes about in his book. Or perhaps what drives him has very little to do with humanity, good, bad or indifferent.

"For the animals," is how Keith Mann ended the acknowledgements in *From Dusk 'til Dawn*. And, as we part with another hug on New Oxford Street, "for the animals" is what he answers when I thank him for coming all the way from whatever undisclosed location to meet with me.

IV

IN THE SPRING OF 1868, on a tract of land near Sheridan, Kansas, William Frederick Cody challenged his rival Bill Comstock to a competition to determine which of the two deserved the "world championship in buffalo-hunting." At that time, the honorific "Buffalo Bill" belonged to Comstock, long renowned for his ability to kill the greatest number of bison in the shortest span of time.

But Cody, himself a scout and marksman of no mean repute—as well as a showman in the making—felt it was time that mantle shifted to his shoulders. He had already been contracted to supply buffalo meat to the crews working to complete the Kansas Pacific Railroad. What better way to secure future contracts than by offering a practical display of his prowess?

Interested spectators poured in from far and wide—more than a hundred alone from St. Louis on a specially chartered train—to see which man could kill more buffalo in an eight-hour period. As well, the show-down generated brisk betting across the West. "Buffalo Bill" Comstock was favoured by most of the US Army; Cody, meanwhile, had the confidence of the railroad men. Between themselves, the contestants had made a side bet of five hundred dollars.

Early on the day of the event, a procession of horse-drawn wagons and riders began to pour out onto the hunting grounds. There were elaborate preparations for a champagne lunch to be served on location. A day of exciting spectacle was assured, since the plains that stretched out from Sheridan were rife with buffalo—although somewhat less rife by the end of that afternoon.

At 8 a.m. sharp, the two hunters and the referees assigned to each man galloped toward a herd that had been sighted. When the herd split into two groups, Cody pursued one and left the other for Comstock. At the end of their first run Comstock had felled a respectable twenty-three buffaloes. Cody, however, bagged thirty-eight.

After a second run, a lunch break was called. The two hunters returned to dine with the spectators and discuss the morning's kill. By now, Comstock had thirty-seven and Cody fifty-six.

Perhaps as a consequence of the champagne at lunch, Cody declared he would even the odds somewhat, by hunting all afternoon without benefit of saddle, reins, or bridle. Barely waiting for Comstock's consent, he vaulted onto the bare back of his horse, Brigham, with his rifle—named "Lucretia Borgia"—brandished over his head. A fresh herd, composed mostly of cows and young calves, had been sighted not far ahead, and there was no time to be lost getting in as many good shots as possible.

In the final tally, sixty-nine buffaloes were recorded for Cody, and a mere forty-six for Comstock, who ceded not only the "championship of the world" but also the title "Buffalo Bill." News of the score spread far and wide, thanks to the Kansas Pacific Railroad Company, which employed Cody. The company ordered the heads cut off all 115 bulls, cows, and calves and mounted at various points across the United States, as a way to advertise the new regions of the country over which the Kansas Pacific was laying track.

Colonel William Frederick Cody was simply a man of those times: opportunistic and inventive, with a Barnum-like gift for reading the desires of the public and a military man's confidence that the world and what was in it was his for the taking. In fact—given his times—you could argue that Buffalo Bill was a better man than many.

Despite his early career as an Indian scout for the US Army, he was later lauded as a considerate employer of Sitting Bull and the other Native American and Canadian performers in his Wild West shows. And although he made his name—literally—from his prowess at bumping off buffalo, he eventually campaigned for an end to wanton killing and skinning of this increasingly scarce form of wildlife.

Would the term "guilt" apply to Cody's own later evaluation of his earlier life? Perhaps the answer to the question matters to me a little more than to most people. Since my mother was one of his descendants, Buffalo Bill is my distant relative.

As a child, I found him vaguely embarrassing. After all, I was growing up in Regina—a city formerly known as "Pile of Bones." Mountains of bleaching buffalo skulls and skeletons had once waited in the railyards to be transported east and turned into fertilizer. Cody had done none of his hunting up in Saskatchewan. Still, I couldn't help feeling implicated.

As an adult, I realize my great-great-grand-whatsis wasn't much worse than anybody else's. The only difference is the amount of attention various branches of the Cody family have paid to the privilege of being related to him. But because he was no better than anyone else's ancestor, I figure I have as much right to descendant's guilt as anybody else, for the privileges we all enjoy at the expense of those from whom our forebears wrested them.

For people who care about such things, it seems impossible to figure out how to undo what has been done, if not by us personally, then at least for our supposed benefit. How to rewind the film of history back to that frame just before we came on the scene—waving "Lucretia Borgia" over our heads, shooting at everything in sight, killing most of what we saw, squandering most of what we killed, despoiling most of what we squandered, and making our entitlement the excuse for most of what we shot, killed, squandered, and despoiled.

To some degree, every human incursion since the moment Adam and Eve were expelled from Eden into the wider world has happened to the detriment of Earth. Taking resources, taking down animals, taking advantage of whatever weaker populations get in the way. It's true that animals take resources too, and also take down each other. But they do so with no demonstrable appetite for expansion or increasing efficiency or widening breadth of scale in their operations.

No doubt, aboriginal North Americans were far better managers of resources and respecters of the land than the Europeans who invaded them. But even Indians devised ways to kill buffalo in unnecessary thousands, by driving them headlong over cliffs. When they conquered other tribes, it wasn't necessarily with a maximum of compassion. When they slaughtered animals, it wasn't necessarily with a minimum of pain.

When they employed dogs and horses to pull their loads or carry them overland, they didn't always regard the individual members of species with the same kind of reverence they accorded animal spirits. When they sought to adorn their bodies and beautify their dwellings, they didn't always ask themselves whether those feathers might not be better left on the birds, or that tail left to the wolf or raccoon who originally sported it.

In all times and all over the globe, human populations—whether indigenous or invading—have taken for granted that the landscape and everything on it is theirs to capture, possess, use, and enjoy. Not, of course, on the vast, ungrateful, technologically complicated and environmentally degrading scale that we descendants of European colonists have developed over the last several centuries. But certainly within human beings the world over there is some sense of entitlement to call this planet our own and get some measure of what it has to offer.

That is our nature, we tell ourselves. That is who we are. How else, after all, could we be? It's every breath we all take, every move we all make. We live to despoil. Despoilment is what we do, by definition. Despoilment R Us.

Even attempts to sidestep some of the more rapacious aspects of our relationship with the universe seem like imperfect antidotes. In *Animal Rights, Human Wrongs*, moral philosopher Tom Regan points out that tilling land for plant agriculture, growing cotton for clothing, and bulldozing the landscape to accommodate human development all involve the destruction of animal habitat and animals themselves.

Something dies, something gets destroyed, no matter what. Dairy farming, points out abolitionist Lee Hall, produces conditions destructive not only to cattle, but also our entire society. The pollution of water and air supply by the manure and methane gas produced by the cow, the non-renewable resources required to run the dairy barn and the abattoir where even a milk cow will eventually wind up, the deforestation resulting from the creation of pasture land for the cow to graze, the use of pesticides and other chemicals required both on the land and in the barn—all are unintended consequences of the production of one carton of cream.

Animal ethicist James Serpell writes about "guilt and anger" as the common human impetus for ecologically concerned groups, whether it's animals or anti-nuclear activism or environmental degradation that provides the primary focus. Yet he does not believe we can achieve "global vegetarianism or a complete end to the economic utilization of animals or the natural environment. Paradise, in this sense, can't be regained because it never really existed."

Even a perception of animals as "innocent" and nature as a whole being simple, clean, and uncorrupted doesn't equip us with a way to engage with them. We have expressed our longing to do so by buying SUVs (before the economy began to sputter) with names like "Explorer" or "Sierra," evocative of the untrammeled wilderness and pristine mountaintops that were sacrificed to build the automobile factories and superhighways. We book ourselves on exotic "eco" safaris and out-of-the-way cruises that require an ocean of jet fuel to transport us, and a pile of "carbon credits" to make social restitution for our selfishness.

Perhaps worst of all, we co-opt one animal species to assist us in controlling or extirpating others. Anthropologists speculate that some kinds of prey animals, like cattle and sheep, may have initially been tamed not as a source of food in and of themselves, but as a means to lure others of their species, in order to hunt them. In other words, the original Judas goats. And of course, animals like dogs are actually enlisted in the hunt, even when the species being hunted is the dog's brother, the wolf.

For those who do feel guilty with respect to any and all of the above, there is no easy road to absolution. No way at all, arguably, to expiate guilt or recover an innocence our kind may never have possessed in the first place. Yet, for some perverse reason, some appear prepared to try, even when the weight of caring and the effort of reparation appear to run counter to their own interests.

Such painful prodding of conscience is taken up movingly by J. M. Coetzee, in his novel *Elizabeth Costello*. Far from feeling virtuous about her sensitivity to the plight of animals, Costello, herself a novelist, is mystified, even embarrassed, by the fact that she's used an invitation to lecture on her work instead as an opportunity to decry man's inhumanity to animals.

When her son—who is hosting her visit to the campus where he teaches—confronts her with the bizarreness of her behaviour, she insists that she cannot help it. Indeed, she tells him, she has actively chastised herself for caring, almost inappropriately, about humanity's commonplace use and even abuse of non-human beings.

"'This is life,' she has scolded herself repeatedly. 'Everyone else comes to terms with it. Why can't you? *Why can't you?*'"

Coetzee's fictional mouthpiece Elizabeth is, perhaps, too hard on herself. She may overestimate the degree to which "everyone else" comes to terms with animal use, abuse, and exploitation. In truth, however most of us rationalize, our consciences may be more troubled than we acknowledge, at least consciously.

For those who feel the pain of paradox, stories heard in childhood are hard to forget. Other animals are not the same as we are, but they are equally important, equally interesting, equally worthwhile.

For those people, that childhood faith has never waned. For many, maturing was a process of being conditioned that animals are here for our service, that they matter less. However, even adults can begin to question that inculcation, and look wistfully back at the children they were.

Therefore, it is more and more a culture of polarities that we live in, between the pull of our private consciences and the powerful force exerted in the other direction—toward greater and greater objectification, commodification and exploitation of animal species.

Hence the resurrection of the fur industry after a couple of decades of embarrassed decline. And what about the recent rise of defiantly carnivorous cooking shows and books and recipe columns? Meat is mastery. Let's not forget our proud human inheritance. Whoever heard of a vegetarian master chef? Who'd ever vote a self-confessed vegan President of the United States?

Meanwhile, somewhere deep inside each of us and far back in our collective past, something unresolved continues to clamour for our attention. Innocence is no longer an option. The only choices available are between a sense of responsibility for our actions and a sense of entitlement to do as we please. Either we act to alter what Wilbur the Pig would call our "miserable inheritance," or we accept it as inevitable. Most of us try a bit of both.

AT THE AGE OF FIFTEEN, I at long last wheedled my parents into letting me buy a puppy. Going to school became a necessary annoyance between feedings, trips to the backyard for toilet-training, and tussles with toys on the urine-sprinkled newspapers spread across the kitchen floor.

Before the pup, my dog hunger had been partially assuaged by fraternization with the various canines on my route to and from school. Post-puppy, those good old pals still got a smile and pat, but in a far more perfunctory way. To remain too cozy with other people's dogs—now that I had one at home—bordered on infidelity.

Still, there was one old-timer on my way to school I couldn't resist. I'd known Angus, a Scottish Terrier, ever since our family had moved to the neighbourhood when I was six. Though now elderly, Angus was still an affable soul. Every morning, he'd amble down to his front gate and invite me to scratch his stiff chin whiskers, before ambling back up his walk to sprawl on the doormat.

One May morning, Angus's front gate was open as I came by. After I patted him briefly and headed off, Angus headed off with me. It was uncharacteristic behaviour, though not without precedent. On earlier occasions when his gate was open, he had taken a notion to follow me, just to the end of his block.

However this morning, Angus not only followed me to the end of his street, he continued across the intersection.

"Angus, go home!"

Surprised by my tone, he stopped short. It looked as if he was prepared to turn around and head back to his own front yard.

Relieved, I started off again. But when I next glanced over my shoulder, there was Angus, once more proceeding in my direction. "Angus, damn it! Go home!"

But he wouldn't. Each time I threatened, he'd pause for a moment. But then, as soon as I attempted to carry on to school, there he was, trailing me at a discreet distance.

Eventually, I hurried back the several blocks to his house, with Angus lumbering along behind me at an infuriatingly slow gait. When I reached his front yard, I attempted to coax him back through the open gate. But he wouldn't come.

Clearly, Angus was having the time of his life. But I was really late for school. When I went to his front door and knocked, nobody answered. There was no one at home to entice him inside the gate.

I had no choice but to run for it, hoping to lose him by the time I reached Albert Street. It was a busy four-lane thoroughfare leading out of town. On the other side stood the red-brick convent house where I went to school.

As I ran, I told myself there was no way on earth Angus would attempt to follow me across. I looked for a break in the rushing traffic, and sprinted across, before he even spotted me.

Almost. At the very last second, after I was well and truly across the busy road, I turned to see Angus, with surprising speed, make a dash toward me—straight into the traffic.

The first car hit him only a glancing blow. As I screamed, Angus righted himself, got to his feet—and foolishly continued to cross. The next car ran right over him. Shrieking now, I stepped into the road, not caring whether I got hit and half hoping I would be.

I cannot recall who helped carry him across the lanes of stopped traffic and onto the sidewalk in front of my school. I can remember only how he lay on that sidewalk, tousled black-and-grey coat oozing blood, flanks heaving lightly, more blood streaming from his nose.

Somehow or other, I got myself into the door of the school and made the little novice at the front wicket understand that I needed to use the phone. There wasn't any kind of animal shelter in Regina in those years, or even an animal control truck. I called my mother, who promised to call the police.

By the time I got back outside, a small knot of concerned citizens had gathered around Angus. Almost immediately, a young constable from the Regina Police Department also showed up.

"Please," I said. "Put him in your car and let's take him to a vet."

The constable nudged Angus's inert form with the toe of his boot. "Too late."

"You don't know that!"

As I pleaded with him, he took off his sunglasses, and chewed uncomfortably on the tip of the side piece. "Look," he said at last. "I'm going to call the Department of Sanitation to send a truck. You ought to go to school."

But I couldn't. I went home instead and locked myself in my room with my warm, squirming little pup. I hated myself.

My mother assured me that it really wasn't my fault. When she managed to reach Angus's family on the phone, they didn't blame me either. But it didn't matter. I knew I was responsible for his death.

After my father came home for lunch, he knocked on my bedroom door, commiserated, and then returned to the kitchen. A few minutes later, the doorbell rang.

I looked out my bedroom window at a police car sitting in front of our house. A moment later, my father came again to my bedroom door. "It's the constable from this morning. He feels bad about what happened and he wants to talk to you."

All I could think of was the way he'd poked Angus with his boot, like a parcel of garbage too loathsome to touch. "Tell him to go away," I said.

My dad went off to do that; I could hear more adult palaver at the front door. Then, my dad was back. "You know, he really seems like an awful decent young fella. Why don't you give him a chance to say he's sorry?"

"Tell him I appreciate him stopping by," was as gracious a response as I could manage.

Again, my father went to confer with the cop. In the next minute, I heard the front door close, and I watched as the constable headed back to his squad car. Once inside, he seemed to hesitate for a long moment. Then, there was the sound of the ignition, and his car pulled away from the curb.

My puppy—as well as subsequent dogs—have long since come and gone. Both my parents have died. Perhaps the people who owned Angus are gone as well. And, for all I know, so is that young constable.

But Angus and the last moments of his life live on and on. In every dog I ever see running down a street, looking lost or simply looking too naïve to be loose on his own recognizance. In every heart-stopping moment on a street or a road or a highway, when there is a dog, or a deer, or a cat, or a squirrel, either dazed or panicked in the midst of the traffic. In every Lost Dog or Missing Cat poster I come across, taped to a street lamp or stapled to a tree.

In every one of those moments, I can't help it. I feel responsible. As if through some oversight of mine, some brief infraction, some careless mistake, an innocent life has been imperiled or lost. As if there was something I actually could do to make it okay, to make the world safe for everything innocent or vulnerable or confused or foolhardy or afraid.

Of course, there is nothing I can do—either to alter the past or to make the world safer in the present moment. But like that cop sitting there in his cruiser, taking a long thoughtful pause before stepping on the gas, I can't help thinking that there is.

V

AT THE PARIS SALON OF 1827, sculptor Gregoire Giraud exhibited a small, superb portrait in marble called "Hound." An alert-looking dog reclines on an oval base, around which runs a series of even smaller relief sculptures narrating his life. We see him attacking a bull, although we're not clear why. In another image, however, in which the hound is killing a snake, it's obviously to save a baby's life.

In *Best in Show: The Dog in Art from the Renaissance to Today*, the text accompanying a photograph of that sculpture tells us "the dog is meant to embody all those qualities that give its species a unique sanctity, worthy of the kind of devotion that might be offered to a Christian saint."

Not long after encountering that picture of "Hound," I literally almost bumped into "Bashaw." This life-size sculpture of a Newfoundland dog trampling an enormous snake stands in the Victoria and Albert Museum in London—a huge, arresting, and popular presence there for more than a hundred years.

The real-life Bashaw belonged to the Earl of Dudley. In the mid-1800s, the earl offered sculptor Matthew Cotes Wyatt a commission of five thousand pounds to immortalize his faithful pet. But by the time Dudley died, Wyatt had not yet completed the work. The artist was never paid, and "Bashaw" was eventually sold to the V&A for a mere two hundred pounds.

The actual Bashaw did sit—or in this case, stand—for his three-dimensional portrait. But the snake is a boa constrictor—hardly likely to have been brought into the studio as a life model. Nor is it a type of snake any Newfoundland dog living in England would be likely to encounter, much less choose to step on.

It may be that a snake was simply added to the sculpture as a structural device, to help balance the heavy marble body of the dog. Or perhaps the sculptor seized on the idea of the serpent as a shorthand way to convey the canine as brave protector of hearth and home.

The catalogue entry from the 1851 Exhibition where "Bashaw" was first shown contains a reference to the faithful friend of man trampling the enemy underfoot. And the way the body of the snake coils up from the dog evokes images of England's ever-popular St. George, vanquishing the writhing dragon beneath the hooves of his horse.

In her 1893 animal classic *Beautiful Joe*, Margaret Marshall Saunders uses the real-life biography of a mistreated dog as the basis for a novel narrated by Joe himself. The actual Joe did overcome horrendous abuse to enjoy a lifetime of happiness with a kindly family. But the novel, written for submission to a contest sponsored by the American Humane Education Society, also contains many instructive and edifying stories of animals—including a probably fictitious encounter between Joe and a snake.

The dog has traveled with his mistress, Laura, to visit relatives of hers in another town. There, Laura and Joe are introduced to other visitors. One is a man named Maxwell who keeps his pet guinea pig in his pocket—as well as a strange little being that darts its tongue out at the dog.

"I had never seen such a creature before," Joe tells us. "It was long and thin and of a bright green color like grass, and it had queer shiny eyes. Its tongue was the strangest part of it, and came and went like lightning…"

When the company is invited to the table for tea, Joe creeps from his assigned place in the hall to a spot under the table. He hasn't forgotten about the peculiar little animal in Mr. Maxwell's pocket and wants to be nearby, in case it reappears to frighten Miss Laura. And sure enough:

> When tea was half over, she gave a little cry. I sprang up on her lap, and there, gliding over the table toward her was the wicked-looking green thing. I stepped on the table, and had it by the middle before it could get to her. One of my hind legs was in a dish of jelly, and one of my front ones was in a plate of cake, and I was very uncomfortable. The tail of the green thing hung in a milk pitcher, and its tongue was still going at me, but I held it firmly and stood quite still.
>
> "Drop it, drop it!" cried Miss Laura, in tones of distress, and Mr Maxwell struck me on the back, so I let the thing go, and stood sheepishly looking about me….
>
> I felt that I had done wrong, so I slunk out into the hall. Mr Maxwell was sitting on the lounge, tearing his handkerchief in strips and tying them around the creature where my teeth had stuck in. I had been careful not to hurt it much, for I knew it was a pet of his; but he did not know that, and scowled at me, saying, "You rascal, you've hurt my poor snake terribly."

I felt so badly to hear this that I went and stood with my head in a corner...I would not move till Miss Laura came and spoke to me. "Dear old dog," she whispered, "you knew the snake was there all the time, didn't you?"

Well, the dog suspected as much, at least. And clearly, when Joe leaps onto the tea-table to interpose his body between the snake and Miss Laura, he sees himself in the role of protector. He is the literary incarnation of Giraud's "Hound," and even a bit like "Bashaw"—the sculpture, if not the real dog, positioned like a four-footed St. George, conquering the dragon.

Could we make the same claim for the greyhound in the old, old story? In his quixotic and ultimately disastrous quest to save the child from the serpent, is the dog a sort of noble knight pitted against a scaly, mythical beast?

Yes and no. According to anthropologist Jean-Claude Schmitt, in all of the versions of the two-thousand-year-old dog-and-cradle-and-serpent story, the snake is indeed described as unusually large and venomous. There are even variants of the tale in which it is identified as a representative of Satan. However, Schmitt writes, in none of the versions of the tale with which he is familiar is the reptile ever identified as a dragon.

Presumably, what the dog does in the story is not unusual in and of itself. Dogs guard cradles and dogs kill snakes, however huge, especially when they intrude in the house. In fact, many of us have seen even the most mild-mannered pet assail a snake with a quality of almost righteous wrath—as if he's assigned himself the role of watchdog at the gates of some pre-lapsarian Eden.

There is, however, one thing remarkable about the legendary greyhound in his encounter with the serpent, something that sets him apart from Giraud's hound, from the Earl's Bashaw, Marshall Saunders' Joe, and even your real-life house pet interposing himself between you and a garter snake: the dog in the story kills the snake without witnesses.

————•◆•————

IN IMAGINATION, I VOLUNTEER TO BE THAT WITNESS. Unobserved and uninvolved in the action, I picture myself somewhere out of sight in the child's chamber, where the loyal greyhound, left behind, sprawls on the floor, asleep and dreaming he's out on the hunt with his master, back in the old days.

Being a dog, he doesn't often look back, at least not in waking life. Sound asleep, it's another thing. Paws trembling, eyelids twitching, he can find himself, in one instant, in a dream of the old green world that contained only the game he chased and the man he served.

Yet the dog merely seems to sleep. In the next instant, at the first whispering, slithering sound, he is wide awake—and sees a snake on its way across the floor toward the child.

Even before the greyhound growls, the snake senses he's awake. It pauses briefly on its way to the cradle, to give him a long, cool, calculating look, then continues undulating on its belly in the direction of the child in the cradle.

Now, the dog issues his second warning growl—and his last. This time, the snake stops short, and raises its head and the upper part of its long body from the stone floor, the better to look the dog directly in the eye.

You're a fool, the glint in the snake's eye says, and is meant to say. *To let yourself be shut inside on a day made for the hunt.* The snake cranes its long, strange neck and twists it from side. *I don't see your master anywhere. Of course, I used to see him, and you so often in his company. But nowadays.…* The snake flicks its tongue contemptuously in the direction of the child and advances once more on the cradle.

More than anything, it is the serpent's contempt the greyhound finds infuriating. Instantly, he leaps at the snake, with such force he knocks the cradle right over. *Uh-oh.* The snake hisses in amusement, and slithers into a corner, out of reach of the dog. *Better not let your friend the master see how you treat his child, or he'll jump to the wrong conclusion. Or maybe … the right one?*

For reasons he doesn't entirely understand, the dog is even more enraged. Once again, he goes for the serpent, digging frantically with his claws at the corner of the wall where it's disappeared, and snapping his jaws on empty air. The snake, meanwhile, reappears from a chink in another part of the wall, and continues gliding toward the overturned cradle, aiming to slide beneath it, to the warm place where the child, nestled in his blankets, still slumbers undisturbed.

But the greyhound snatches quickly at the tail of the snake beginning to disappear under the cradle and manages to grasp it. Firmly, he grips the muscular, undulating body in his jaws.

Wait! The snake twists its head, so as to fix the dog with one glinting eye. *Stop and think for a moment*, urges the unblinking gaze. *With the child dead, think what your life might be like....*

The dog's teeth are poised to bear down on the spine of the snake. But for a moment, he unclenches his jaws just a little. What if he were to let the snake go and do its worst? In that moment, it's as if he can envision himself, and his master, just the two of them, running through the woods.

Ah! The snake's rigid body relaxes in the dog's grasp. *There, you can see it, can't you?*

For just that one moment, the temptation is almost overpowering. Then—crack! The greyhound clamps his jaws on the snake and snaps its spine with a sickening crunch. Then he shakes and shakes and shakes the body, spattering its blood in all directions. Finally, he flings it away, as if to throw off all evidence of temptation—then turns his attention, gratefully, to the sound of footsteps approaching the chamber.

Little does the dog know there's worse to come. But I know it, and can hardly bear to witness what will happen next: the servant's screams, the master's return, the blade of his sword whistling through the air and down upon the unsuspecting animal. In that split-second, I know, the greyhound will barely have time to recognize the man with the weapon raised against him as the same man he has loved and served, both out in the field and in the child's bedchamber. In that last instant of his life, the dog will likely not have a chance to wonder where the master who loved him has gone—much less where he himself has gone wrong.

The death of the snake is by no means the end—nor even the climax— of the story of the dog by the cradle and the serpent beneath. Even the death of the heroic greyhound is really just the beginning. The real drama centres around what happens next, with the master's discovery of his mistake and the remorse that follows.

In his book *The Others*, ethologist Paul Shepard conjectures what animals might say to each other, at the point when humans have driven them all to the brink of extinction: "When we have gone they will not know who they are."

Or perhaps we would rather not know. Perhaps one of our greatest sources of unease about animals is exactly that: the fear that somehow, even fleetingly, they recognize in us what we prefer not to see in ourselves; that it is not their muteness but our own willful obliviousness that prevents us from hearing the truth about who we are.

———◆◆◆———

PART FOUR

Dubious Distinctions:
A Story of Voluntary Conscription

IN HUMAN SOCIETIES, PERSONAL IDENTIFICATION with certain animals has been and continues to be a persistent theme. The horse, however, occupies a position of particular precariousness in our estimation. Because of its speed and remarkable beauty, we are eager to glorify it. Yet horses can be made to give us what we want from them. In many cultures, that includes their flesh—whether as a restaurant delicacy for our own consumption or down-market meat products to feed our pets.

Therefore, in almost every way, human association with the horse is fraught with ambivalence. Because of our close identification with its noble character and our admiration of its grace, we find it difficult to treat this species as an expendable object. At the same time, that very identification makes the horse a perfect victim for sacrifice in our name.

To resolve our ambivalence, we have always had to seek ways to enlist the horse's complicity in its fate at our hands. Whether in ancient rites of ceremonial slaughter, or on the thoroughbred racetrack of today, we make a special point of reassuring ourselves that the role we have selected for this animal is not only honourable, but that the outcome—whether glorious triumph or gory death—is what it would choose for itself.

In spite of that, horses and the other animals with whom we identify leave us with a lingering paradox to ponder: If we do indeed see them in some ways as surrogates of ourselves, how successful can we ever be in distancing ourselves from the fates to which we consign them—fates we would seldom choose for ourselves?

I

PROPERTIES OF A GOOD GREYHOUND

A greyhound should be headed like a Snake,
And necked like a drake,
Footed like a Cat,
Tailed like a Rat,
Sided like a Team,
Chined like a Beam.
The first year he must learn to feed,
The second year to field him lead,
The third year he is fellow-like,
The fourth year there is none sike,
The fifth year he is good enough,
The sixth year he shall hold the plough,
The seventh year he will avail
Great bitches for to assail,
The eighth year lick ladle,
The ninth year cart saddle,
And when he comen to that year
Have him to the tanner,
For the best hound that ever bitch had
At nine year he is full bad.

About two hundred years after the Lord of Villars so profoundly mis-judged his dog, on the other side of what will later become known as the English Channel, Dame Juliana Berners (or Barnes) sets herself a similar task of judgment. In rhyming couplets, she too addresses the question of what constitutes a "good" greyhound and how humans can tell.

For Dame Juliana, however, the question is not a matter of punishment, but a matter of practicality. Like the eventually unfortunate Lord of Villars, she is a person of noble birth. She was, in fact, brought up in court, which is no doubt where she developed her love of hawking, hunting, and fishing.

These passions are unusual enough for a woman. They seem even more startling when you consider that Juliana Berners is a nun—the prioress of the Sopwell Nunnery in St. Albans, a day's ride north of London.

Some of her time in the convent is spent working on her writing. For example, her book on fishing is the first treatise on this subject ever written by a woman. But what she would herself likely regard as her magnum opus is her *Boke of St Albans*, which, in addition to being a study of heraldry, "sheweth the manere of hawkynge and huntynge."

Understandably, a book of this type includes many tips on that most useful of hunting animals, the greyhound. How Dame Juliana may have felt about her directive to take a dog who has rendered honourable service for nine years to be himself rendered at a tannery, she doesn't indicate.

What she might have made of the Lord of Villars' faulty judgments about his greyhound, two hundred years before her time, is impossible to know. What she would make of our treatment of greyhounds, is equally hard to imagine. But it seems like a good bet that the Prioress of Sopwell would recognize that paradox of exploitation and exaltation at the heart of her assessment of the breed.

"I'M WAHNIN' YOU, you're gonna fwall in love with my dwogs!"

The voice on the other end of the phone is rich with the orotund vowels and overlooked "r"s of the American Northeast. I found June's phone number on the website of a large dwog—I mean "dog"—track, casino, and family entertainment complex in southern New England. She is an employee who "adopts out" retired greyhounds right at the track.

Dog racing in North America is in general decline, except in Florida and Mexico. In the US, more than thirty states have banned the sport. In Canada, there is only one dog track, as far as I'm aware, in central Alberta. But retired racers are available for adoption almost everywhere across this continent, thanks to the efforts of adoption groups.

Of course, I could easily find such a group in Toronto, and learn how they prepare prospective owners for the particular challenges of taking a working animal with zero social skills and turning him or her into an acceptable pet. But I want to see where these animals come from, who they are on the track, and how a trackside adoption operation like June's handles folks who turn up to inquire about her dogs.

Perhaps most of all, what I want is to meet the modern counterpart of the dog who kept watch by the cradle and battled a snake to the death in a contest that proved, in the end, his own undoing. If I look into those far-sighted eyes, I figure, I will be able to see where he's been in the eight hundred or so years it's taken him to make his circuit around a long, long track stretching from the diocese of Lyon to a kennel behind a casino complex near the Massachusetts–Rhode Island border.

JUNE'S ADOPTION OFFICE is in the same small building as an indoor kennel for a dozen or so dogs freshly retired from the nearby track. Their smell permeates the common wall which, on the office side, is covered with paintings, photos, plaques, and shelves of knick-knacks, all with a predictably greyhound-related theme.

June herself is more of a surprise: a startlingly tiny elderly woman, with an explosion of white hair and an expression of sad-but-wise. Her head bends forward on a severely curved neck, like a blown dandelion on a drooping stalk.

All I've told her over the phone is that I'm interested in learning about her adoption program. I did not say a single thing about seeking to adopt a dog. Even so, on the way here, there's been some debate between my partner and me. Shouldn't I have told her I'm engaged in research? he, the ethical journalist, wonders.

No doubt, he's right. But if I'd put it to June like that, I suspect that would have ended the phone call. As it was, all she asked was where I was calling from, and when I told her, she was delighted. "I've adopted some very nice dwogs to people up there in Tahr-ahn-toe! Wait'll you see my sweethahts. You won't be able to go home without one!"

She was, I thought, speaking only figuratively. The animals in her kennel are fresh from the track, not even neutered, much less socialized. In person, however, June is the hard sell personified. She is sincere in her ferocious passion for the "dwogs," but also frightening in her intense desire to move the merchandise.

"Come see my babies." June opens the door that separates her cubicle from theirs to reveal a room full of greyhounds in two-storied rows of mesh-fronted crates. Some are brindle, some are fawn, some are black, some are grey, some are spotted, some are all white. There are barrel-chested dogs, scrawny dogs, anxious dogs, indifferent dogs, and smiling dogs. True to the reputation of their breed, not one of the dozen or more utters a sound.

"What do you like?" June asks, spreading her arms expansively.

She has asked us nothing about our previous history of dog owner-ship, how and where we live, what other animals we have in our house. Her assumption is we've stopped to shop.

My partner gives me a chastising look. There is no way on earth he intends to leave this place with a racing greyhound.

"Now, here's a real hunk of mee-yan…" I don't immediately recognize the word as "man," nor realize that the hunk June refers to is a particularly tall and robust-looking greyhound. His name is Bird Dog and he is as aloof as a horse, looking down from his crate on the upper tier.

June has already told us about her own succession of greys, acquired over the twenty-seven years she's been running the adoption program at the track. She assures us she has loved each and every dog of the four al-most as much as she loved her departed husband, whom the dogs have all "gone up to join."

Now, she has all the dogs she could want right here at her office. Each of the "dwog men," she tells us, at the twelve kennels that operate at the track, gives her dogs on an ongoing basis. As soon as one is adopted, he or she gets replaced by another.

At any given moment, therefore, June has at least a dozen dogs. Of course, what she wants most for them is homes of their own. And she finds them homes. More than two hundred, she tells us, every year.

My God, I think, that's almost four a week! How many come back as returns, she doesn't say.

As we stand gazing up at Bird Dog, June's handler arrives. The dogs,

so silent up until now, break out into a din of barking, and scratch frantically at the wire-covered doors of their crates with long elegant forepaws,
as if suddenly transformed from remote works of art into an eager pack of
pups in a pet-shop window.

Margaret the handler, it turns out, has been summoned to the kennel
expressly to help June help us to a dog. In a businesslike way, Margaret
opens Bird Dog's crate, slips a collar and lead on his neck, and eases him
down to the ground. Like a shot, he's surging at the end of his leash, out
the back to a small fenced area of sand that serves as the run. The other
dogs continue to bark in protest at his special privileges.

"Take him for a walk," June directs us.

My partner takes the loop end of the leash and more or less follows
Bird Dog around the small run. He looks like a man cooling down a horse
he's never met before. I sit down next to Bird Dog, and attempt to engage him with a word. Nothing. His gaze, along with his interest, is elsewhere.

"So?" demands Margaret forthrightly. "You taking him?"

Another poisonous look from my partner. Quickly, I protest that I
have a few questions. How would Bird Dog cope with my cat? Or with
housebreaking? Or with stairs?

"We'll tell you everything you need to know," Margaret assures me.
"Well?"

Despite the pressure, we don't take Bird Dog—to Margaret's disgust.
From June, it's more like disappointment in us for passing up such a bar-
gain. Not only do the dog men supply her with top-flight dogs, they contribute 450 dollars per animal, to cover neutering, dental work, and
anything else it might need in order to be adopted.

"So the hundred dollars you'd pay me is quite a steal. Our program
accepts no donations, holds no fundraisers. Everything comes from the
dwog men."

And that's the way June likes it. She has no interest in working
through larger adoption groups. For her, it's important to carry on the
program she pioneered at this track, back in the days when greyhounds
were routinely "retired" with a lethal injection or some kind of shot far

less humane. There's vindication for the sport, it seems, in every dog she's able to hand off to a new owner.

Perhaps that's why, for all the hard sell, we can't help but like her. Meanwhile she, despite our failure to "fall in love" with Bird Dog, still likes us enough to take us to the track, where she spends her time when not giving out dogs.

The tables overlooking the track are equipped with TV monitors, both for close-ups on the action below and also to beam other dog and horse race events going on across the country. In contrast to June's office with its kitschy pet memorabilia, this is the world of inveterate bettors who wouldn't look at a greyhound unless it had a number on its back.

At the table, June introduces us to one of the inveterates—a bespectacled, wizened friend named Joe, who says he owned racing greyhounds himself once, and respects June for her dedication to finding homes for the retirees.

"Would *you* ever have one as a pet?" I ask.

"Nah," says Joe. Clearly, it's an absurd question.

His attention turns trackside, as t-shirted handlers parade dogs on leashes to the gate. Eight dogs to a race, no more and no fewer. Blanketed and muzzled they walk, stately and grave as thoroughbreds. But when they reach the gates, each is inelegantly shoved into place—the same way you and I might push our pet into his crate for a trip to the vet.

Once they've loaded the dogs the young men hustle out of the way as the mechanical lure—a plush bone, rather than a rabbit—comes rocketing around the inside rail, just ahead of the release of the greyhounds. The buzzer sounds, the gates fly open, and out shoot the dogs, legging it for all they're worth.

The race is short, almost ridiculously so, compared to the time it takes to get the dogs to the post and loaded—under seven hundred yards in length, in this case. No jockeys on board to call the shots, not enough time to concoct strategy. The greyhounds simply race toward a lure they can never catch. When they reach the end of the track, the lure is whisked out of their reach, they break stride in disarray, and once more the handlers step in to clip on their leashes and take them away. That's it. It's over in seconds.

It might be days between races for a dog. In between those brief out-ings, it's life inside a small cage in the backstretch. There, all that happens are meals and quick turn-outs in the run, before being crammed back inside to wait until it's post-time again.

Perhaps the closest parallel is to research animals in laboratories, lim-ited to life in cages, utilitarian interactions with human beings, and almost no involvement with members of their own kind. At the end of the line, there are two possible outcomes: for the lucky, retirement; for those not so fortunate, extinguishment.

At trackside, June kibitzes with a group of Runyonesque regulars scattered around the various tables before she places her succession of two-dollar bets. Each time she fails to win, she castigates herself good-humouredly: "Why didn't I bet my numbahs? Why? Today is the day I'll kill myself, I sweah."

Her attitude about greyhounds has become shrewd and businesslike, now that she's away from her "babies" back at her office and is assessing them only as potential pay-offs. She and Joe confer earnestly about whether such-and-such bitch can perform while on hormones to keep her out of heat. Or why some big "hunk of mee-yan" looks so good, but has a record of fading in the stretch.

After a half-dozen or so races, my partner and I have had enough.

"Promise me," says June, as she walks us out of the stands, "that when you get your greyhound, you'll get it from me."

We are on a carpeted walkway that looks down onto the casino floor. Rows and rows of slot-machines spread out below us; in front of each stands someone intently feeding it chips, in lonely communion.

Most of the dogtrack fans are equally solitary at their individual tables. Meanwhile, somewhere out of sight are the kennels. Each separate cage houses a dog, each dog an individual study in ethereal grace. The cages are stacked in rows, and each animal is an isolated part of the same vast, impersonal machine.

To June, the way to appease the machine—and to make peace with it—is by moving those dogs, two hundred or more a year, from the racing kennels in the backstretch, to the quarters attached to her office, and then into homes as rapidly as she can. To her, this is the system that pays off more reliably than playing her "numbahs." That's what she takes home at the end of the day, to discuss with her departed husband and the four greyhounds who have gone, in succession, to join him up there.

This moment, if any, would be the time to come clean about my reasons for being here. Either that, or placate my conscience by announcing I'll take Bird Dog after all. However, I elect to do neither. Instead, as I shake her hand, I promise June that when I do decide to adopt a greyhound, I will get in touch with her first. It's an honest pledge, and she appears to take it as such, before turning to head back across the walkway where her betting cronies and the racing greyhounds are waiting for the call to the post.

AT THE RAYNHAM GREYHOUND PARK in Raynham, Massachusetts, the fourth annual Greyhound Adoption Expo is in full swing. Adoption clubs from all over the United States have set up booths to hand out literature about their activities and to raise funds by hawking everything from greyhound-shaped soaps to greyhound-headed coathooks to greyhound sock puppets, and—for some reason—rhinestone tiaras and feather boas intended for greyhounds to wear.

Almost as numerous as the greyhound advocates are the dogs themselves. Herds of them, roaming like tame antelope, standing (they never sit) to receive whatever attention strangers wish to bestow as their due, or reclining with their preposterously long, bony legs arranged like driftwood. Just as I can't help staring at them, so are they staring too—off into the middle distance. Life on the track may be long since over, but they remain on the lookout, even in retirement, for something running just out of reach.

"Living sculpture," is how my friend Mary, a former greyhound rescuer, describes their allure. There is something about those hypnotic faces, that gait that floats on air, that otherworldly gaze—either into the middle distance, or else into the Middle Ages.

"Aid4Greys.Com, Bolingbrook, Illinois" reads a banner above a table presided over by a couple from the Chicago area. Their own dogs, the couple explains, are back home in Bolingbrook, being cared for by other members of Aid4Greys. Greyhound adopters support each other, just like parents, by swapping dog-sitting duty, arranging playdates, sending someone over to offer counsel if any problem arises with anybody's grey.

Not that problems arise often, they are quick to assure me, adding almost by rote: "Notice how quiet it is in here?"

I have to agree. There is the friendly chatter of human voices, the occasional amplified announcement on the PA, the periodic chiming or chirping of someone's cellphone. But not a single dog bark, not a one. Well, okay, one. But the noise, it turns out, has emanated from a Boxer who's somehow managed to infiltrate.

"Once you adopt a grey, you'll never want another breed of dog." Almost everything the couple from Bolingbrook says sounds like a well-rehearsed pitch. Unlike June in nearby Rhode Island, however, they're not selling dogs here, just dog-related merchandise. Yet, like all devotees to a worthwhile cause, they can't help reaching out to the uninitiated.

"How many greyhounds do you have?" I ask.

So far, only two. "But they're like Pringles. You can't have just one."

"No problems with housebreaking, learning to climb stairs, and not to chase the cat?" From June and Margaret, I had received no acknowledgement of what are supposedly major problems for animals in transition from a life on the track to the low-key existence of a house pet. Surely from these people—with no dogs to peddle—I will hear the truth.

"No problem," the couple asserts as one. "In fact, greyhounds are real couch potatoes."

"IF I HEARD 'COUCH POTATOES' once from those greyhound adopters, I must have heard it thirty-five times."

Some days later, in a diner in neighbouring New York State, I am telling my friend Mary about the Raynham Adoption Expo and asking her to compare it with her early days in greyhound rescue. At "couch potatoes" she smiles and shakes her head as she recalls her own first encounter with dogs straight from the track.

"About twenty years ago, I read a story in the paper about how race tracks just offed these dogs—some as young as a year—when they weren't any good for racing." In the same article, she learned some forty greyhounds had been housed in a barn not far from where she lived, "freezing to death, waiting for adoption."

Mary took on two of them, with bedsores on their skinny, close-haired bodies from a lack of bedding, slash marks from other dogs, and bloody clumps of ticks. "I brought them home. They just floated into the house, like royalty come for a visit. I had no idea what I was getting into."

Nor did she have any crates for them, so she tied them to chairs. "They ate the woodwork, they couldn't climb stairs, they had no idea about paper-training. So there was no way I could just let them loose. They'd never had anything to chew on, besides the strips of paper they used for bedding at the track. I was working on a book at the time, and were they ever terrible dogs for a writer: They chewed up my writing and my books—just like those strips of bedding."

She and her fellow rescuers didn't really know how to go about getting these bizarre creatures adopted. "We used to pitch them to people as if they were Cocker Spaniels, for God's sake. They're not."

THE RAYNHAM PARK ADOPTION EXPO is held right at the track—with the promise that "veterans" will get the chance to race later in the day, just for fun. But some of the greyhound adopters have never seen a race. One woman tells me emphatically she wouldn't want to. It's as though she'd prefer not think about the world her dog came from.

Yet, it *is* the world they've come from, as well as the reason behind their very existence. And whatever individual adoption groups and their myriad members might think of the "industry" and vice versa, the organizations representing the interests of both bodies have, in recent years, adopted, as you might say, a policy of mutual cooperation.

For a panel discussion at the Raynham Park event, entitled "Adoption

Groups and the Industry: How can we improve how we work together?"
Gary Guccione, the communications coordinator for the American Greyhound Council as well as executive director of the National Greyhound
Association, is on the podium with Cynthia Branigan, the *grande dame* of
greyhound adoption in the United States.

There are some questions from the floor about performance-en-
hancing drugs rumoured to be in use at some tracks, and concerns about
chronic injuries in racing dogs. However, the overall message from both
industry and adoption is upbeat and positive. Because, Gary Guccione
explained, fewer dogs now needed to be put down at the end of their
racing careers, "we see more injuries in adopted dogs." He went on to add
proudly that 93 percent of racers are now made available for adoption.

"Word of mouth is more effective than anything," Cynthia Branigan
agrees. Especially the right kind of word. "When someone asks 'Is that a
rescue dog?' I tell them: 'This is a retired professional athlete who now
lives in my home.'"

Yet despite the friendliness between industry and adoption personified by the panel, a vast uneasiness about the racing aspect seems to prevail.
"We are neither in favour of racing nor are we against it," the Chicago-
area couple has told me in their rehearsed-sounding way. That, I gather,
is the approved message—like Cynthia Branigan's insistence an adopted
greyhound should not be termed a "rescue" but a "retired professional
athlete." In the US election campaigns of both 2000 and 2004, animal
activists attempted to persuade Massachusetts voters to ban greyhound
racing in this state, one of only ten that still sanction the sport. Neither
initiative made it into law, but here at the adoption expo in 2007, it's likely
nobody—adopter and industry advocate alike—is oblivious to the fact that
there's another racing-ban campaign already gearing up in Massachusetts
for the November 2008 ballot. (Indeed, on November 4, 2008, the Massachusetts electorate did vote by a margin of 56 percent for a ban that
would put the Raynham Park track out of business by 2010, as well as the
state's only other greyhound track, Wonderland.)

When Raynham Park announces the start of its official racing day
shortly after noon, only a few adopters bring their retired racers to the rail

to watch their younger brethren speed after a mechanized bone. Nor do those canine spectators evince much interest in looking on from the sidelines—a perspective they would never have had, back in their own day as professional athletes.

MARY'S INVOLVEMENT WITH GREYHOUND ADOPTION goes back to the early nineties, and lasted only about four years. Many things are different now in the adoption-industry relationship, as she's the first to admit.

A generation ago, dogs whose careers on the track were over, as well as dogs who simply didn't show promise, were routinely euthanized by various means, some less humane than others, depending on the track. When adoption groups formed and approached the tracks, the racing industry saw an opportunity to put an end to the expense and bad press of killing off dogs and look good doing it. While some tracks, such as the one June works for in Rhode Island, still fund their own adoption programs, many more now elect to work through the myriad of adoption organizations.

But it's still "a symbiotic relationship," Mary points out, given that adoption groups get dogs from the tracks as well as money from the industry, on the condition that they take a neutral position on racing. Yet, she envies the level of organization among adoption groups nowadays. "They have an 'Amber Alert' set-up when dogs go AWOL." It wasn't like that, she says, back when a black greyhound she'd helped find a home escaped from his new owner.

"A bunch of us went looking for him. I'll never forget it. I found him, right out there on Route 22, in the dark—a pitch-black dog!—standing on the highway, looking *exactly* like a deer in the headlights. How the hell he survived, I have no idea."

BACK AT THE RAYNHAM PARK Greyhound Adoption Expo, there is a strong sense of fellowship, based on the same underlying idea: these dogs are like no others. Beautiful they may be, but it's not about beauty. Nor about calmness, nor tractability, nor their apparent desire to do nothing all day but loll on the couch.

Following the panel discussion, a trio of personable young women from Greyhound Adventures of Greater Boston get up to present some fun things to do with greyhounds—including winery tours, the Christmas Jingle Bell Walk featuring "fifty-four greyhounds on Boston Common with elf hats and antlers," and the Greyhounds Reach the Beach event in Delaware. But at the same time, the women present "hardware" tips about double leashes for "spooks and newbies," who could give a faulty leash the slip.

"You can never, ever let them go," is the repeated refrain—right up there with "couch potatoes" and "retired professional athletes." Greys, they emphasize again and again, simply can't be allowed off the leash. As docile as they seem, as calm, as Zen-like, as dreamily meditative.... True as all that may be, there is something else about animals bred to race after a lure. You can't let them loose. Not at Dewey Beach, not on Boston Common, not even in your local dog park. Not ever. A flash of movement on the other side of the street, and they might be gone; a sudden taste of the freedom to run and run, and they might not come back.

As I sit listening, a black greyhound suddenly appears at my elbow and fixes me with that peculiarly formal gaze.

"Holly wants you to pat her," a woman leans toward me to whisper.

I give Holly a couple of pats on her bony skull and smooth black back. She stands there politely enough. But to me, her mind seems elsewhere. When I stop patting, she moves away from my chair to gaze thoughtfully out the door.

"They're wonderful dogs," Holly's owner assures me, rising to get a firmer grasp on Holly's leash and lead her back to the chair. "Once you adopt one, you won't ever want another breed. It's just that ... you can never, ever let them go."

II

BUT THE PEASANTS, hearing of the dog's conduct and of how it had been killed, although innocent, and for a deed for which it might have expected praise, visited the place, honoured the dog as a martyr, prayed to it when they were sick or in need of something, and many there fell victim to the enticements and illusions of the devil, who in this way used to lead men into error.

Even for an experienced inquisitor like Stephen of Bourbon, the story must have been a stunner. He may have heard it in the confessional of the church in Chatillon-sur-Chalaronne, or learned it from some loquacious old woman on the market street in Sandrans, or had it whispered to him in confidence by a concerned citizen in Neuville, Marlieux, or even Villars. However the Dominican priest sent by the Pope to weed out heresies, sorceries, and assorted other abominations in an area north of Lyon called the Dombes acquired this information about the cult of the martyred greyhound, he must have been amazed. To think that a dead dog could wield such power from the grave!

More than seven centuries after it was written, the part of Stephen's exemplum called "De Adoratione Guinefortis Canis" that deals with the worship of a dog in a well is as startling as the day the Pope's inquisitor first heard the story. And, to me, just as fresh.

To come up against the unexpected bedrock of historical fact beneath what I've taken as merely mythical is like stumbling upon the remains of that well, deep in that grove of trees. I feel as if I've looked down to see that pile of stones—actual stones—covering up something else equally real.

So, let me see if I've got this right: After stuffing the dog down the well, the lord departed with his lady the ruin that had lately been their home, leaving their lands to be reclaimed by the forest. Where they disappeared with their child and servants, nobody seemed to know. It was as though the master, not the dog, had been slain and interred.

Meanwhile, around the abandoned well, the trees that the Lord of Villars had so hastily planted before his departure continued to grow. With them grew the fame of the greyhound whose body lay at the bottom of that well and under those stones. What could it be about that story of the faithful dog unjustly killed by his master that would strike such a chord with the common people, and elevate an animal's death to the level of Christian martyrdom?

That's the question at the heart of French anthropologist Jean-Claude Schmitt's book *The Holy Greyhound*. That's where I have found the text of Stephen of Bourbon's exemplum concerning his inquisitional examination of this canine "saint" in its entirety. And in Schmitt's detailed study of the entire affair and the culture from which it comes, I have received what the author himself terms "some insight into the class-consciousness of the peasantry and ... the profoundly religious nature of ideological conflicts in feudal society."

Most important to me is the way those conflicts seemed to impel the peasants to identify themselves with the dog. Like him, they frequently suffered at the hands of their betters, with unfair punishments and routine indifference to their service.

As well, there were political grievances to nurse. At that time, chief among abuses perpetrated by the seigneurial class was destruction of peasant farmlands, in order to create fishponds (*étangs*) for the nobility's exclusive enjoyment. When the Lord of Villars' manor house came crashing down around his ears, how the peasantry must have rejoiced. How reassured they must have been to perceive, in God's retribution for the wrongs against one dumb animal, the possibility of divine redress for their own just grievances.

The dog buried in the well was proclaimed not only a local hero, but a bona fide martyr. His unsung act of courage and ignominious death were now to be celebrated far and wide.

With celebration came supplication. As the horrified Stephen of Bourbon wrote in his account of the cult, the locals actually *prayed to it when they were sick or in need of something.* It was as if the greyhound not only had posthumous power to help them, but also felt their pain and suffering as he would his own.

THE VENERATION OF A MARTYRED GREYHOUND in medieval France may well have been the first instance of an animal emerging as a symbol for the masses. However, it was not the last. Early in the twentieth century, in the working-class Battersea area of south London, an abused brown dog briefly served a similar function.

"The Brown Dog Riots" were a skein of feminist issues, workers' rights, and the elitism of medical science, all hopelessly ensnarled over a bronze statue of a dog, with a drinking fountain for people and animals at its base. "The Brown Dog" briefly overlooked the Latchmere Recreation Ground, as a symbol of opposition to animal vivisection—until it was deemed too incendiary a symbol for a public space.

It was two female medical students at the University of London who supplied an anti-vivisection group with the factual story of a dog victimized by multiple surgeries before being crudely euthanized. After reading the women's eyewitness account, the group lit upon the idea of erecting a statue to honour the little terrier, drolly named Fun by the physicians who sequentially tortured and eventually killed him.

In Latchmere, a particularly impoverished area of Battersea, the statue went up with an impassioned inscription:

> In Memory of the Brown Terrier Dog Done to Death in the Laboratories of University College in February, 1903, after having endured Vivisection extending over more than Two Months and having been handed over from one Vivisector to another Till Death came to his Release. Also in Memory of the 232 dogs Vivisected at the same place during the year 1902. Men and women of England, how long shall these Things be?

What ensued was a clash between upper-class medical students—marching from the university to the "wrong side of the river"—and equally well-born opponents of vivisection. There was also a third element: trades-unionists and other working-class folk from the borough of Battersea. According to literary scholar Coral Lansbury, this group identified their own oppression at the hands of the upper classes with the cruelties inflicted on animals at the University of London and elsewhere.

After the first of two riots, the army of medical students was in disarray and the statue of the dog still overlooked Latchmere. However, in the following year, 1908, political forces opposed to the continued display of the statue gained control of municipal government in Battersea.

At that point, a compromise was proposed, through which a doctor well-known for his pro-vivisectionist views was allowed to present an alternative to the incendiary description at the base of the statue. "The dog was submitted under profound anaesthetic to a very slight operation in the interests of science," the proposed new inscription began, and went on:

> In two or three days it was healed, and remained perfectly well and free of all pain. Two months later it was again placed under profound anaesthesia for further experiment, and was killed under the anaesthetic. It knew nothing of what was being done to it on either occasion. None of us can count on so easy death. We doubtless shall suffer pain or distress, both mental and physical. This dog was free alike from fear and suffering. It died neither of starvation nor of overfeeding, nor of burdens from old age. It just died in its sleep.

Ultimately, the issue of the proposed new inscription became moot. Suddenly and surreptitiously, the entire statue was removed under order of the new, unsympathetic Battersea Council. What became of it, nobody is actually sure. Most likely, it was broken up in pieces in the Council yard or melted down. But for a brief season, the inscribed lines "Men and women of England, how long shall these Things be?" served as a rallying cry in Battersea for downtrodden workers and oppressed animals alike.

"DO YOU THINK," I ASK animal activist Ronnie Lee, "that people here have some particular concern about justice for animals?"

"You mean, 'Why Britain'?" Clearly, it's a question foreign visitors have asked before. "Well, that's a mystery, isn't it? We've been bad with respect to colonialism and waging war, after all. So why should we be any good about animal rights?"

Ronnie is an undersized, mild-looking man with wire-frame glasses, scruffy stubble, and a ball cap that makes him look a little like Radar on the old M.A.S.H. TV series. But I can't help thinking he looks even more like Squirrel Nutkin.

Appearances, however, are deceiving. As a co-founder of the Animal Liberation Front—a loose affiliation of direct-action groups branded "extremist"—Lee has been someone to be reckoned with. Like Keith Mann, he's done considerable jail time—well over a decade, when you tot it all up. And now, though similarly retired from the front lines of the ALF, he is still a custodian of its conscience.

"Maybe," I suggest helpfully, "it's that class consciousness that seems to inform everything here. Like the fox hunt." Ronnie got his start in activism as a fox-hunt saboteur—surely a textbook example of class warfare, if ever there was.

"Fox hunt's finished now," he replies instantly. "At any rate, in the kind of hunt that goes on now, killing by dogs isn't allowed. They can use up to two dogs, mind you, to flush out the fox, but they're obliged to shoot him."

Yet, back when Ronnie Lee and Keith Mann were actively involved in "sabbing," it seems to me the pink-coated, stirrup-cup wielding, horsey types they confronted must have been the logical successors of the barons and squires who once rode roughshod over the small acreages of the poor. "The unspeakable in pursuit of the inedible," as Irishman Oscar Wilde characterized the English aristocracy riding to hounds.

I tell Ronnie what I'm wondering about is a kind of working-class identification with animals. "You know, like the residents of Battersea during the Brown Dog Riots?"

"No." He cuts me off firmly. "Some poor people—like badger-baiters—are the most terrible animal abusers, others aren't. It's not about class."

Ronnie's own background is ordinary London middle-class, which may be why he isn't eager to foster the notions of some particular bond between the downtrodden of our species and any other. However, even Keith Mann, who grew up working-class in the North and describes animals as "the bottom of the heap," doesn't make any special claim for kinship on that account.

Yet I still find it hard to let my question go. I mention to Lee footage smuggled out of chicken slaughterplants and *foie gras* operations in Canada and the US showing workers literally stomping on chickens, or grasping ducks by their necks and slamming them against walls. "Some people speculate that because those jobs are the lowest of the low, workers take out their own degradation by degrading the animals. What about that idea?"

Ronnie continues to resist any identification, positive or negative. "Plenty of poor people would not stomp chickens," he assures me. "The ones who do are just bad people, really. They exist across classes."

In his view, "human supremacism" is what keeps members of our species—whatever our class—from identifying with non-humans. "Anything different is automatically inferior. We're better; therefore we can do what we want to them."

Religion, he feels, is more to blame than class distinction for robbing us "of independent thought." As he reflects on that, he shudders eloquently. "Brrr. If we're made in God's image, He must be so ugly."

Yet the news, according to Ronnie, is by no means all bad. Improvement in racist attitudes among humans and the fact that Britons today are altogether more accepting of difference will, he feels, inevitably have an effect beneficial to animals.

As if to applaud that thought, his mobile phone rings brightly. "Hallo, luv!" He mouths to me "Mother-in-law" with a shrug, then returns to the call. "How are you getting on, then, Mum?"

On a morning that's as sunny as Ronnie Lee's chat with his mother-in-law, I am sitting across a round table from him in the sky-lighted, aqua-coloured tea room of the Royal Pump Rooms, on the main street (called "the Parade") in Leamington Spa.

A mineral-bath resort town south of Birmingham seems like a rather genteel location for a meeting with an animal rights activist, as well as a bit of a hike for me from London. But it's fairly close, as I understand it, to where Lee lives. Like Keith, he doesn't readily specify his exact home address. However, he was happy to meet me at the train, repair to the

Pump Rooms cafeteria—"they have some vegan choices"—and give me all the time I want.

"Bye-bye then, Mum." His accent, to my ears, is mostly London, except for the long "u" sound he gives to words like "Mum." It's an inflection he thinks he may have picked up in prison in the North.

"Whoops, sorry." He's no sooner rung off with Mum than his mobile clamours anew. "Hallo? Ah, right." His tone has shifted into something smoother and more PR-like. Someone from the media is on the line, asking him about greyhound rescue, one of the legal forms of animal activism to which he now confines himself.

"Well, almost twenty thousand greyhounds are killed every year. Fifteen thousand of them before they even race. Breeders can tell at an early age if they're good for racing, you see. Then, of those who do race, even by the industry's own estimate, about three thousand get put down annually. It might be more. So that's at least eighteen thousand and maybe as many as twenty thousand per year who get put down.

"As there are thirty tracks, that means each one is responsible for the death of up to six hundred dogs per year. It's something people aren't even aware of, to be honest. It's an horrific statistic. Which is why people should boycott the industry."

Ronnie rattles through all of this briskly and brightly, as if commenting on trends in sportswear design. Finally, in response to a comment at the other end, he says: "That's brilliant. Cheers. Bye bye, then."

A radio station, he explains as he clicks off his phone. There are, he says, people involved in animal activism who don't like dealing with the media. But in his view, that's an opportunity lost.

It sounds to me as if he is not so much into greyhound adoption as greyhound racetrack abolition. I tell him about my observations at American tracks of the necessarily cordial relations between those who breed and race the dogs, and those who take them on afterward. Ronnie replies that adoption groups in Britain can also wind up "in cahoots with" the industry through their need to maintain goodwill. This is why the organization he works with here—Greyhound Action—has a long-term interest in an end to racing.

In the UK, he says, the industry is roughly the same size as in the US, with about thirty major tracks concentrated in southeast England. Just as in the States, dog racing has declined from its heyday in the 1950s, and now is trying to reposition itself, with affiliation to casinos and a new family orientation.

"Loads of them have closed," he says. Seventeen the previous year alone, as a result of demonstrations by Greyhound Action and other groups.

I can't envision protesters being permitted to accost would-be patrons at any US. track. But he assures me demonstrators here don't encounter as much trouble from police "as you might expect" because they are careful to stay on public property and leaflet in a peaceful way.

It's at the racing-industry events like dinner dances, Lee adds almost gleefully, that the demonstrators go to town a bit. "You know, shout at them and whatnot. But we don't want to alienate the public. We want them on our side."

For a moment, I have a mental image of industry nobs—if the dog-racing world does indeed boast such—dressed to the nines for a dinner dance, and being jeered on their way in by anti-racing protestors in cloth caps and rubber boots, standing at the gates in the English rain. If accurate, it's a picture that satisfies my notion of the exploited working-class getting their own back. In my mind, the workers include the dogs on the track, as well as the protestors moved to identify with them through feelings of solidarity in a larger struggle.

Of course, Ronnie Lee would not agree it's a matter of class identification. All the same, it's my mental image and I'm sticking with all of it, including the English rain—even with a brilliant sun shining down through the skylight on our table in the tea room at the Royal Pump Rooms in Leamington Spa.

DRIVING THROUGH SARATOGA SPRINGS, on my way to the National Museum of Racing and Hall of Fame, I typically misread the map and overshoot. When I stop in at the actual racetrack to get re-directed, the guard points in the direction from which I came.

"About a quarter mile back. Don't know how you missed it. There's a horse right out front."

In Saratoga Springs, *no* horse out front would constitute a more striking landmark. As well as boasting mineral waters as salutary as any in Leamington Spa, this upstate New York resort town is home to the oldest thoroughbred racetrack in North America and the National Museum of Racing and Hall of Fame. In every way that matters, it is a town about horses and the horsey set.

All down the main commercial thoroughfares are life-size plaster replicas of horses, each one decorated by a different artist. As well, there are super-realistic bronze horse sculptures, some with jockeys aboard, and abstract equine forms in ironwork.

The windows of most stores are keyed into the theme. Horse effigies in stained glass compete with horse-painted plates and horse-head potholders. Even in displays of merchandise not remotely equestrian, little plastic horse models cavort.

On the racetrack guard's instructions, I turn around and drive back the way I came. Sure enough, here is the racing museum—with a horse out front, cast in bronze.

Not just any horse, either. It's the great Seabiscuit, standing squarely on a granite pedestal, free of rider or saddle or bridle or fetter of any kind. The inscription on the pedestal extols him as one of the "immortals" of turf history, thanks to "courage, honesty, physical prowess—and also intelligence and understanding almost spiritual in quality."

A separate plaque nearby explains how this former claiming horse rose to greatness during the Depression, and went on to unprecedented achievements, even after "what should have been a career-ending injury." Then, as perhaps the definitive accolade: "Seabiscuit retired with world-record earnings of 437,730 dollars."

And there we have it: the perfect summation of the people's equine prince. From nothingness, to an unlikely but fabled career, to adversity overcome, to enormous wealth—all of it earned for the benefit of others.

Only in his memorial does Seabiscuit stand alone, without accoutrements or encumbrance or any emblem of fame and majesty and accomplishment. A bare-backed symbol of hope in a time when Americans went largely without, a representative of aspiration, and a four-legged repository of the dreams of millions of people at a point in history when they lacked everything else.

Not far away stands a statue of a more recent titan, the great Secretariat. Like Seabiscuit, his idealized likeness is unencumbered by saddle or bridle. But unlike his predecessor, Secretariat is depicted in full gallop. It's as if he's running across a meadow—for himself, and not for the money. However, there was money aplenty for others in his long career.

In terms of physical prowess, Secretariat was a competitor favoured by the gods: he was big and bold and sturdily enough built to withstand the terrible physical pressures on long bones and delicate ankle joints and tender hooves pounding on the hard surfaces of North American tracks.

By no means a tragic hero, Secretariat was a hero nonetheless, especially during a tarnished time in American life. It was during what Gerald Ford called "the long national nightmare" of the Watergate scandal that the big red horse won the Triple Crown, and somehow or other, served to brighten the otherwise black American mood.

Within his lifetime, Secretariat inspired a species of adulation equivalent to a rock star's. His devoted groom, Eddie Sweat, was besieged by requests for souvenirs, including combings from the famous chestnut mane and tale. Once, a woman even asked Sweat for some of Secretariat's droppings, which she planned to encase in glass. "And of course," writes Lawrence Scanlan in his book *The Horse God Built*, "Eddie obliged when the horse did."

Secretariat's death was hastened by a hoof disease called laminitis. However, he outlived Barbaro, a later victim of the same condition, by close to two decades, during which Secretariat was happily at stud and completely out of the public eye. Even so, the outpouring of public grief over his passing was impressive—and long-lasting.

To illustrate the emotional power of this thoroughbred, Larry Scanlan repeats a story told by one of the staff at Claiborne Farms, where Secretariat is buried. One day long after his death, a couple from Texas came to pay their respects.

"It was an extraordinary thing," the employee told Scanlan. "They had come a long way and the woman just broke down at the grave. She lay over that stone and wept, just shaking and trembling. You would think her own son was buried in the ground below."

Ten years after Secretariat's death, the United States Postal Service issued a stamp with his likeness, making him the first thoroughbred to be so honoured. In that same year, the TV sports network ESPN included him in its list of the top fifty athletes of the twentieth century. He is the only animal ever to enjoy—at least *presumed* to enjoy—that distinction.

To this day, almost two decades after his death, you can go to his website to buy a bobblehead Secretariat, a DVD of his racing career, or any of a vast array of other memorabilia. In an age of online immortality, Secretariat gallops on, across an expanse far vaster than the specialized confines of the National Museum of Racing.

Long before and far beyond the elite world of American thoroughbred racing, there is the shared history of New World frontiersmen and their horses that began on the long way West. Thanks to that relationship, it should come as no surprise that, even today, Americans postulate a partnership between their own national identity and the animals who most helped them shape it.

Even city slickers who never so much as rode a carousel horse feel a sense of solidarity with the trail-riding cowboy, out there in the yonder with a bedroll, a campfire, and Old Paint grazing under the stars. In the words of Republican Congressman John Sweeney of New York, horses "are American icons that deserve to be treated as such." Sweeney has been the chief sponsor of the American Horse Slaughter Prevention Act, designed to: "prohibit the shipping, transporting, moving, delivering, receiving, possessing, purchasing, selling or donation of horses and other equines to be slaughtered for human consumption, and for other purposes."

As of this writing, the legislation is still awaiting passage by the US Senate. However, already the effect has been to shut down American horse-slaughter operations, and divert their business to plants in Canada and Mexico. If and when the American Horse Slaughter Prevention Act becomes law, shipping US horses to other North American plants will no longer be legal; however, opponents of the bill fear the result of its passage will be to increase illegal smuggling of horses into Canada and Mexico to be stunned, bled, and butchered.

Congressman Sweeney is explicit about why he views that as inappropriate treatment of an American icon. "Would we ever think of slaughtering and serving a bald eagle in this country? The same should be true of the horse."

Whether the congressman realizes it or not, bald eagles—millions of them—*have* been slaughtered in America, to the point where their populations are only now recovering. It just so happens cooking and eating them has less appeal than stuffing them as trophies, poisoning them with pesticides, exporting their parts as aphrodisiacs and appropriating their feathers for costumes and decorations.

The horse, on the other hand, suffers an almost singular misfortune among creatures made use of by man. No other animal is so personable, so beautiful, so strong, so swift, so amenable to training, so useful as human transport—and at the same time so good to eat.

In France, *viande de cheval* has long been on the human menu; in fact, horsemeat is being heavily promoted these days as part of a French cultural heritage which should not be imperiled by the homogenization of standards among the nations of the European Union. In the United States, however, and in much of Canada, the United Kingdom, and Ireland, the public resists the idea of human consumption of horseflesh.

Other uses of horse by-products, including as pet food, glue, and a source of human estrogen replacement, continue largely unquestioned, even in America. Yet, that powerful identification with the horse, that notion of partnership, somehow puts eating horseflesh out of bounds.

In the Canadian province of Quebec—as in France—horsemeat is more prevalent on the menu than in the English-speaking world. At the same time La Belle Province reverences its history of fellowship with the horse. In his book *Little Horse of Iron: A Quest for the Canadian Horse*, equine historian Lawrence Scanlan documents the affinity that the *habitants* of eighteenth-century Quebec had with these animals. So much so, that when the English tried to starve out the inhabitants during the siege of

Quebec, they refused to slaughter their horses for food. That, writes Scanlan, would have been "like killing a member of the family."

There's "lots worse than slaughter," is how Temple Grandin summarizes her objections to a bill that makes no other provision for horses that are unwanted. "Sure, there was bipartisan support in Congress for banning horsemeat export, but it comes down to what do you do with all those horses nobody wants? Politicians won't pay the practical costs, like keeping 'em in sanctuaries. Politicians only deal in abstracts. So, we got unwanted American horses turned out to die, or smuggled in reefer trucks south of the border—or up to Canada, for all I know. Just 'cause a bunch of politicians think it's un-American to sell American horses for meat."

Nor does the legislation offer acknowledgment of the wide gap between the romantic image of man and mount and the sad reality of how many thoroughbreds, saddle horses, and feral ponies actually wind up.

The Misfits, a film Arthur Miller wrote for his then-wife Marilyn Monroe, captures the association between an aging cowboy named Gabe and the wild mustangs he captures to supplement his income. For Gabe (Clark Gable, in his last film role) the fact that the horses he ropes are now sold for dog food is a terrible truth he has to face about himself and his entire way of life.

It wasn't always that way, he tries to make clear to Roslyn, played by Monroe. Back in the day, the mustangs he rounded up in the Nevada desert were turned into "sweet" saddle horses. Through no fault of his, things aren't like that any more.

"I'm doin' the same thing I ever did but they changed it around," Gabe explains. "There was no such thing as a can of dog food in those days." The meaning of his own life, he implies, and the West in general, have been no less cheapened and traduced.

In *Neither Man nor Beast*, feminist philosopher Carol J. Adams recalls herself as a child who rode and loved horses. So much so, that she would not allow her mother to feed the family dog canned food made from horsemeat.

Yet, Adams also remembers how she would regularly watch pigs going to slaughter at the end of her street—just before she'd head home for a meal of pork chops. How, she wonders now, had such unquestioning distinctions already been made, even in childhood?

She concludes that her culture—American culture—fosters the view of certain animals like pigs, cows, and poultry as "appropriate victims," designated for death and consumption. As a child, she had already received that message and accepted it—but not regarding horses. However, Adams adds, as an adult it was the death of her horse—and the sight of its meaty, inert corpse—that prompted her to become a vegetarian.

In Canada, there is a similar sense of horses not as "appropriate victims" but as animal companions. In the western provinces of British Columbia, Alberta, and Saskatchewan there are particularly strong historical affiliations with the horse—as well as the majority of Canada's horse-slaughter plants.

In June 2008, a graphic documentary feature aired on CBC Television's *The National* showing horrific conditions in some prairie horse-slaughter facilities and linking the increase in slaughter horses coming to Canada to the American Horse Slaughter Protection Act. Viewer response to the gruesome footage suggests that, like their American cousins, Canadian legislators may soon be engaged in the same struggle between sentimental support for a cherished animal and the current practice of disposing of unwanted horses through slaughter for foreign consumption.

But what's the alternative? In the United States, the American Veterinary Medical Association and the American Association of Equine Practitioners echo Temple Grandin's concern, should the American Horse Slaughter Prevention Act prevail, that many fates worse than slaughter await old and undesirable horses.

"Who knows how they'll be put down in the future?" asks John Block, a former US secretary of agriculture opposed to the ban. "It's not going to achieve the objective that it's more humane for horses."

Not only is the proposed legislation deficient in alternatives to humane slaughter, it has nothing to say about numerous other kinds of abuse and exploitation of horses. How do Americans—or Canadians, or Britons for that matter—feel about mares kept perennially pregnant and urinating for the production of commercial estrogen? Or carriage horses stumbling down automobile-congested streets in the tourist districts of many large cities, ponies who plod in endless circles at amusement parks, and the hundreds of thoroughbreds who die annually of their injuries on the track?

Similar to much of our identification with animals, the partnership we've formed with the horse appears to be a limited one.

SOMETIMES, OUR SENSE OF KINSHIP with animals is actually painful to acknowledge. In *Survival*, Margaret Atwood's landmark treatise on Canadian consciousness as exemplified in the country's literature, the author devotes an entire chapter to what she dubs "animal victims," and how Canadian writers and readers relate to these frequently doomed literary figures.

Atwood thinks it's not so much that Canadians feel guilty about the highly publicized seal hunt, or warfare waged on wolves and other animals almost to the point of extinction—even if she considers this country's history with respect to animals "as bad as the slave trade or the Inquisition." What she does find "much more likely" is a direct identification with animal victims because Canadians feel "threatened and nearly extinct as a nation."

"The animals are us," declared naturalist Ernest Thompson Seton, to which Margaret Atwood adds: "And for the Canadian animal, bare survival is the main aim of life, failure as an individual is inevitable, and extinction as a species is a distinct possibility."

No doubt, many Canadians shrink from such a description of themselves as almost inevitable losers in a Hobbesian battle for "bare survival." However, as a Canadian herself, Atwood is entitled to editorialize. Harder for any national or ethnic community to accept is an association with animals made by an outsider.

In J. M. Coetzee's novel *Elizabeth Costello*, the protagonist gives a university lecture in which she compares the process of animal transport and slaughter to the treatment of Jews by the German Third Reich. After the lecture, a Jewish poet angrily confronts Costello: "The Jews died like cattle, therefore cattle die like Jews, you say ... if Jews were treated like cattle, it does not follow that cattle are treated like Jews."

But Costello can't shake her equation of the enormity of the mass marginalization, isolation, persecution, and execution of one life form with that of another. Later, she confides to her son that she has imagined herself going into someone's well-appointed bathroom and picking up a bar of soap with a wrapper that reads: "Treblinka—100% humane stereate."

To Elizabeth Costello—and presumably to her creator, J. M. Coetzee—nothing pejorative is intended by this cross-species identification. To the contrary, the plight of the Jews of Europe under the Nazi regime is made more poignant by the comparison to animals abused and slaughtered daily in their millions around the globe. Yet, to the Jewish poet, the "cattle-car" analogy is reprehensible—no doubt in part because, in Hitler's Germany, it was intended to be.

Long before the German war machine was even beginning to rev up, European Jews were accustomed to negative comparisons to animals—especially pigs. It is, according to Claudine Fabre-Vassas in *The Singular Beast*, an anomaly in the ugly annals of prejudice that Jews are most closely identified with the animal they themselves do *not* eat. While the French were derided as "frogs" and the English identified as "beefeaters" on the basis of their respective diets, Jews were denoted by a creature considered repulsive to them.

Perhaps, Fabre-Vassas suggests, the epithet "pig" reflected the sense of insult Gentile peasants felt in the Jews' refusal to partake of European Christianity's staple meat. In which case, the best way to return the insult was for Christians to push the identification between Jews and pigs to the utmost.

One of the most hideous examples of this negative identification comes from Italy in the fourteenth century. At the beginning of Lent, Christians would sometimes cram a Jew into a barrel and roll him down a mountain slope—to his death or at least serious injury.

Eventually, that custom was refined to permit a Jew to pay to have a pig take his place. The pig would be dressed in clothes identifiably Jewish, carried in an ornate carriage or sedan chair to the edge of the slope, and then hurled down to its death.

To be replaced by a pig surely constituted an aspersion. To also pay for that privilege must have added, in the eyes of the local Christian population, an element of particular richness to the insult.

But for Gentiles themselves, identification with swine had an entirely different meaning. As previously mentioned, *The Singular Beast* details Christian rituals connected with pig slaughter and consumption that involved the sons of the family. Almost invariably, the relationship between the boy and the sacrificial animal was sympathetic, even intimate.

III

IN MAINSTREAM WESTERN CULTURE, the notion of "blood sacrifice" is now largely incomprehensible. Most non-Muslims can understand it—sort of—when a Muslim neighbour tells them he has bought a goat to sacrifice in commemoration of Ibrahim and Ishmael, or to mark the birth of a child. But understanding is predicated on the hope of some quick, painless process with a sharp knife, preferably conducted where no one else can see it, as well as the idea of meat to eat—not killing for ritual's sole sake.

Rites that involve animal sacrifice in a strictly propitiatory way strike many of us as…well, "unsettling" would be the least judgmental way to put it. The thought that this sort of sacrifice is rooted deeply in our unconscious is something we'd like to *keep* unconscious, deep, and dark, far back in the mind.

However, right at the front of historian Richard Bulliet's mind are thoughts about the importance of prehistoric animal sacrifice to who we are. In *Hunters, Herders and Hamburgers*, he looks at the wonderfully evocative cave drawings of Lascaux and elsewhere—artwork up to 35,000 years old—and sees something quite different from what many archaeologists and anthropologists have concluded.

The first cave drawings—indeed the first human artworks—were of animals, most frequently horses. Generally, scholars view them as expressions of aesthetic appreciation by our earliest ancestors. Or else, this primitive artwork may represent man's attempt to "capture" prey animals in pictures, as a means of ensuring success on the actual hunt.

Bulliet, however, sees in those earliest subjects of art the evidence of their importance as objects of sacrifice. The ritual killing of animals—principally horses—he maintains, pre-dates their domestication as beasts of burden or haulage.

Even meat eating, he suggests, may have been a kind of afterthought, a mere by-product of the main purpose of propitiation. Perhaps it was the hunters who got first crack at the meat after an animal was slain, as well as the privilege of participating directly in the ceremony of sacrifice. Lesser members of the tribe merely got to enjoy the gory spectacle.

Certainly, in Bulliet's view, gratification of bloodlust was the prime motivation in singling out animals for sacrifice. Everything else followed from this primary activity, including the eventual domestication of animals. Having captive creatures handy to human encampments made them more quickly available for ceremonies of slaughter than wild creatures that first had to be spotted, tracked, and killed before bringing them back to the communal altar.

However, writes Bulliet, even in the era of domestication, the ritual killing of animals was set up to simulate the hunt. The captive creature would be released, pursued throughout the settlement, and tormented in ritual fashion before being dispatched.

In ancient India, for example, a sacrificial ox would first be slathered in grease, then chased, hit with sticks, stabbed, slammed in the forehead with a live puppy, hamstrung—and finally, after three days of this gruesome torment, put to death. In such grotesquery, it's possible to trace the roots of modern-day rites in Spanish-speaking and other countries, which involve driving bulls through village streets and into a ring. There, they are taunted, tortured, and finally slain in a ritualistic, almost religious, manner.

Other scholars of the ancient world disagree that blood sacrifice was an end in itself. James Serpell, for example, does not connect the earliest sacrificial rituals of the reindeer-herding Tungus of Siberia to bloodlust. Rather, he says, the Tungus needed to concoct ceremonies that would render acceptable the killing and consumption of animals they had raised with real affection.

What we do know for sure is that, in societies from ancient Egypt to pre-Christian Rome to North American native cultures, sacrifice of a particular animal was associated with the reverencing of some specific deity—such as the cult of the dog-headed Egyptian god Anubis. In hunting cultures, the sacrifice of a representative animal of the species sought as prey was intended to ensure the successful capture of other members of that species, or to guarantee their continued abundance.

According to Paul Shepard, the rise of agrarian cultures changed the identity of deities and, in consequence, the types of animals deemed sacred to them. Gone were lion, bear, and other predator deities of hunting cultures. Frequently, cattle became the new objects of worship. Even where cows or bulls were not specifically worshipped, they were made sacred through sacrifice to particular gods, to keep the herds safe from predators, and to assure their continuation.

Exactly *why* did the ritualized selection, killing, and in many cases consumption of the body of a chosen animal ever come to represent expiation, redemption, salvation, celebration, and all the other values associated with sacrifice? No one is sure.

Equally obscure is why some religious cultures—such as Islam—have retained live animal sacrifice for commemorative purposes, and why others have developed wholly symbolic rituals to take its place. In some way, blood sacrifice comments upon or elevates the more quotidian kinds of animal slaughter and consumption that it both represents and legitimizes.

In ritual contests, where an animal is faced as an actual adversary, says Paul Shepard, the spectacle serves as "a re-enactment of the struggle of men to wrest power from animals as a continuing measure of civilization." In other words, it would seem we must be prepared, periodically, to fight for our entitlement and the right to use animals as resources.

The bullfight culture of Spain is a particularly ritualized example, both in the selection of the sacrificial victim, and in the preparations the matador makes before taking the animal's life. Not only does the bullfighter proclaim his purity by abstaining from sex prior to an engagement in the ring, he also prays for forgiveness before heading out to the anticipatory cheers of the spectators in the arena.

Some curious kind of honour accrues to the victim of the bloody ritual that follows. This may arise from what Georges Bataille has termed the destruction of the sacrificial object's "realities of subordination." Sacrifice, he writes, "draws the victim out of the world of utility and restores it to that of unintelligible caprice."

But if the sacrificial animal enjoys a kind of release from the everyday exploitation of the species to which it belongs, it is still powerless to control the proceedings. This appears to hold true whether the animal is merely an object of sacrifice to a particular god, or whether it actually represents the deity to whom its death is consecrated.

In *The Golden Bough*, his exhaustive compendium of recurrent myths across many cultures, J. G. Frazer details a ritual from ancient Rome, in which, every October 15, the right-hand horse from a chariot team that had run on the Field of Mars was sacrificed for the purpose of ensuring good crops. Frazer describes how the horse's head and tail were cut off and distributed, and how its blood was mixed by Vestal Virgins with the blood of unborn calves, in order to create a concoction used by shepherds to fumigate their fields, and for other rites.

The sacrificial horse, Frazer makes quite clear, was honoured as the embodiment of a god, both in its slaughter and its dissection. And yet, it's a peculiar form of honour that culminates in the death of the honoree.

At the same time—despite the favour it conferred on the victim—ritual killing was, in some cultures, attended by an element of blame. Across the ancient world, those who took the role of butcher were usually highly respected priests. Yet, some rites required them to shift blame for what they were about to do—for instance, by whispering "it's not me, it's the gods," to the animal, before delivering the fatal cut.

In an iron-age feast called the Bouphoria, Paul Shepard tells us, dispensation was sought after the animal—a bull—was slain. In that rite, the executioner would pretend to flee the scene so that he could be "tried" and then exonerated of the killing. In other cultures, the weapon itself took the blame for committing the act. After being passed from hand to hand, the knife was "convicted" of the crime and then thrown away, as if to absolve the entire assembly of the death of the animal.

Such exculpatory rites suggest that guilt frequently attended animal sacrifice, however ennobled, and that ceremonies of expiation were required to help humans grapple with their ambivalence about the bloodiness of the business. In our own more secular time, the nature of the animal sacrifices may have changed, but the attendant need for sanctification remains.

As mentioned previously, early in the twentieth century, Delia Akeley, the first wife of hunter and taxidermist Carl Akeley, posed in Africa for a photograph to document the downing of her first elephant. In the picture, Delia is being "anointed" with the bloody pulp from the tusk of that elephant. Behind her, an improvised arch of tusks is supported by native bearers.

This is how philosopher Donna Haraway describes that photograph:

Here, the image is of a sacrament, a mark on the soul signing a spiritual transformation effected by the act of first killing. It is a sacred moment in the life of the hunter, a rebirth in the blood of the sacrifice, of conquered nature.

Consciously or not, Delia Akeley's baptism by blood recalls the ancient world, where religious ritual served to elevate animal death to sacramental heights. Meanwhile, in the secular scientific laboratories of Akeley's time and earlier, a similar effort to ennoble the dispatch of animal "specimens" is reflected not in pictures, but in the words of the experimenters themselves.

"When animals are sacrificed on the altar of science that Nature may reveal her secrets, the means are consecrated by the end," wrote James Blundell. Blundell was an obstetrician in the early nineteenth century who conducted experiments on animals in order to develop techniques of blood transfusion for his patients.

Around that same time, anti-vivisectionists and abolitionists employed religious terminology and scriptural references to further their own opposite ends. Perhaps scientists like Blundell thought to do an end-run around the pro-animal lobby by co-opting God to their side. Or perhaps the physician was reaching back into the collective unconscious for that image of "the altar" of science, and blood offerings being made upon it.

Nowadays, when modern experimenters talk of animal "sacrifice" in the laboratory, they refer primarily to the act of killing the experimental subject either to end its suffering or to conduct a post-mortem on the remains. Philosopher Bernard Rollin suggests the choice of that word, with its "religious, sacerdotal connotations," is quite deliberate. How better to emphasize the high-mindedness of their experimental purpose? "To sacrifice is to make sacred," he writes, in *Animal Rights and Human Morality*.

In a face-to-face conversation on that point, Rollin put it even more bluntly. "It's a euphemism," he told me. "Along the lines of 'work makes free.'"

IN THE LEAD-UP TO THE BOUPHORIA RITUAL of animal sacrifice described by Paul Shepard, the altar was baited with grain, in order to entice candidates for slaughter to volunteer. Whichever bull stepped forward first was deemed to have consented to his own death. In other cultures, different devices were employed to extract the necessary okay from the victim—such as lightly sprinkling the animal with water, until it tossed its head in a manner that could be interpreted as assent.

Where does that need for the complicity of the sacrificial animal come from? After all, if there is honour in it for the victim and expiation available to the perpetrators, requiring the animal to be onside seems unnecessary.

Perhaps the contradiction is best understood by considering whether that sense of identification our species sometimes feels with animals might operate in conflict with our enormous capacity for entitlement. Born of that struggle between our sense of sympathy and our sense of superiority, the concept of animal as willing participant emerges as a child of human necessity.

Among the Ainu of Japan, it was a long-time custom in small villages for the men to capture a bear as a cub and let the women raise it like a child—even to the extent of suckling it at their breasts. As the bear grew, he was penned and fattened. Once mature, he was prepared for sacrifice.

The first step was to tell him the "good news" of his upcoming death:

he would be sent back to his real parents, in the spirit world. (The Ainu word for "sacrifice" in fact means "send away.") As well, the bear was briefed on what to say on arrival among the spirits. "Please speak well of us and tell them how kind we have been. Please come again to us and we shall do you the honour of a sacrifice."

Before dispatch, the bear was subjected to a lengthy ordeal of "honour," much like the torment of the sacrificial ox in ancient India. After being led through the village, he was taunted. After that, he was strangled, and finally—depending on whether it's James Serpell or J.G. Frazer telling the story—either shot through the heart with an arrow or squeezed to death between two poles.

Perhaps these rituals, James Serpell speculates, helped to "distance the killers, both emotionally and symbolically from the animal." Certainly, they were rites calculated to remove any element of identification with the victim.

After all, this was no wild bear the Ainu hunters had captured and submitted to sacrifice. This was a trusting pet they had reared like a child—before turning on him. No wonder the human participants con- cocted what Serpell calls "self-justifying fantasies" to transform their betrayal of a former friend into a sacrifice even the victim was expected to celebrate.

After his death, the bear was drained of blood, which the villagers then drank for strength. Finally, the victim was decapitated, and his head set up at the table with some of his own flesh on a platter under his nose, as if he were a guest at a feast not—as Shakespeare might have put it—where he ate, but where he was eaten.

To our ears, the Ainus' observance sounds quaintly gruesome. Yet, this method of coaxing complicity from animal victims may not be as far removed from us as we think. In the whole long history of humans' relationship with animals, right up to the present moment, such fantasies of coopera- tion accompany many situations in which non-human creatures act as donors of resources we feel we require. When the animal itself fails to give ready consent, it's up to us to supply that readiness.

During the sacrificial killing of the bear, the Ainu women—some of them those who had once suckled the cub—were prompted both to laugh and to cry. It was not just a way for them to signal their ambivalence, but also a means to release the community at large from any guilt over killing an animal they had known, fondled, raised, spoiled, and loved.

For those of us who live in more sophisticated societies, there is still a dependency on what James Serpell calls "the exploitation of domestic species." With the need to use animals comes the same age-old conflict between engagement with them and detachment from those we raise to fill our needs for food, entertainment, solace, and spiritual communion.

Donald Watson, who founded the vegan movement in the US in the 1940s, wrote about his own childhood recollections of the family farm—and his gradual realization of the illusory nature of the animals' consent:

> They all "gave" something: ... the cows "gave" milk, the hens "gave" eggs ... the sheep "gave" wool. I could never understand what the pigs "gave," but ... then the day came when one of the pigs was killed: I still have vivid recollections of the whole process—including the screams, of course.

Those who remember the 1960s may still chuckle at the recollection of Starkist Tuna's spokesfish Charlie. Charlie's highest aspiration was to be good enough to be chosen by Starkist—to be caught, killed, canned, and consumed. Today, images of smiling cows outside cheap eateries or pigs in chefs' hats wielding butcher knives send the same message: animals are happy to serve us, and to be served.

More and more in the twenty-first century, we rely on the media—particularly daily newspapers and television current affairs shows—to help reinforce a sense of animals' complicity in how we treat them. As the primitive Ainu of Japan needed to laugh and cry as a way of dealing with the bear's transition from lovable mascot to ritual sacrifice, so do we require humour and harmless pathos to help us to a necessary sense of detachment about the uses we make of non-humankind.

Every couple of weeks, it seems, there is a lighthearted story of a cow or pig escaped en route to the abattoir, and cheered on by humans as he or she dodges death for one extra hour. Moose are featured running comically amok in urban areas, while hungry bears are ideal to lead the six o'clock news, if they can be videotaped jimmying open the back door of a bakery to scarf down a tray of muffins. And what local newspaper can resist a lively feature on the runaway shenanigans of the kangaroo who went AWOL from the petting zoo and managed to tie up six lanes of commuter traffic?

In reality, most of these escapades end, at best, in capture. At worst, the final frame or closing paragraph deals—as briefly as possible—with the animal's necessary demise. But even with the worst outcomes, wire copy services and TV networks categorize such stories as "brites" or "animal oddities" and use them to enliven a dull news day. Just as they count on their reporters to capture the event in a breezy "human interest" way—as if hijinks are what animals like to get up to, strictly in order to hand us a cheap laugh.

HOW DIM A VIEW THE THIRTEENTH-CENTURY Dominican cleric, Stephen of Bourbon, took of a dog "honoured as a martyr" is clear from his exemplum inveighing against worship of the slain greyhound. It was, he notes, only a short step from the peasantry's identification with the way the animal had been "killed, although innocent, and for a deed for which it might have expected praise"—to the common people's falling "victim to the enticements and illusions of the devil" by praying at such an unhallowed burial site.

Yet even the regional representative of the Pope's inquisition may have had some inkling of how such a heresy might take root. As a mere servant to a nobleman, a greyhound would be on a footing similar to the peasants themselves. At the same time, given that breed's exclusive association with nobility, the dog would have the necessary cachet to qualify as a hero. And not just any hero, but a martyr put unjustly to death, and then resurrected through the posthumous devotion of the masses.

No other version of the dog-cradle-snake fable appears to have spawned a real-life cult following like the one Stephen uncovered in the diocese of Lyon. No other version expands to mingle so freely with a religious paradigm. And there's yet more to Stephen of Bourbon's account, as he expands upon what went on in the grove that had grown up around the well where the body of the slain greyhound had been entombed:

Above all, though, it was women with sick or weak children who took them to this place. They would go and seek out an old woman in a fortified town a league distant, and she taught them the rituals they should enact in order to make offerings to demons, and in order to invoke them, and she led them to the place. When they arrived, they would make offerings of salt and other things; they would hang their babies' swaddling-clothes on the bushes roundabout; they would drive nails into the trees which had grown in this place; they would pass the naked babies between the trunks of two trees—the mother, on one side, held the baby and threw it nine times to the old woman, who was on the other side. Invoking the demons, they called upon the fauns in the forest of Rimite to take the sick, feeble child which, they said, was theirs, and to return their child that the fauns had taken away, fat and well, safe and sound.

Having done this, the infanticidal mothers took their children and laid them naked at the foot of the tree on straw from the cradle; then, using the light they had brought with them, they lit two candles, each an inch long, one on each side of the child's head and fixed them in the trunk above it. Then they withdrew until the candles had burnt out, so as not to see the child or hear him crying. Several people have told us that while the candles were burning like this they burnt and killed several babies.

Stephen makes it sound as if the children themselves became incidental victims of sacrifice. The cleric's characterization of the mothers as "infanticidal" notwithstanding, sacrifice of their offspring was not the intention when women brought their ailing infants to be cured by the dog who had once saved a child, only to be slain for his pains. More likely, earlier pagan rituals became conjoined, by the "old woman" Stephen mentions, with a bastardized form of Christian liturgy, and any deaths that occurred in the performance of these ceremonies were purely accidental.

Eventually, the well in which the dog was interred became the focal point for rites much older than the events that had occurred in the manor house of the Lord of Villars—rites older even than the original fable of the dog by the cradle and the snake beneath; rites older, in fact than Christianity itself.

The paradigm is one we know well: a hero noble in origin, yet raised to a life of humble service. Misunderstood in his actions, summarily judged, and unjustly put to death, he is hastily interred, but later brought back to life by the devotion of the faithful in whose hearts he dwells for all eternity.

Like any inspiration figure we create, the greyhound who took hold of the imagination of the public in a certain small corner of thirteenth-century France followed in the footsteps of those who had preceded him. He made the requisite journey along a road of earthly tribulation and satanic temptation that led, at last, to wrongful death.

But a story like his never ends in death. In fact, it's a story that never ends at all, but merely begins over and over again at the beginning—with an unassuming hero, born to lay down his life so that others might live to exalt him.

—————————

IV

THERE ARE STILL MANY OF US old enough to remember Laika, the canine cosmonaut. But most were likely too young at the time to understand what her heroic exploits in space actually consisted of, and how they ended.

In the USSR's Space Dog program, there were nine dogs—mostly strays scooped up from the streets of Moscow. But Laika was the first to go into orbit. Her name meant "barker," and perhaps it was appropriate not only because she was a dog, but because she served as a pitchman for the entire notion of space exploration.

Despite the cold war tensions of the 1950s, the Western world made as much of Laika and her stunning achievements as the Russians did. The American press nicknamed her "Muttnik" for the Sputnik 2 capsule in which she was confined, and breathlessly reported her successful launch from the Baikonur Cosmodrome into an orbit nearly two thousand miles above Earth. And they continued to report—for the several days it took the batteries that operated Laika's life-support system to run down.

Adults at the time must have known what that would mean for the dog. But for us kids, the idea that she slowly suffocated while hurtling around alone in space failed to really register. Years passed before I understood Laika had died in orbit.

In the United States, early space efforts gravitated to primates, rather than dogs. But the outcomes for those animals were often as bleak as Laika's. In 1949, two monkeys, named Albert 1 and Albert 2, were poised to be fired into suborbital space in the nose cones of captured German V-2 rockets. However, both died during test launches.

Subsequent Alberts survived the trip up into the atmosphere—only to perish when parachutes failed to open and the nose cone containing the monkeys "impacted" the ground. In 1951, a subsequent parachute failure killed yet another primate astronaut, along with several mice. Finally, in that same year, the US Air Force launched a rocket to "near space" forty-five miles up. A monkey named Yorick and the eleven mice who were his companions in flight survived.

Undoubtedly, the best-known non-human American astronaut was a chimpanzee named Ham. After being conditioned to pull levers to obtain rewards, Ham blasted off from Cape Canaveral on January 31, 1961, inside a capsule atop a rocket. His "mission" was to perform a series of tasks while in flight, so that scientists could determine the effects of launch, weightlessness, and re-entry on performance.

Because of a technical miscalculation, Ham's capsule wound up traveling at a rate of speed far faster than planned, which meant the chimp was weightless longer than anticipated. In spite of that, he managed to continue performing his tasks successfully. After landing in the Atlantic, his capsule took more time to recover than expected, and it leaked. Nevertheless, Ham survived the experience.

Headlines heralded Ham's "heroism," while newspaper photos and TV footage carried images of his grinning face as he sat at the controls. But as British writer Erica Fudge has pointed out, there were other aspects to Ham's historic space voyage which received less media play.

Rocketry was expensive business. There could be no allowance for monkeying around up there in the stratosphere. While being rewarded with banana pellets for pulling levers correctly, Ham was also punished when he made wrong moves, by having electric shocks applied to his feet. What the public did not realize was that Ham's much-vaunted smile was actually a chimpanzee's typical grimace of fear or pain.

Nor did Ham's name refer, as popularly supposed, to his gung-ho, attention-grabbing, born-for-showbiz nature. H.A.M. was an acronym of the Holloman Aerospace Medical Center in New Mexico where chimpanzees were trained—through a system of rewards and punishments—in preparation for space flight.

WHEN IT COMES TO MYTHMAKING IN THE MEDIA, not even a chimpanzee astronaut comes close to the heroic cachet of a horse. That may be because chimpanzees and monkeys are inevitably seen as droll, slightly wacky knock-offs of human beings, always grinning and clapping when they should be turning a noble profile to the camera.

Horses, meanwhile, tend to go about their brave business in silence and look good doing it. They possess an elegance of face and form that is almost awe-inspiring, along with a remote quality that gives the impression that they take their orders not from mere mortals, but from a higher authority. And perhaps uniquely among four-footed things, horses seem to run for the sheer undirected joy of running—as if eating up the ground beneath their hooves was intrinsic to the pleasure of living a life that knows no human bounds.

But as with any animal, horse heroes must be seen as eager participants in the human-directed exploits for which they earn their immortality—even when those exploits are acts of felony that end in death. Such is the case of Black Bess, the legendary mount of eighteenth-century English highwayman Dick Turpin.

In reality, Turpin was a standard-issue bad boy who likely stole the black mare on which he made his renowned ride—and who likely didn't make the ride at all. Indeed, it seems he was not actually hanged as a romantic highwayman, but as a horse thief. Yet none of that matters in the mythology that's grown up like ivy to obscure the real story.

The ivy-covered version is largely derived from a nineteenth-century novel called *Rookwood* by Harrison Ainsworth. Turpin is presented as a Robin Hood-style robber of stage coaches. After one escapade, he's forced to elude the ever-unpopular "King's men" by riding Black Bess at a headlong gallop for fifteen uninterrupted hours, all the way from London to York.

Turpin makes it, but Bess does not. I recall, in Grade Two, being set up at the front of my class by the teacher to read aloud a cut-down kids' version of *Rookwood*, while she hurried off to the staff room for a much-needed smoke. As I reached the exciting conclusion of the ride, my eyes skimmed ahead on the page—to the paragraph where gallant Bess collapses of heart failure. I immediately burst into tears.

"What is it? What happened?" the other kids clamoured.

"Black Bess is dead!"

Tearful pandemonium broke out among the entire class. Our teacher, redolent of cigarette smoke, came hotfooting it back from the staff room, convinced that a murder had occurred among us.

In *Rookwood*, Dick Turpin is as inconsolable about Bess as my Grade Two class. As for the horse, the author depicts her refusing to slow her stride until her great heart gives out. Undoubtedly, it's that image of Black Bess's loyalty to her rider—however he acquired her—that has helped elevate Dick Turpin from common criminal to dashing outlaw.

Yet a tapestry displayed in 1879 at the York Exhibition offers a more cynical opinion of Turpin. Beneath the image of Dick Turpin and Black Bess is woven a poem:

> May the steed that comes nigh her in courage and fire,
> Carry rider more worthy to make her heart tire;
> Though she saved him and died to prove what she could do;
> Yet *her* life was most precious by far of the two.

In our own time, it's still easy to embrace the image of a horse giving his life to gallop that extra mile. And in an age where such images become iconic in the millisecond it takes to beam them around the globe, it's easy to fall in love with four-footed heroes at long distance. Especially when they fall first, like the thoroughbred racer Barbaro.

Whether you saw his fateful stumble live during the televised running of the Preakness Stakes in 2006, or whether you caught it later in endless rerun in the frenzied weeks that followed, chances are you remember Barbaro. After a sensational first-place finish at the Kentucky Derby two weeks earlier, the handsome three-year-old colt was heavily favoured to win the Preakness in Baltimore, and then go on to take the Triple Crown. But at Baltimore's Pimlico racetrack, virtually out of the gate, Barbaro shattered a rear ankle in three places.

With more than a thousand pounds of horse held up by four long legs that seem fragile as wineglass stems, the terrible vulnerability of thoroughbreds stands in poignant contrast to their speed, their material value, and the much-touted privilege of their lives. Or perhaps it was simply the sight of an elegant animal holding up his injured leg at an obviously excruciating angle that prompted instantaneous and enormous public response.

Certainly, by the time Barbaro commenced prolonged medical treatment after his "misstep" on the track, his health and welfare had become a matter of urgent concern to thousands of people—including those who'd never heard of him before the accident. The surgeries he underwent at the University of Pennsylvania's New Bolton Center school of veterinary medicine to repair his fractured foot and ankle with a titanium plate secured with screws, the laminitis that afflicted his left leg as a result of his favouring the injury, the ups and downs of his hoped-for recovery over many subsequent months were all tracked from afar by breathless emailers, who sent hundreds of thousands of "hang in there, champ" good wishes to Barbaro's special message board at the New Bolton Center, along with apples, carrots, candies, postcards, and flowers.

Then, on January 29, 2007, that vast outpouring of support was eclipsed by a veritable tidal wave of human grief. Nine months after the original injury, the horse's owners, Roy and Gretchen Jackson, announced their decision to end Barbaro's ordeal by putting him down.

"Goodbye, brave and beautiful boy," one email tribute read: "Go back to the wind, and nevermore have to tolerate the weakness and ignorance of mortal man." "Happy grazing in horse heaven," ran another, "Long may you gallop."

Writing about the Barbaro grief phenomenon in *the Los Angeles Times*, T. J. Simers sounded a somewhat less elegiac note, when he observed that the majority of such messages were from women. "What is it about women and dead horses?" he asked plaintively, and then went on to joke: "Don't get me wrong, when it comes to horses, I've cried too—one big lug coming to mind that went off at odds of three to five.... only to finish last."

More pointedly, Simers observed that every racing season sees about seven hundred horses who die as a direct result of racing, along with numerous others put down after training accidents. So why the big deal about Barbaro?

Other detractors in print and online went even farther by ridiculing Barbaro as "dog food" or 1,500 pounds of horsemeat. Some accused the Jacksons of keeping the horse alive all those painful months in hopes he'd recover sufficiently to stand at stud. (In the thoroughbred realm, artificial insemination won't do. The stallion is literally required to stand and "cover" the mare—for fees that, in Barbaro's case, would recoup his lost value as a competitor.) Still others analyzed the phenomenon of grieving for a mere animal as further evidence of a society with hopelessly misplaced priorities.

By far, the eulogies—from blogging fans and renowned writers alike—outnumbered the jeers. The word "hero" was invoked again and again. Even those who acknowledged the hideously unbalanced priorities of the world of horse racing—as well as of the world the rest of us inhabit—couldn't help succumbing to the tragic allure of Barbaro.

He was beautiful, he was long-suffering, he was talented, he was brave. Yes, brave. Somehow, it seemed as if the horse had chosen long months of surgery over euthanasia directly at trackside. Or, perhaps that notion of bravery came from an idea that Barbaro, at the outset of his career, had weighed the dangers of running on a hard turf track for a living, and decided to go for it.

In the 2008 Kentucky Derby, two years to the day after Barbaro's promising victory, Eight Belles, the only filly in the field, suffered a calamity, just after she crossed the finish line in second place. In thoroughbred parlance, she "broke down." To the rest of us, that meant both front ankles snapped.

So spectacularly awful was the injury that Eight Belles could not even be splinted, then euthanized somewhere out of sight. Instead, the filly was put down right there on the track, eclipsing the worthy victory of a much-touted colt called Big Brown.

Perhaps because the protracted Barbaro saga had paved the way for recriminations, Eight Belles' ignominious exit inspired even more pointed questions about the so-called "sport of kings." William C. Rhoden of *The New York Times*—a sharp critic of thoroughbred racing at the best of times—demanded to know why there was no pressure to put the Eight Belles disaster under "the umbrella of animal cruelty, as there is with greyhound racing or dog-fighting. . . . Why do we refuse to put the brutal game of racing in the realm of mistreatment of animals?"

In the same newspaper a few days later, writer T. D. Thornton reminded fans of the thoroughbred track that Eight Belles was only one of fifteen horses on May 3, 2008, at thirty-nine US tracks who didn't finish his or her race. Those other, less glorious, steeds, Thornton wrote, would be "only a cryptic footnote . . . distilled into a single line of agate type . . . 'trailed, pulled up 1/2.'"

Meanwhile, Big Brown, who'd won the Derby handily, romped on to take the same Preakness Stakes, which had proven to be Barbaro's Waterloo two years earlier. However, before the third leg of the Triple Crown, at Belmont racetrack in New York State, the handsome chestnut-bay colt was diagnosed with a "cracked hoof." Amidst stories of anabolic steroids and forecasts of extreme heat for the running of the Belmont on Long Island, Big Brown entered the annals of thoroughbred ignominy when he became the first Triple Crown contender to run dead last in the conclusive race.

The "booster rockets," according to Joe Drape of *The New York Sunday Times*, never engaged, and Big Brown disappointed a crowd of close to one hundred thousand, who "stood and roared, anticipating that he would swoosh past the grandstand into immortality." No definitive diagnosis of his lameness has been offered since. All we know is that Big Brown's stallion rights, luckily, had already been sold before he failed to clinch the Triple Crown. (Some months later, in October 2008, after suffering an injury to another hoof during a workout, Big Brown was officially retired to stud, to the relief of anyone concerned about his apparent fragility.)

Even in the competitive category of over-the-top tributes to fallen horse heroes, some distinctions are definitely more dubious than others. Before the running of the 2007 Kentucky Derby—a year after Barbaro's sensational first-place finish—a conglomerate called Yum Brands Foods came up with a unique way to commemorate the bay colt's achievement and at the same time publicize their own brands, which include Pizza Hut, Taco Bell, A&W, and KFC: Yum offered a one-million dollar bonus to any horse in the Derby field who could better Barbaro's six-and-a-half length lead of the year before.

Somehow, it escaped Yum's notice that Barbaro's spectacular Derby performance very likely contributed to the fracture that not only hobbled him in the Preakness two weeks later, but led to his death. Veteran sports reporters from TV's Bob Costas to *The New York Times*' George Vecsey deplored Yum Brands' insensitivity in encouraging riders to goad equally fragile competitors into the same kind of life-ending injury.

For anybody of an ironic turn of mind, there also seemed something egregious about a huge corporation built on battery-raised chickens, factory-farmed pork, and feedlot-finished beef seeking to further exploit an already exploited event involving a fallen animal. Especially on a day when each horse in the 2007 Derby on his or her way to the gate was required to pass under an archway inscribed "Barbaro 2006."

It may have been fortunate for all concerned that Street Sense won that day by a mere two-and-a-half lengths. In the end, Yum Foods' "Barbaro Bonus" went unclaimed.

THE *VEDAS* ARE A BODY OF TEXTS from Ancient India, dating from about 1400 to 900 BCE and comprising the oldest sacred texts of Hinduism. From the *Rig Veda*, American historian Wendy Doniger has translated a Sanskrit passage concerning horses as objects of blood sacrifice. In that ancient world, horses enjoyed a particular status of honour, even when— perhaps especially when—they were slated to die. Back then, Doniger tells us, in order to elevate the quality of the offering, the priests would promise the sacrificial animals a painless passage and a kind of eternal glory.

"You do not really die through this," officiants sought to convince the horses, and perhaps themselves. "You go on paths pleasant to go on."

Like the sacrificial bear the Ainu assured a speedy return to his parents, the horses of the *Rig Veda* had to be persuaded to consent to the sacrifice. The journey to those pleasant paths was presented in the positive terms modern-day parents might use to assure their child that a departing pet is slated for "doggy Heaven."

Yet, the words of the priest to the horse are touching, too, with their assurance that the animal does not "really die." Perhaps because the priest speaks directly to the animal, the effect is of a whispered conference between partners.

It's that suggestion of consultation that elevates the horse's death from mere slaughter to supreme sacrifice. A sacrificial victim who volunteers for the job becomes something more than an object on the altar. He becomes an equal participant in the ritual.

One morning early in March 2006, a public memorial was held in Toronto to celebrate the life and mourn the death of a police horse named Brigadier. He had been euthanized on the Toronto street where an angry motorist had deliberately driven his van at the animal and the policeman on his back—shattering Brigadier's front legs and sending the cop up onto the hood of the vehicle.

About 1,200 ordinary citizens made their way, along with uncounted members of the media, to the Ricoh Coliseum at the Exhibition Grounds. There, they joined mounted police officers and horses and dogs from the Toronto force, the Royal Canadian Mounted Police, and other forces from across the country in a solemn service that included bagpipers, an emotional eulogy from Brigadier's horseless rider, and a well-worn saddle on display at centre stage.

Brigadier was cited as a fallen hero of the force. There was wistful speculation that—in taking the brunt of an automotive assault—Brig may have saved his human partner's life. That partner, still braced and bandaged, moved painfully to the podium, and struggled through tears to bid goodbye to a colleague and friend.

Altogether, Brigadier's eight short years on earth and sudden death were celebrated with the same solemnity police forces accord human members of their ranks who die on duty. A procession of pipers and mounted officers, a montage of film clips and still photographs all marked the passing of an animal who, in life as well as death, would surely be unaware of the meaning behind the big fuss.

Like the vast majority of his kind, Brigadier chose neither the circumstances of his life, nor of his death. As much as he was loved by his partner and the entire Toronto force, nothing about Brigadier offered evidence that, if consulted, he would have volunteered to put himself on the line.

It was public outrage at the manner of Brigadier's death that had created the need for a memorial. But for some in attendance, that indignation was not entirely assuaged by ceremony. The motorist who'd driven his van into Brigadier had done so with impunity. Animal lovers worried aloud that their presence at an event laying him to rest like a fallen warrior might make the horse's senseless slaughter seem somehow okay.

But perhaps the only homage we know how to pay is through taking something senseless and investing it with meaning. Hence, the little copies of Brigadier's picture passed out like holy cards at a First Communion service, the tributes of his comrades, the pomp of the proceedings, the sincere hope that this high-flying homage to an animal's life might countervail the lowly inconsequence of his death.

Such memorials are becoming increasingly common, and not only for police animals. The University of Guelph in southern Ontario is only one of a growing number of research institutions where animal technicians and experimenters gather annually for a ceremony of public thanks to each and every laboratory rat, rabbit, bird, and cat sacrificed over the past year on the altar of science.

Is the human community finding it ever more important to extol the heroics of animals and to invest their passing with elements of voluntary sacrifice? Or are we merely putting a modern spin on rituals devised many centuries, even millennia, in the past, to help human beings deal with the ambivalence that has always accompanied the life and death choices we make on non-humans' behalf?

Perhaps we have not come as far as we think from the days when ancient Hindu priests looked into the eyes of horses about to be slaughtered, and murmured into their ears that the best was yet to come. Whatever was about to happen, they would not die, but merely go down different, more pleasant paths.

V

TOWARD THE END OF HIS LIFE, the Dominican cleric Stephen of Bourbon recalled stories from his own experiences as a devout priest, a doughty traveler, and a tireless investigator on behalf of the Church of dangerous superstitions and potential heresies. These he wrote down as exempla— or, as we call them today, teaching tools. They were parables in anecdote form, full of memorable details and vivid situations tailor-made for an uneducated audience.

As his exemplum called "De Adoratione Guinefortis Canis" reveals, Stephen had a real narrative gift. He also had a way of commanding immediate attention, with what newspapermen in later centuries would come to call a "grabber lede."

"Sixthly," begins "De Adoratione Guinefortis Canis," "*I should speak of offensive superstitions, some of which are offensive to God, others to our fellow men. Offensive to God are those which honour demons or other creatures as if they were divine; it is what idolatry does, and it is what the wretched women who cast lots do, who seek salvation by worshipping elder trees or making offerings to them; scorning churches and holy relics, they take their children to these elder trees, or to anthills, or to other things in order that a cure may be effected.*"

I can hear Stephen, inveighing from the pulpit against demons, or "other creatures" being declared divine. And by the time he gets to those "wretched women" who put their faith not in holy relics like sensible folk, but in trees and anthills. . . . Well, what can I say? I'm sucked right in.

And Stephen knows firsthand whereof he speaks.

"*This recently happened in the diocese of Lyon where, when I preached against the reading of oracles, and was hearing confession, numerous women confessed that they had taken their children to Saint Guinefort. As I thought that this was some holy person, I continued with my enquiry...."*

Now I can picture him, in the confessional: this honoured visitor, listening attentively as not just one but "numerous" women admit they'd sought cures from St. Guinefort. The mere fact that they'd found it necessary to include visits to this saintly someone on their list of sins to confess would have piqued Stephen's curiosity right away.

Still, this kindly priest was not one to apply pressure. Instead, he would likely have leaned a little closer to the latticed window that separated confessor from penitent, to murmur—in a low voice, calculated to convey neither censure nor alarm—some casual questions about the identity of St. Guinefort, *"and finally learned that this was actually a greyhound, which had been killed..."*

Now that, as later generations would say, must have been a real stop-press. This St. Guinefort, this supposed "holy person," is actually a...what?

How Stephen responded in that moment, he doesn't elaborate in the exemplum. From there, he goes on to retail the manner in which the greyhound had been killed, and how the remorseful master then flung its body down the well, before departing with his wife and child.

Yet it's impossible not to divine between the succinct lines at least some residue of his amazement that any dog—even one killed "unjustly"—would pass on to an afterlife as the centrepiece of a pagan cult. Much less a pagan cult headed by an animal with the name of a bonafide Christian saint.

WHY THE NAME "GUINEFORT" for a slain greyhound? wonders anthropologist Jean-Claude Schmitt. For one thing, at least one human version of St. Guinefort was already well-known in that area of France, courtesy of monks who came from Cluny to educate the locals about this early martyr. Like the better-known St. Sebastian, Guinefort was challenged to abjure his Christian faith by soldiers serving pagan Rome. When he would not, he was shot full of arrows.

As St. Guinefort de Pavie, this early martyr was credited with healing children. Two centuries before Stephen of Bourbon showed up in the Dombes region on his inquisitorial mission, mothers were making pilgrimage to the chapel of Guinefort in Pavie, in the l'Isère area, to beg him to restore their children's good health. "*St. Guinefort, St. Guinefort, Pour la vie et pour le mort*" ran one invocation to this saint. Later, in the grove by the abandoned well where the dog was buried, the women of the villages bordering the Chalaronne River offered the same incantation on behalf of their children.

"The murder of the greyhound that saved the child," writes social anthropologist Jean-Claude Schmitt, "sanctioned his veneration as a martyr and saviour of children. Planting trees by the well where the greyhound's body was buried preserves the 'memory of the dead' and initiates a wooded place where the rite occurs."

Whether the monks of Cluny ever heard about this appropriation of the name of a particularly venerated martyr—and if they had, how they might have felt about it—we can only speculate. If the reaction of their clerical colleague Stephen is anything to go by, it's safe to say the monks would not have been favourably impressed.

But the reasons behind the peasants' choice of "St. Guinefort" as the name for the martyred dog run deeper than Christianity, and intertwine with the roots of far earlier traditions. Not only did the human St. Guinefort share the greyhound's proprietary concern for children, his feast day coincided with rituals more ancient even than his martyrdom in the fourth century CE.

The feast of St. Guinefort falls on August 22, toward the end of a period known then—and now—as "the dog days" of summer. Far back in the pre-Christian era, those weeks between July 25 and August 24 marked a time of celebration of the dog-star Canis Major, which rose and set within those dates.

In ancient Egypt, the cult of Anubis, the dog-headed god, commemorated the rise of Canis Major with canine sacrifice. Around that same time of year in Greece, dogs were massacred in a similar observance. Later, in Rome, red-haired dogs were singled out for sacrifice during the dog days.

Not surprisingly, the early Christian calendar shows the influence of these pagan rites. Though observances did not take the form of blood sacrifice, saints with dogs as their "attributes" were celebrated in that month. The feast day of St. Bernard, the pioneer of the breed of rescue dogs named for him, was celebrated on August 20. And, in a further connection to the canine Guinefort, the July 25 feast of St. Christopher— sometimes depicted with a dog's head—was observed by placing the image of a serpent at the saint's feet.

MEANWHILE, BACK IN THE CONFESSIONAL, sitting in the semi-darkness, Stephen of Bourbon is still in a state of shock at what he's heard about this cult of dog worship. On the one hand, the inquisitor in him is aroused, perhaps even slightly titillated. On the other hand, the priestly part of him is utterly appalled.

For all his outrage, Stephen is not one to act hastily, nor punitively. Nor would that be the best way to draw out the locals about their alarming customs.

I hear the kindly priest—at least I think I do—with his voice still at the low murmur of the confessional and his tone carefully crafted to reveal nothing apart from earnest concern for the well-being of the women whispering their admissions. Already, Stephen knows what he must do: persuade these women to take him to this place in the woods where the dog supposedly lies at the bottom of an abandoned well. Make them show him exactly what it is they get up to.

Not that he isn't already familiar with pagan rites involving demons and fauns and changeling children. Such rituals, far older than the grove that's grown up to reclaim the ruined manor house of the Lord of Villars, sometimes involve endangering the child more seriously than any illness.

"*When a mother returned to her child and found it still alive,*" he later recounts in his exemplum, "*she carried it out into the fast-flowing waters of a nearby river called the Chalaronne and plunged it in nine times; if it came through without dying on the spot, or shortly afterwards, it had a very strong constitution.*"

Yet of all the bizarre bits of business described to Stephen of Bourbon in the confessional on that day in a village church about forty miles north and slightly east of Lyon, only one was novel enough to shock and astound him: the fact that the centrepiece of these godless carryings-on was a dead dog.

AS A TALE OF HEROISM, sacrifice, victim complicity, and the power of ritual, the legend of St. Guinefort stands out, even in a field crowded with timeless stories. For one thing, there are the enduring mysteries at its heart: How the connection developed between the unjust killing of a dog—if there was indeed such a dog—and his veneration by the peasantry in a society not renowned for its reverence toward animals. And, more importantly, how it was that an ancient and almost universal fable about a greyhound protecting a child from a snake came to be connected to the specific story of the Lord of Villars.

We have no idea how long before Stephen of Bourbon visited the Dombes region it was that this particular dog supposedly killed a snake and was then killed in turn by his master. However, what is apparent is that the death of the dog and the subsequent destruction of the manor house occurred early enough for that grove of trees around the well to have grown into a full-fledged wood, and for the type of worship that went on there to have become well-established by the time Stephen of Bourbon came to the Dombes—probably about ten years before his death in 1261.

At that time, European Christendom was rife with rumours of various cults, pagan rituals, and assorted other heresies practised by unlettered peasants in contravention of Church doctrine and entirely outside the auspices of ordained clergy. When Stephen of Bourbon showed up in the area north of the city of Lyon, on the banks of the Chalaronne River, what he heard about demonic rituals involving the spirit of the dead dog and the parents of ailing infants must have struck him instantly as the kind of heretical practice the Inquisition (only one of several across Europe in the Middle Ages and throughout the 1500s) had been devised to root out.

The "old woman" or *vetula* referred to by Stephen—the neighbour-hood crone who taught anxious mothers the rituals that would invoke demons for the purpose of "changing" their ailing children for the healthy beings they had previously been—was probably accustomed to clerical interference of one kind or another. The history of Christianity is also the history of the persecution of "demons" and "witches"—the latter usually women living outside the pale of society either alone or in groups. They were often said to be attended by animals, whose role as "familiars" became yet another trumped-up reason for persecution.

There is no evidence in Stephen's account that he actively prosecuted either the old woman or any of the women who enacted the rites for the sake of their children. Most likely he regarded them merely as deluded peasants, not dangerous heretics. When he acted to put an end to the cult, however, the ringleader would probably have lost, if not her life, at least her livelihood.

Whatever short-term effect the cleric's subsequent actions may have had on driving the rituals underground, it was the peasantry who prevailed. From the thirteenth century until almost the mid-twentieth, the holy greyhound Guinefort was indeed—as anthropologist Jean-Claude Schmitt has dubbed him—the "healer of children" and an unofficial martyr of the Catholic Church.

It was around 1940, Schmitt has determined, that the last child was taken to those woods for healing by his or her grandmother. Who might have officiated at this event is not known. Schmitt was able to unearth the name of one Francoise Tremblay, the *vetula* who "facilitated" the cult until about 1930. But he arrived on the scene too late to locate Tremblay's grave, which he says had been "flattened" in 1974. Nor was he ever able to determine who, if anyone, had taken over from that woman.

In Stephen's story of Guinefort, Schmitt finds an unusual opportunity to examine both a folk legend and a religious ritual. The legend of the dog, the rites by which the children were "reclaimed" from the devil, as well as the reclamation of the wood by the peasants from the "desert" it had become after God destroyed the castle.... All these elements come together tantalizingly in a single narrative.

However, it was a story misunderstood by Stephen of Bourbon—even after he became a character in its development, and even as he recounted it for the edification of the faithful. "For," observes Schmitt, "the peasant rite was intended to drive back the dominion of evil, but the inquisitor saw it as depending upon a complicity between women and demons.

"For the peasants," he continues, "there was no contradiction between the notion of sanctity and the memory of a dog, even if the theology of the period and modern rationalism have nothing to gain from such a primitive belief system." In other words, the women were enacting a ritual to save their children, through a form *they* recognized as religious observance, even if Stephen did not. In the cleric's mind, no rite connected with a dog could ever be anything but devilry; no invocation of an animal under a saint's name could ever be anything but a shocking blasphemy.

Ironically, Schmitt points out, the Church itself edged into the realm designated as "superstition" as time went on, in a process begun by the Reformation and advanced through the Enlightenment, the French Revolution, and onward. At a certain point, there becomes little to choose between some of the arcane rites of traditional Catholicism, such as exorcism or transubstantiation, and semi-pagan rituals performed in a rural wood.

Common people, however, take their martyrs where they find them and flock to memorials that commemorate them—be they a statue of a vivisected brown terrier, or a solemn ceremony attending the death of a police horse, or an abandoned well rumoured to contain the remains of a slain greyhound.

"CHURCHES WERE BUILT ON THE SACRED SITES of wrecked pagan temples," ethologist Paul Shepard reminds us. "It took centuries to recruit enough converts to go out and cut down the sacred trees, smash the effigies and burn the drums." To him, the medieval Church smacks of a particularly anti-nature ethic, and an obsession with notions of pacification and control of animals—as opposed to respectful interaction with another realm of being.

However, even within the strictures of medieval Christianity, there was some latitude when it came to employing pre-Christian symbolism and ceremony for purposes of religious recruitment. It was, for instance, permissible to ascribe animal attributes to Christian saints. The dog-headed Christopher was the one entrusted to bear the Child Jesus across a raging river. As well, the Church co-opted earlier rituals of animal sacrifice to illuminate Christian mysteries, such as the invocation of Christ as "the Lamb of God" in the sacrament of the Holy Eucharist.

But it was just as important for clerics like Stephen of Bourbon to dissociate the faithful from pagan forms of animal worship by associating animals with devilry. In "De Adoratione Guinefortis Canis," Stephen describes one particularly wanton danger to which mothers allegedly exposed their children when leaving them to be healed in the woods.

"*One woman also told me that she had just invoked the fauns and was withdrawing from the scene when she saw a wolf come out of the forest towards the baby. If maternal love had not made her feel pity and go back for him, the wolf, or as she put it, the devil in the shape of a wolf, would have devoured the baby.*"

Jean-Claude Schmitt thinks that Stephen may simply have invented the detail of the wolf-as-devil. Certainly, it would have helped the cleric to underscore the danger of the practices in the woods, if he managed to debunk the "holy" greyhound as the devil's creature by linking him with the much-despised wolf.

But is it also possible that, in evoking the image of the wolf—actual or invented—Stephen of Bourbon may have himself become caught up in the world of transformation embodied by those woods? Just as sickly children were exchanged for healthy ones, so too might the noble greyhound—the protector of the cradle—be transformed, in an instant to an earlier, darker self: the very devil in disguise.

ONE WAY TO LOOK AT THE STORY of the slain greyhound is as a tale of sequential transformations, beginning with the dog himself. First, there is the faithful pet, trustworthy enough to be left in sole charge of a child.

But when the master comes home, it is to discover a different animal on the family hearth. Gone is the reliable dog servant and in his place stands some wilder, more wolfish creature. His jaws drip with blood; his gaze boldly and—it seems—defiantly meets his master's eyes.

Now, it is the master who suddenly transforms himself from a reasonable man, to the savage slayer of his good and faithful servant. In that single, ill-considered act, he is changed in the eyes of man and God into a felon. And at last, he turns into a dispossessed vagrant, bereft of land, title and future, condemned to oblivion with his wife and child.

From there, the transformation of the land can commence, as well as an alteration in the common people who inhabit it. As the lord's castle crumbles, drought devastates his land. Only the trees planted in and around the well that houses the dog's corpse appear to thrive. Gradually, those saplings transform into a grove. To that spot, peasants come, emboldened by the disappearance of the nobleman to honour that dishonoured man's dog.

Only at this point does the greyhound acquire a name. As "Guinefort," he begins the journey that will transform him into a patron saint. A dog becomes enshrined not only as a martyr, but as the helpmeet of parents whose healthy children have mysteriously turned weak and ill.

At last, the stage is set for the greatest transformation of them all: The wooded place grown up from the ruins of the abandoned manor becomes the focal point for rites older than time.

Once those transformations have occurred, they set the stage for older stories of alteration. One such story begins with the capture of the first wild wolf. After that, comes taming, first through confinement, next by restraint, and at last through love. The tamed wolf becomes a trusted servant—no, more than a servant: a colleague on the hunt, a helper in the fields, a companion by the hearth, free to come and go, but pleased to stay. Then, a day arrives when the man, interpreting an act of courage as treachery, no longer sees the dog as he is, but as the wild wolf he confined and tamed through fear so long ago. In slaying the wolf, he sets the dog free.

Free again to come and go, yet still pleased to stay. This time, the dog entity chooses to abide at the right hand of Heaven, bidding all the men and women and children to come and be healed, through his special intercession as one of God's creatures turned holy martyr.

—

PART FIVE

Bound for Freedom:
The Paradox of the Leash

J UST THIS MORNING OUT MY WINDOW, I saw a man trying to stop
and smell a rosebush, until his dog pulled so impatiently on the
leash that the man was dragged away. Next, a fat jogger ran by, with an
equally fat Lab in tow, both breathing laboriously. And finally, I
watched a young Filipina nanny escort her employers' huge Neapolitan
Mastiff down the street, as nervous as a woman trundling a bomb in a
wheelbarrow.

All of these sights—seen in a matter of seconds, I swear—argue to the
increasing integration of pets, particularly dogs, into our lives. Critics of
that trend would say that the dogs I saw out my window are far too much
in control of their owners' lives, as well as public space.

Yet whatever your perspective on dogs and other animals in contemporary urban society, you probably agree that humans are actually the ones
still in charge. We're the ones who will go on deciding what's best for them
and for us. Whether it's regulations to govern the size of fishbowls, leash
laws for housecats, or legislation regarding the treatment of apes in
Spain—or, for that matter, legislation regarding the treatment of *bulls* in
Spain—the ways we deal with animals will continue to require us to walk
them, on leash, into deeper and deeper ethical thickets.

Paradoxically, whatever measure of freedom animals enjoy is predicated on human control. For that reason, debates about nature versus
nurture, or rights versus obligations, or moral responsibility versus mental
competence will always be held on their behalf, not with their involvement.

As directly affected as animals are by what we decide for them, they will never be what George W. Bush might term the "deciders."

I

ACCORDING TO HISTORIAN WENDY DONIGER, "The ideal state of humans among animals in not one in which wild animals become tame. It is a state in which a human becomes one of the animals." Maybe that's not the ideal of every human, but it's probably safe to say most animals would agree with Doniger. Having it our way—obliging the animals among us to become, if not tame, at least under our control—has not necessarily been to their benefit.

At some level, most of us are aware of that. One way we deal with the guilt it engenders in us, both as individuals and as a species, is by making arbitrary distinctions among the animals involuntarily under our aegis. A few, we take into our homes and hearts, as proof of our goodwill toward all. But most we hold at a distance—and sometimes in disdain—in order to make it easier to use and even abuse them according to our needs and desires.

Perhaps no animal, wild or domestic, exemplifies the arbitrariness of our choices as readily as the pig. Certainly no other animal is as universally derided—and with less reason. Far from being "fat and lazy and extremely rude," according to his characterization in the song "Swinging on a Star," the pig is clean, benign, intelligent, affectionate, and—when not stuffed with nutrients and hormones intended to pack on the pounds—inclined to be trim.

Though there is no good reason that swine are maligned, there is a good explanation: we like to eat them. So much that, over millennia, we've converted the pig from a forest boar, living happily in a pack, to the bloated, lethargic, swill-encrusted, sedentary animal of song and story.

Nowadays, even that popular image of the pig, wallowing in his pen as he roots noisily with his snout, is idealized. Pigs who live—or exist, anyway—on what are called "intensive" farms don't get much chance to root or wallow, or to come in contact with honest dirt. Nor do they spend much time hanging out with their fat friends.

From birth to death—often a short trip—today's pigs live under a regime of high hormone intake and rigid constriction in cramped separate stalls, sometimes numbering thousands to a barn, and overly heated to keep the animals lethargic. Procedures like tail-docking, castration, and snapping off tusks are performed on juvenile animals without anaesthetic.

Still at a young age, most get unpacked from the barn in order to be repackaged for transport by truck or freight car. This can mean confinement for days on the road without food or water or shelter or shade. Eventually, those who survive the trip arrive at a facility where—if they're lucky—they will be accorded the kind of "good death" that meets the humane standards set by Temple Grandin. The best moment, possibly for many of them, saved for the last.

In many ways, a dog is not unlike a pig. Both are of roughly equal intelligence, amenable to training, and capable of great affection. The main difference between them resides in the way humans have chosen to treat each species.

However, in the view of animal ethicist James Serpell, the existence of a companion animal is hardly more natural than that of livestock. "The inconsistencies inherent in our treatment of these two separate classes of domestic animals are only paradoxical when it is assumed that both types of treatment are normal. The contradictions are resolved by viewing either extreme or the other as odd, unusual, exceptional and therefore unimportant in the overall scheme of things."

The dog, it seems, has profited at the expense of the pig. Treating the dog well—in those lucky instances where he is well-treated—enables us to treat the pig poorly. In effect, we punish the pig for appealing to our palate, just as we reward the dog for appealing more to our visual aesthetic—and, at least in most cultures, appealing less to our tastebuds.

Pigs also have the misfortune to be extremely similar to human beings in physiological and genetic structure. This makes them ideal heart-valve donors, as well as military training "models" for battle-field medical tactics. According to *The New York Times*, pigs are routinely anaesthetized, shot, and even set on fire, before being "stabilized" by American army medics in training. (In Canada, at a training base in Suffield, Alberta, military spokespeople have assured the media that pigs wounded for those kinds of simulated battlefield scenarios are tranquilized before undergoing general anaesthesia, and are only *surgically* wounded, as opposed to shot or burned.)

The genetic structure of dogs is also remarkably similar to ours. Just as frequently as pigs, dogs are used as experimental subjects for medical research, product testing, and invasive cognitive studies. Yet for most people, the image of a beagle puppy wide-eyed in terror in the lab is a far more affecting symbol of unacceptable suffering than a passed-out pig being pumped full of bullets by an army medic.

Over the centuries, we have done a good job of desensitizing ourselves to pigs as objects of legitimate concern. Perhaps the increasing amount of love, money, and media attention our society lavishes on dogs is proportional to the degree to which we've increasingly diminished, depersonalized, and distanced ourselves from swine.

But even designating pigs as "appropriate victims" (as Carol J. Adams has called them) has not rescued humankind from historical ambivalence about them. In her exhaustive study of the treatment of pigs in medieval Europe, Claudine Fabre-Vassas digs down into the motives of Christians who punished Jews for abstaining from pork.

"By a complete turnaround," Fabre-Vassas writes, "the Jew bears the burden of the question that is always hovering over Christian homes, where issues concerning the consumption of this so human-seeming animal are so definitely unsettled."

In other cultures, ambivalence about eating pigs has expressed itself in other ways. The Negrito women of Malaysia traditionally made pets of piglets, and even suckled them, much as Ainu women in Japan nursed the bear cub they would later help kill. However, among the Negrito, young animals reared this way were never slaughtered and eaten, like other swine.

Among some tribes of New Guinea, women also treated young pigs like babies. But their men, holding different views, would periodically kill, cook, and serve their wives' piglets to honoured male guests.

Not surprisingly, anthropologists found that relationships between the sexes in these New Guinea tribes were generally strained. The women lived separately from the men—perhaps not only to signal their disap-proval of the way their pets were treated, but also to draw some physical distinction between the locations in which pigs were reared and the place where they were killed and eaten.

In *Charlotte's Web*, as previously mentioned, E. B. White presents pig slaughter as an inevitable fact of twentieth-century American farm life. But the author does allow Wilbur, the runty piglet, to buck the inheri-tance to which every member of his kind is supposedly heir. Why?

Perhaps Wilbur's singularity—the exception made of him by a spider clever enough to weave his praises into her web—is merely that: an excep-tion that underscores the inexorability of the rule. While not sacrificed through slaughter, Wilbur is made special in another way, by being pro-claimed so in words, and thus spared the fate of the rest of the herd.

In some cultures, there is a practical connection between hunting and pet-keeping. In a study of Amazonian Indians, anthropologist Philippe Erikson observes that "pets help future hunters acquire basic ethological knowledge and . . . provide an elegant solution to the ethical dilemma faced by people whose livelihood depends on the periodic enterprise of killing animals. . . . Feeding some members of animal species certainly makes eating others appear more legitimate." Also, prey animals, once tamed, can act as a lure to bring others of their kind within the range of hunters' arrows or spears.

Sometimes, the act of sparing can itself be a form of sacrificial offer-ing—as in the Old Testament story of Abraham and his son Isaac. Abra-ham was prepared to offer his only son to God, until God intervened to cancel the sacrifice He had demanded. A hapless ram was hastily substi-tuted for Isaac, as proof of Abraham's good intentions. (In the Koran, Ibrahim's son Ishmael is similarly spared from sacrifice, when Allah settles for the substitution of an animal. To this day, an annual ritual slaughter of goats and cows occurs across the Islamic world during the festival of Eid ul Azha, in commemoration of Ibrahim's near-sacrifice—and Allah's sparing—of his son.)

Even in a secular sense, the concept of sparing has enormous currency.

A powerful recent example appeared in media coverage of the 2001 foot-and-mouth disease outbreak among livestock in Britain.

Three and a half million cattle, sheep, and pigs were slaughtered in an effort to stem the tide of infection, and their carcasses disposed of through burning on enormous pyres. Haunting film footage and stark photos of those smouldering piles of animals—stiffened legs clearly discernible among the flames—pervaded television and newspapers. Billows of smoke across the countryside added a quality of pestilence to an already-grim scene.

Among few "good news" stories in that dark period was the discovery in a Devonshire slaughterhouse of one small Charolais calf, still alive under a pile of corpses awaiting disposal. According to some reports, the calf was attempting to nurse on her dead mother, and would shortly have succumbed to starvation, had she not been found—by the very farmer who had given her and her mother up to slaughter.

In contravention of the rules, farmer Philip Board and his family took the calf back home. They bottle-fed her and fought off attempts by authorities to have her returned to the place of execution.

In an interview with the BBC, Farmer Board said he'd initially thought of calling the calf "Lucky." But then, he said, the name "'Phoenix' just came into my head because of all the pyres of dead cattle around us." From a media perspective, the choice of such a regenerative name couldn't have been better.

With journalists and camera crews sparking the outcry, Britons rallied around Phoenix, and importuned the government to spare her life. The pleas to exempt one small but symbolic calf turned into a general clamour to end the preventive slaughter of livestock in response to the epidemic.

Phoenix *was* spared, and went on to have at least four calves of her own. (What has happened to her in recent years, I haven't been able to discover. However, it seems likely that—being a beef cow—Phoenix may at some point keep that deferred date with the abattoir, unless the Board family decides to extend her special status indefinitely.)

In her book *Animal*, British scholar Erica Fudge points up the irony at the centre of the Phoenix story: despite the widespread carnage caused by attempts to end the foot-and-mouth outbreak—and ignoring the fact that cattle in their millions are slaughtered routinely for consumption in Britain—the media invariably referred to the British public as "a nation of animal lovers" for rising up to defend the right to life of this particular calf. It was as if the high-profile sparing of one served to countervail the inglorious deaths of all the nameless others.

For his study of animal abuse stories that make for good media campaigns—so-called "beautiful cases"—sociologist Arnold Arluke interviewed publicists and marketers at various humane societies and animal shelters in the US. Arluke determined that a "poster pet" needs the right sort of physical appeal and the right kind of background story. As well, the animal has to have an appealing name.

In one case, a dog who was ideal in every other respect had come to the shelter with an unfortunate name. "Lusty" was quickly rechristened "Hope," and the campaign machinery began to roll.

Had that small Charolais calf in Devon been presented to the British public with the moniker "Lucky," would she have appealed as powerfully to the press as a symbol of hope to rally around? Possibly not. One animal viewed as merely lucky is, at best, media fodder for a single news cycle. A calf named "Phoenix," on the hand, summons powerful images, both ancient and modern, of miraculous rebirth from the flames, of regeneration on a national scale.

MODERN HOUSE PETS such as dogs and cats are, in most cases, the descendants of entire species singled out for special treatment. Some others—like tame birds or reptiles—may have originated with individual members of a species spared the fate of the rest of their kind. But for what sort of life have we singled out these special animals?

In *Dominance and Affection: The Making of Pets*, Chinese-born scholar Yi-Fu Tuan looks across the spectrum of our development and treatment of numerous animal species. In four basic ways, he says, we've tinkered with the biological makeup of the animals we've chosen to tame not for consumption but companionship.

First, we have diminished their size. The word "pet" is itself a diminutive of "petite." Next, we've tampered with their sexuality through neutering, both to control their numbers and their behaviour. Third, we've selectively bred them for a less wild appearance—softer fur, for example, or spotted coats instead of solid colours.

And perhaps most importantly, we've sought to foster juvenile traits that make them seem submissive rather than threatening: rounded muzzles, large neotenous eyes, floppy ears, even smaller teeth than their non-domestic counterparts.

As well, we have made certain pet species the focus of particularly intensive breeding techniques to produce variations of all kinds, both practical and aesthetic. The dog is the best—or the worst—example of an entire species subjected to our mania for manipulation. And within that species, the Pekinese is a prime example of a breed created to represent an ideal.

Tuan's description of how the so-called "lion dog of Peking" was developed is a sometimes grisly cavalcade of breeding and mutilation. To produce the flat face—meant to recall artists' depictions of a lion that allegedly trotted after the Buddha like a lapdog—reputable breeders patiently selected for this characteristic through successive generations. However, unscrupulous members of the profession, unwilling to wait, would break the unformed cartilage of an infant Pekingese's nose, or tie tight bands around its head to squash the face.

The creation of the Peke's characteristic rolling gait—again, supposedly leonine—was partly achieved through stunting puppies in cages to bow their legs. It's impossible not to draw a comparison to similarly brutal techniques used in the Chinese courts to modify the human female foot to conform to the "lotus" ideal.

These crude practices were by no means exclusive to China, nor confined to the benighted past. Today, they find their modern equivalents in genetic tinkering which sometimes produces physical characteristics deemed "desirable" at the expense of a dog's ability to live a healthy life. Bulldog breeds, for instance, are notorious for their respiratory problems and their inability to deliver their pups naturally.

As certain breeds become too popular—Collies and Golden Retrievers, for example—they also become overly inbred, which increases the risk of congenital disorders like hip dysplasia and optical problems. On puppies of numerous other breeds, surgical alterations like the "trimming" of ears and "docking" of tails are still performed, not always under anaesthetic.

In an essay called "Companion Animals as Mediators," James Serpell questions the means we've employed to turn pets into "cultural artifacts, incapable of existence outside the human domain. By doing this...we not only turn a blind eye to the welfare of these animals, we simultaneously destroy their capacity to mediate [i.e. between us and other animals] on our behalf."

Paul Shepard takes an even darker view. "Pets are no part of human evolution or the biological context out of which our ecology comes. They are civilized paraphernalia...ambiguous tyranny.... Indeed, the domestication of animals has never ensured their tender care. In recent Anglo-American tradition the dog is 'man's best friend,' but it is abhorred in the Bible. In Muslim tradition the dog's saliva is noxious and contact between people and dogs requires ritual cleansing..."

The situation, he contends, only gets worse: "Even modern pets are property that is bought, sold, 'put down,' and neutered. Pets are deliberately abandoned by the millions and necessitate city-run slaughterhouses, shelters, and 'placement' services...."

Like James Serpell, Shepard puts the blame on our failure to find within pets a way to get ourselves back to the natural world that pre-dates our enslavement of any animal species. "The pet," Paul Shepard concludes, "cannot restore us to wholeness any more than an artificial limb renews the original; nor can it do more than simulate the Others among whom our ancestors lived for so long.... They are monsters...biological slaves...wholly unlike the wild world."

However much we might reject a designation like "monsters" to describe the pet animals we love, it's difficult to dispute Shepard's indictment of our terrible inconsistency. Without doubt, the earliest humans sacrificed animals in ritual ways I find abhorrent, and dealt with their own ambivalence through methods that seem to me bizarre. Nevertheless, when compared with the spasmodic nature of a modern "pet-crazy" culture that alternately embraces and rejects the animals in our midst, the ancient methods at least seem small-scale, personal, and sincere.

We, on the other hand, are disingenuous when we pretend it is our pets who control us. In truth, more now that at any previous point in human history, the very existence of the animals we've claimed to befriend is left entirely to our arbitrary whim.

Despite similar concerns, James Serpell ends his book *In the Company of Animals* on a more hopeful note. Like Shepard, he ponders what he calls the "paradox" of pet-keeping. But he suggests that pets have actually played a role in the "downfall" of the notion of human superiority.

"For when we elevate companion animals to the status of persons," Serpell writes,

> It becomes obvious that the notion of human superiority is a phantom: a dangerous egotistical myth that currently threatens our survival. Ironically, as the forerunner of livestock domestication, pet-keeping led us to our present destructive phase of history. Perhaps by making us more aware of our biological affinities with animals and the natural world, it will help lead us out again.

To me, it's significant that Serpell chooses to consider pets not as frivolous luxuries, or as evidence only of the horrors of human caprice, but as potential saviours of a species in danger of self-destruction through its own hubris. He looks ahead to some unspecified catastrophe from whose brink only animals can lead us—back to that point in history when it was for his usefulness to man that the household pet was most highly prized.

II

I IMAGINE MYSELF SETTLED in a back pew of a church in one of the many villages where the itinerant Dominican cleric, Stephen of Bourbon, might plausibly have dropped by to deliver one of his famous pronouncements against consorting with demons. In my mind's ear, I am doing my best to listen to his sermon the way those parishioners would have taken it in, more than seven centuries ago, in a remote backwater of a country not yet incorporated as "France."

"One day," Stephen begins, translating rapidly into the vernacular from his own Latin text, "when the lord and lady had gone out of the house, and the nurse had done likewise, leaving the baby alone in the cradle..." *Alone?*

Whoops. Already, I've reverted to my twenty-first century sensibility, and have been stopped short by words that sound unthinkable to a modern ear. The mother, the father, and the baby's nurse all off for the day, leaving an infant unattended in his cradle? My God, what could these people have been thinking? Asphyxiation on a crib toy, a violent stomach cramp, Sudden Infant Death Syndrome...surely any and all of these were as likely—likelier!—back then as today.

"...a huge serpent," Stephen is explaining, as I struggle to tune back in, "entered the house and approached the baby's cradle." Well, sure. A giant snake. Why not? Probably a commonplace event, in those days. But hey, no reason for all the responsible adults in the house *not* to go out, leaving the child to the mercies of every passing reptile.

"Seeing this, the greyhound, which had remained behind, chased the serpent and, attacking it beneath the cradle, upset the cradle and bit the serpent all over, which defended itself, biting the dog equally severely." The greyhound, *which had remained behind....* Ah!

Now, in the space of four short words, I suddenly grasp what would have been evident all along to Stephen's contemporaries: the child has not been left alone, at least not entirely. A dog has been posted at his cradle, precisely to deal with this sort of venomous invasion.

"Finally, the dog killed it and threw it well away from the cradle. The cradle, the floor, the dog's mouth and head were all drenched in the serpent's blood. Although badly hurt by the serpent, the dog remained on guard beside the cradle."

All in a day's work, in other words, for the valiant family dog. One demon dispatched, he continues on watch, in the event of any other—But wait. There's more to Stephen's story, it seems.

"When the nurse came back and saw all this she thought that the dog had devoured the child, and let out a scream of misery. Hearing it the child's mother also ran up, looked, thought the same thing, and screamed too. Likewise the knight, when he arrived, thought the same thing and drew his sword and killed the dog."

No! I'm wrong. Dispatching a serpent was *not* all in a normal day's work for this dog. Otherwise, the nurse would have immediately suspected why the dog was covered in blood. The knight, when he arrived on the scene, would have immediately looked for clues, instead of damning the dog, no questions asked.

"But the peasants," Stephen goes on, "hearing of the dog's conduct and of how it had been killed, although innocent, and for a deed for which it might have expected praise, visited the place, honoured the dog as a martyr, prayed to it when they were sick or in need of something…"

That at least is straightforward enough. Except, maybe, just there at the end, when the dog makes that transition from a creature wrongly slain to a full-scale intercessor whose resting place is a destination of pilgrimage for the ailing and the needy.

"Above all, though, it was women with sick or weak children who took them to this place. When they arrived, they would make offerings of salt and other things; they would hang their babies' swaddling-clothes on the bushes roundabout; they would drive nails into the trees which had grown in this place; they would pass the naked babies between the trunks of two trees—the mother, on one side, held the baby and threw it nine times to the old woman, who was on the other side. Invoking the demons, they called upon the fauns in the forest of Rimite to take the sick, feeble child which, they said, was theirs, and to return their child that the fauns had taken away, fat and well, safe and sound."

There. That's the exact spot in the woods where I become completely and entirely lost. The precise moment in the narrative when an ancient and oh-so-familiar story of a dog, a cradle, a baby, and a serpent becomes intimately associated with a particular cult in a particular part of France at a particular point in the Middle Ages. What can a martyred greyhound possibly have to do with esoteric rites, in which fauns and satyrs and fairies of the forest are beseeched to return healthy babies illicitly replaced in their cribs by sickly changelings?

That would not be a matter of puzzlement for Stephen of Bourbon. Stephen and the congregations to which he preached took for granted knowledge of a common practice of the time and place which, more than seven centuries later, is all but obsolete.

"The presence of the dog," explains Jean-Claude Schmitt, in *The Holy Greyhound*, "recalls one of the protective measures customarily taken against changelings, in which an animal, generally a dog, is left near the cradle."

And there it is. The explanation of why the only child of a nobleman would be left slumbering in the sole care of the family dog.

It wasn't the likelihood of a marauding snake or a wolf or even a human intruder that prompted the master to leave his dog at the baby's cradle. It wasn't only the greyhound's skill and courage that proclaimed him "so useful" a dog. It was his value as a deterrent of demons bent on making mischief by substituting sickly children for healthy ones.

Even long after the notion of changelings had gone out of style, Jean-Claude Schmitt tells us, the ritual invocation of the dog known as St. Guinefort continued, as always. As late as the 1970s, when Schmitt visited that region of the Dombes, he interviewed adults who could recall as children being brought for healing to that same spot in those woods near the mill-course at Crosat, not far from the banks of the Chalaronne.

Every one of them cited the story of the greyhound, the snake, and the cradle as the starting point for the superstitious rite. No mere ornament to the family hearth, the dog, then as now, was most valued when he paid his way with loyal service. Even after he was proclaimed a "saint," the faithful continued to regard Guinefort as an animal created and designed to be a helper to man.

———◦•◦•◦———

THE CHRONIC CARE WARD of any hospital is a sobering place. Many patients aren't so much hopelessly ill as just hopelessly old. Their families are mostly dead or dispersed, their spouses long since buried or bitterly forgotten, their peer group gradually edging toward extinction. The young—in some cases even their own—are uninterested in spending time in the company of someone whose vital presence has long since fled, leaving only a husk of humanity behind.

For some, this hospital ward is the last stop on the road, bypassing the seniors' residences that, somehow or other, never wound up figuring in their calculations. For others, the dream of eventually returning home lingers—or at least the hope of graduating to a room of one's own. For all, days and nights are a constant barrage of compromise and impingement: the din of the TV set attached to the next bed; the proximity of someone else's garrulous visitors; the pervasiveness of the odour of someone else's lunch tray or bedpan, or incipient death.

Into a world like this, ambulatory and energetic life enters like the proverbial shaft of light into a tomb. It's life, in this case, in the shape of my effervescent friend Kelly and her two dogs, Porter and Lucy, whom she brings once a week to make the rounds of the Chronic Care Ward.

Porter is a particularly large and calm Shetland Sheepdog, with gentle-manly manners and an air of sincere concern. Lucy, the West Highland Terrier, is a peppery little soul—sharp, alert, and utterly dominating, despite her size. At least, that's how she is in her home environment, ruling a household of two human adults, several cats, innumerable tropical fish—and Porter, of course.

When we reach the first of the four-bed wards on Kelly's regular roster, Lucy immediately makes for Merle, a small porcelain doll of a woman, with a sad, furrowed brow. As soon as Kelly lifts her up onto the bed, Lucy sprawls on her back in Merle's frail arms and remains there until Kelly returns to collect her at the end of her rounds.

"I always ask people first whether they want me to bring the dogs over to see them. I never let the dogs stay too long with any one person—well, except for Merle. Lucy will lie like that for as long as I let her, and it really does seem to do Merle a world of good."

As Porter makes the rounds with Kelly, he gives anybody who wants it the benefit of his vast benevolence. He'll crawl into their beds to cuddle, if that's what they seem to crave. In the case of one stroke victim who moans "No, no, no" over and over, he elects to position himself next to her wheelchair and lick her hand in endless consolation.

"God!" A skeletally thin but still beautiful woman named Mary rolls her eyes in the direction of the moaning woman. "I wish she'd damn well knock it off."

When Porter comes over, Mary holds out one of her rail-thin hands, deeply tanned and wrinkled like brown crepe paper. She is more interested in telling her own tale than patting Porter. Still, the dog provides a way into that conversation with me, a newcomer.

Mary turns her arresting blue eyes on me as she recollects how her adult son's dog was run over. "He phoned me right away, and he was crying. Crying like a little boy."

Later, I learn that in the six years Mary has been in the Chronic Care Ward, her son—in faraway Vancouver—has never once come to visit. But you'd never know that from her tone. It's her beloved son, of course, whom she wants to talk about. Yet Porter is the place to start, and pet stories are the way to go forward into reminiscences that actually have little to do with dogs.

When we arrive at the men's ward, Porter heads to a spot between two wizened old men, sitting side by side in silence. One is Greek; the other, who I'm guessing is Polish, takes a firm grip on Porter's muzzle. As he holds and strokes and croons sweet Slavic nothings to the dog, the other old man—apparently oblivious to his fellow patient—also leans over, to murmur to Porter in Greek, equally convinced the dog understands him if no one else does.

Once back in the room where we started, we find Lucy still lying motionless in the arms of silent, sorrowful Merle. Two other patients chat as they watch TV. The fourth woman lies in bed, looking on, but apart from the proceedings.

She doesn't get any visitors, she says, even though her children live within easy distance of the hospital. When I ask, she flatly refuses to have Porter lifted up onto her bed. But then, as if not wanting to lose my good-will, she starts to tell me about a Cocker Spaniel from her childhood. "It was my dad's dog, actually," she corrects herself. "Wouldn't let anybody get between it and Dad."

Like the dog who had belonged to Mary's son, the spaniel was run over. Right in the driveway, she recalls, by the next-door neighbour. "Of course, it was an accident. But we couldn't eat our supper that night, we were so upset."

I sense it's important to her to make clear that she cared—if not about the dog, per se, then certainly about that long-ago family group arranged morosely around the supper table. Like Mary's story, this recollection has little to do with the dog's misfortune.

Still, it is an illustration of the different ways therapy dogs work on different patients. For those who love animals, there are straightforward physiological and psychological effects, including a slowed heart rate and a cheered outlook.

For those who don't, the benefits may be of a less obvious kind. Porter and Lucy's presence has prompted this woman to rummage her memory for a reminiscence she thinks will interest a stranger who seems interested in dogs. And even a memory culminating in death in the family driveway comes from a better time, a more companionable place.

Once their shift is up, Porter and Lucy flop down in the back seat of the car, evidently exhausted from hours of being cuddled and coddled and stroked and exclaimed over in a number of languages. As sociable as they are, this weekly trip to the Chronic Care Ward constitutes work for them.

As soon as they get back home, however, they revive and revert to the self-directed house pets I recognize: mooching for scraps, standing alert and ready to growl at neighbourhood noises, or nosing over their toes the way dogs do, to make sure all are present and accounted for.

Kelly has a demanding life beyond her weekly volunteer stint. We talk about how hard it is to shrug off the sad confinement of the people we've just been with, and return to a pace that may be hectic but is at least satisfying. For us, it's impossible not to identify with people who could be—perhaps inevitably will be—us, somewhere down the line.

For Kelly's dogs, however, there seems no space within this present moment for introspection, or backward reflection. In their minds, there may well not be room to extrapolate from the bleakness of where they've just been to the likely shape of their own unspecified future.

Perhaps that's what makes many pets so much better at this kind of work than many people are: offering empathy that takes no lasting toll, lending presence devoid of ego. Giving exactly what is needed in the moment, taking nothing away that won't be forgotten after a good night's sleep. Above all, relying on us to value the currency in which they pay their way.

THE IDEA OF ANIMALS AS THERAPY for humans is nothing new. More than two hundred years ago, British Quakers opened the York Retreat as a progressive antidote to the lunatic asylums of the day, and offered their patients gardens populated by rabbits, poultry, and other small domestic animals as alternatives to locked cells.

In 1844, invalid poet Elizabeth Barrett published a poem dedicated to the tireless sick-room vigilance of her Cocker Spaniel, Flush: "But of thee it shall be said, This dog watched beside a bed Day and night unweary." Less than two decades later, Florence Nightingale's "Notes on Nursing" included the recommendation that "a small pet animal is often an excellent companion for the sick, or long chronic cases, especially."

In the United States, it wasn't until the 1940s that pet therapy caught on in any official way. And only in the last couple of decades has recognition of the measurable physiological and benefits of animals to the physically and mentally ill and the aged truly become commonplace across the Western world.

For one thing, animals' medicinal kit includes the soothing balm of a particular kind of silence—benign, companionable, non-judgmental. At least, that's how most pet-lovers describe the wordless support they feel from animals and how they choose to interpret it.

For whatever reason, the positive medical effects of pets on everything from cardiovascular health, attitude toward treatment, prognosis for recovery, and general outlook have been conclusively demonstrated. Consequently, pet therapy has become a recognized industry, one labeled by Paul Shepard as "the corporate use of animals in health care."

And a huge industry it is, according to Shepard, encompassing vast breeding programs, development of "R and R" initiatives for clapped-out canine and other animal caregivers, and even support services to console long-term patients when their favourite therapy animals die. To Shepard, there are some positive elements for society in these increased opportunities for interaction with animals. However, he also expresses concern that "underneath there remains the shadow of utility, and the animal commodity dressed out as medical treatment."

That concern is part of Shepard's general discomfort with the net loss to animals by their incorporation—one might almost call it co-optation—into the industrialized, anthropocentric world. "Animals were present at the center of human life for thousands of centuries," he writes, "before anyone thought of taking them captive, making them companions, forming the 'friendship loops' of which animal-facilitation therapists and ethicists speak."

It's true, there does seem to be an enormous need in our culture not only to put pets at the centre of our lives, but also to justify their presence there by extolling their "helper" roles in the real-life medical, social, and personal dramas in which we humans star. This is especially so with dogs. As journalist Alison Gillmor pointed out in an article for *The Walrus* magazine, bookstore shelves buckling under the weight of bestsellers about dogs reflect our increasing tendency to regard them as teachers, social convenors, family therapists, and more.

Gillmor suggests that dogs offer a "reassuringly physical and direct" antidote to the rushed and transient nature of our urban culture. As well, there is their appeal as "blank slates" on which we can inscribe whatever we need. Dogs' ability to reflect us as we want to see ourselves no doubt accounts for innumerable memoirs about beloved dogs who saved the writer's emotional life in the wake of some personal cataclysm, and dogs whose gentle wisdom taught the true meaning of love, or Christmas, or family—or all three.

I would add the thought that the canine-as-mentor concept is also fuelled by the pressure animal lovers feel to defend their best friends against critics who decry the expense, belittle the sentimentality, and dismiss the anthropomorphism at the heart of pet ownership. In a culture that reckons worth in monetary terms and now cultivates consumerism the way previous generations inculcated good citizenship, a dog must not only pay his way in affection to his owner, he must also be seen to pay his way.

Just as shopping, jogging, cooking classes, yoga, fine dining, new hairstyles, and gardening now all come under the heading of "personal therapy," so too must pets. As a bonus, the demonstrated usefulness of animals in hospital and other clinical settings helps bolster the wider perception that pets are therapeutic by definition. If companion animals contribute to the well-being of their owners as well as the health of the patient community, such selling points can be—and are—marshalled as proof of their practical value to society at large.

III

A NUMBER OF YEARS AGO, I wrote a novel called *The Hidden Life of Humans*, which traces a relationship between a woman and a dog from mutual suspicion, through tentative cohabitation, to eventual acceptance on both sides of a fundamental bond. In part, I based the book on my own experiences with a wonderful but badly behaved dog left in my temporary custody.

Shannon was a Collie—a breed of dog jokingly ridiculed for its potential to "get lost at the end of a leash." But I didn't find Shannon in the least stupid. Full of phobias, okay. Inclined to hysteria, sure. Humper of legs, chewer-off of buttons, gnawer of crotches of panties left on the floor.... yes, yes, and yes again. He was all that and worse.

But he always struck me as a dog deliberately playing the part of the Dumb Blonde. Somewhere inside that narrow skull and its tightly-housed brain, I felt certain, he knew what I wanted. Just didn't want to give it to me. But surely with some training, he would.

I found a trainer named Bob, who was of the big, burly school of "hard" men still much in vogue at that time. A man of choke chains and reproving raps on the nose with the loop-end of the leash and sudden *volte-faces* south just as the dog was deciding to bolt north. Luckily, Bob deemed Shannon less in need of raps on the nose than immediate cessation of "coddling."

Eventually, Shannon stopped being terrified of elevators and open staircases. He gave up jumping on people while they were standing, and having simulated intercourse with their arms while they were sitting down. He could accompany me into stores without adverse incident. And in advance of people arriving in my home, it stopped being necessary to shut him away like that embarrassing brother-in-law who makes fart noises with his armpit.

True, he never totally got the hang of Recall when off-leash. But at least he got the point of the idea behind the leash, and helped me to see it for the paradox that it is. Therefore, when it came time for me to write my fictional dog Murphy's meditation on this theme, it was really Shannon I was paraphrasing—if not echoing, word for word:

> Why is it when she reaches my leash down from the shelf, I surge with such excitement? Even though the leash represents what reins me in as much as what sets me free. That's the mystery inherent in my leash, both my liberation and my oppression, my boonest companion and my strictest chaperone...
>
> Without my leash, let it be clearly understood, there is no such thing as a walk. Yet with my leash, there is no such thing as a walk on the wild side, ever. And for me, the wonder of that contradiction will never cease.

Of course, for other writers and other dogs, the leash may represent a different kind of bond. Rhoda Lerman writes in her book *In the Company of Newfies* about watching her dog Celeste "pick up a bright pink leash and walk around the driveway with it in her mouth, head held high, making believe she was on lead.... She creates a tether between us, holding me so I don't stray from her... She holds the leash in her mouth so we are holding each other... The leash is both faith and connection."

But for both parties, equally a symbol of freedom and restraint. After all, what we are asking of the animals most in our midst—particularly dogs—is a species of good citizenship in which we share. A contract that requires them to feel free to do what we want, thereby allowing us to do what they want while telling ourselves it's our own idea. License to be licensed, as you might say.

WOOFSTOCK, AN ANNUAL ONE-DAY EVENT in Toronto, is exactly what the name conjures up: a milling throng of mostly amiable souls on hand to gawk, groove, and take in the entertainment. Apart from far better weather here, the only real difference between this highly urban event and that iconic rainy-day love-in on Max Yasgur's farm is demographic: of Woofstock's approximately 300,000 attendees, half are dogs attached by leashes to the other half.

On a sunny Saturday in June, a length of several blocks of downtown Toronto is roped off to traffic, so that what promoters estimate to be about 150,000 dogs—roughly 50 percent of the entire canine population in the Greater Toronto Area—and attendant human personnel can wander at will. Or at least, to the length of their leashes.

The abundance of dogs is overwhelming. Big dogs in bandanas panting along the pavement, little dogs sporting peaked caps peering out of backpacks, medium-sized dogs being continually extended and retracted on their Flexi-leads like trout in play at a fly-fishing derby. Dogs stealing ice cream from kids; kids stealing ice cream from dogs. Small comedies of strangers becoming entangled in each other's leashes; small dramas of strangers failing to become disentangled from each other's leashes.

I spot a man carrying a beautiful Shiba Inu pup, so well-behaved in its owner's arms that its harness and leash seem superfluous. The puppy swivels its head left and right and back again, surveying its surroundings from the heights.

Suddenly, it dawns on me: the Shiba Inu is a robot. Why would someone bring it here, of all places? Although, come to think of it, in this crowd, a man with a fake dog in his arms seems less sadly deficient than those of us wandering around Woofstock with no dog at all.

In fact, Woofstock is so doggone dog-friendly, it seems to be about more than itself. Maybe a model for what urban Utopia might look like—perhaps from the perspective of a pet, as re-imagined through the eyes of its owner.

Yet, given the enormous numbers of humans and animals on the move, there is remarkably little aggression. The only dust-up I witness is between two humans: a couple, each with a small dog in tow. The man snaps at the woman and then turns on his heel, dragging his dog with him. Whereupon the woman picks up her dog, and heads off in the other direction. A moment or two later, I see them back together again. Still snarling at each other while the two little dogs, at the farthest extent of their leashes, pointedly pretend they're not with these people.

Dog trainer Dale Stavroff agrees about the remarkably high level of canine accord. With so many obviously untrained dogs in the company of so many apparently inexperienced owners, he says, it's almost miraculously harmonious.

Stavroff has flown in from British Columbia to promote his recently-published training book, *Let the Dog Decide*. Earlier in the day, I saw him on stage demonstrating his techniques on about a half-dozen "problem" dogs. One dog was billed as excessively shy; another was a biter; still another a jumper-upper.

Essentially, Stavroff dealt with all of them the same way: proffering chunks of cooked beef sausage, looking away from the dog until it was comfortable with eye contact, squatting down to lure the dog closer with more treats, quickly gaining its cooperation with positive reinforcement.

The idea, he explained, is to get the dog to choose good behaviours that come with a reward versus bad behaviours that don't. In *Let the Dog Decide* and in his website videos, he speaks of "compassionate compulsion"—a Zen koan if ever there was one. In fact, the very concept of "letting" the dog "decide" hints at the contradictions his method must straddle. Still, with its emphasis on positive reinforcement to draw out the dog's co-operation, Dale Stavroff's method is certainly on the benevolent end of the spectrum. He opposes techniques of outright mastery, such as throwing the dog on its back to assert your dominance, or positioning yourself as the "alpha" member of the pack.

This is in direct opposition to the leader-of-the-pack image cultivated by celebrated Mexican-American "dog-behaviour expert" Cesar Millan. Within canine society, Stavroff points out, alpha males and females come and go, and are always in danger of losing their dominant status to an up-and-comer. Instead, the role of the human in a household that includes dogs, he says, should be of the "wise elder" whose authority is ongoing and unassailable.

Millan is one of those success stories other trainers like to challenge— an alpha in the dog-trainer world constantly vulnerable to usurpation by his competitors. Although he writes little about Millan in his book, in conversation Stavroff is willing to make specific criticisms of the "old-fashioned stockman" image that has made Millan a star on National Geographic Television with *Dog Whisperer* and a bestselling author of a book that claims to "rehabilitate" dogs while training their owners.

According to Stavroff, Cesar Millan's philosophy is one of "dominance and push," successful only in fixing problems in the short-term and doomed finally to fail, once the "blow-back" occurs. What seems to bug Dale Stavroff most is that Millan "never talks about a positive result, like getting a dog to sit. He's always just stopping dogs from doing annoying things."

Dale Stavroff isn't the only dog-training expert who criticizes Millan for achieving short-term results that don't stick. Dr. Nicholas Dodman, a professor of animal behavioural studies at Tufts University, refers to Millan's methods—such as "flooding" a dog with what he already fears— as "inhumane."

Dr. Ian Dunbar, a British-born veterinarian and advocate of positive training methods for dogs, attacks Millan's pack-leader persona. "Dogs aren't wolves," Dunbar declared to the *San Francisco Chronicle* not long after the SPCA in that city petitioned the National Geographic Channel to stop running *Dog Whisperer* on the grounds that Millan's methods constituted "abuse."

Nor are dogs pack animals at all, according to San Francisco SPCA Academy for Dog Trainers founder Jean Donaldson. In a recent installment of the column she writes for *Dogs in Canada* magazine, Donaldson sought to explode that "behaviour myth" along with nine others, including another Cesar Millan favourite: the idea that letting a dog go ahead of you through a doorway gives it dominance.

Perhaps this struggle for dominance among dog-training experts is understandable. For one thing, their field has become one multi-million dollar arm of the almost fifty billion-dollar a year North American pet industry. Even more importantly, the conflicting and conflicted ways in which we view animals—as well as how we view ourselves—are bound to be reflected in the schools of thought on how they should be schooled.

Vicki Hearne, who died of cancer at a fairly young age in 2001, is remembered variously as a poet, a philosopher, a psychologist, and an old-fashioned animal person. Her views on training perfectly summarize the conflict between restraint, control, and conditioning on the one hand, and on the other all the Zen paradoxes inherent in letting the animal decide to do what you want. Each of those selves is on view in her books, of which *Adam's Task: Calling Animals by Name* is probably the most widely quoted and enduring.

Much of her philosophy of dog-training Hearne credits to William Koehler, long the chief trainer for Walt Disney Studios. For her, there was no question that Koehler was a genius when it came to dogs and how to acquire the appropriate mindset in order to deal with them. "Corrections in Koehler's vision," she declares early in *Adam's Task*, "are administered out of a deep respect for the dog's moral and intellectual capacities."

Similarly to Koehler, that notion of "respect" for Hearne rules out cooing and treats. "It is usually a diet of syrup, bribery and choked rhetoric, rather than physical abuse, that creates character disorders such as viciousness and megalomania in a dog. Biting is a response to incoherent authority."

Because she was also a philosopher and a poet, Hearne gets to fold in words like "rhetoric" and "incoherent" along with references to Wittgenstein's lion. Allusions to "shared language" and invocations of "respect" coexist in her work with some fairly old-school—and fairly aggressive—animal wrangling.

Her writing is far more literary than Cesar Millan's, and heavily peppered with quotes from writers and philosophers Millan may never have heard of. Still, like him, Hearne manages to make an old-fashioned I'm-in-charge approach okay, by plugging it into the owner's brain in a new-age animal-centred of way.

While advocating for his tough tactics, Millan salves the consciences of soft-hearted, pet-sensitive owners by insisting that America's dogs are "suffering" from "lack of leadership," and long only for some common sense at the other end of the leash. Hearne successfully soothes the same animal-loving liberals by depicting punishment as "respect" for the dog's essence and "coherent authority" as a more satisfying reward than a cookie.

When setting out to train a Pointer named Salty, Hearne cures the dog's tendency to dig holes by filling the holes with water and immersing Salty's head in them until she is gasping for air. "This has nothing to do with either punishment or authority," Hearne assures the potentially squeamish reader, "and if it is corrupted by either, then it becomes cruel."

Hearne goes on to correct other unacceptable behaviour by pinching Salty's ear so that "she screeches with the sting and indignation of it." Which, if it is not punishment, certainly comes close enough to merit a cigar.

In specific moments, Hearne's viewpoint can be expressed in ways that slip out of reach even as you read the words. For example, her opinion of what constitutes animal rights: "This is the first right, the right from which all others follow, for them and for us, the right to be believed in, a philosophical right to freedom of speech, the right to say things the philosopher has not taught them or us how to say."

Or, if philosophy fails, you can always pinch their ear or immerse their face in a hole full of muddy water and as deep as respect.

"You're not actually a psychologist, are you?" Deborah Solomon asked Cesar Millan in her weekly interview column in *The New York Times Magazine*.

"No. Not by a school," answered Millan. "There is no college that teaches you how to control a pack of dogs."

Yet, by setting up his Dog Psychology Center in Los Angeles, Millan has invited the inference that there's more to developing the "calm assertiveness of a natural pack leader" than always preceding your dog through the door. At the same time, the emphasis on the "natural" is an integral part of a mystique calculated to lull uptight, uncomfortable, urban dog owners to see themselves out there on the mountain slope, running at the head of the pack.

However, that's not the reality of the lives of most of the dogs and owners Millan or any other trainer deals with. Today's "pack of dogs" usually comes at the end of a bunch of leashes held in the hand of a paid dog-walker, or else meets up during off-leash hours in the dog-designated area of their neighbourhood park.

THE PUBLIC INFORMATION MEETING in the lobby of City Hall in Toronto is entitled "People, Dogs & Parks." Of those three, only people are actually in evidence to discuss the logistics of creating new off-leash areas in Toronto. This is a city with about two and a half million humans in its greater urban area, at least 250,000 dogs, 1,500 parks, only thirty-two off-leash areas, and at this point no "harmonized strategy" as the Parks and Environment Committee likes to put it, for creating more places for dogs to run free without pissing off others in the park.

Of such widespread concern among dog owners, parents of small children, and other park enthusiasts is this issue of off-leash areas, that neither the temptation of a beautiful, bright, early June evening, nor the telecast of what will turn out to be the final game of the Stanley Cup hockey series can serve to keep a couple of hundred people from showing up at City Hall. And this downtown session is only one of several similar meetings in the Greater Toronto Area. Clearly, when it comes to People, Dogs & Parks, Torontonians are there.

What also becomes clear only minutes into this information meeting is how carefully it is controlled. Much like a well-run off-leash area. People are invited to speak up, but only within "breakout" groups, urged to break out but only within the confines of the stated rules, and encouraged to run with some fresh ideas but only so far and for so long, before they're reeled back in on their figurative Flexi-leads.

In fact, the Parks and Environment Committee already seems to have a pretty good idea of what it wants to recommend to City Council, with respect to what kind of parks make for good off-leash areas, how the dog-owning community should be involved in the development of rules, and who exactly is going to enforce those rules in a large urban area with no existing policy already in place and an increasingly cash-strapped administrative budget.

Onstage is a facilitator with some PowerPoints outlining what she calls "Rules of the Pool." ("Rule one: Show Respect; Rule Two: One Conversation at a Time"...) Meanwhile, each of the tables at which participants sit awaiting the cue to break out into small-group discussion has been supplied with a Parks Department employee as a mini facilitator.

Carol, the facilitator at the table I've joined, says she'll soon leave her desk job as Parks Supervisor Horticultural in order to spend each workday traveling the entire extent of the Toronto waterfront with three Border Collies she's trained to disperse the overly-aggressive Canada Geese who frequent the Lake Ontario shoreline. Carol doesn't take her Border Collies to off-leash areas in any of the city's parks, because there are so many badly-behaved dogs.

A disabled man at the same table agrees. Richard tells us his assistance-dog Piper gets hassled so much by other dogs in the local park, they've given up going there. Piper is at this meeting—a black Labrador lying on the floor behind Richard's wheelchair. We learn that Piper can open the fridge and bring Richard a Coke or beer, or the phone, or anything else that he needs. The Lab can even do laundry. Surely someone who works as hard as Piper deserves a little no-hassle time in the park.

Of course, we humans on hand are working hard right now too, to resolve these contentious questions that arise in off-leash areas. Ironically, our labour is mainly for the benefit of underemployed urban dogs with too little exercise and nothing to do. These are not canine helpers dispersing geese or fetching Cokes for a man who can't walk, but typical house pets who need somewhere designated to go, in order to run around in groups—in wistful simulation of the wild state their kind enjoyed, long before there were parks or even people with a roster-sheet of tasks useful to humans that dogs might sign up for, such as hunting, herding, hauling, or guarding the cradle.

The break-out discussion now turns to creating designated areas for dogs, and how to separate those from areas dedicated to kids. Geoff, a young parent with a lawyerly manner, is all for proper enforcement of separation of children and dogs. His daughter, he says, had a "negative experience" with a dog on the loose. Mark, a dog owner, is also a parent. Sounding a bit harried—even a tad hysterical—from the pressure of multiple demands, he declares himself dead-set against splitting up exercise time for his dog and kids. He wants to be able to "wear out" all of his charges on the same outing to the park, in the same area.

This notion of needing to make provision to wear out ourselves and our pets is unique to modern society—and affluent society at that. In an earlier time in Toronto, Mark's children would have found themselves sufficiently exhausted by chimney sweeping, or changing bobbins at the woolen mill. Their dog, meanwhile, would be condemned to pull a cart until he dropped in the shafts, or run himself to a shadow turning the spit at the family hearth.

Almost a month later to the day, Council approves new rules for off-leash areas in Toronto parks. According to the newspapers, everything in the resolution that passed is virtually identical to the proposals in the handouts distributed by the Parks and Environment Committee on that warm June night, when summer sunlight and hockey both took a back-seat to the question of canine freedom and human rights. However, Council's enthusiasm for the proposed plan is tempered by the observation that "there may be no funds in the 2008 budget for the one-million dollar cost."

Bob Dylan once observed: "If dogs run free, then what must be, Must be and that is all." Well, maybe not quite all. In today's urban society, it seems if dogs run free, it's not *for* free.

WITH ALL URBAN PETS, there exists a tension between freeing them to play the role of the untrammeled Other in our lives, and the need to rid them of whichever aspects of their untamed Otherness don't work for us. Nowhere is the contradictory quality of that relationship more in evidence than in the way we elect to spend our money on them.

According to statistics from the US Census Bureau for 2007, pet ownership is booming in the United States. More than 60 percent of all households have at least one pet. (In Canada, census figures for the same year are roughly similar, with Canadians showing a slight preference for cats over dogs as compared to their American neighbours)

In 2007, American consumers spent a record forty-nine billion dollars on all pet products and services combined—fifteen billion dollars more than a mere two years before. Since at least 2004, pet-related expenditures have comprised one of the largest sectors of the US economy—exceeding what is spent on home hardware, jewelry, or candy in that same year. And the billions spent on pet food alone easily surpass the amount of money Americans spend on baby food.

In fact, apart from computer electronics, pet products are the fastest growing retail segment in the country. And with the possible exception of nutritional products, the animal-oriented items and services that make up those billions have been developed to gratify our desire to make pet animals' lives more like our own.

Stefan Wiesen is a Canadian who gave up being a financial consultant to become the owner of a dog bed company. He believes that the best pet-industry investments today are in companies with that humanoid hook.

"A few years ago," he told *Dogs in Canada* magazine, "it was unheard of for people to have pet insurance. Now most pet owners 'need' it. . . . Today, we are seeing dog greeting and condolence cards, and pet funeral services. I would look at any company that can capitalize on the humanization of pets, through a product or service that enhances this mega trend."

"Humanization" is the marketing term for treating animals the same way we treat ourselves. A third of what is now spent on pets in the US—the most rapidly-expanding category—is on health care. That includes root canal surgery, chemotherapy, liposuction, and behavioural pharmacology. In 2005, American pet lovers spent fifteen million dollars on behaviour-modification drugs alone.

According to a 2006 survey conducted by the American Pet Products Manufacturers Association, 77 percent of dog owners had administered some form of medication to their pets. Among cat owners, the percentage was considerably less but still more than half.

In July 2008, the mainstream *The New York Times Magazine* regarded the issue as sufficiently newsworthy to devote a cover story to "Pill Popping Pets." David Lummis, a pet industry analyst for a market research firm, told the author of the piece, James Vlahos, that owners' desires for more tractable pets fuel the increasing demand for medications that modify animal behaviour. "Our expectations are going up. Owners want their pets to be more like little well-behaved children."

In a society where even well-behaved children seem harder to come by, such high expectations of pets are often unrealistic. Though himself a pioneer in behavioural pharmacology, Dr. Nicholas Dodman of Tufts University's veterinary school cautions that pills are no more a cure-all for pets than they are for people. Animal behaviours—such as aggression, food-guarding, and marking of territory—may be inconvenient to owners but they are perfectly normal for dogs and cats.

Meanwhile, dog training expert Dr. Ian Dunbar claims, "I have never in my life had to resort to using drugs to solve a behaviour problem." It is, Dunbar suggests, humans' own reliance on drugs to manage problems rather than solving them that has produced this spike in pharmacological cures for their pets.

For those unwilling to resort to chemical answers for either themselves or their animals, the pet industry provides other therapeutic options, from various methods of training, to psychological intervention, to the services of animal healers and psychics. Despite innumerable articles, TV specials, and in-depth interviews with practitioners of extra-sensory approaches to behavioural issues in animals, nothing conclusive about the efficacy of these methods has been established. However, it's probably safe to say that the kind of people who seek out palmists, tarot-card readers, and tea-leaf experts for insight into their own problems are the same kind of people who will invite a psychic over to assess their dog's aura, or mail a photo of their cat to someone offering a diagnosis from afar, or change the position of their pet's bed because a Feng Shui practitioner has assured them the animal's incontinence problem will be solved thereby.

At an even more esoteric end of the pet-industry spectrum, business is also booming at a small biotech company in California that produces "lifestyle pets." These are not robotic animals, like that Shiba Inu puppy I noticed in the crowd at Woofstock. Allerca of San Diego is in the business of creating and supplying living animals. In this case, they are cats genetically modified to make them tolerable for allergy sufferers.

The development of the hypoallergenic cat has gone on over the past few years at what Allerca's chief executive terms "a secret undisclosed location." But despite the sinister sound of that, these cats are not produced in Petri dishes or courtesy of Frankensteinian bolts of electricity. A population of cats who naturally carry a mutant gene that makes their protein less allergenic to humans have been mated with ordinary cats the old-fashioned way to produce hypoallergenic kittens.

These kittens—neutered before delivery to prevent, uh, copycatting—retail for about four thousand dollars apiece. The enormous demand even at the price makes clear how far humans who can afford it will go for a living, breathing animal in their household that also allows *them* to live and breathe.

"You're not just buying a cat," is how the Allerca CEO justifies the company's elaborate screening of prospective buyers. "It's a medical device that replaces shots and pills. At the same time, this is a living animal, so the well-being of our product comes before our customers. This is not some high-priced handbag that you put back on the shelf if it doesn't match."

Would-be Allerca cat owners are interviewed for "motivation and warmth." Their willingness to tolerate a cat who behaves like a cat—by having an "accident" on the floor or clawing the furniture—is evaluated, along with other possibly allergenic materials in their homes.

Because the cat may not be safe for people with the most severe forms of allergy, the company insists on indemnifying itself with a rigorous screening process. A US Food and Drug Administration allergy test kit is sent to the home of the potential purchaser in order to test all family members. As well, a collection system is installed on the family's vacuum cleaner, to detect the presence of other allergens.

But even that is not the end of the story. Clients who successfully jump through all of Allerca's hoops still have to wait up to fifteen months within the States, and up to eighteen months in Europe for their four-thousand-dollar kitten to arrive.

For people who already regard the passion for pets as "crazy" and "out of hand" the combination of artifice and animalism represented by the Allerca cat must seem incomprehensible, as well as perverse. For people among the 70 percent of Americans surveyed who regard their pets as family members, the idea of scientific research making available something furry yet sneeze-free to cuddle might seem simply like another example of better living through chemistry.

Perhaps the only conclusive thing to say about the Allerca story is that it perfectly represents that paradox of freedom and control that operates at the heart of our modern relationship with household animals. Our freedom to associate with them is predicated on control—whether in the form of a leash, a behaviour-modification drug or genetic alteration. In the end, we may be the ones who pay the bills, but they are the ones who pay the price—by yielding up some of the essential animal qualities that attracted us to them in the first place.

IV

LI'L ABNER CARTOONIST AL CAPP once described children as "midgets with no money." By that token, animals could be called illiterates with no money, unable either to document their grievances or purchase their independence. The best they can hope for is that some human "friend" will write the story of their lives, the way Anna Sewell did for Black Beauty and Margaret Marshall Saunders did for Beautiful Joe. Even in those well-intended offerings, the authors essentially presented their animal protagonists as people in order to have them empathized with as animals.

In *Black Beauty*, a mare narrates the story of her life. All of Beauty's fortune—both good and bad—is directly dependent on the whims of human beings. *Beautiful Joe* also offers the animal's point of view, to trace the real-life story of a dog first abused by a cruel owner, then rescued and rehabilitated by the pet-loving family of a minister.

Anna Sewell intended her book as a teaching tool for children and adults in her lifelong campaign against the "hell for horses" England was deemed in the first half of the nineteenth century. From a horse's perspective, Sewell effectively conveyed how a creature under saddle or in harness might feel, right down to the excruciating, ongoing pain of having her head held at an unnatural angle by what was called a bearing or check rein.

Along with her Quaker mother, Sewell was an activist against all kinds of cruelty to horses. Together, these small, frail gentlewomen regularly confronted carters and cab-drivers in London and remonstrated with them about their harsh treatment of the animals in their charge.

However, once *Black Beauty* was published, its wide popularity proved a more powerful form of advocacy. The book became a byword for humaneness toward horses, and was credited with, if not entirely transforming, at least reforming equine welfare in Britain and elsewhere.

Though the infamous check rein fell mostly out of fashion, it did not entirely disappear. Ironically, in the funeral procession for Anna Sewell— who died shortly after *Black Beauty* was published—the horses that drew her hearse, as well as the rest of the carriages in the procession, had bearing reins. Sewell's mother, bereaved of her daughter, had to stop the cavalcade and go from carriage to carriage, requesting that the offending reins be removed. Only then did Anna Sewell's body continue on its way to interment.

Margaret Marshall Saunders, a Canadian, was also involved in advocacy for animals, along with women's rights and the cause of temperance. When she heard about a contest sponsored by a US animal welfare organization looking for a manuscript that would do for animal welfare in America what *Black Beauty* had done for horses in Britain, Saunders decided to enter. She felt she might do worse than to borrow a leaf from Anna Sewell's book and present events from an animal's perspective.

In both books, the narrative "voice" is identifiably human. Yet the point of view captures something uncannily animal. Not only does Anna Sewell convey what Beauty feels when she's first saddled and shod and subjected to a check rein, the mare's emotional attachments to the other animals she encounters are palpable too, and sometimes unbearably affecting.

In *Beautiful Joe*, Saunders captures the dog's terrible night of throbbing misery, with his freshly severed ears and bloody stub of tail burning under the bandages. Again borrowing from Sewell's earlier novel, she also ventures to humanize her hero, by imbuing Joe with emotions of love, loss, anxiety, and even hate that are as complex as our own.

Much of the success of these books is achieved by putting words into the mouths of creatures whose principal difference from us is that they don't speak our language. As Saunders says in her book, real animals suffer not only in silence, but "in bitter, bitter silence." Their lack of ability to state their own complaints eliminates them, de facto, from any hope of audience, much less redress.

Yet, by giving their fictional protagonists not only the gift of speech but written speech at that, it's possible that Anna Sewell and Marshall Saunders have diminished some of the pathos of the wordless plight of real-life "dumb" creatures. Paradoxically, the fact that both Beautiful Joe and Black Beauty have literary means to get our attention and "tell" us about the good and the bad treatment they have witnessed may somewhat undermine the authors' case for the mute helplessness of animals.

IN THE BOOK OF GENESIS, animals are created before man. However, right from the moment Adam and Eve come on the scene, other creatures are relegated to the backseat, like the family dog. "First come, last served" seems to sum up the place of animals in the Bible.

Yet in nineteenth-century Britain and America, not all religiously inclined thinkers regarded that view as either just or inevitable. Anti-slavery crusader William Wilberforce, social philosopher Jeremy Bentham, animal welfare advocates Henry Salt and Anna Kingsford, among many others, felt that moral concern for one's fellow man in no way precluded moral concern for non-human creatures. In fact, for some of those nineteenth-century firebrands, the inclusion of animals among the disenfranchised was a legitimate tenet of true Christianity.

Thus it was that in Britain, from about 1800 on, a broad coalition of abolitionists, anti-vivisectionists, and other activists campaigned for improvements in a number of areas involving animal welfare. The mistreatment of cart and cab horses, widespread wagering on bull, badger, dog and cock fights, the live skinning of cats for their pelts, the desperate lives of many cart and turnspit dogs, the cropping of canine ears and tails were all subjects of discussion and legislation in this period.

In America, animal activists similarly arose from the ranks of the socially conscious and also connected their advocacy for women, slaves, and other disadvantaged humans to their concern for better treatment of animals. In fact, both in the United States and Britain, formalized organizations for the prevention of cruelty to animal species pre-dated—although did not by any means prevent—the creation of similar protection agencies for children.

Then as now, advocates for animals were not uniform in either their approaches or motivations. Some expressed concern about the "degradation" of humanity caused by tolerance of cruelty to lower species; others were outraged on behalf of the creatures themselves. Still others, as animal historian Erica Fudge has observed, were most caught by the aesthetics of the thing—for instance, wishing to clear London's streets of diseased-looking or half-starved animals and the stench of their manure.

Among those committed to improving the lot of non-humans, there were also differences of interpretation. Despite his oratory on behalf of suffering animalkind, Jeremy Bentham never did give up eating meat—at least, that of domestically raised animals which, he insisted, enjoyed far better lives and more humane deaths than creatures hunted in the wild. As mentioned earlier, even Darwin, who wrote and spoke so movingly about "a matter of degree, not of kind" with respect to the relative intelligence of humans and animals, could not bring himself to sign a petition opposing vivisection.

Nevertheless, the mid-to-late nineteenth century both in England and America was remarkable as a period of activism on behalf of animals as well as underprivileged humans. So conjoined were the goals of anti-slavery and animal welfare movements that *The Abolitionist* was the first name chosen for their publication by the British Union for the Abolition of Vivisection. Only later did they change the name to *The Liberator*.

Looking back on that period in Britain and America—at the nexus of human abolitionism, the advancement of women's rights, and advocacy on behalf of animals—what is most striking is a general strain of optimism. Once the slaves had been freed and female suffrage accomplished, so the thinking went, improved welfare for animals undoubtedly would be next.

Today, at our twenty-first century remove, we might feel that some measure of the optimism of those times has been justified by subsequent events. If slavery has not been entirely abolished, at least the practice of slavery is universally condemned. While many women around the world continue to live in conditions of helpless disenfranchisement, at least women's right to vote is now largely taken for granted.

However, if we glance back at those long-ago crusades on behalf of animals, and then look around at the current condition of most non-human beings, we might be forgiven if we find ourselves wondering what, if anything, has actually changed for them. What exactly happened to that revolution that has always been just around the next corner?

Abolitionist Lee Hall ends her book, *Capers in the Churchyard: Animal Rights Advocacy in the Age of Terror*, with an expression of cautious hope that we may at least be approaching that corner. After running through several models of cooperative, egalitarian societies in both the animal (bonobo) and human (Muscogee Indian) domain, she concludes:

> Of course, it takes time to unlearn the patterns of interacting that we've been brought up to accept as the norm. . . . It would mean giving up the human clubs of whiteness, of maleness, and even of humanness, kicking the habit of defining ourselves as possessors of dominion over all that fly, walk, swim and crawl over the contours of a weary planet. It would mean the most comprehensive peace movement ever known.

As I closed the book, I wondered how anyone who cares for animals as much as Hall obviously does can bear to think of living without their guaranteed proximity in our homes and access to their presence in the outdoors. And even if we all agreed it was time to end animal enslavement and let them live their lives according to their own lights, how might that actually be brought about?

I put my question to her in an email:

How do we loose those bonds, forged by fifteen thousand years of history, and let those companions go?

And if simply opening the corral gates, livestock barns and urban apartment doors to let the inmates go is premature, what is the gradual process by which that end could be led up to?

Her response, when it came, was disappointingly unspecific:

Yes, opening the door would be wrong. If we put other animals into positions of dependency it is our moral duty to care for them and provide for their needs. (Notice how we fall terribly short of the mark here and indeed we fall short of the mark of caring for each other, including when other humans are put into harm's way by our own actions.) As for animals in agribusiness, phasing out demand for the products would phase out a reason to breed them. On cats, neutering and trap-neuter-return seems to be the best way to go.

Her reference to "other humans put into harm's way" was a swipe at animal liberationists who use violence and intimidation to achieve their goals. The "capers in the churchyard" of her book title refer to a 2004 campaign in Britain, in which animal activists sought to intimidate a family who supplied guinea pigs for biomedical tests to nearby Huntingdon Life Sciences, a large commercial lab. As one of their tactics, the activists disinterred the remains of the mother-in-law of the guinea-pig farmer, carted them away, and, as Hall writes, demanded "a stop to the breeding of guinea pigs in return for the bones."

This is only one of numerous incidents she cites to illustrate the inhumanity and brutality of this brand of "direct action." She feels it gives a bad name to all advocacy efforts on behalf of animals, especially in the post-9/11 "age of terror."

Hall also observes that "Huntingdon Life Sciences goes on performing tests for drug companies, food industries, and agribusiness, albeit mainly by moving repeatedly out of the protesters' way." By 2001, HLS had already relocated its head office from England to the United States, as a result of earlier break-ins and other acts of intimidation by animal activists.

But if the violent activism of British animal rights groups doesn't achieve real progress for animals, what would Lee Hall recommend instead? In her speech at the Vegetarian Expo I attended in Saratoga Springs, she put heavy emphasis on a vegan lifestyle as a centrepiece of any program dedicated to what she calls "kicking the habit of dominion."

She's been vegan herself since living in Britain in the 1980s. "London was a great city for vegans," she told me when I met her in Saratoga. "It still is."

Of course, London in the eighties was also a great city for animal liberation activists, and still is. Their numbers include the kind of activists she criticizes in her book: the kind who rob graveyards, send letter-bombs to scientists and intimidate the families of low-level lab technicians. And, in many cases, also adhere to a strict vegan diet.

Months after meeting with Lee, I am in England myself, on a fast train racketing back to London from Leamington Spa. I think back on my conversation with her and suddenly wonder if that peculiar intersection of violence and veganism also strikes her as at all ironic.

I have just spent most of today with Ronnie Lee, one of the founders of the Animal Liberation Front, an animal-rights alliance associated with those "capers" involving an old lady's remains referred to in Lee Hall's book. Ronnie is as firmly vegan as Hall is. So much so that he's brought his own soy milk with him to the tea room at the Royal Pump Rooms at Leamington Spa.

As he pours it into the first of endless cups of tea, he offers his perspective on that grave-robbing incident.

"Of course, I'm not saying I was involved. Nor do I even know for sure it was ALF-connected. Still, I was interviewed about it at the time, and I do remember saying that the dead body of one human was surely less important than the living bodies of those animals at Huntingdon, involved in experiments."

He thinks he even recognizes "Lee Hall" as the name of some animal advocate in America who had taken issue with that comment. But to this day, he's not in the least sorry he made it.

Ronnie's only regret about the entire episode seems tactical. Digging up some guinea-pig farmer's mother-in-law is not as effective as targeting homes of laboratory "abusers." Since they "live for the pleasure of their accumulated wealth, make them into pariahs. You have to make them seen like pedophiles, preying on the helpless."

What sort of targeting?

"A certain level of violence" directed against abusers, he says, would be acceptable. For example: beatings. Whereas he feels letter-bombs involve too many risks for innocents, like postal employees or children. However, direct action of some kind is definitely required. "I don't believe in appeals to people's better nature," he says flatly.

He goes on to talk about being bullied when small—he still *is* small—and learning to take the offensive. In this vein, he is very much the diminutive "General Ronnie" of his old ALF action days, rather than the media-friendly greyhound rescuer he's since become.

"How would you ever get the public to support treating scientists that way?" I ask. "Surely most people feel that if experimentation can cure cancer, what are a few mice?"

Instead of answering, he poses a question of his own: "Do you know that the pharmaceutical industry is the second biggest in the world, after the military?"

Then, in the next moment, he reverts to what I think of as his "Squirrel Nutkin" persona—fussing and chattering and benignly British, as he describes the difficulties of trying to keep one's pets vegan, whilst having to "put some meat in" for one of the dogs who can't stomach the vegetable stuff. Of course, that only sets all the others to demand meat as well.

I can't feature Lee Hall fretting so comically over the petty taste preferences of pets—not when, in her view, they shouldn't be in our homes in the first place, waiting for us to determine who or what they can eat. Nor can I picture Lee cracking me up, as Ronnie does when he talks about his first prison stretch.

When the other, more hardened, inmates asked him what he was in for, he told them he'd broken into a lab and stolen a hundred mice.

"They couldn't grasp it," he recalls. "'Oh, valuable mice, were they?' they kept asking me. You know, sort of hopeful. Because otherwise, it made no sense."

From his late teens—first as a vegetarian, then as a vegan, later as a saboteur of fox hunts, then as an acknowledged rustler of laboratory animals, and an unacknowledged sender of letter-bombs and burglar of human bones, and ultimately as chief strategist for the ALF—Ronnie Lee has spent most of his life involved in animal advocacy and activism. Apart from brief and meaningless clerical jobs after leaving school, his almost six decades on the planet have been devoted, both inside and outside prison, to editing animal-rights newspapers, organizing actions against targeted animal "abusers," dealing with the media on animal-related issues, and campaigning on behalf of animal causes, including picketing fur shops, passing out brochures against badger-baiting at village fetes and booing lab workers as they filed into plants where animal testing went on.

Aside from his long involvement in the animal rights movement, Ronnie has never had any long-term career. At the present moment, he lives on state benefits which include recognition of his role as "carer" for his wife, who has cerebral palsy.

To interviewers who question this *modus vivendi*, he likes to say: "Look, the government puts millions of pounds into animal abuse—why shouldn't they pay me a bit to fight it?"

Nowadays, however, he keeps a low profile and operates mostly as an armchair strategist. "The key is to get the potentially good people to follow the activists; after that, the vast majority will go along. Then you can just seize political power."

And do what with it?

Nothing revolutionary, he assures me. "There won't be an uprising in

the streets here. Change will only come through established channels."
Currently, Ronnie prefers the Green Party to any of the others in Britain,
but its current leadership "would have to go" before an effective coalition
could be forged between them and militant animal activists.

He seems to enjoy donning his General Ronnie uniform, and laying
out his long-term philosophy, which begins with "rolling back" current
population levels, to fifty million—worldwide. (It's worth noting that, at
present, the population of Great Britain alone is somewhat more than
that.) "There would have to be vasectomies at puberty, with sperm saved
in banks until it's needed—if ever."

Nor would violent means be required to achieve this. "Even in the
ALF, most people are followers. You need education and coercion." And
at that, he appears to view coercion as a last resort. "I would sooner give
out leaflets now than hurl a brick," he says, apparently forgetting his earlier comments about forgoing appeals to people's better natures in favour
of targeting vivisectionists.

My train is slowing down for its arrival into Marylebone Station, and
I'm still transcribing at top speed notes from my recent encounter with
Ronnie. How to summarize someone so meek and homey on the one
hand, and so grandiose on the other?

Like Lee Hall, he believes in middle-of-the-road strategies like spay-
neuter clinics for homeless cats and an end to the exploitation of "working" animals. Also like her, Ronnie subscribes to some edgier policies, such
as the elimination of complicity between welfare groups and exploiters,
and the idea of returning to "pre-invasion borders" to recreate human-
free habitats for animals such as existed before we came along. And just
like Hall and many other activists across a broad spectrum of beliefs and
degrees of radicalism, Ronnie Lee rejects "bigger cages," a term which
serves as shorthand for all small and meaningless attempts to ameliorate
conditions he regards as innately unacceptable.

"People understand best," says Ronnie, "if you put the animal situation
in terms of a slavery analogy. To have said of African slaves, 'Right, we'll
give them more room in the hold of the ship, fewer beatings and comfier
shackles,' would not have satisfied the proponents of abolition. Well, it

won't satisfy us either, when it comes to animals."

That's another sentiment I'm sure Hall would have no trouble agreeing with. Yet, what separates commitment to a cause from choice of means to achieve it seems like a wider gulf between her and Ronnie than the ocean stretching between here and America.

The train eases to a standstill. I stuff my notebook into my satchel and head out into the London dusk. If Lee Hall were with me, I can't help but think she would be protesting all the way along the platform that irrespective of whether or not he always makes sure to pack his own supply of soy milk, Ronnie Lee is one vegan who still has a thing or two to learn about what she's termed "kicking the habit of dominion."

WHEN I INFORM KEITH MANN that an American abolitionist told me she regards London as a vegan Mecca, his eyebrows go up. "Actually, given the demand here, I'm always surprised about the lack of options."

Even this particular Red Veg where we are lunching in Deane Street in Soho—part of a small chain—is a dreary little place, with dingy plastic tables, a clouded coffee pot that the waitress tells me hasn't seen action in a year, and the faded logo in need of a coat of red paint.

"Maybe your next project could be a line of spiffy new vegan restaurants," I suggest.

Keith grimaces. "I've enough on my plate with this little lot." By which he means touring to promote his book on the animal liberation movement, *From Dusk 'til Dawn*. At many of the events, the DVD of a documentary called *Behind the Mask* is also screened and offered for sale. Like his book, it presents direct action—even illegal action—as a sometimes necessary response to animal cruelty. "We all want to change the world legally," Mann observes in the film, "But it just doesn't work like that."

Today, he has on him a copy of another DVD, which lays out how the United States government concocted the attacks in New York and Washington on 9/11. "I bang on about it all day long," he tells me cheerfully. He also wonders whether I've seen a brilliant film which debunks the 1969 landing of US astronauts on the moon.

Initially, I am somewhat bemused by these sideline interests, so apparently removed from causes involving animals. Then it occurs to me that, like his colleague Ronnie Lee, Keith in his post-activist years has come to link the struggle for animal rights with a more generalized debunking of conventional wisdom and the official version.

He tells me he's just returned from the Netherlands, and on re-entry into the UK braced himself, as always, for a hassle about his criminal record. He despairs of ever getting a visa to go to the States to take up numerous invitations he's received to speak and flog his book there.

Obviously, Keith Mann has a vested interest in questioning authority, especially with respect to the notion of what constitutes a "terrorist." As Lee Hall's book cautions, in the post-9/11 era, animal activists look like enemies of the State—particularly when, as in Mann's case, their criminal records include details about acts of sabotage against private property, even to wearing a balaclava in the commission of many of these offences.

Keith also professes contempt for what he regards as Britons' general willingness to place unquestioning trust in officialdom. He worries that his fellow Brits are far too ready to trust in an omnipotent "they" who would as happily hoodwink the public about 9/11 or the moon landing as pretend that no *real* abuse of animals would ever be allowed in the UK.

I remind him that Britons are also renowned for their sense of "fair play." Back in the late nineties, secretly filmed scenes of lab workers at Huntingdon Life Sciences abusing and mocking beagle puppies who struggled when their blood was drawn or refused to cooperate in painful experiments were smuggled out and shown on television with sensational results. The public reacted with mass outrage, and several of the lab workers were arrested and convicted of a peculiarly British-sounding offence—"terrifying dogs." HLS's decision to relocate its head office from England to the United States was largely motivated by Britons' response to that footage.

Keith agrees. "But there is a backlash problem as well. People still point to that episode as proof that the system deals with the 'bad apples.'"

He adds that the beagle-puppy affair resulted in an increase in security at facilities where animals are abused. As well, the fact that now all

Britons are under regular surveillance, thanks to the CCTV cameras on almost every corner, means direct action against abusers is harder and harder to pull off. All of which he decries as increasing repression of the populace by government.

That rapid oscillation between upbeat showmanship and a kind of wariness—almost a paranoia—seems at the heart of Mann's own personal paradox. On the one hand, there is his apparent conviction that, on numerous fronts, progress not only has been made but will continue. On the other hand, the core belief that brought him to this work—"animals are at the bottom of the heap"—carries with it the implication that, the fix being in, they always will be.

"Why do you think," I ask him—as I'd asked Lee Hall—"that animal rights is always the next revolution?"

Keith doesn't hesitate for a nanosecond. "Because everybody benefits from animals. Freeing the slaves didn't adversely affect everybody—only slave holders. And giving women the vote didn't destroy anybody's way of life. But abolition for animals? It affects everybody in some way or other. If we change things for them, we change things for everybody. They're everywhere."

He's right. Even in the Red Veg, they're here, if only because they aren't. Simulated beef burgers made of soy, pretend hot dogs, and vegetarian versions of minced-meat favourites. And however relatively vegan-minded London as a whole may be, food free of animal products is still harder to come by here than bangers and jellied tongue and ox-tail and mutton—and what is reportedly nowadays the meal most frequently ordered by Londoners: chicken masala.

In the UK generally, the concepts of "bigger cages" and "free range" still presuppose that raising animals in confinement is an article of faith. True, fur is no longer for sale here, except at Harrods, and cosmetics claim to be "cruelty-free." At the same time, the farming industry, the horse-racing industry, the pharmaceuticals industry, the book-binding industry, the restaurant industry, the pet industry . . . all of these and more—as well as the vast public that supports them—continue to depend on the confinement and control of animals.

Let them go? Not likely, not without a fight. It's no wonder we'll continue to postpone that revolution for as long as we can.

V

IF ANY WIDE-SCALE ANIMAL RIGHTS REVOLUTION is ever to erupt, humans will have to run it. That, perhaps, is the element that makes legal and legislative change involving non-humans different from any social movement on behalf of any other oppressed group in history.

The recent trend toward courses at more and more North American universities in the field of animal law does not necessarily indicate that animals themselves are increasingly beneficiaries of legal reform. Most laws regarding animals are not *for* them, merely about them: custody disputes over who gets Rover after the divorce; claims for financial compensation involving the loss or damage to pets or livestock; patent arguments about the ownership of genetically manipulated lab mice. In cases like those, it's the legal rights of human beings at issue, with respect to the disposition of a living piece of property. Even in high-profile legal battles, such as around the late Leona Helmsley's bequest of millions to her dog, the question of whether the hotel heiress was entitled to dispose of her estate as she wished easily overshadowed consideration of her canine heir's right to inherit.

Arguably, however, any increased focus on legal issues to do with non-humans is of long-term benefit to those interested in advocating animal rights. Toronto criminal lawyer Clayton Ruby—who has acted on behalf of owners in several high-profile cases—likens the current state of animal law to where gay rights activism was a quarter-century ago. Asked to comment on a rise in the number of animal-law courses being offered by Canadian universities in the fall of 2008, Ruby told the *Globe and Mail* newspaper, "People sense this is going to be an area of importance in the future."

For now, in Canada, both animal welfare advocates and activists for animal rights have to be content with only periodic glimpses of the potential importance of animal-related legal issues. When the death of

Toronto police horse Brigadier hit the news in 2006, some members of the public likely were surprised to learn that the man who drove his vehicle into horse and rider was charged only with causing bodily harm to the mounted officer and failure to remain at the scene of an accident. Canada's Criminal Code makes no provision for animals killed or injured in the line of duty as law-enforcement personnel.

During the memorial service for the slain police horse, no mention was made of the disparity between Brigadier's lofty status as a fallen officer and his lack of importance under law as a wronged animal.

Following the service, mounted police from various forces across Canada milled around his empty stall—decorated with a wreath of carrots, as well flowers and hundreds of cards and letters—and gave vent to some of the bitterness they'd kept in check during the memorial.

More than half of the fifty United States of America have laws on the books criminalizing the wilful killing of law-enforcement animals—most often as a felony. In 2000, the US Congress enacted legislation to protect animals working for federal agencies. Even if nothing was going to bring back Brigadier—or any of the other police dogs and horses killed in the line of duty over the years—at least, agreed the officers gathered outside his stall, beefed-up legislation would provide them the satisfaction of knowing these animals' death counted as a crime.

In June 2006, just three months after that Brigadier's memorial, the Toronto Police Services Board (which provides civilian oversight of the police force) called for a law making it a criminal offence to harm an animal used for law enforcement. "Right now," said a Toronto city councillor lobbying in favour of the law, "police service animals are considered no different than barnyard animals. We all know this is not true. They are highly trained and serve alongside our officers to protect the public."

The careful separation of service animals from mere livestock is, of course, telling—and understandable. In Canada, strengthening any federal legislation aimed at curtailing animal cruelty and abuse is almost invariably opposed by the farming lobby. Therefore, the proponents of "Brigadier's Law" needed to make crystal clear the very limited and specific scope of the Criminal Code changes they had in mind.

On October 24, 2006, Brigadier's Law was introduced in the House of Commons in Ottawa and passed first reading. However, as of this writing, there has been no further progress of this bill through Canada's Parliament. For the time being—at least in the eyes of the law—police service dogs and horses in Canada are still no better than barnyard animals.

Canada's federal anti-cruelty laws have long been criticized by animal welfare and advocacy groups as antiquated and inadequate. Attempts to update the legislation began in 1999 under a Liberal government, and in 2008, culminated in Bill S-203, introduced by a Liberal senator John Bryden and supported by the Conservative government of the day and some members of the opposition. However, the bill's opponents both in the House of Commons and in the ranks of many animal advocacy groups accused the bill of failing to provide anything but cosmetic upgrades to sentencing guidelines for cruelty offences. Liberal MP Mark Holland tried and failed to introduce a much more comprehensive bill, C-373, with stiffer penalties and provisions for prosecution of a wider range of offences.

In April 2008, Bill S-203 passed into law. Though criticisms of its inadequacies persist among advocates of animal welfare, further revamping of Canada's anti-cruelty laws does not appear to be a high priority for any major federal political party. Therefore, with no provision for proving intent to harm, no reference to the prosecution of trainers of fighting dogs, no attempt to regard animals as anything besides property—and nothing to say about rights to protection of non-human law-enforcement personnel—animal-related legislation in one of the world's most highly respected countries continues to lag behind many other nations, including Ukraine and the Philippines.

In the Canadian federal election campaign in the fall of 2008, only one registered party—and a minuscule one at that—made animal cruelty a central plank of its election platform. The Animal Alliance Environment Voters Party of Canada fielded four candidates, all of them in southern Ontario ridings deemed easy wins for mainstream opposition parties to the governing Conservatives. The goal, explained Liz White, leader of the AAEV Party of Canada, was not to send herself or any of the other three candidates to Ottawa. "I don't have a hope in hell of getting elected," she told me cheerfully, as I went door-knocking with her one October night close to Election Day. What she and her fellow party members wanted was to demonstrate voter support for the AAEV party's goals.

In White's view, "change occurs on the edge," rather than within the mainstream parties. As we walked through a gentrified downtown Toronto neighbourhood called Cabbagetown, I took a look at one of the pamphlets White was sticking into the mailboxes of houses with nobody home, or proffering to residents who responded to their doorbell or knocker. "Climate Change" rather than a more specifically animal-related issue led the parade of concerns on the pamphlet, but that struck me as perhaps a necessary concession in the AAEV's transition from an animal advocacy group to a registered political party.

Right after "Climate Change" came "The Commercial Seal Hunt," not simply decried in the campaign literature as cruel, but also criticized as an environmentally-insensitive policy supported by all the major parties, despite good evidence of global warming as a threat to seal populations. Only at the end of the pamphlet was reference made to the passage of Bill s-203 and the inadequacy of Canada's current legislation to prosecute perpetrators of animal cruelty in a meaningful way.

When introducing herself at the door, Liz White invariably identified her party in a single breath as one promoting "action on the environment and animal protection." Particularly at those households where dogs answered the doorbell chime along with their owners, I noticed how the word "animal" got her in the door. Elsewhere, it was "environment" that did the trick.

"The environment is not one of a list of issues," White told me along with prospective voters on the doorstep. "It's *the* issue, taking in everything from health care to the seal-hunt." As we walked from house to house, she told me that though she is a long-time animal activist, she sees nothing wrong in addressing animal issues in a more widespread way, as part of this larger environmental concern. Since the formation of the Animal Alliance almost two decades ago, her goals have included drastically reducing the use of research animals in Canada, promoting a vegan diet, and re-examining our relationship with pets. But she saw it as "strategically a mistake to be sanctimonious" about any of that, and—within this more recent context of electoral politics—appeared willing to focus on more general precepts.

The incumbent Liberal candidate in the riding, she explained patiently at each doorstep, was a shoo-in for re-election. "So if you vote for me, you can send a strong message to Ottawa about animal protection and the environment without worrying that you're splitting a tight vote and electing a Conservative." Having already run in this riding in a previous by-election, White told me that she has much more influence with the incumbent now than she would ever have had as a non-candidate. "At least I've succeeded in getting him to *mention* animal rights in the House."

When one homeowner offered to put one of her party's lawn-signs in his yard, White thanked him, but said she hadn't had any made up. "Too costly?" I asked sympathetically as we headed on to the next house. "Yes, for the environment," she replied. "They're coated in Plastisol. Non-recyclable."

It must be tough, I thought, to get the environmental message out, when just displaying the message is destructive of the environment. Still, Liz White seemed confident, out here at the edge, that the changes she seeks will happen, however incrementally. On Election Day, when I emailed her to wish her good luck, she emailed back, jokily: "I've rented an apartment in Ottawa just in case I shock everyone and win Toronto Centre."

The next morning, a quick check of the election results revealed that neither she nor any of the other three Animal Alliance Environment Voters of Canada Party candidates would be imminently house-hunting in Ottawa. Garnering under two hundred votes apiece, they hadn't even made themselves eligible for the federal funding available to parties polling more than 2 percent of the vote nationally. Clearly, an end to the seal-hunt and amendments to Canada's Criminal Code with respect to animal cruelty are still on hold, and the emphasis on animal-related law that attorney Clay Ruby foresees as "an area of importance in the future" in Canada remains in the future—at least for now.

IN OCTOBER 2005, the Italian newspaper *Il Messaggero* reported that the city council of Rome had voted to ban spherical goldfish bowls in that city. Not only do round bowls cause blindness in fish, according to fish experts consulted by the councillors, they also restrict oxygen.

"The civilization of a city can be measured by this," declared one member of council, when the ban passed into municipal law. Rome invited further measurement of its level of civilization through other animal-related reforms voted in along with better goldfish bowls. Docking dogs' tails was declared illegal, along with trimming cats' claws for "visual appeal," and leaving animals in hot vehicles or in store windows. As well, any dog owner who denied his pet a daily walk would be fined a sum equivalent to seven hundred dollars US.

Laws enacted for the direct benefit of animals themselves—especially laws that might come into conflict with the convenience of the humans to whom they belong—are rare any place. Even in traditionally "animal-loving" nations such as Britain, seldom has there been much reluctance to flush an unwanted guppy down the toilet. Such scruples on behalf of goldfish and other pets in Italy—where animal rights had not previously been in the forefront—seemed remarkable enough to merit headlines.

Similarly, in 2008, when a committee of Spain's parliament recommended granting rights to great apes, animal lovers elsewhere couldn't avoid making withering reference to the country's entrenched bullfight culture, or commenting on the fact that Spanish hunters are notorious for the routine hanging of hunting dogs from trees at the end of each season in order to spare themselves the cost of off-season upkeep.

Instead of waiting for governmental action on apes' and other animals' behalf, some activists have sought redress from the courts. In April 2007, a chimpanzee named Hiasl was poised to become the centre of the biggest legal proceeding involving an ape since the Scopes Trial eighty-two years before.

Hiasl was born in Sierra Leone, where he was captured, then smuggled to Austria. There, he was slated to join the ranks of animal experimental subjects at a research lab outside Vienna. But before that could happen, the chimp was intercepted by customs, confiscated, and turned over to an animal sanctuary, where he remained for years. It was only when funds required to keep him housed at the shelter threatened to run out that Baxter—the laboratory originally intended as his "home"—requested the return of the now twenty-six-year-old Hiasl, to take up his long-interrupted career in research.

Animal activists from Britain and across Europe rallied with the intention of securing "human" rights that would prevent Hiasl's being turned over to Baxter. A British woman named Paula Stibbe sought to adopt the chimp legally, in order to qualify him for consideration under law as a human.

However, when a birth certificate demanded by the judge proved impossible to locate for an animal born in the wild, Hiasl's claim was rejected by the lower court. At that point, his supporters began making plans to take the case to Austria's Supreme Court in hopes of a more sympathetic hearing. Since that time, I am unaware of any further updates on the status of the case, or the chimp's current whereabouts.

Since long before Hiasl, moral philosophers have been looking at the question of loosened bonds and elevated freedoms as they apply to animals. American philosopher Martha Nussbaum speaks of animals' entitlement not to "compassion" but to "justice."

Andrew I. Cohen, of the University of Georgia's philosophy department, argues in favour of "secondary moral standing" for animals similar to what is accorded human infants—in effect, a form of guardianship that protects their interests even as it recognizes the inferiority of their moral standing to that of adult humans. Meanwhile, Abraham Rudnick, of the Departments of Psychiatry and Philosophy at the University of Western Ontario, suggests "other consciousness"—i.e., the perceived ability of higher animals like apes to recognize the consciousness of other beings—as grounds for legal consideration.

In issues of law as well as concerns about morality, our determination of intelligence and/or consciousness in certain animal species is the usual criterion for consideration of their rights. However, Bernard Rollin has objected that an alien species arriving on Earth would have no moral authority to oppress human beings even if the new arrivals were superior to us in intelligence. For that reason, Rollin argues in favour of legal rights for animals on the basis not of intellect, but their worthiness of moral consideration. Being "property" rather than "persons" forever denies rights to animals, he says, unless the legal definition of what they are is changed.

He deems subjective terms like "kindness" and "cruelty" inadequate for determining our moral or legal obligations to them. Even people who purport to love animals can treat them badly, in somebody else's estimation. Nor does simply extending a sort of bountiful compassion respect the essential features of an animal's "telos"—meaning its goals and purposes as an individual.

However, that same concept of telos is at the heart of the essential dilemma in granting legal rights, even to the so-called "higher" mammals: How do we go about holding animals to the same legal and moral standards that we are prepared to confer on them?

Rollin offers the example of an urban house cat killing songbirds. While he believes that "any animal has the right to the kind of life its nature dictates," he also points out that the competing interests of cat and songbird have to be weighed. When the cat hunts, it is only pursuing its telos. On the other hand, should a cat's right to hunt trump a bird's right to life?

Rollin does not recommend making a moral judgment on an animal that is itself incapable of appreciating a human definition of morality. Instead, he suggests a common-sense approach, such as keeping the cat from that form of predation. However—as any town council that has ever been embroiled in a heated debate about indoor-versus-outdoor cats could tell you—such an approach is far easier proposed than enacted.

Indeed, when we begin to talk about legal rights for animals, animal historian Erica Fudge wonders from whose perspective we should speak. In the same way that we invent notions about what animals think about us, so do we supply ideas about their motives and intentions on a whole host of topics—with no way of verifying the accuracy of our perceptions about what they perceive.

Then there is the matter of prejudice in favour of animals who most resemble us. British social philosopher Ted Benton takes issue with the "rights view" of Peter Singer, for example, whose Great Ape Project (GAP) initiative advocates legal consideration for primates on the grounds of their perceived similarity to us. In Benton's opinion, that perspective "remains anthropocentric." He believes we would do better not to think in terms of rights for animals at all, but in terms of what would best serve their needs. In that respect, animal welfare specialist Donald Broom is on the same page, when he speaks of honouring obligations to animals, rather than addressing their rights.

In *Rattling the Cage*, lawyer and author Steven M. Wise makes the same case as Singer for the legal rights of great apes both on grounds of intellect and genetic similarity. Additionally, Wise supports what he calls "liberty rights" for chimps and bonobos, species he regards as particularly deserving of at least some limited form of autonomy, based on the potential of their consciousness. He advocates guaranteeing these primates reproductive rights, as well as the right to keep their own offspring and habitat.

Although Wise marshals good arguments for such legal consideration, he doesn't explain how these developments might be effected. Nor does he determine whether rights for chimpanzees would best be developed in conjunction with human society, or by leaving these animals strictly on their own, in their own species habitat.

Perhaps the knottiest questions of all are tied around that problem of animals' inability to seek rights for themselves, or speak up for their interests under law—or, indeed, participate in human society as anything like equal citizens or like-minded colleagues. Eighteenth-century philosopher Immanuel Kant believed that absence of language disqualified animals as candidates for legal consideration, period. Two centuries later, French philosopher Jean-Francois Lyotard expressed that disqualification differently. An animal's lack of means to "bear witness," in Lyotard's evaluation, rendered it the "paradigm of the victim": someone who suffers wrongs yet can't claim damages.

Yet, such basic deficiencies have not prevented animals from ever being brought to trial. Nor has lack of human status under law excluded them from sentencing by human courts. According to Steven Wise, both the Hammurabic and Old Testament laws made provision for the lawful stoning to death of any ox convicted of goring any human being—even one as marginally human as a slave. Later records from the Middle Ages detail a proceeding against a mother pig and her piglets accused of killing and eating a child. As a concession to their extreme youth, the piglets were let off. However, the sow paid the ultimate price.

In another case from the same era, pigs who merely witnessed the trampling of a pig-keeper's son by some of his charges were condemned to death along with the perpetrators, on the grounds that "their cries and aggressive actions showed that they approved of the assault." Even if unable to bear witness, in Lyotard's term, to their own benefit, animals can apparently, from time to time, find themselves hanged by self-incriminating remarks.

At certain times and places in history, it has not even been necessary for an animal to be in the dock, in order to be prosecuted, judged, and sentenced. Across Europe of the sixteenth century, huge colonies of rats were tried and convicted for raiding granaries and eating up the barley— without ever showing up in court. Infestations of locusts and plagues of snakes were similarly dealt with, and "executed" in absentia.

In our own time, while the legal status of animals has not significantly changed, our perception of due process has perhaps altered somewhat. Nowadays, in those rare instances when animals get their day in court, they are more likely to be represented by independent counsel. However, just as in previous centuries, the arguments presented for and against them are invariably made by human beings, in accordance with man-made laws. And the verdict, when it comes, is based on what the court deems best not for the animal on trial, but for the humans in whose interest court has been convened.

FILING INTO COURT ROOM 4-4 of the Ontario Superior Court at 10 a.m. on a mid-May morning, I am quite excited to find myself, for the first time, in a court of law—and Superior Court, no less. I have commenced my career as a legal observer right at the top: with a challenge under the

Canadian Charter of Rights of Freedoms to the Dog Owners' Liability Act—better known to its opponents by the lachrymose-sounding acronym DOLA, and best known to the public and the press as Ontario's "pit bull ban."

On August 29, 2005, the province of Ontario became the largest jurisdiction in the world to put in place breed-specific legislation (BSL, to the initiate) that expressly forbids possession of a pit bull terrier, a Staffordshire Bull Terrier, an American Staffordshire Terrier, an American Pit Bull Terrier, or a dog that has an appearance and physical characteristics that are substantially similar to those dogs, unless said dog is kept muzzled and leashed when not on the owner's property, or the property of someone who allows the owner's dog to be unmuzzled or unleashed. The dog must be sterilized; it cannot be sold in Ontario nor given to anyone who already owns a similarly restricted dog; it can be surrendered to a pound which may sell it to a research facility or destroy it; and it cannot be permitted to have puppies. Any puppies the animal does have must also be surrendered.

As well, under the provisions of the Dog Owners' Liability Act, a peace officer may seize any dog in public if that officer believes the owner is or has at any time been in violation of the act, regardless of the breed of said dog. Also under the act, a peace officer may obtain a warrant to enter any premises to seize a dog suspected of being in violation, and may use as much force as necessary to seize the animal. If the officer believes immediate action is required, he or she is entitled to enter any premises without a warrant.

Even before the DOLA (or pit bull ban) came into effect, a coalition of concerned groups started figuring out how best to challenge the constitutionality of this sweeping legislation. Literally the day after the DOLA passed, the five member-groups of the coalition—The Dog Legislation Council of Canada, Advocates for the Underdog, The Golden Horseshoe Pit Bull Terrier Club, the American Staffordshire Terrier Club, and the Staffordshire Bull Terrier Club of Canada—announced they had engaged prominent Toronto criminal lawyer Clayton Ruby to mount a challenge based on the Charter of Rights and Freedoms included in the Canadian Constitution.

In addition to a long and mostly successful career defending the accused of the two-legged variety in some of Canada's most prominent criminal cases, Ruby is also well-known both as an advocate of civil rights and as the chief advocate for a number of earlier cases involving animals. For instance, a year or so before taking on this charter challenge to the DOLA, Ruby successfully defended Sabrina, a flying squirrel, against deportation back to the United States (where she had been purchased) after she was brought into Canada, where it is illegal to capture one of her species.

In a young woman named Catherine Cochrane, Ruby and the coalition—by now known collectively as "Banned-Aid"—found the perfect pit bull owner to take on the Ontario government in court. A small, shy twenty-three-year-old anthropology student of mild aspect, Cochrane had adopted her dog, Chess, from the Toronto Humane Society before the ban came into effect. She has no idea whether Chess—not present in Superior Court for the arguments—qualifies as a pit bull or not. What Cochrane does know is that her dog came to her with no record of bad behaviour, and has never, in her own experience, been anything but an exemplary pet.

By no means do all of the spectators in court personally own pit bulls. There is a representative from the Canadian Kennel Club, for instance, whose Airedale jewelry advertises her own breed affiliation. But like most in the courtroom, she expresses concern during a courtroom recess about the implications of legislation imposed on any type of dog simply because of its breed characteristics. A animal welfare advocate from small-town Ontario agrees, although she admits she worries about people on "social assistance" with badly bred pit bulls.

Among the self-confessed pit bull owners—like the aptly named Steve Barker of the Dog Legislation Council of Canada—there is an apparent determination to buck the stereotype about the breed and its fans by appearing neat and normal for this event. The designer of a readily available button—"My Ontario Includes Pit Bulls"—is fresh-faced and wholesome as can be, despite the fact that not only her Ontario but her household includes a pit bull.

The woman sitting beside me in the courtroom says she owns a Bull

Terrier, a breed related to some of those which fall under the ban, but not itself on the proscribed list. The arbitrariness of that is not lost on her.

"I am firmly convinced," she tells me, just as we rise for the entrance of Madam Justice Thea Herman, "that if Don Cherry wasn't a Bull Terrier man, Bullies would be banned too."

Don Cherry is a bluff, unabashedly right-wing television hockey commentator and popular Canadian contrarian. I had almost forgotten that, years ago, Cherry was equally famous for his white Bull Terrier named Blue, who showed up frequently on Cherry's TV segments and was prominent in publicity pieces about his master.

Michael Bryant, the Attorney General of Ontario, is not here, but has sent three government lawyers to respond to the charter challenge on his behalf. They've brought with them plenty of copies of the "Factum of the Respondent" to hand out to any of us who want them. These stapled documents run to more than sixty pages, printed on both sides with ammo to support the ban: "Pit bulls are dangerous animals that pose a public safety risk . . ."; "Mauling of Darlene Wagner by two (2) pit bulls in Chatham, Ontario . . ."; "Killing of a child by two (2) pit bulls in Hamburg, and Germany's statutory import ban on pit bulls . . ." As well, there is a recapitulation of the government's case that led, the previous summer, to the passage of the DOLA.

Meanwhile, the "Notice of Application" from Clay Ruby and his co-counsel Breese Davies is printed on only one side and runs to a mere four sheets. It states the grounds for the application: "restricts the liberty of dog owners of Ontario . . ."; "unconstitutionally vague in that it does not provide sufficient guidance"; "The definition of 'pit bull' in s. 1 of the Dog Owners' Liability Act is unconstitutionally overbroad . . ."; "impermissibly shifts the burden of proof from the prosecutor to the defendant . . ."—and provides a list of documentary evidence that will be used at the hearing on the application.

In every sense, the proceedings promise to be a classic underdog-vs-overbearing match-up, with the three government attorneys in the role of the black-hatted heavies, backed by the limitless power of the public purse. Virtually everybody in Court Room 4-4 of the Ontario Superior

Court—with the possible exception of the handful of media and a few non-aligned spectators—is rooting mutely but with visible fervour for the dog of the Applicant not only to have her day in court, but to carry it.

Despite the inherently theatrical nature of the courtroom set-up, the proceedings prove disappointingly devoid of pyrotechnics. No witnesses are called; testimony from the brief period of public hearings that preceded the imposition of the legislation the summer before is merely recounted by counsel.

Occasionally, Madam Justice Herman referees a brief wrangle between opposing counsel or interrupts the presentations to request clarification on some point or other. Most of the time, however, there's just a lot of chin-wagging about what breeds are or are not "captured" by this legislation, how society's interests measure up against the rights of individuals, whether the impossible onus of proving one's dog *isn't* dangerous renders the stipulations of this legislation unconstitutional, and if—as Ruby contends—this legislation is or is not a case of using a hammer to hit, well, a flea.

For all the sessions' *longueurs*, however, there is something innately remarkable in the very fact that here are learned counsel in black gowns and white stocks, begging leave to acquaint the judge with such niceties of the case as specific height at the shoulder of certain breeds of dogs, structure of various types of canine jaws for the purpose of biting and holding, and the precise definition of the word "brindle." At moments, it's feels like watching the Westminster Kennel Club Dog Show crossed with *Court TV*. At other moments, it's like being on the set of one of those 1940s movie melodramas in which a dog is on trial.

It must be *Courage of Lassie* I'm thinking of. That's the one with Frank Morgan as a small-town lawyer who gives the closing argument of his career in order to save the reputation and life of a shell-shocked Collie whose World War II exploits have left him with peace-time behavioural issues that the community he's come home to does not properly understand.

Unlike in the movies, the lawyers for the Applicant may not be able to secure a happy ending for opponents of the DOLA. Pit bulls are far from the public's image of Lassie—even Lassie on a bad day. They are best known as the type of dog favoured by dog-fight enthusiasts and drug lords. Aggression is not only bred into them, it is widely known to be enhanced with forms of "training" that include fatal attacks on other animals, including smaller dogs and even kittens, and systematic beating by their handlers.

As a result, pit bulls are generally regarded as loaded guns just waiting to go off. Certainly, that was the picture painted by the Ontario Attorney General in seeking passage of the breed-specific ban against them. And it's the same picture that enlivens the pages of the government's thick "Factum of the Respondent" today, replete with stories of pit bulls locking their jaws onto steel cables, hanging on, and refusing to let go even when bristling with tranquilizer darts fired into them by animal control officers.

Attempting to countervail such images is no easy task—especially when you're trying at the same time to dispel the idea that such an entity as a pit bull even exists. By citing examples of valour, kindness, gentleness, and general canine good sense displayed by these dogs, Clayton Ruby is, however unwillingly, bolstering the government's claim that the term "pit bull" is one that can be defined and described.

At base, the problem with both the Applicant's argument that pit bull-type dogs suffer unfairly from guilt by association and the government's "if it walks like a duck" approach is that the underworld of dog-fights and drug dealers is so remote from constitutional arguments and charter challenges, and so far out of reach. Despite the DOLA, unmuzzled and arguably dangerous pit bulls—whatever a "pit bull" might or might not be—have not disappeared in Ontario. Nor will they, regardless of whether the ban is upheld or not.

Down in the substratum of fight rings and drug drops and in the backyards and garages where dogs are reared to be aggressive and trained to kill, business will go on as usual. Instead of putting muzzles on their dogs, those owners will confine the animals' exercise to the treadmills where they build their endurance. Or simply trade in their pit bulls on Presa Carnarios or Dogos Argentinos—even bigger breeds with reputations for aggression which, so far, have not been targeted in Ontario for breed-specific legislation.

It's the middle-class breeders of Staffordshire Terriers—"the nanny dogs of Britain"—who stand to be driven from their formerly legal means of livelihood. It's their dogs who must be sent out of the province or surrendered to pounds if they can't be sold or given to anyone in Ontario willing to keep them muzzled in public and have them sterilized. It's their sort of people who think of raising money via a black-tie "Bully Ball" to pay even the specially reduced rate of a lawyer as prominent as Clayton Ruby.

Of course, there was no ending—happy or otherwise—in court that day. Almost ten months passed before Justice Thea Herman announced her ruling. Perhaps to nobody's great surprise, the judge did not find the Dog Owners' Liability Act of Ontario in violation of the Canadian Constitution or any of the provisions of the Charter of Rights and Freedoms cited by the application made on Cochrane's behalf.

Justice Herman did, however, agree with the Applicant to the extent that one definition of "pit bull" in the DOLA is too vague, in its reference to a dog that has "an appearance and physical characteristics that are substantially similar to those of" the specific breeds of Staffordshire Bull Terrier, American Pit Bull Terrier *et al* referred to in earlier definitions of breeds covered by the DOLA.

Predictably, both Applicant and Respondent claimed victory. According to lawyer Clayton Ruby, Madam Justice's dismissal of the term pit bull as "unconstitutionally vague" rendered the entire Dog Owners' Liability Act impossible to enforce. "The words 'pit bull' are all over that law," Ruby averred. "Without the words 'pit bull' ... there is no legislation left."

For his part, Attorney General Michael Bryant noted the judge's ruling had struck down only two of the 117 provisions in the DOLA. "This means that the law continues, which means no more pit bulls in Ontario."

In September 2008, Clayton Ruby made an appeal to overturn the ban to the Ontario Court of Appeal, based on the possible unconstitutionality of the vagueness of the term pit bull, as noted by Madam Justice Herman in her decision. Little more than a month later, the appeal court judges ruled to reject the Applicant's assertion that the scope of the DOLA is too broad. At the time of this writing, Ruby is still considering the possibility of appealing their ruling to the Supreme Court of Canada.

More than a decade ago, my friend Mary in upstate New York left greyhound rescue to work with a pit bull adoption organization. Not long after the Ontario legislature passed the DOLA, Mary sent me a video of herself and another member of her pit bull adoption group on a local TV news show. The two women are showing the host of the program a litter of American Pit Bull Terrier puppies available for adoption. The pups are described in a voice-over as having been smuggled out from Ontario where to remain, under current legislation, "would have resulted in their death."

Even where these dogs are legal, their lot is not always a happy one. "Therapy dogs straight out of hell" is how Mary characterizes some of the pit bulls she has known and either placed with other people or kept for herself. One of her own is, in fact, a therapy dog.

Callie is a white pit bull possessed of popping pink eyes and a comically soulful look—like one of those character actresses in forties films who specialize in wordless mugging. Mary thinks the fact that Callie is deaf may give her an extra element of empathy for the limitations of the humans with whom she visits regularly. As well, it was probably her deafness that saved her from being "trained" by dog-fight aficionados for a short, brutal career in the pit. She was lucky enough to be abandoned instead.

Whichever particular hell Callie emerged from has not left her with any discernible scars on her character. And in that respect, says Mary, this dog is typical of the breed—if it *were* a breed, which of course it's not. What endears pit bulls to Mary and the rest of her rescue group is that Velcro clinginess to humans that motivates them to want to please, whatever the task. Of course, that same fervour to do man's bidding is also what has made some of them so dangerous to other dogs.

"They're not bred or trained to attack humans," Mary says. "In fact, that would be a bad thing in the ring. And of course, as fighters, they have to be literally ready to die for their handlers. Which they do, all too often."

Mary has a sense of mission about pit bulls beyond what she felt in her earlier work as a rescuer of retired racing greyhounds. To explain it, she quotes animal trainer Vicki Hearne: "It is true that pit bulls grab and hold on. But what they most often grab and refuse to let go of is your heart, not your arm."

In *Bandit: Dossier of a Dangerous Dog*, Hearne documents the rehabilitation of an alleged pit bull named Bandit that spared him a death sentence. She also manages to lay out a case against racial and social profiling of humans and dogs. Almost twenty years later, journalist Malcolm Gladwell took up the same theme, in a piece for *The New Yorker* titled "Troublemakers."

Gladwell does not so much attack the Ontario pit bull ban as worry it to tatters, by applying dog-bite data to owner types, rather than breed types. Like Hearne—whom he quotes on the subject of pit bulls' aptness as therapy dogs—Gladwell comes to pretty much the same conclusion as Clayton Ruby before Madam Justice Herman: When a hammer-sized law is fashioned to stamp out a flea, it might also wind up doing in the dog the flea rides on.

IN AN EFFORT TO UNDERSTAND the circumstances that prompted worship at the shrine of an unjustly slain greyhound in the diocese of Lyon in the thirteenth century, anthropologist Jean-Claude Schmitt examines some of the political and social upheaval at that time. He speculates that the peasants' "resurrection" of the dog as a religious idol served to connect the notion of the punishment of the killer—a nobleman—with an affirmation of their own rights.

The greyhound's rights, however, were not at issue, neither before nor after his death. Posthumous veneration was the only form of compensation he received for the injustice he suffered. Nowadays, a dog deprived of life under similar circumstances would be unlikely to end up with even that much.

PART SIX

Gods and Monsters:
Everywhere and Nowhere

I N EARLIER TIMES AND OTHER CULTURES, relics of animals have been
viewed as objects of reverence, mystery, and even worship. Nowadays,
in a modern and mostly urban realm, apart from attention to the various
ways we prepare the carcasses of creatures we intend to eat or wear, the
remains of animals are often deemed beneath our regard. Increasingly,
however, there are striking exceptions.

More and more, for instance, animal lovers are inclined to revere the
cremated remains of deceased pets, much as they would pay respect to
what is left of members of their own species. As well, interest in animal
art, animal imagery, and animal representations of all kinds seems increasingly to transcend childhood and accompany us along our journeys
as adults.

Because animals are so strongly defined in our consciousness by their
corporeal presences, honouring their absence is mostly tied up to physical objects. From totemic creatures, to fluffy mascots, to whimsical souvenirs, to the photos or ashes of bygone pets, we experience a degree of
spiritual satisfaction in evocations of animal bodies that rivals our attachment to images and mementoes of absent human beings.

Yet because animal bodies are also conspicuously present in our world
as pieces of meat, as furs, as leather handbags and stuffed trophy heads,
we are desensitized to their significance as relics. What does it cost us
emotionally to reverence the physical essence of animals, yet in other circumstances to use, abuse, and traduce their corporeal remains? To approach

the question is to engage the ultimate paradox: How can animals be both everywhere and nowhere in our emotional calculations?

I

FROM THE OUTSKIRTS of the beautiful village of Chatillon-sur-Chalaronne, a narrow highway—unevocatively known as "D-7"—leads more or less southeast, in the direction of Marlieux, another charming hamlet in the Dombes region north of Lyon. But well before Marlieux, we've been led to understand, there should be a *panneau* by the roadside to denote the place.

That the place still exists to be denoted must be a posthumous piss-off for Stephen of Bourbon. After all, look at all the trouble he took, more than seven centuries back, to obliterate it and excise everything to do with the dog.

There is no more dog. I have to remind myself of that, as we head along D-7 in our rental Citroën, past ancient fields silver with morning frost and the ponds whose creation upset the peasantry so long ago glinting with tourist-brochure beauty in the sun. The dog's remains were disinterred and burned.

Even so, I can't quell the excitement I feel, approaching the place with all the eagerness of a horse heading for home and a big bag of oats. Because, of course, in his zeal to obliterate the holy greyhound, Stephen of Bourbon accomplished exactly the opposite.

BY THE TIME STEPHEN HAD HEARD a few more confessions, he knew what had to be done. "*We went to this place,*" is how he later reported these events, "*We called together all the people on the estate, and we preached against everything that had been said.*"

Who "we" were, he doesn't elaborate; possibly himself and some of his clerical underlings. Or perhaps simply Stephen on his own, speaking in the magisterial manner of the Pope he was pleased to represent.

"*We had the dead dog disinterred, and the sacred wood cut down and burnt, along with the remains of the dog.*"

What a scene that must have been, with the inquisitorial visitor, Stephen of Bourbon, directing a party of local men to dislodge the stones from the abandoned well, pull out the trees that had taken root, and dig down, down, down until they came upon.... What? The corporeal remains of a greyhound, buried under layers of dirt and rock and rotted twigs and the duff of disintegrated leaves from who knows how many years.

Whether any of the women who'd prayed to St. Guinefort were on-site to witness the disinterment, Stephen doesn't say. If any of the children miraculously cured by the dog's intervention ("*St. Guinefort, St. Guinefort, Pour la vie et pour le mort*") came out to witness the disinterment, no mention is made of them either. But on anyone present, the effect of seeing those flattened, musty remains—probably no more than strips of hide stained dark like the earth and clinging to various lengths of bone— would surely have been nothing short of colossal.

This? Everyone, including the Pope's inquisitor, must have asked himself the same question. This mouldering, compressed piece of matter is what our worship has been based on?

At the same time, the remains were actually there to be found. That fact must have been impressive to everyone—perhaps most of all to Stephen. Even more impressive, surely, would have been contemplation of the continuing power of these inconsequential remnants to influence the course of human events.

For the death of his dog, the Lord of Villars had been punished by the disproportionate destruction of his entire way of life. And in the wake of that destruction, the dog had become the focal point for religious cere-monies older than that way of life, older than Christianity. So much the centrepiece of it all, in fact, was the dead dog, that when Stephen of Bour-bon acted to eradicate the pagan rituals root and branch, it was not the fauns or the demons or even the old woman behind the rites that he tar-geted, but the woods themselves and the corpse of Guinefort. *There really was a dog.*

Quickly, as if there was no time to be lost, Stephen began ordering the men to move on to the next task: burning the body they'd disinterred, along with the grove of trees that had sprung up around the well. Within an hour, nothing would have been left of the holy greyhound's desiccated relics except a smouldering mound of grayish ash, with a chip of bone here, a charred tooth there. The grove would take more time to burn. But by the end of the day, even that would have been reduced to blackened stumps, singed grass, and branches turned to charcoal sticks.

Even so, Stephen was taking no chances on leftover black magic or pagan energy lurking among the burnt-out remains. "*I had an edict passed by the lords of the estate,*" he later wrote, "*warning that anyone going thenceforth to that place for any reason would be liable to have his possessions seized and then sold.*"

That, in his view, was evidently that. You can almost hear him dusting his hands, loudly thanking the locals for their cooperation, inwardly congratulating himself for the way he'd put the entire business to rest. What Stephen of Bourbon would not have known—as he rode away from the Dombes region, smiling the smile of satisfaction that comes with a job well done—was that devotions centred around the dog who had killed the snake were slated to continue on that selfsame forbidden spot for more than another seven hundred years.

EARLY IN THE TWENTY-FIRST CENTURY, American photographer Sally Mann undertook a project from which more weak-kneed pet lovers might shrink: Mann disinterred the year-old remains of her beloved pet greyhound, Eva, salvaged what fragments she could, and took them back to her studio to reassemble and photograph. Eventually, those photographic studies of Eva's hide and bones became part of a larger exhibition Mann called "What Remains."

That 2004 exhibition at the Corcoran Gallery in Washington, D.C. was subtitled "Matter Lent." As art critic and scholar Alice Kuzniar points out, "Lent" conveys a sense of gravity, similar to the forty-day period of mourning called Lent that precedes the resurrection of Christ. Perhaps that sober subtitle was necessary to dispel any sense of sensationalism inherent in "What Remains." In addition to the bones of her dog, Mann's exhibition included studies of human bodies photographed in varying stages of decomposition.

The subtitle "Matter Lent" also serves to evoke the fleeting way in which pet animals—especially in view of their comparatively short lifespans—are "lent" to us, only to be taken away too soon by mishap, disease, or decrepitude. The bleakness of that little pile of bones and hair that Eva has dwindled down to in her posthumous photos strikes Kuzniar as "suggesting an unutterable, choking grief that can only put on display but not verbally express what essentially is a void."

To me, Mann's pictures of Eva's bones also hint at an element of comfort. More than human beings, animals impress themselves upon our memories by virtue of their corporeal qualities. The text Sally Mann wrote to accompany the images of Eva's remains documents her wanting to find out what had "finally become of that head I had stroked, oh ten thousand times, those paws she so delicately crossed as she lay by my desk, rock-hard nails emerging from the finest white hairs."

Whether consciously or not, Mann has echoed Hamlet's reaction to the skull of Yorick, the jester he remembers from his own childhood: "Here hung those lips that I have kissed I know not how oft." Then, when Mann contrasts the sleek, soft tactility of the living Eva's fur and flesh with the "tiny pieces that remained—tail bones, teeth, claws…" she shares with Shakespeare that sense of wonderment that what was once so warm and lively, so fine and firm and strong, can now be summed up in a few decayed remnants.

However, when the species is our own, that contemplation of the difference between the quick and the dead, the fleshly and the merely skeletal, is tinged with a kind of dismay at what has been lost. Not only is Hamlet revolted by the earthy odour of Yorick's remains—"And smelt so? Pah!"— his ever-ready melancholy is kindled by the recollection of the "man of infinite jest" whose grinning, witless skull so inadequately evokes the deceased.

In contrast, Sally Mann's memories of Eva don't appear to be betrayed by those few, physical remnants. It's Eva's body that Mann remembers, how it felt to stroke and fondle and press against her own. For that reason, it seems to me there might be some elements of consolation available to Mann in those "tiny pieces" of Eva that the remains of a human companion could never supply.

For humans in general, the extent to which we summarize animals in terms of their physical essence may cause us to treat their remains either as enormously significant or as completely inconsequential. On one end of the spectrum, there are pet cemeteries and Sally Mann's photographed remains of her beloved Eva's bones. On the other end, there's the commodified carcass hung in the butcher's window or the meaningless tuft of fur on the roadside that once was a chipmunk.

Surely Stephen of Bourbon's decision to dig up and incinerate the "relics" of the holy greyhound was complicated by concerns rooted in that ambivalence about the body itself. One the one hand, the message the cleric wished to send by unearthing the dog's remains was one of contempt for the unworthiness of the object of the peasant's worship. On the other hand, he must have worried, at least fleetingly, about the importance he might confer on those remnants of bones and fur by the very act of disinterring them with such fanfare.

In his 1999 novel *Disgrace*, J. M. Coetzee invests the inconsequentiality of animal bodies with redemptive power. In so doing, he elevates the remains to a level of almost religious significance.

Coetzee's protagonist, David Lurie is, as the title indicates, a man in disgrace with fortune and men's eyes. He has committed a shameful assault on a woman for which he is attempting to atone. One of his acts of penitence is to volunteer at an animal clinic full of unwanted dogs that are most often euthanized. Lurie's task is to drive the dead bodies to the entrance of an incinerator. There, they are loaded onto trolleys and hauled to the furnace.

He becomes aware that, if he leaves the corpses for workmen to load and incinerate, they frequently lie waiting so long that rigor mortis sets in. Lurie has been horrified to discover that, when the workmen finally arrive, they often snap the dogs' bones in order to cram their stiffened forms onto the trolleys. He can't bear to think about the bodies being treated that way. Now, when he arrives at the incinerator, he places the freshly deceased dogs onto the trolley himself, arranging their still-limp corpses with gentleness and respect. It is the least he can do—both for the dogs and for the salvation of his own sense of grace.

Because animals' bodies are so regularly cut up for consumption or any number of other human uses, the connection with their original owners is not always obvious. Sometimes, it's difficult even to identify them as parts of an animal that was once alive.

When I was about ten, a sudden rage among girls at my school was "lucky" rabbits' feet. You could buy them at the five-and-dime—and probably still can, in the dollar stores that have replaced Woolworth's and Kresge's. These were the feet of actual rabbits, with their fur and toenails intact, cut off just above the ankle and grafted onto a metal cuff. The cuff was fitted with a beaded chain that could be attached to the zipper of your ring-binder or pencil case.

My own rabbit's foot was dyed bright blue. That may be why I did not immediately grasp that it was from a real animal. Or maybe I didn't want to grasp it, because to do so would lead to all kinds of distressing speculations about how that lucky foot had been obtained from the unlucky rabbit.

Therefore, it was quite a while before I allowed myself to acknowledge the fact that the fur—apart from its lurid colour—was suspiciously genuine. And even more time elapsed before it occurred to me how realistic were those claws, and that hard, slightly irregular bone beneath what I had taken for plush.

I was horrified. The girls who were lucky with their rabbits' feet, it seemed to me, were the girls who didn't yet know or who didn't care that their favourite charm had once been a living thing.

BY THE TIME WILLIAM COWPER'S favourite spaniel Beau died in 1796, the dog had been the subject of a number of his master's poems. However, that was not regarded as sufficient immortality. Beau's remains were stuffed, perhaps to help Cowper deal with his grief. One friend, a Mr. Hayley, expressed the hope that the preserved body of the beloved pet might "make a pleasing and salutary impression on the poet's reviving fancy."

Whether that might have happened, we'll never know. Unfortunately, Cowper's devoted companion, Mary Unwin, died in the same year, and that was a blow from which the mentally fragile writer never did recover.

Needless to say, there's no record of anybody in Cowper's circle suggesting that Mary should have been preserved in order to revive the poet's interest in writing. But the practice of stuffing favourite pets for consoling display was common right into the nineteenth century.

Nowadays, the most familiar examples of taxidermized animals are mounted heads of deer and bear and other large wildlife. Occasionally, a famous domestic creature will get the nod—like Roy Rogers' palomino, Trigger, stuffed in his entirety and on display at the Dale Evans Museum, along with the cowboy star's German Shepherd, Bullet.

Even more gloriously on view are two celebrated members of the USSR's Space Dog program of the 1950s. One of the cosmonaut dogs who survived her space flight was Belka—Russian for "Squirrel." Belka's preserved remains are in a glass case at the Memorial Museum of Astronautics in Moscow.

Another of the space dogs, called Strelka—or "Little Arrow"—not only made it back to Earth alive, she later had puppies. One of her litter was given to Caroline Kennedy by Soviet Premier Nikita Kruschev. But Strelka has been perpetuated by more than her offspring. Her preserved body is part of a traveling exhibition that has visited the US, China, and Israel, among other countries.

To me, there is something almost eerily indecent in the idea of exhibiting the body of any dead hero. However, when, as in the case of animals, heroes are so entirely defined by their physical selves, I can better comprehend the impulse to give a kind of permanence to the especially ephemeral quality of their lives.

That may be even more important when there are no actual remains to enshrine. As I mentioned earlier, Laika, the first and most famous Russian dog cosmonaut, suffocated in orbit, in a capsule that was not recovered. It wasn't until forty years after her famous and fatal space flight that a lasting way to honour her was devised. Today, on the outskirts of Moscow, you can find a statue of Laika standing audaciously on a rocket.

That simulation is all that remains of a genuine media star and martyr to the unmanned space program of the Soviet Union.

Perhaps the most telling comment on the evocative power of animal remains is provided by Venezuelan artist José Antonio Hernandez-Diez, in an astonishing 1991 installation called "San Guinefort." The actual cadaver of a canine—not a greyhound, but a small brown dog of indeterminate breed—is sealed inside a septic glass container which is fitted with rubber sleeves. The viewer is able to put his or her arms into the sleeves, and thereby reach inside the glass case to touch the animal's body.

According to the New Museum of Contemporary Art in New York, where the piece was exhibited in 2001, "San Guinefort evokes South American Catholic faith and superstition—the proof of touch is considered a remedy for religious doubt."

Taking away such proof was, of course, at the heart of Stephen of Bourbon's decision to disinter the remains of the original canine St. Guinefort and destroy them. Just as supplying justification for faith is at the heart of the preservation of animal bodies, like Strelka's, like Trigger's, like Beau's.

Even when the body itself is no longer available to be permanently memorialized, alternatives may be supplied, as in the memorial to Laika. Or, as in the case of the greyhound known as St. Guinefort, pilgrimage to the tomb may continue, just as before, despite the fact that the body itself, the well that housed it, and the grove of trees that surrounded it were dug up and put to the torch in a wholly inadequate attempt to disinter superstition and incinerate faith.

WITHIN A KILOMETRE, SURELY, of the promised roadside *panneau*, and it's only now dawning on me: What if we can't find it—neither the roadside marker nor the place that it marks? To have come so far, only to drive endlessly and fruitlessly around and around the (admittedly beautiful) French countryside, and yet end up nowhere.

Rueful recollections of that long-ago hunt for Greyfriars Bobby using a faulty Edinburgh map flood unbidden into my mind. And much more recently—no more than a week ago—wasn't I traipsing through the

London borough of Battersea, in quest of the resurrected statue of the Brown Dog? Just another reiteration of that wretched "life motif" of mine: forever doomed to hunt and hunt for canine markers and memorials, dogged by the fear of never finding them.

Back in 1910, the controversial Brown Dog sculpture—commemorating a terrier subjected to numerous vivisections before being released by death—was dismantled by four workmen under the guard of 120 policemen, and hidden in a bicycle shed. Nobody has seen it since. It took until 1986 for a new Brown Dog memorial to be erected, a work by sculptor Nicola Hicks Brown. Through advance reading, I had learned this new monument is regarded as a far cry from the old. Instead of a defiant little dog with an inscription documenting his abuse and appealing to the public—"How long shall these Things be?"—the new Brown Dog is an ingratiatingly humble little figure with no political or social context, modeled on one of the artist's own dogs.

Nevertheless, I was in London and I wanted to see it, the same way that Greyfriars Bobby's memorial had been a must, all those years before. The same way—should I ever find myself in Salt Lake City—I would want to take in that city's monument to the seagulls who saved the Mormons' crops by eating up a plague of katydids. Examples of public memorials to honour animals are rare enough that I'm prepared to go looking, whenever I get the chance.

Besides, the Brown Dog—even in his newer and blander incarnation—felt like a particularly apt way-station along the road to the elusive non-remains of St. Guinefort. Both dogs were put to use for the protection of the weak and ailing—the greyhound first as a guardian of the cradle, then as a posthumous healer in death; the poor terrier named Fun as a living tool to advance medical knowledge. The fact that the vivisected dog was memorialized specifically to end the practices that made him famous is no more and no less ironic than the fact that Stephen's immolation of the unholy greyhound actually helped the dog's cult to flourish for another seven hundred years.

So there I was on a sunny Saturday, traipsing the Old English Garden in London's Battersea Park, among the absurdly early crocuses and roses, trying and failing to locate the Brown Dog. Finally, it was a family with a real-live black Labrador who came along to put me right.

At first, as Mum and Dad disagreed over the statue's presumed location, I feared there might be a new Brown Dog Riot. However, Dad and Labrador Millie eventually parted from Mum and the kids to lead me to Hicks Brown's much-disputed sculpture.

I could see what the critics are on about. The pose of the dog is servile and tentative—a riff on the theme of Dog, not the embodiment of an outrage. Even more significant is the fact this statue is hidden away among the roses and the holly of the Old English Garden, rather than set out on a main street to challenge the onlooker.

At the very least, I decided, I owed it to the memory of the original Brown Dog to search out the spot where he'd stood. I left the new Brown Dog in his leafy hideaway, and went back to busy Battersea Road. At the intersection of Latchmere Road is the Latchmere Pub. According to what I'd read, somewhere nearby, a raised piece of pavement marks the spot where the statue stood, in the now-disappeared Latchmere Recreation Grounds.

Inside the pub, a pleasant young trio of employees was getting ready to open. None of the three had any idea where a statue of a brown dog might once have stood. However, they told me, there was quite a nice sculpture of a little dog across the way in Battersea Park, near the English Garden. Perhaps I might like to take a look at that?

I thanked them, went back outside, wandered a ways, located a worn patch of uneven paving brick—and pretended to myself it was the base of that original Brown Dog sculpture and drinking fountain. As close as I might be to the actual spot—or as far off—I knew it was as near as I was going to get to the abused brown terrier whose likeness had become such a *cause célèbre* that not a trace was permitted to be left behind.

No statue, no inscription, no marker, no memorial.... As my partner and I pass yet another road-sign on D-7, and slow down to read yet another notification of a local attraction that has nothing to do with Guinefort, I try not to remember how bereft I'd felt in London, failing to find any palpable proof of the Brown Dog.

There really was a dog, I remind myself fiercely. And perhaps nobody in

Christendom was more surprised than Stephen of Bourbon to have that confirmed, when the peasants he'd set to digging into that well hit pay dirt.

II

IN *THE GOLDEN BOUGH*, J.G. Frazer recounts how mystified Jesuit priests were when they first came to Canada and confronted the natives' attitudes to dead animals. After catching a beaver, for instance, Indians always ensured that the bones were treated with respect, and not left for the dogs to gnaw.

"How could a beaver possibly know what had become of its bones after death?" one of the Jesuits chided. To which the Indian replied:

> Before the beaver is stone dead, his soul takes a turn in the hut of the man who is killing him and makes a careful note of what is done with his bones. If the bones are given to the dogs, the other beavers would get word of it and would not let themselves be caught. Whereas, if their bones are thrown into the fire or a river, they are quite satisfied; and it is particularly gratifying to the net which caught them.

In contrast, consider a modern media account of a "bear dump" at Esker Lakes Provincial Park in northern Ontario. In September 2007, the bears' bones made headlines all over the province. When officers working for the provincial Ministry of Natural Resources had been faced with a sudden influx of hungry black bears in settled areas, their solution was to capture the animals, take them to the edge of town and shoot them—then distribute their carcasses to various dump sites in the area. A photo on the website of the local Member of Parliament—outraged to hear about this method of "animal control"—shows some strewn bones and large fragments of skulls.

A spokesman for the Ministry of Natural Resources explained to Charlie Angus, the angry MP, that a tight budget and an increase in the number of invading bears had forced the ministry to cut back its program to relocate them. They couldn't even afford to hire a backhoe to dig a pit to bury the remains.

Perhaps those on-site problems could be answered with an infusion of cash. Still, a larger point seems to have been missed: one difference between "advanced" civilization and the unsophisticated lives of the original inhabitants may be the difference between a pile of dishonoured animal remains scattered here and there, and a culture of reverence for what those bones symbolize and to whom they belong—and where.

Perhaps about as far back as we can dig into the mist-shrouded consciousness of our ancestors in Western Europe is the period of time from roughly 75,000 BCE until about twenty thousand years ago. It was during that time that the animal of chief interest to them—the cave bear—became extinct.

Like the predecessor of the modern horse in North America, the cave bear of Europe—along with other mammalian species—was most likely wiped out by the climate changes that occurred at the end of the Pleistocene glacial period. While some theorists suggest that over-hunting by humans accounted for the disappearance of such mammals as cave bears and woolly mammoths, the majority of opinion still seems to weigh in on the side of the glaciers.

The cave bear was about 30 percent larger than the North American black bear, and mostly vegetarian. However, the animal was fierce enough to inspire shock and awe in the human inhabitants of modern-day Switzerland and France, judging from sites of apparent worship that have been uncovered and examined.

Readers of Jean Auel's *The Clan of the Cave Bear*, the first novel in her Earth's Children series, will recall that when a child named Creb is attacked by a cave bear, the assault by such a revered animal figure, although frightening, confers special status on the victim. Auel depicts a world in which Neanderthals identify with and worship this animal. However, there are conflicting schools of thought on whether these early humanoids had actually developed the sort of consciousness that would admit of a symbolic or religious relationship with animals.

As well, among those who doubt Neanderthals had the "theory of mind" necessary to construct the kinds of shrines found at Drachenloch or Regourdou there is skepticism that skeletal remains of cave bears found at those sites are proof of animal worship. Nevertheless, there seems enough support for the idea of primitive perception of the cave bear as a god to warrant taking a figurative look inside the caves.

At Drachenloch in Switzerland, what some term "relics" of cave bears were discovered, organized neatly under slabs of stone: a stack of bear skulls, deliberately arranged, along with one skull of an adult bear pierced by the leg bone of a cub.

Meanwhile, in caves at Regourdou in the south of France, skeletons of cave bears were unearthed—minus their skulls. Ten or more bears have been found under a single slab. In both sites, there are strong indications that the organization, decapitation, and concealment of these skeletal remains could not be accidental. Some archaeological and anthropological expeditions have also identified what they believe to be altars where burnt offerings were made, and small stone carvings that are somewhat bear-like.

This evidence at least suggests that the bear was among the very first animals to be worshipped, back in the infancy of human habitation on Earth. As with later evidence, from more advanced cultures ranging from the Egyptians, to the Greeks, to New World aborigines, to the ancient Indians of the Subcontinent and others, the holy relics—or mere remains—of cave bears unearthed at Drachenloch and Regourdou hint at a pronounced ambivalence in the way humans have regarded and treated sacred animals, right from the dawn of human consciousness.

In some instances, animals have appeared like divinities to be feared and appeased. In other cases, humans see in them emissaries from another world—to be sacrificed and sent "home" in order to insure a continual stream of their kind to Earth, for man's comfort, companionship, sustenance, and worship.

Looking at animals from the youthful perspective of such early humans, it is impossible not to identify the seeds of a great contradiction between reverence of animal species as gods and their almost simultaneous banishment. Captured, killed, and sacrificed on ground that was theirs long before it was ours, they are then sent back where they came from long before we did. Subsequent rituals return them to Earth again—so that cycle of appeasement, sacrifice, banishment, and the quest for home can begin all over again.

WITHIN HUMANS AS INDIVIDUALS, as much as within our entire species, the patterns of our quests are set early. My own adult pilgrimage to the heart of the Guinefort myth began with a story read in childhood. But the seeds of that mission may have been sown even earlier by another book: Margaret Marshall Saunders' *Beautiful Joe*.

As in my later encounter with Guinefort, it was some years before I realized that the dog at the centre of Saunders' novel had actually existed. In the case of Joe, many more years passed before I learned that his gravesite had not only been preserved, it had become the centrepiece of a public memorial in Meaford, Ontario—no more than a hundred miles from where I now lived in Toronto.

When I finally made the trip to Beautiful Joe's grave, seeing that actual plot of earth surrounded by a fence gave me an unexpected jolt. It was a feeling similar to what I could recall of my first visit to Boston, walking along the Freedom Trail and coming upon a small tombstone inscribed "Paul Revere."

Like Beautiful Joe, Paul Revere was a character I had met through childhood reading—at an age when the lines between fact and fiction are notoriously blurry. Somehow, I had not thought of Revere as someone who had actually lived—until I saw proof that he had actually died.

Next to the gates of Beautiful Joe Park is a small pink house where a family named Moore once lived. Joe came into that house pretty much as described in the 1893 novel by Margaret Marshall Saunders, an in-law of the Moores who learned the story while visiting from the Maritimes. Mutilated as a young dog by a brutish owner, Joe was rescued and lived with the Moores until a ripe old age. The fenced gravestone that's now within the park perimeter is where the family buried Joe in the early 1900s.

By that time Saunders' novel had already made him famous. But Beautiful Joe Park in Meaford has been known by that name only since the 1960s. Even then, you get the impression that it may have required some convincing before the town fathers would agree that it was high time they memorialized Meaford's most celebrated resident. And at that, beyond fencing off the land and putting up a plaque, nobody at that time seemed to know what more could be done to honour a dog. It was only in the mid-1990s that a local heritage society formed to try to widen recognition of the park and sustain interest in a book already a century old. And it has only been in the last decade or so that a board really committed to that mission has been in place.

To look down at the grave and imagine those mouldered bones lying beneath that ground gives rise to feelings more complex, in their way, than the contemplation of the tombstone of Paul Revere—or, for that matter, William Shakespeare or Peter the Great or Tutankhamen. Death reduces us all, of course, great and small. But because a dog is so comparatively inconsequential to begin with, Joe seems oddly magnified by this unusual homage to his earthly remains.

Here he is, with a park named for him, a marked gravesite, and—since 2006—a bronze sculpture of himself on a pedestal at the entrance. Like the Brown Dog, like Guinefort, Joe makes his claim to fame not on the basis of what he did, but what was done to him—in his case, by the anonymous brute immortalized as "Jenkins the milkman" in Saunders' novel.

Margaret Saunders is buried in Mount Pleasant Cemetery in Toronto, not far from where I live. But I have never gone there to search out her tombstone. Yet here I am in Meaford, a hundred miles from home, looking down at the stone that marks the remains of a dog no one would know were it not for Saunders.

In its heyday, *Beautiful Joe* became the first Canadian novel to sell more than a million copies. For years after, it continued to top children's book lists around the world. In recent decades, the novel has given way to juvenile literature that is less didactic and more colloquial. When the copyright was allowed to lapse by the original publisher, the Beautiful Joe Heritage Society put out its own edition in hard copy and online.

Some board members express hope of restoring the novel to its former glory by making it more widely available through libraries and getting it taught in schools. However, that's not likely to happen. *Beautiful Joe*— though still beautiful to those who loved it as children and continue to revere it—is a book of a bygone era.

What remains is the truth behind the tale. There once was such a dog abused in such a way, who was taken in by a family of animal lovers, given a happy home, and christened "Beautiful" Joe because the mutilations to his body had left him so ugly.

Even now, when people journey to the place where the dog is buried it is for the affirmation the story affords: a moment's terrible injury may be requited by an eternity of benefice; the reward of humble service may be lofty renown; what begins in brutality and bitter, bitter silence may end in peace, amity, and—at long last—the sweet repose of home.

IT WAS STANDING AT THE GRAVESIDE of Beautiful Joe that I made the decision to find "Le Bois de Guignefort." At least, that's how I am recalling it now, as my long-suffering partner continues to drive us up and down the byways of what the tourist literature persistently refers to as "the undiscovered Dombes," in search of that as-yet-undiscovered roadside marker.

The way to those woods that Jean-Claude Schmitt describes in *The Holy Greyhound* is more or less chiseled into my memory—as is my recollection of myself looking down on Joe's gravestone, while murmuring Schmitt's directions like a litany: "Three-point-six kilometres southeast of Chatillon; three-point-six kilometres southwest of Romans; four-point-eleven kilometres north of Sandrans, and four-point-three kilometres northwest of Le Chatelard...." Schmitt reckons it's only a few dozen metres from the Chalaronne River, "in which the women immersed their children, at the point where the Crosat mill-course flows into the river, at the point where it comes closest to the hills fringing the riverbed to the northeast...."

Now that we're more or less here, however, it's not nearly as simple as the book made it sound. Now that we're here, and I have started asking myself what I'm going to do if we can't find the place we have come all this way expressly to find, it is becoming increasingly hard to ask myself anything else.

In this one corner of the world where Guinefort is everywhere, how can it be that he seems to be nowhere at all? And why has my urgency about tracking him down started to feel not so much like hurrying home, as like trying to go home and failing to find the place?

I am, I realize, no longer thinking about Beautiful Joe, and the far simpler journey to his grave that felt like stepping neatly back into childhood. Now, I am thinking about the more complicated steps required to reach a destination more distant in every sense.

In *Elizabeth Costello*, J.M. Coetzee's title character imagines the life of a chimpanzee in an experimental lab, being investigated by his human keepers in every way except the ways that matter to him. What does he care if he can solve the problems they pose to him or communicate responses to their queries? "The question that truly occupies him," says Costello, "as it occupies the rat and the cat and every other animal trapped in the hell of the laboratory or zoo is: 'Where is home and how do I get there?'"

That is, Coetzee's character feels, the query most central to the lives of all displaced animals. As I gaze at the wooded farmland that stretches out on both sides of the D-7, I think about the cornfield at faraway Fauna, stretching out beyond the enclosure occupied by Theo, the solemn baboon.

Just as the sun was going down, Gloria Grow told me, Theo always seemed to recollect some mysterious sorrow. He would stare out across the field and give voice to a long sad cry.

But Theo was not the only primate on the place who seemed intent on broadcasting his whereabouts to some unseen listener. Tom, the oldest chimpanzee at Fauna—with his mottled upper lip and air of ancient gravitas—also set up a cry at the end of the day, and then again just before dawn, Gloria reported. "It's as if he's saying 'Here I am!'"

WHEN JEAN-CLAUDE SCHMITT was sifting through old documents, interviewing locals old enough to recall the rites in the woods, and driving up and down these same roads trying to determine precisely where the dog was interred, he must have had days like this. There must have been times when, more than anything, all he wanted was for the ghost of Guinefort to abjure that silence greyhounds are so renowned for keeping, and set up a howl a living human could hear: "Here I am!"

Where are you, Guinefort? Hey? Where's the boy? Dug up from the well and burned to ash. Your corporeal remains, at least. But where are *you*, God's holy greyhound, with a better master now that you had before?

The destruction of the Lord of Villars' manor house by God, Schmitt observes in his book, actually abets the process of the dog's resurrection. The woods open up to the common people, to create a place where the rituals can occur, in Guinefort's name.

His name. That's what truly sends him to heaven. He's more than a saint—almost a dog spelled backward. At the very least, he's a demi-god, capable of intercession on behalf of children when they fall ill, and seem to slip out of their parents' hands, and into the grasp of malevolent fairies.

And even if he's only a dog, at least a dog by his nature is loyal, and courageous against serpents. Just like St. George. Or what about St. Michael, who drove Lucifer down to hell and turned him into a legless thing, doomed to slither on his belly forever more, calling out to God who was now deaf to his name?

But not deaf to the name of Guinefort. Isn't that right, boy? You were called by name by the common people, and called home by their prayers to your rightful dwelling place. Now if only I knew how to find that spot.

III

IN GERMANY, THE LAST WILD BEAR was hunted and killed around 1835. After that, the sad, oddly humanoid upright figure with a ring through his nose, shuffling through the village at the end of a chain, was the only contact most Germans had with a once-sacred animal. In Berlin—a city named for the bear in the early Middle Ages—images of bears on flags and statues of the city's namesake have remained prominent right up to the present. But apart from captives in animal parks and zoos, there were no living representatives of the species anywhere in Germany for 170 years. Until Bruno.

In the spring of 2006, a brown bear who'd escaped from an Italian sanctuary wandered across the border into Bavaria, and thereby created a sensation. Coincidentally, the previous year had been proclaimed the Year of the Bear in Germany, and now lo and behold, the bear was back! How cool is that? Let's call him "Bruno."

However, euphoria at the news of the bruin's repatriation to German soil rapidly turned to consternation. As Naomi Buck, a Canadian journalist based in Berlin, reported: "After he had made mincemeat of nine sheep, six chickens and four pigeons, the mood in Bavaria changed." All told, on a five-week rampage across Bavaria Bruno killed thirty-one sheep, thirteen chickens, four goats, four pigeons, and even a few guinea pigs.

On one of his raids, Bruno left a sample of fur behind. DNA testing identified him as the son of two brown bears who'd been relocated from their native Slovenia to the Italian sanctuary whence he had escaped. Other members of that particular family of bears had proved similarly problematic. Open season was declared on Bruno.

At that point, the emphasis was still on tracking him, not whacking him. Karelian Bear Dogs, a bear-human "mediator," and an anaesthesia specialist with narcotics-filled darts were all dispatched to find Bruno, tranquilize him, put him in a cage, and get him back to Italy. Alive.

Seeing a marketing hook, Baerenmarke, a Nestle-owned manufacturer of condensed milk with a mama bear as its logo, paid for transport of a cage all the way from Montana. That, in turn, prompted the World Wildlife Fund—to whose resettlement program in Italy Bruno belonged—to launch a campaign to capture the bear. Alive.

Given that, what followed is almost impossible to believe—especially in an era with a declared emphasis on preservation of disappearing species.

On May 22, 2006, Bavaria's Environment Minister Werner Schanappauf suddenly gave hunters the go-ahead to take Bruno down. Little more than a month later, on June 26, the bear himself became the final item on the tally of casualties incurred in his rampage. Before the mediators or tranquilizer darts could get to Bruno, a hunter did, and shot him. Dead.

The following winter in Munich, the Bavarian capital, the curator of the city museum mounted an exhibition rich with imagery related to bears and their history in Germany. It was dedicated to Bruno's memory. "A martyr, a holy animal who stands for all others," was how the curator Helmut Bauer characterized Bruno in a conversation with Naomi Buck.

I didn't get a chance to see the exhibition myself, but a friend in Munich sent me a copy of the museum catalogue. Using materials from the permanent collection as well as some borrowed items, Herr Bauer managed to find representations ranging from bearskin rugs to *Baerendreck*—the southern German term for licorice, literally "bear crap"—to illustrate his own belief that, "Erotic, hagiographic or satirical, the bear has always been an important symbol here. But Germans have forgotten what the bear really is, as an animal."

The exhibits included photos of bears kissing their trainers; there was an 1835 engraving of the (previously) last bear killed in Germany being brought into the village—his body sprawled ingloriously across a wagon, while the hunter who killed him is borne in triumph on the shoulders of his compatriots. There were bears with nose rings riding motorcycles or being subdued with whips; there were gummy bears, and bottles of beer with polar bear logos, and mechanical bears, and masks depicting sacred bears, and teddy bears, and every kind of bear imaginable.

I emailed curator Helmut Bauer to ask him what the brief return, and even briefer reign, of a wild bear had meant to modern Germans, and how they now felt about what had happened. Bauer replied:

> Bruno did not fit into the concept of a natural world that is totally cultivated. People go for walks, enjoy lovely views, and are sure that nothing dangerous with happen to them. We view the wilderness on TV, perhaps with an aperitif, while sitting in a comfortable armchair.

Bruno's murder, however, upset a lot of people. Bruno became a symbol for the oppression of nature. Everyone can do a good job, pay their insurance premium, or buy a ticket to the zoo. But no one dares to behave according to their wild nature. The wild in man should appear only as rarely as a wild bear in the beautiful countryside.

"Bruno is dead. But he lives on in our hearts." We hear this phrase again and again. People have suddenly realized through Bruno's death that they themselves are imprisoned in a comfortably sheltered system. Bruno does not fit into such a system. There is only room in such a world for a standardized life. It is sad for Bruno, but also sad for us, because we no longer can or dare accept the power of the wild.

Less than a year after Bruno was consigned to an afterlife in the hearts of the German public, another bear appeared to challenge his solo occupancy there. In December 2006, twin polar bear cubs were born in the Berlin Zoo to a mother named Tosca—who rejected them. To the public's dismay, zoo officials decided not to intervene, even after one of the cubs died.

But at that point, Heiner Kloes, the curator of bears, took matters into his own hands, and made a decision to try to save the other cub. A sympathetic keeper, Thomas Doerflein, was assigned to bottle-feed the little bear, named Knut, cuddle him, and play with him behind closed doors at the zoo. When Knut made his debut in March 2007 with Doerflein at his side, public outrage turned to international ecstasy. Suddenly, the entire world seemed to be in love with Knut.

As the love affair continued with long lineups to catch a glimpse of Knut wrestling in his cage with his keeper, the polar bear cub turned into an unprecedented media and marketing bonanza for the Berlin Zoo, where visitorship rose by 27 percent, resulting in a ten-million-dollar profit. In November 2007, Thomas Doerflein was awarded Berlin's medal of merit for his service to the zoo and to Knut.

Inevitably, Knut grew up and became so strong and unruly that, in July 2008, the so-called "Knut show" had to be shut down, for the sake of

Thomas Doerflein's safety. The public was still welcome to flock to the polar bear's outdoor enclosure, but the beloved spectacle of Knut and his keeper in daily wrestling matches was no longer on offer.

In an unfortunate footnote, the keeper took his own life in September 2008. By that time, Knut had been openly criticized by some of Doerflein's fellow keepers as a "psychopath" so addicted to human adulation, that, in the words of keeper Markus Roebke, "he actually cries out and whimpers if he sees that there is not a spectator outside his enclosure." Whether those harsh assessments in any way influenced Thomas Doerflein's decision to kill himself remains a matter of speculation.

At least in his first year of public life, Knut the exotic Arctic polar bear cub managed to succeed as a media phenomenon where Bruno the native European brown bear failed. Knut captured hearts around the world exactly as the World Wildlife Fund had dreamed of capturing Bruno: in a warm, friendly, non-violent manner—and above all, alive.

THROUGHOUT HIS LIFE, ethologist Paul Shepard—who died in 1996— claimed a strong attachment to bears. In numerous books, he wrote about the glory days of their earliest mythology, as well as what he viewed as their sad decline into mere plush toys. Whether you are a bear hunter like Shepard or simply someone interested in the variegated fortunes of this interesting animal, one thing seems clear: at every stage of the bear's history, his visual resemblance to us, when standing upright, has shaped his fortunes—both as a god and as a monster.

Not so eerily similar to humans as to make us uncomfortable, like great apes, bears are still not enough unlike us to escape a particular kind of exploitation, as dressed-up human surrogates. Yet, their humanness, combined with their size, strength, and unpredictability, has also inspired a level of near-universal worship not shared by any other animal species.

Beginning with the cave bear in Europe of the early Paleolithic period, reverence of various ursine species arose on every continent where their kind existed. In ancient Greece and pre-Christian Europe, the constellation Ursa Major connected the bear to the goddess Artemis. In Crete, Artemis was worshipped in a cave called "Arkoudia," meaning "cave of the she-bear."

Gradually, the popularity of the hunting goddess spread across ancient Europe and Britain. Among the Helvetians, Artemis was called Artio, and the name of their chief city, Bern, meant "she-bear." To the Celts, she was Art, mother of Arthur, their "bear king." And when Christianity arrived, Art was rechristened "St. Ursula" so that pantheistic reverence for the bear could carry on under another name. Meanwhile, on another continent and long before the Europeans arrived, the Navajo identified the same constellation of stars with the bear.

In Paul Shepard's view, it is the bear's human-like posture when on hind legs that contributed most to the native North American image of a shaggy sage, reading the forest as if it were a book, and exhibiting an elder's knowledge of which plants to eat as medicinal and which to avoid as poisonous. Shepard also describes the image of the sacred bear as "maternal," which he believes contributed to the general public's embrace of the toy "teddy bear" early in the twentieth century. The bear's fur, he writes, "reminds us we are primates with a much longer memory of clinging to a mother's fur than being held against a naked breast."

If that were so, it seems to me Shepard could make a better case for a teddy *gorilla* than a teddy bear. Yet, while toy monkeys and little stuffed apes have long enjoyed some popularity as children's cuddle creatures, it's the teddy bear that outstrips all others, even today.

He is, in fact, the ultimate "transitional object," in the phrase made famous by Donald Woods Winnicott in the 1950s: an inanimate object that evokes the softness and warmth of a mother, and sometimes the smell of "home." At the same time, it is something that belongs to the child, and can literally and figuratively accompany him or her in the transition to a completely developed sense of a separate self.

Why bears, in particular, got the nod seems easy enough to figure out. They are wild animals when required to be—threatening to enemies, if a child is longing for a powerful protector. But because the teddy bear stands erect like a doll he also resembles a human infant, if a dependent companion is what the child most craves.

Only a die-hard believer in the collective unconscious would suggest that every child's affinity for his or her teddy bear connects to ancient, un-surfaced recollections of a primitive realm in which bears were worshipped as divine. Still, any of us might be tempted to align the desires and dreams of childhood with the infancy of our entire species. Every human infant's task of separating individual identity from the larger realm that is "not-me" readily serves as a microcosm for the process of development of consciousness in humanity at large.

However, that is not to say any individual child's transitional object gets instantly dumped the moment he or she develops a distinct sense of self. Some children—most notably, though by no means exclusively, girls—take the teddy bears of their babyhood away with them to college, as companions on a journey to new realms that echoes that earlier psychic journey from infancy to personal identity.

In 1956, British playwright John Osborne gave a theatrical twist to the idea of teddy-bear as "transitional object" in his blockbuster play *Look Back in Anger*. The antihero Jimmy Porter is the character for whom the description "angry young man" was invented. Disaffected from what he views as an England still infected with class-consciousness, Jimmy takes out both his peevishness and his rage on his wife, Alison.

Alison is a product of the English upper middle class. Curiously, the fact that Jimmy has chosen to eschew the kind of white-collar work his middling college background has prepared him for in order to sell sweets at an outdoor market stall doesn't appear to bother her. At least, it doesn't bother her half as much as her snobbish family background bothers Jimmy.

Numerous events in the play serve to drag this unhappy couple from battleground to battleground. Yet even in the midst of the maelstrom, they find moments of conjugal accord. Jimmy has a small stuffed bear and Alison owns a toy squirrel. The couple uses these plush toys as surrogates for themselves, in order to make sexual overtures to each other.

The scenes in which Jimmy and Alison reach out through their avatars are fascinating. In her squirrel persona, Alison postures seductively, miming her huge bushy tail, while blandishing Jimmy as a "great, sooooper bear!"

Jimmy plays both familiar aspects of bears. Sometimes, he is a solitary, empathetic woodland animal. At other points, he acts the part of the cranky sorehead, reaching out to swat with an unpredictable paw. Clearly, the bear-and-squirrel games are not only sexual role-play, they are expressions of love, choked and suppressed in their everyday lives, unless filtered through the one fanciful medium left to a couple bereft of any other kind of communion.

As a squirrel, Alison embraces a role that is part cuddle-toy and part baby vamp—not unlike Nora, the central character of Henrik Ibsen's much earlier play, *A Doll's House*. Almost a hundred years before *Look Back in Anger*, Ibsen's Nora mimes the twitching and capering of her husband Torvald's "little squirrel," in order to keep him falsely secure in his role as the head of the household.

Eventually, Nora abandons those games. At the end of the play, she famously "slams the door" on everything infantalizing and controlling that her marriage to Torvald represents.

The ending of *Look Back in Anger*, however, plunges Osborne's totally incompatible couple into permanent occupation of the only realm where their relationship has ever worked: that make-believe domain in which Alison is a sleek and bright-eyed squirrel, and where Jimmy forever remains her unpredictably cross but fundamentally well-meaning bear.

"We'll be together," Jimmy's bear promises Alison as the curtain falls on the shambles that their adult lives have always been and will remain. "You're a very beautiful squirrel."

IV

I MAY NOT HAVE BEEN THE LAST middle-aged, middle-class, non-internet-savvy urban adult to hear about Furry Fandom, but I was far from the first. Back in the fall of 2005, I was working on a series of short programs about animals and humans for CBC Radio in Toronto. The melding of human and animal characteristics seemed like an interesting theme to explore.

"Have you heard about Furry?" my producer asked.

I had not. But after she explained to me the (admittedly) little she knew, I was hooked. A subculture of adult humans who dress up like cartoon animals and hold conventions and communicate online in their plushy personae? My God. I couldn't wait to hunt one down and stick a microphone in his or her face.

Finding stuff about Furry on the internet was easy—including the information that this subculture pretty much evolved on the internet. Since the early 1990s, Furry MUCKs (Multi-User Chat Kingdoms) began appearing, along with Furry MUD (Multi-User Dimension) avatar games, and eventually postings of pieces by "Mundanes"—non-Furries—about the cult.

Furry really became mainstream when an article about a 2001 Furry convention ran in *Vanity Fair*. Not long after, Furry-oriented storylines featured on two popular American network television series, *CSI: Crime Scene Investigation* and *ER*. None of these incursions into Furry by the Mundane media went down well with Furries themselves—particularly the *Vanity Fair* piece written by George Gurley.

Even a Mundane like me could understand why. "Judging from the Midwest FurFest," shrieked the subhead of Gurley's feature article, "this is no hobby. It's sex; it's religion; it's a whole new way of life."

The truth is, Furry—like most phenomena—is more or less what you want it to be. For those who get off having sex dressed up in timber wolf suits with long bushy tails, no doubt there are "virtual" partners aplenty to be found in chat rooms, or direct encounters to be had at "conFurences" and elsewhere. But in *Vanity Fair*, the entire Furry Fandom comes off sounding like a gang of particularly uninhibited drag queens, all wrapped in outrageous fur stoles, and a majority having simulated sex with stuffed toy animals.

As I phoned around to find someone willing to come on air to talk to me, I began to get the impression most Furries were just regular folk who liked to imagine themselves as animals and didn't make that big a deal about it. Some of them said they didn't even dress up as animals, and in numerous cases it sounded as if sex had little to do with a fetish that was more cuddly than carnal. Nevertheless, none of the Furries I contacted appeared eager to talk about their harmless pastime on air.

Eventually, I found Roo, right there in Toronto—which, along with

L.A. turns out to be one of the Furry capitals of North America. Roo described his own Furry alter ego as a "punk kangaroo with facial piercings and a Mohawk." He lived in a Furry household, he told me, with five other members of the Fandom, each with his or her own animal persona. And yes, he was willing to say all that on the radio.

In other words, Roo was perfect. How perfect? After we'd arranged when and where he would come for the taped interview, he asked: "Would you like me to wear my tail?"

I had learned that many Furries keep their tails—much the way male Mundanes might keep their tuxes or "tails"—in the closet for special occasions. "I would be so honoured," I said.

On the appointed day and time of the interview, I met Roo at the elevator in the CBC building. Sure enough, a long, slightly curved, plush kangaroo's tail protruded from the back of his jeans.

As we got into the elevator car, I watched him flip the tail adeptly, to make sure it didn't get caught in the door. Out of the corner of my eye, I saw another passenger—one of the younger, hipper radio producers—raise her eyebrows.

"Was that guy a *Furry*?" she hurried over to me later to ask in hushed tones.

"Oh yeah," I replied nonchalantly. "You know, Toronto's one of the Furry capitals of North America."

In the studio, Roo talked about the fact that he was "out" at work—in a suburban Toronto restaurant—but didn't ever wear the tail there.

"What do you tell your co-workers when they ask about Furry?"

"I tell them what I'd tell anyone: Furry isn't defined in any narrow way. It's about anthropomorphic animals, and for most of us, it's more of a community to hang with than a sexual orgy kind of thing. The media wants to see it as a kink, but it's just another way of living, that's all."

"What drew you to Furry?"

Way back when, Roo explained, it was the Walt Disney animated version of *Robin Hood*. In fact, he was not the first Furry I'd come across who'd cited the inspirational power of that film. In an article from *L.A. Alternative Press* published not long after the infamous *Vanity Fair* piece appeared, writer L. J. Williamson's first paragraph began: "Todd says he first realized he was a Furry when he saw Walt Disney's 'Robin Hood,' an animated movie in which Robin Hood and Maid Marian are foxes, Little John is a bear and King Richard and Prince John are lions."

According to Roo, *Robin Hood* achieves a perfect union of cartoon animal character types with human counterparts familiar from the tale of Merry Men in Lincoln green jerkins and feathered hats. And though his own inner animal turned out to be a kangaroo with a pink Mohawk and piercings, the way he conceived his Roo self intermingled the same smiling type of Disney cartoon animal with the human accessories and emblems of Punk.

"So what do you see yourself as?" I wanted to know. "Human or animal?"

The answer, as you might expect, was somewhat complicated. "I am a kangaroo in my head," Roo said. "In my head, I see you seeing me as a kangaroo."

As he spoke, he smiled confidently at me across the console table. What I saw was a pleasant-faced young man, somewhere around thirty years old, with a three-inch-high stand of hair bristling along the top of his otherwise close-cropped skull. A few small rings and studs glinted from one eyebrow, one side of his nose and on both his entirely human-looking ears. Of course, there was that tail to consider, but it was below my line of sight.

However, he was right. In my head, I *was* seeing him seeing me seeing him as a kangaroo. Not only did I know what he meant, I was a touch envious of his ability to imagine himself in another shape—and a peculiarly layered hybrid shape at that—and still seem perfectly sane while saying so.

When I was very little, long before I conjured imaginary horses to ride, I found it natural to *be* a horse. I could sense the feeling of my iron-shod hooves ringing on frozen ground and my neck stretching out, as I galloped full-tilt. Sometimes, that horse was all animal, like a wild mustang on a TV nature show. At other times, I saw myself as a prancing baby Pegasus straight out of *Fantasia* with long eyelashes and a bow in my mane. Either way, I was confident that other people looking at me would see me precisely as the horse I was in my head.

"It's like," said Roo, "when I head home in the subway, wearing this tail, right? I'll get a kick out of thinking some little kid is going to notice and feel good that there are people in society who live some other way. You know, live out loud."

Avoiding the somewhat pole-axed expression of the technician on the other side of the control-room glass, I thanked Roo and walked him back to the elevator. Before the door shut, I got a glimpse of the faces of the other occupants as Roo stepped inside the elevator car and instinctively whisked his tail out of harm's way.

I thought about him going home on the subway, quietly delighted with the attention his tail would undoubtedly attract. Then I imagined him reporting on his day to the Furry housemates. One was a panther, another was a giraffe. The other two were a cross of squirrel and coyote, and a jackal-wolf-hybrid.

Typically of Furries, Roo had told me, they all got along. "Mind you, when you've got somebody who's a Jackawolf and somebody else who's a Kangaroo ... In the wild they wouldn't be sitting together, talking about this great new CD one of them bought or whatever. So, once in a while, we maybe make a joke about somebody getting eaten."

SOME MONTHS LATER, I experienced a brief, reverberative echo of that conversation with Roo. I was reading about members of different Ojibwa clans identified by allegiance to different totems. According to the account, they would periodically tease each other in their animal personae: "My totem is the wolf, yours is the pig ... Take care! Wolves eat pigs!"

What exactly is the relationship between a human clan and its particular totem animal? Structural anthropologist Claude Levi-Strauss rejected the traditional view that an animal only becomes totemic if first judged "good to eat." Not at all, declared Levi-Strauss. Certain species are chosen as totems "not because they are 'good to eat' but because they are 'good to think.'"

In his essay "The Totemic Illusion," he explains that the word "totem" means "he is a relative of mine" in the Ojibwa language. Clan membership and relationship are expressed by reference to that particular group's totemic animal, not through bonds of matrimony or consanguinity.

Levi-Strauss also cautions against confusing the "collective naming system" of totemic clan membership with the identification of an individual animal as a "guardian spirit." That personal kind of relationship, he says, has nothing to do with the animal designation of a clan. Among the Ojibwa, even when the specific representatives of the totemic species disappeared—as, for instance, the caribou from southern Canada—the relationship to the totem was unaffected. "It is only a name," Ojibwa members of the Clan of the Caribou explained to an inquiring anthropologist named Landes.

To Levi-Strauss, it's not a case of "only." The symbolic, rather than literal, quality of the clan or totemic name opens up an imaginative realm of almost unbounded thought:

> The animals in totemism cease to be solely or principally creatures which are feared, admired or envied: their perceptible reality permits the embodiment of ideas and relations conceived by speculative thought on the basis of empirical observations.

Sigmund Freud also explored totemism—most notably in *Totem and Taboo: Resemblances Between the Mental Lives of Savages and Neurotics*. In his view, totemic cultures deal with the guilt (common to all cultures and to all individuals) that arises from the killing of the father. That "killing" can take the literal form of expulsion and/or murder of the alpha male from the tribal group, or the child's symbolic murder of the father through incest fantasies. The totem can also, at certain times and in certain situations, become an object of deflected blame or responsibility for this death of the father.

For my purposes, Freud's perspective is useful mainly to reinforce the idea that the infancy of cultures and the infancy of individuals follow similar patterns. As to what constitutes a totemic animal or a sense of identification with that animal, I am quite unabashedly cherry-picking among some of the ideas advanced both by anthropologists and psychologists.

Perhaps Paul Shepard's straightforward description of West Coast Indian totem poles makes it easier to look at these metaphorical animal figures in their broadest spectrum. "To the American Indian," writes Shepard, "the figures on the poles are those about whom traditional stories are told. They are not only components of a visible structure but players in a heard tale."

The avatar-like quality of the totemic figures on, for instance, the great Haida or Kwakiutl poles of coastal British Columbia encourages us to connect them to giant theatrical forms in some cosmic puppet play. They exhibit the animated expressions of the creatures they represent, and yet also possess a kind of mystic potency that is far beyond the realm of the individual.

Given the abstract, spiritual nature of the relationship between clan members of totemic tribes worldwide, from Polynesia to Parry Island, it's clear that tribal cultures—perhaps all cultures—make a definite if unconscious distinction between animals as individual beings and animals as conceptual figures. How and when such distinctions arose is not nearly so clear. However, *why* they arose may be easier to ponder.

In native North American cultures where the spirit form of an animal— buffalo, bear, and others—is invoked for help in the hunt, the animal spirit of necessity must be kept distinct from earthly representatives of its kind killed for their hides or horns or meat. The Great Spirit is seen as eternal, constant, and undiminished by the deaths of individual animals—so long as those animals are taken respectfully, with pleas for forgiveness beforehand and with appropriate thanks after the fact, thereby assuring the spirit's continued cooperation in supplying fresh members of its own species for human use.

As both James Serpell and Joseph Campbell have observed, the need to assuage guilt is intrinsic to ancient hunting cultures. And that assuagement of guilt through propitiation of animal spirits is greatest in societies where nature is severe and game comes and goes. Among the Inuit, Campbell points out, where the caribou is one of few species, the need for propitiation is far more obvious than in equatorial areas with a wide variety of prey.

In cultures like the Inuit, those few dominant species seem like close friends. Conceiving of slain animals as rejoined in the afterlife with the great spirit animal operated much as religious notions of the next world always operate: as compensation for suffering on Earth.

To the Jesuit and other white missionaries, the notion of beavers looking across from the Great Beyond to note what happened to their bones, or departed bears dwelling cheek-by-jowl in the afterlife with the bravest human warriors, seemed patently ridiculous. Nonetheless, the equally fanciful concept of a bountiful eternity as redress for earthly travail was the mainstay of Christian indoctrination of the Indians of North America.

Looking strictly at our own times, we can still see wispy traces of totemic animals and guardian spirits in the form of animals. From lucky charms to team mascots and logos on running shoes, we have adopted animal symbols and adapted them to our own secular purposes. Perhaps we are reaching back in search of guides and fellow travelers on our own journey—these days, a journey most often undertaken on our own four wheels.

In 2005, Andy Newman of *The New York Times* reported numerous sightings of teddy bears, fuzzy rabbits, and even rubber spiders jammed up under the bumper guard or bungee-corded to the grille-work of a wide variety of trucks in New York City. These vehicles ranged from an iron-monger's pickup, to large municipal dumptrucks, to long-distance semi-trailers.

That's not to say animals were the only form of truck adornment Newman observed. He also noted stuffed clowns and Baby Stewie dolls and bodacious babes serving—like all automotive adornments—as comments in passing to other drivers. However, toy critters seemed to occupy a niche all their own, leading the *Times* reporter to ask various truckers: "Why use beat-up stuffed animals?"

The answer was almost unanimous: "Chicks dig them."

Digging deeper than chicks, art historian Morton Denton speculated to Newman that the animal connection might reach all the way back to the serpentine figureheads on the mighty ships of the pharaohs. "You would have these humanizing forms, anthropomorphic forms—a device that both proclaims the identity of the machine and conceals it."

From that thought, I would venture a possible link to the heraldic animal emblems on the visors and shields of medieval knights in Europe. Not only did such symbols identify individuals in battle or a friendly joust, they aligned the rider with a particular patron, virtue, strength, or cause. Meanwhile, crests and coats of arms emblazoned on the sides of royal coaches and other conveyances also featured lions and more fantastical beasts as a way of indicating the identity and importance of the passengers.

Newman's interviews with truckers revealed that many of the stuffed animals strapped to their vehicles were rescued from the garbage or picked up along the road. No surprise there to Mierle Laderman Ukeles, who is (believe it or not) the New York Department of Sanitation's artist-in-residence. "I always felt," she says, "with these creatures that they withdrew from the garbage and refused to let go of, that there was an act of rescue involved."

If so, such a gesture would again recall those knights of old, pledged to chivalric deeds along whatever roads they happened to travel. What better way for a sanitation worker to advertise his similarly chivalrous nature than by affixing evidence of past rescues to the front of his "charger"?

Of course, the parallels between modern-day truck drivers and medieval knights have to break down someplace. That point may come in the contemplation of the "mistreatment" of some of these plush truck adornments. Many of them, reports Andy Newman, have been "tied to grilles in positions that recall the rack, and exposed to the maximum amount of road-salt and mud-spray. Why do this? Whence the urge to debase an icon of innocence?"

"There's a transference in this," is how Mierle Ukeles explained it to Newman. "There's this soft, flesh-and-bone sanitation worker, who knows very well they could be crushed against this truck. The creature could be the sanitation worker in a very dangerous position, so the animal could be a stand-in."

Whatever these ornamental items represent to its workers, the Department of Sanitation in New York City no longer permits stuffed animals or any other objects to be attached to city trucks. Even back in the 1970s, when Mierle Laderman Ukeles first clocked the phenomenon,

Newman says, the garbage collectors were flouting the rules. And nowadays, stuffed animals on garbage trucks in the city are "nearly impossible to find."

There are, however, still myriad other types of work vehicles to which soft little creatures are bound. Newman suggests they "may reflect the driver's frustrating position in society. Stuffed animals are found mostly on the trucks of men who perform hard, messy labor, which, despite the strength and bravery it demands, places them on the lower rungs of the ladder of occupational prestige."

If Andy Newman's supposition is correct, it opens up a further possibility: like totemic figures, these animals may also serve an identifying function. By denoting a particular clan, little Pooh Bears, Bugs Bunnies, and Scooby-Doos could advertise like-minded labourers to each other, whenever they pass on the road or encounter each other's rigs in a parking lot.

If so, it's surely a hangover from childhood. Then, the particular kind of toys for which each of us felt a special affinity helped advertise us to other kids with similar sentiments. The identifications we made with each other through those (frequently) animal-like objects surely constituted— and still constitute for today's kids—a clan membership, albeit of a small, exclusive, and limited sort.

When I was in Grade Five my best friend and I initially bonded over the tattered collections of dogs, bears, rabbits, and assorted other animals we had amassed separately since babyhood. Other girls our age had already moved past stuffed toys and baby dolls, to high-heeled "Ginger Rogers" dolls, and even beyond. So Paula and I were thrilled to find in each other a ready collaborator in setting up a library for our teddy bears or building cardboard hutches for the rabbits.

But we were also at an age when, in our Catholic school, we were being prepared for the sacrament of Confirmation. In order to become a "soldier of Christ," each Grade Five pupil required—among other things—a sponsor, who was, in turn, required to come up with a gift.

For her sponsor, Paula chose my mother, and I selected my Aunt Beth. Shrewd choices, since both women were notorious pushovers in the gift department. The usual roster of Confirmation presents ran to rosaries or missals covered in mother-of-pearl. However, what Paula and I had our hearts set on were two small, identical, stuffed Wirehaired Fox Terrier dogs we'd spotted in a downtown toy shop.

Despite the unorthodoxy of the request, my mother and aunt were both easily persuaded to buy us the dogs. We named them Rover and Clover, and incorporated them into our respective menageries.

Only a few months later, Paula's parents suddenly announced that the family was leaving Regina and moving to Ottawa—a considerable distance, even in adult terms. To Paula and me, it might as well have been Ulaanbaatar. Still, we vowed to write to each other, and we did. Occasionally, Rover or Clover got packed in a small box cushioned with Kleenex and posted across the country for a visit with his twin.

Eventually, as their owners grew, the dogs' trips dried up, along with Paula's and my letters. Apart from one brief re-encounter as university students—when neither Rover nor Clover was even mentioned—Paula and I lost contact for more than forty years.

When she did get in touch, it was the proverbial bolt from the blue: an email message to a CBC Radio program on which I had been filling in for the regular host. It turned out that, like me, Paula had lived in Toronto for years.

Once reconnected, we emailed further, to explore the idea of getting together. After so many years and such different lives, it felt like a gamble, but one worth taking. Each of us described her current appearance and what she'd be wearing, and agreed to meet on the steps of the Royal Ontario Museum.

On my way out the door, I suddenly worried that, despite the descriptions, we wouldn't recognize each other. Then I remembered Rover. Although threadbare in spots, with mangy, hairless patches and glass eyes somewhat dulled by age, he had probably changed less over the years than I had.

I plucked Rover from the shelf and tucked him in my purse. If all else failed, I figured I could hold him aloft outside the ROM, like a tour guide's umbrella, in hopes my long-lost friend would spot him if not his owner.

As I approached the museum, I picked out among the throngs a woman about my own age sitting on a step. Could it be ...? I wasn't sure. Then I got close enough to make out an object in her hand: a small stuffed fox terrier, as threadbare as his still-identical twin. On an inspiration exactly like mine, Paula had brought Clover along.

She and I did, of course, find each other very different after so many years. Not only changed in appearance, but altered in outlook, choices, and personal style. Yet still with that unique basis of affinity forged so many decades ago.

Now, whenever we get our respective families together at either her house or mine, Rover and Clover invariably adorn the dinner table. As everyone present well understands, they serve as mute testimony to the fact that, come what may, Paula and I are still members in good standing of the Clan of the Wirehaired Fox Terrier.

V

IN HIS RENOWNED ESSAY "Why Look at Animals?" critic John Berger writes that the lifelike animal toy as we know it was a product of the nineteenth century. The mass production of these objects occurred about the same time as the proliferation of public zoos in major cities around the world put wild, caged animals in close proximity with ordinary people. To Berger, the timing is more than coincidental. "Zoos, realistic animal toys and the widespread commercial diffusion of animal imagery all began as animals started to be withdrawn from daily life."

He suggests all of these developments speak to the marginalization of "real" animals and the inadequate substitution of stuffed toys, pets and controlled outings to the local wild animal park. However, toy animals may provide at least one benefit that perhaps hasn't occurred to Berger: pet reassurance. At best, representational creatures permit us— as children and even as adults—to take our ambivalence about our living animal companions, as well as our concerns for their future and our terror of their departure, and put them someplace safe and comforting.

In *Melancholia's Dog*, Alice Kuzniar discusses both dogs and dog "collectibles" as stand-ins for the "lost object" of Freudian psychology, the mother. Just as the live animal helps provide compensation for that original lost object, so do inanimate canine models act as "safeguards or antidotes" against the loss of our real live pets.

Collectibles do this, Kuzniar suggests, by evoking "a pleasurable but imprecise nostalgia, a melancholic dwelling on the reminiscences of the pet." As well, it seems to me that toy animals have this positive effect on collectors even when the actual pet they represent is still very much alive and well. Though Kuzniar does not take her idea in this direction, I do think she'd agree there is significance in the extraordinary availability of animal memorabilia at events aimed at owners of living, breathing, non-human companions.

Dog shows in particular are rife with vendors of dog statuettes, paintings, cushion covers, stained glass windows, and more. People seem to gravitate toward artistic representations of the breeds of real-life dogs they prefer and indeed may well already own. French Bulldog fanciers will buy tiny toy French Bulldogs, just as breeders of Basenjis and owners of Owchars are on the lookout for fresh figurines of their darlings to take home. Some satisfaction is innate in the object itself, a satisfaction not superior to, but entirely separate from, the living animal who inspired it.

Of course, nostalgia plays a role, too. Stuffed animals and animal figurines not only remind us adults of the real family pets of our childhood, they remind us of similar but long-lost toys that were equally integral to that childhood. Like living pets, these inanimate representations keep us in direct contact with who we were then and how we saw the world.

Their function needs no further justification. Yet, I think there *is* more—beyond both nostalgia and replacement of lost pets. If humanity as a species has been unkind to animals as a group, if our decisions about them have left us in a permanent state of ambivalence, and if our individual choices on their behalf continue to make us uneasy, then there surely is relief to be had in uncomplicated, guilt-free affection for images and representations of animal species we admire.

Real animals can be, variously, good to eat, good to think, good to love, and good to tell. In all cases, the satisfactions come at some emotional cost, either acknowledged or repressed. Replica animals, on the other hand, are good to have and to hold without penalty. And the only cost is what's written on the price tag.

Over about the last dozen or so years, I have been developing a collection of miniature plastic farm animals—the kind that come in various sizes from various manufacturers. Of course, meticulous agrarians like me make a sincere effort to keep to a consistent scale, so that our stock will look plausible grazing together in the field, pecking in their pens and nickering over the corral fence.

During that decade-and-some that I've been gradually acquiring livestock, I've amassed a dozen or so cows and calves of breeds ranging from Holsteins to Herefords, and a small herd of horses encompassing foals, mares, and stallions of several breeds. Of pigs, sheep, goats, and fowl, I also have a decent sampling, as well as a few oddities—including a spotted mule, a burro, a roe deer, and even a llama.

I also keep a couple of dogs about the place—or I would, if there *was* a place. Perhaps like some others involved in "hobby farming" on a miniature scale, I never quite get around to buying the farm. But I can't resist purchasing livestock and setting them out on a display surface, however barren.

Probably, my original impulse was to recreate that pleasure I'd known as a child, playing with my toy farm animals on the back lawn, raking grass cuttings into make-believe haystacks. I was an urban kid, and even as an adult too much of my life has been spent in cities. But then as now, I loved the idea of being out among the honest cow-flop and the chortling chickens and the big, quiet beasts switching flies.

However, in recent years I find myself growing increasingly ambivalent about real farm animals and the uses to which their lives are put. Time was, one of my great annual pleasures in Toronto was a visit to The Royal Winter Fair where—as they say in the ads—"Country comes to the City." Now, an annual exhibit there called "From Farm to Fork"—featuring a sow nursing a swarm of small piglets under the glow of a warming lamp and some wall text that recounts the matriculation of pigs from weanling to wiener—puts me right off.

Similarly, whenever I'm out in the real countryside, I feel less and less comfortable with the cows I encounter on country roads—those modest herds of milkers the farmers still claim to "know by name." In the small dairy yards, it's hard to overlook the livestock trailer drawing up to load some unwitting elderly Bossy—out of milk and therefore out of luck—for her one-way trip to the abattoir. Out on the highway, it's even harder not to notice the transport trucks, like multi-decked cruise ships crammed with doomed passengers, barely visible except for a glimpse through a porthole of an occasional snout or inquiring eye.

Meanwhile, however, down on the farm—down on *my* farm—everything is always copacetic. Okay, so maybe nobody moves, nobody so much as moos and nobody's more than an inch or two high. But at least nobody dies. The worst that can happen is that my cat might leap up to deal some poor piglet a vicious blow or send the Indian Runner ducks plunging over the edge of the table and down to the floor below.

It is, in short, a farm conceived not for consumption but for contentment. A menagerie assembled for its amity, its permanence, the appeal of its wide mixture of attractive inhabitants. No fences needed, because nobody's leaving. No castration required, nor artificial growth hormones, nor scientifically-based breeding.

If more stock of any species is desired, it is easy to find at the nearest toy store. In fact, during the Royal Winter Fair, you'll easily locate the booth of miniature farm animals for sale. It's just this side of "From Farm to Fork."

THE VILLAGE OF VILLARS DES DOMBES boasts an ancient church with Romanesque details dating from the eleventh century. Despite the name, however, there is no reference anywhere to the late Lord of Villars. Perhaps that's not surprising, considering the cloud under which he and his family left town.

Not far to the northwest is another similarly small community, Chatillon-sur-Chalaronne. That's the same Chalaronne River which, a few kilometres beyond the village, runs alongside the grove of trees where tens of generations of mothers gathered, to immerse their children in the water as part of a superstitious healing ritual.

There is no specific mention of Chatillon in Stephen of Bourbon's list of local place-names. But a large outdoor map near the ancient marketplace vaguely indicates that "*Le Bois de Guignefort*" (the local spelling of "Guinefort") is somewhere close by. So clearly, Chatillon is at the heart of all the Guinefort action.

Before coming here, I inured myself to the very real possibility that modern Chatillon-sur-Chalaronne might be a hideous strip of cheesy malls. Or perhaps a *zone industrielle* paved over the holy greyhound's one-time burial place. At the very least, I was braced for souvenir shops hawking t-shirts declaring: "*J'ai Survécu le Bois de Guignefort.*"

What I had not dared to hope for was what I found: a serenely picturesque, tastefully cobbled village with a market dating from medieval times, a few quaintly ruined chateaux, and not much new in seven-plus centuries. Nor, beyond that lone reference on an outdoor map, does Chatillon-sur-Chalaronne offer any evidence of commercial homage to the miracle dog killed and resurrected in the immediate environs.

I confess, the cornball, tchochke-loving North American part of me had secretly hoped for souvenir greyhound key-fobs on offer, or a Stephen of Bourbon action figure to dangle from the rearview mirror, or a "*Je ♥ Mon Saint Lèvrier*" bumper sticker—or even the presence of a local doggy daycare called "Le Spaw de Guinefort." Something, anything to indicate that I'd come to the right place. But St. Guinefort was nowhere to be seen in Chatillon-sur-Chalaronne, and nobody in town seemed to have any idea he was the heart and soul of the local tourist industry.

Even on a sleepy Saturday in February, when many tourist sites were shuttered for the "*Fermeture Annuelle*," the restaurants in Chatillon were doing land-office business among the locals. In an overcrowded pizzeria, a kindly couple offered to share their table, and ultimately their fellowship, with us. What were foreign tourists doing here in the off-season? was the first thing they wanted to know.

"*Nous cherchons le Bois de Guignefort,*" we answered.

"*Le bois de . . . quoi?*"

Well, like, duh. *C'est évident, n'est-ce pas?* The holy greyhound? In the best

French I could muster (none too good) I attempted to sketch the bare outlines of the story, in hopes of jogging the couple's memory. But either my French was worse than I thought, or else they had never heard the story before. In which case . . . was it possible we'd arrived at a village on the banks of some *other* Chalaronne?

But that couldn't be. There was, after all, the big tourist map with the woods clearly listed—just no indication of how to get there. Nor did the directions from Jean-Claude Schmitt's book seem to correspond to any-thing on our Michelin map of the Ain and Haute-Savoie region that in-cluded the Dombes.

For by no means the first time in my long, inglorious history of fail-ing to locate dog-related markers, monuments, and memorials, I experi-enced a sinking sensation. I ducked into a nearby stationer, thinking that, at this point, even to blunder upon a small souvenir greyhound would be better than nothing.

Inside Le Papier Rouge, a shelf of tourism books caught my eye. I went over to investigate—and came face to face with a glossy brown-and-off-white pamphlet entitled *Saint Guignefort Légende, Archaéologie, Histoire*.

Translating the introduction as rapidly as I could, I grasped that I had in my hands a monograph put out in 2005, to commemorate the twenty-fifth anniversary of l'Association Saint Guignefort. The organization had been founded in Chatillon-sur-Chalaronne following publication of an-thropologist Jean-Claude Schmitt's book, *The Holy Greyhound*, which had postulated the exact location of the "sacred grove" to which the faithful had been flocking from at least the mid-1200s to pray to a martyred dog on behalf of their ailing children.

Prompted by Schmitt's directions to the site—the same directions I had been trying and so far failing to follow—archaeologists in the late 1970s unearthed sound evidence to support his claims. Of course, in Schmitt's book, there was no reference to this dig, which had been undertaken only as a result of what he had written and published. Until this moment, I had no idea any such excavation had ever taken place, let alone where.

Good dog, Guinefort, I thought as I carried the monograph to the cash. What a good dog, to come when you're called by name—even in a foreign tongue.

VI

"GOOD FOR YOU!" SAYS MY PARTNER GENE, as I emerge from Le Papier Rouge, waving a monograph emblazoned with the name "Saint Guignefort." "That's what I call old-fashioned reportorial legwork."

He can call it that. He's a trained journalist, wheelman, reader of maps, sharp-eyed observer of the passing scene, whatever scene he happens to pass. "You went to the location with an inquiring mind," he praises me. "You scouted out the local scene."

A "Nancy Drew moment" is what I prefer to call my surprising stumble upon a salient clue. The worst kind of Nancy Drew moment. "After all," I point out as we head in the car (I *won't* call it the "roadster") back toward D-7 with renewed purpose, "I went into that shop looking for some sort of kitschy little dog figurine."

"It counts," Gene insists. "Journalism, detection, call it what you want: it's 99 percent perspiration and 1 percent blind, dumb luck."

That would be my method. The blind, dumb part, that is—with a modicum of luck thrown in.

We drag the Saint Guignefort society monograph, like a freshly-killed springbok, back to our lair. It's a red bordello-like room at the Hotel de la Tour, full of clever pillows, lampshades hung with feather boas, and promises of "*la gastronomie et le cocooning*"—the latter a concept too ineffably French for mere North Americans to decode.

In our cocoon, we pore over descriptions in the monograph of the archaeological dig inspired by Jean-Claude Schmitt's research. Even with his completely competent French, it takes Gene some time to sort through arcane terminology describing ditches and layers and artifacts, and get to the gist: We've been looking in the wrong place.

Not only are the woods farther from the river than Schmitt's *The Holy Greyhound* seemed to indicate, they are on the opposite side of the road. However, the good news is the archaeologists' reference to the location on the property of a family named Clerdan corresponds with a tiny dot near the D-7 on our Michelin map marked "Clerdan."

There is, adds Gene—with the air of a man leading up to the big finish—even better news: Back in the late 1970s in the course of their dig, the archaeologists reported locating the foundations of what was probably a ruined house. And near it, fragments of stone that almost certainly had been part of a well.

No remains of anything resembling the bones of a dog were unearthed. But why would they have been? According to Stephen of Bourbon, the body of the greyhound had remained in the well only until he had personally supervised its disinterment and incineration.

THERE IT IS. We haven't missed it. The *panneau* is a rusted-looking plaque, with the same Gothic script as the other official markers we've seen in Chatillon-sur-Chalaronne and other ancient towns in the region.

"Bois de St Guignefort" it reads. Quite dazed, I get out of the car, to take a picture and to scribble a literal translation of the French text into my notebook. "The Woods of St Guinefort. Site of the legend where during the centuries the masses gave themselves over to practices of the Gallic mythology. Worship of waters and of the forests, against which Étienne of Bourbon the inquisitor of the faith preached in the XIIIth century."

The first marvel, of course, is that it is here. Were it not for this plaque at this particular curve in the D-7, one would have no idea that he or she had found the place. A ditch runs along the roadside, and beyond that ditch, a meadow crosshatched with tire tracks leads into a wood of not particularly ancient-looking trees.

But the second marvel is that the woodland is still here—rather than a housing development or a gas station or a plant nursery. This rural part of France, with fields and streams and abundant stands of trees, is in certain basic ways not much changed from the days when Stephen of Bourbon journeyed along a distant ancestor of the D-7 toward an earlier grove of trees, with the intention of cutting it down. The *étangs* are the same bodies of water that raised the peasants' ire in the days of the Lord of Villars, after good farmland was flooded so that noblemen could fish.

Except for an occasional car whipping by at startling speeds along the narrow, curving road, there is no one else in the vicinity. And nowhere on the sign does it warn that this is private property. However, Gene—more precise in these matters—reminds me that the archaeologists had to get permission to dig here, all those years ago. The Clerdan family still owns these woods. Just to go barging in would be trespassing.

Trespassing? By now, I feel the way all groupies and cultists and amateur explorers must feel: that I've earned the right to be here.

However, I decide to compromise by walking in only so far and no farther. Beyond the meadow with its tire tracks are bits of soiled paper that make it look as if travelers might have pulled off the D-7 at this spot from time to time, not so much to pay their respects to the shrine of the dog martyr as to relieve themselves.

A small junked refrigerator not far from the car tracks gives further evidence that this has become something of a nuisance ground. One part of me is saddened, on behalf of Guinefort and all his followers over the centuries. Another part of me exults that these intact woods, the description of the dig, the existence of a sign marking and describing the place, all add up to so much more than I expected, with my bleak premonitions of strip malls and filling stations.

A car comes around the bend and angrily honks at us for not pulling our Citroën entirely off the road. Yet with our Canadian reticence, we're reluctant to park on private property, however unmarked. Walking into the woods, however, is, for me, another matter.

It's a morning that promises to be sunny later, but with lingering mist for now, and white hoar frost on the ground. Those trees beckon, and I find it impossible not to venture a bit closer to where all the action must once have been.

Of course, any evidence of the dig has long since been covered up and made indistinguishable from the rest of the landscape. Yet, this is the place. I know it. Site of the legend and the ancient practice, just as the *panneau* declares for all to see.

———◆———

WHAT DOES IT MEAN TO HAVE FOUND THE PLACE? What would it have meant *not* to find it? Suppose Stephen had ordered the locals to dig for the corpse, and they had turned up nothing. Would he have felt better or worse than he wound up feeling, once those decayed bits of bone were brought to the surface?

It is forbidden. That's what Stephen preached. An animal may not be dressed up as a holy martyr; a saint is not permitted to be disguised as a dog. *It is forbidden,* said this cleric, who came to spy on the peasants' rite, desecrate the shrine, and burn the unholy relic.

Yet . . . what is forbidden need not end. It may merely be kept under wraps, by keeping secret. The Pope's man has come, but he will also soon go. Meanwhile, the holy martyr dwells among us, regardless of the fate of his earthly remains.

Late at night, in this grove where the old woman—the *vetula*—has led the rituals to restore the sick, nothing need alter. With no light but a burning torch, here and there the glinting eye of a wolf will look on while his better brother is invoked. *St. Guinefort, Pour la vie et pour le mort,* always and everywhere. Though they've taken your body from us, they cannot take you from our hearts, nor take us from this place.

Here in the woods, far from the prying eyes of our betters, we are *better* than our betters. With the flaming torch and the eyes of the wolf, and the old familiar ritual, let us pray: Saint Guinefort, Saint Guinefort . . . The dog, the martyr, the god, though he dwells in dust, and in what some would call a monster's disguise.

———◆———

"BOIS DE ST GUIGNEFORT—*Lieu de légende où durant des siècles des foules livrerent aux pratiques de la Mythologie Gauloise. Culte des eaux et des forêts contra lesquels Étienne de Bourbon inquisiteur de la foi prêcha des le XIIIième siècle."*

It's not until I have returned to the roadside to copy down the exact French wording on the plaque that it hits me: Nowhere does it say that this "St Guignefort" happened to be a dog. "A cult of waters and forests," is what it says. Not a word about a cult built around worship of a sacred greyhound.

If Stephen of Bourbon was shocked to discover that the "holy person" whispered about in the confessional was a dog, I am twice as shocked to learn that the dog on the *panneau* is merely some unspecified figure from

"Gallic mythology." The greyhound has disappeared, as entirely as his disinterred body did—as mysteriously as the original statue of the Brown Dog.

Yet *there really was a dog*. Stephen knew it then, and I know it now. Not an animal spirit out of Shintu, or a dog-headed deity in ancient Egypt, or some romanticized wolfhound who may or may not have been mourned by the last Welsh king. Not even a mythologized dog whose courageous story of battle against a snake is universal, but a mortal greyhound whose remains truly were dug up from this specific spot in a grove of trees, where they'd been buried, hugger-mugger, by a guilty master.

His name may have been borrowed from a human martyr, but the story is his own. It's a story unique in the annals of reverence, and a status as healer of children unrivalled by any other dog. And yet ... the fact that he was a dog is nowhere in evidence on the plaque next to the woods consecrated to St. Guinefort.

"Animals are at the bottom of the heap." I can almost see Keith Mann at my elbow, nodding sagely, not at all surprised by this startling turn of events. "We all have to do with them. If we change things for them, we change things for everybody. They're everywhere."

Everywhere and.... nowhere.

Everywhere and nowhere. Could it be the biggest paradox of them all? The ubiquity of animals, their indispensability, is their downfall—along with the fact that they are also easily replaced. Because they are so central, they must be entirely marginalized. Because they are everything, they must be as nothing.

The secret, in the end, is that we can't do without them, although they could have done so easily without us. To admit our greater dependency would be the end of us. So we hush up the truth and put it in the same place we put the animals—right at the bottom of the heap.

This, I now realize, is what the journey to *le Bois de Guignefort* is about. This is what the ending of the story signifies. This is the truth I've found at the heart of the old, old myth: Not even the most exalted among them are exempt from the terrible, limiting truth of their inconsequential consequence. Animals are everywhere and nowhere.

VII

PAUL WATSON, founder of the Sea Shepherd Conservation Society, has made a career of inveighing against our system of valuation based on human self-interest. In his crusades against the destruction of marine life by man, Watson draws distinctions between what he calls "deep" and "shallow" ecological motives. In 2007, he told *The New Yorker*: "A 'deep' ecologist would clean up a pond because plants and animals deserve to be free of pollution; a 'shallow' ecologist would preserve the pond so that his grandchildren could have a nice place to swim."

Few of us, however caring, can come to terms with the fact that, deep down, we are shallow ecologists. However vociferously some of us decry the exploitation of animals, mostly, it's not in our interest to end it. Not only have we so far failed to come up with adequate substitutes for all the ways we employ animals for our benefit, we have barely begun to address the implications of relinquishing our vast sense of entitlement.

Never mind the knotty practical question of how we could give back to the non-human world what is rightfully theirs. We aren't ready to address the more basic question of whether we want to.

Previously in human history, almost every surrender of exploitative control has been accompanied by some practical inducement to facilitate that change in philosophy. Abolition of slavery in America was achieved not only by a combination of enlightened ethics and military might, but also by a realization that the industrial landscape was changing, in ways that made it possible to contemplate large-scale cotton harvesting and production without the requirement of unpaid labour.

In the late 1960s, the so-called "second wave" of the women's liberation movement did indeed draw momentum from the larger revolutionary spirit of the times—just as the first wave, in the 1850s and '60s, was galvanized by the energy of the abolition movement. However, that second wave was abetted by the realization that our culture would benefit from "letting" women knock themselves out both as over-achievers in the workplace and guilt-driven supermoms at home.

In North America, the grudging gestures we've made to our indigenous

peoples have cost our dominant culture less in returned land and resources than we've gained in good public relations. A burial ground here,
a lakefront development there, a much-ballyhooed apology from the
government of the day ... In the end, it's unlikely much significant real
estate will revert to its original owners.

When it comes to the interests of animals there's even less uptick in
broadening their rights, assuming we could figure out how to do it. Open
up the doors of the research apes' and rabbits' cages? Slap our cattle on
their rumps and send them out to graze in whatever unclaimed pasture
land they can find? Replace all the trees we logged from various species'
habitats, return all the non-indigenous animals to their countries of origin, undo all the genetic upgrading we've performed to make it more con-
venient to harvest their milk, meat, eggs, and organs, or more fun to bet
on their lightning speed?

What a relief to realize we couldn't manage it, even if we wanted to.
Because the truth is that, deep down among our deepest fears, lurks the
nagging suspicion that we lack the will to try.

IN THAT SPLIT-SECOND, as the blade of his master's sword came whistling
through the air and down upon him, did the greyhound recognize the man
with the weapon as the same man he had loved and served? And if he did
not, would that instant have been long enough for the dog to wonder
where the master he loved and who loved him had gone?

Or perhaps it was a moment later, as the dog lay dying on the stone
floor of the child's bedchamber that he found the answer staring at him
from the open, unseeing eyes of the serpent he had worried to death. In
that moment, the greyhound may have thought he glimpsed something of
his master in that empty gaze.

But maybe not even then would the dog recognize the man in the serpent, any more than the master had recognized his faithful dog in that
wolfish beast with bloody jaws he mistakenly believed had killed his child.
And now that his dog is dead and he is full of remorse, how can the man
bear to recognize himself as the enemy?

If he does not, we can hardly blame him. In the various accounts of the greyhound, his master and the snake—and in the larger story that is us and animals—there are not many of us who could bear to see ourselves cast in the role of the villain, whether with two legs or four legs or no legs at all.

Yet we can't have the dog by the cradle without the serpent beneath. Without the two together, along with the child in the cradle, there would be no story. And without the master of the dog and the father of the child, the story would end very differently. Not only for that one particular snake and that one unfortunate greyhound, but for the master and his family, and for all the successive generations of families who came to worship in a grove made sacred to St. Guinefort.

Without question, the master is as essential to the story as the dog and the serpent. The sad fact is that, of the three of them, the man seems to be the one with the least clear idea of what the real story is and where it may lead.

——————◆•◆•◆——————

ACKNOWLEDGEMENTS

F IRST OF ALL, my thanks to all the animal-engaged people named in
the preceding pages, who gave me their time, their opinions, their
assistance, and the benefit of their expertise in my exploration of some of
the complex relationships between animals and us. I hope that these scientists, scholars, welfare advocates and rights activists, along with those
otherwise involved with animals whom I also describe and discuss in this
book, will feel that I have represented them and their work and beliefs
accurately and with understanding.

I also offer my gratitude to the authors, living and dead, of the books,
films, plays, research papers, and journalistic articles that I cite and refer
to throughout. These novelists, ethologists, anthropologists, historians,
artists, reporters, legal experts, screenwriters, psychologists, poets and
pundits have provided me with illuminating perspectives from which to
develop my own ideas and opinions about animals and us.

My thanks to my agent, Hilary McMahon of Westwood Creative
Artists, for her belief in this project from the beginning, and to everyone
at Key Porter Books for sharing that belief early on and advancing this
labour of love to completion between handsome covers. I would also like
to acknowledge the assistance of the Canada Council for the Arts and the
Ontario Arts Council. Although the writing of this book was not directly
funded by these agencies, their assistance to me on projects past has helped
make my development as a writer possible, and their ongoing support of
the Canadian publishing industry makes writing a possible profession in
this country for me and many others.

As well, thanks to those in radio program development at the Canadian
Broadcasting Corporation who provided me with resources and encouragement for audio exploration of human-animal relationships, first in a

2004 half-hour pilot called "The Ark Gallery," and then in a series of four half-hour radio programs which aired in 2006 on CBC Radio One as "Noah's Arkade." It was through researching, devising and developing those shows, first with producer Kelly Galbraith and then with producer Nancy Watson, that I began to get some inkling of the endless complexities of animals, as well as the inexhaustibility of human interest in them.

On a personal note, I am enormously indebted to the many friends and colleagues who have encouraged me in researching and writing this book. There are too many caring people in this category to list individually, but I do hope those who proffered everything from information to inspiration to commiseration know who you are, and will not be disappointed by the results of the work to which you contributed so much over the past two years.

I owe particular thanks to Deirdre Kessler, a wonderful writer and a wise friend, for her insights into both animals and artistry, and her invaluable comments and encouragement, after careful contemplation of my manuscript. I am also profoundly grateful to my mate, Gene Allen, for his good literary instincts, his sound journalistic sense, his shrewd advice, his warm wit, his unfailing patience with my technological bewilderment, his unflagging faith in my work, and his unstinting love in our life.

Last, but by no means least, I would like to express my thanks to all the non-human animals—past and present, real and imagined—who have enriched my spirit, inspired my thought, and touched my heart.

SELECTED BIBLIOGRAPHY:
books directly quoted from and/or referred to.

Adams, Carol J. *The Sexual Politics of Meat: A Feminist-Vegetarian Critical Theory.* New York: The Continuum Publishing Company, 1990

———. *Neither Man Nor Beast: Feminism and the Defense of Animals.* New York: The Continuum Publishing Company, 1994

Ainsworth, W. Harrison. *Rookwood: A Romance.* Philadelphia: Carey, Lea & Blanchard, 1834

Arluke, Arnold and Sanders, Clinton R. *Regarding Animals.* Philadelphia: Temple University Press, 1996

Arluke, Arnold. *Just a Dog: Understanding Animal Cruelty and Ourselves.* Philadelphia: Temple University Press, 2006

Atkinson, Kate. *Behind the Scenes at the Museum.* London: Doubleday, 1995.

Atwood, Margaret. *The Edible Woman.* Toronto: McClelland & Stewart, 1969

———. *Survival: A Thematic Guide to Canadian Literature.* Toronto: House of Anansi, 1972

Bekoff, Mark. *Animal Passions and Beastly Virtues: Reflections on Redecorating Nature.* Philadelphia: Temple University Press, 2006

Bowron, E.P., Rebbert, C.R., Rosenblum, R., Secord W. (eds) *Best in Show:*

The Dog in Art from the Renaissance to Today. New Haven, Conn.: Yale University Press, 2006

Bulliet, Richard. *Hunters, Herders and Hamburgers: The Past and Future of Human-Animal Relationships*. New York: Columbia University Press, 2005

Chamberlin, J. Edward. *Horse: How the Horse Has Shaped Civilizations*. Toronto: Alfred A. Knopf Canada, 2006

Coetzee, J.M, and Garber, M., Gutmann A. (ed) *The Lives of Animals*. Princeton: Princeton University Press, 1999

Coetzee, J.M. *Disgrace*. London: Penguin, 1999

———. *Elizabeth Costello*. London: Penguin, 2003

Cooper, William W. *Curious and Instructive Stories About Wild Animals and Birds*. Edinburgh: W.P. Nimmo, Hay & Mitchell, 1897

Fabre-Vassas, Claudine. *The Singular Beast: Jews, Christians and the Pig*. New York, Columbia University Press, 1997

Frazer, James G. *The Golden Bough: A Study in Magic and Religion*. New York: The MacMillan Company, 1942

Fudge, Erica. *Animal*. London: Reaktion Books, 2002

Gipson, Fred. *Old Yeller*. New York: HarperCollins, 1956

Gotfredsen, Lise. *The Unicorn*. Translated by Anne Born. London: The Harvill Press, 1999

Grandin, Temple. *Thinking in Pictures: And Other Reports From My Life with Autism*. New York: Vintage, 1996

Grandin, Temple, and Johnson, Catherine. *Animals in Translation: Using the Mysteries of Autism to Decode Animal Behavior*. New York: Scribner, 2004

Griffin, Donald. *Animal Minds: Beyond Cognition to Consciousness*. Chicago: University of Chicago Press, 1992, revised 2001

Hall, Lee. *Capers in the Churchyard: Animal Rights Advocacy in the Age of Terror*. Darien, Conn.: Nectar Bat Press, 2006

Haraway, Donna J. *The Haraway Reader*. New York: Routledge, 2003

Hearne, Vicki. *Adam's Task: Calling Animals by Name*. New York: Alfred A. Knopf, 1986

———. *Bandit: Dossier of a Dangerous Dog*. New York: HarperCollins, 1991

Kalof, L. and Fitzgerald, A. (eds). *The Animals Reader: The Essential Classic and Contemporary Writings*. Oxford and New York: Berg , 2007

Kuznetsov, Anatoly. *Babi Yar: A Document in the Form of a Novel*. New York: Farrar, Straus and Giroux, 1970

Kuzniar, Alice A. *Melancholia's Dog: Reflections on Our Animal Kinship*. Chicago: University of Chicago Press, 2006

Leonard, R. Maynard (ed). *The Dog in British Poetry*. San Francisco: Chronicle Books, 2005 (originally pub. 1893)

Mann, Keith. *From Dusk 'til Dawn*. London: Puppy Pincher Press, 2007

Podberscek, A.L, Paul, E.S. and Serpell, J.A. (eds) *Companion Animals and Us*. Cambridge: Cambridge University Press, 2000

Pollan, Michael. *The Omnivore's Dilemma: A Natural History of Four Meals*. New

York: Penguin Books, 2006.

Rawlings, Marjorie K. *The Yearling*. New York: Charles Scribner's Sons, 1939

Regan, Tom. *Animal Rights, Human Wrongs*. Lanham, Maryland: Rowman &Littlefield, 2003

Rollin, Bernard E. *Animal Rights and Human Morality*. Amherst, NY: Prometheus Books, 1981, revised 1992

————. *The Unheeded Cry: Animal Consciousness, Animal Pain and Science*. Ames, Iowa and Oxford: Iowa State University Press, 1989, revised 1998

Sacks, Oliver. *An Anthropologist on Mars: Seven Paradoxical Tales*. New York: Alfred A. Knopf, 1995

Saunders, M. Marshall. *Beautiful Joe*. Toronto: McClelland & Stewart, 1934

Scanlan, Lawrence. *The Horse God Built: Secretariat, His Groom, Their Legacy*. Toronto: HarperCollins, 2006

————. *Little Horse of Iron: A Quest for the Canadian Horse*. Toronto: Random House Canada, 2001

Schmitt, Jean-Claude. *The Holy Greyhound: Guinefort, Healer of Children Since the Thirteenth Century*. Translated by Martin Thom. Cambridge: Cambridge University Press, 1983

Serpell, James. *In the Company of Animals: A Study of Human-Animal Relationships*. Oxford: Basil Blackwell, 1986, revised 1996

Sewell, Anna. *Black Beauty: The Autobiography of a Horse*. London: Jarrold & Sons, 1877

Shepard, Paul. *The Others: How Animals Made Us Human*. Washington, D.C.: Island Press/Shearwater Books, 1996

Singer, Peter. *Animal Liberation*. New York: New York Review/Random House, 1975, revised 1990

Spiegel, Marjorie. *The Dreaded Comparison: Human and Animal Slavery*. New York: Mirror Books, 1996 (revised & expanded edition of original 1988 version)

Stavroff, Dale. *Let the Dog Decide*. Toronto: HarperCollins, 2007

Taylor, Angus. *Magpies, Monkeys and Morals: What Philosophers Say About Animal Liberation*. Calgary: Broadview Press, 1999

White, E.B. *Charlotte's Web*. New York: Harper & Row, 1952

Wise, Steven M. *Rattling the Cage: Toward Legal Rights for Animals*. Cambridge, Massachusetts: Perseus Books, 2000

Wolfe, Cary. *Animal Rites: American Culture, the Discourse of Species and Posthumanist Theory*. Chicago: University of Chicago Press, 2003

SELECTED BOOKS OF GENERAL REFERENCE:
helpful background reading, not directly quoted from or referred to by title.

Amory, Cleveland. *Man Kind?: Our Incredible War on Wildlife*. New York: Harper & Row 1974

Cavalieri, P. and Singer, P. (eds). *The Great Ape Project: Equality Beyond Humanity*. London: Fourth Estate, 1993

Dunayer, Joan. *Animal Equality: Language and Liberation*. Derwood, Maryland: Ryce Publishing, 2001

Montgomery, Charlotte. *Blood Relations: Animals, Humans and Politics*. Toronto: Between the Lines, 2000

Niven, Charles D. *History of the Humane Movement*. London: Johnson Publications, 1967

Noske, Barbara. *Humans and Other Animals: Beyond the Boundaries of Anthropology*. London: Pluto Press, 1989

INDEX